BACK-TO-BASICS AMERICAN COOKING

Anita Prichard

with illustrations by Nina Clayton

A PERIGEE BOOK

ACKNOWLEDGMENTS

I wish to express my gratitude to the many accomplished American home cooks who have contributed their recipes to this book. I especially thank Ernestine Oliverie Escobar from Brownsville, Texas, and Gwen King from New Orleans, Louisiana, for sharing with me their recipes and regional-cooking expertise.

My grateful thanks to Frances Osgood and Betsy Hartmann for their dedication in helping test the recipes and to their husbands who supported their efforts.

I'm indebted to Betty Wagner, who patiently edited the manuscript for presentation to my publishers, and to Mary Gunther for carefully typing the manuscript. I also thank Libby Hillman, teacher and author, who started me on my teaching career in the field of American cooking.

Perigee Books
are published by
The Putnam Publishing Group
200 Madison Avenue
New York, New York 10016

Library of Congress Cataloging in Publication Data

Prichard, Anita.
  Back-to-basics American cooking.

  Originally published: New York : Putnam, 1983.
  Includes index.
  1. Cookery, American. I. Title.
TX715.P9346   1984   641.5973   84-7640
ISBN 0-399-12806-9
ISBN 0-399-51067-2 (pbk.)

Design by Nina Clayton
First Perigee printing, 1984
Printed in the United States of America

1 2 3 4 5 6 7 8 9 10

CONTENTS

BACK-TO-BASICS AMERICAN COOKING

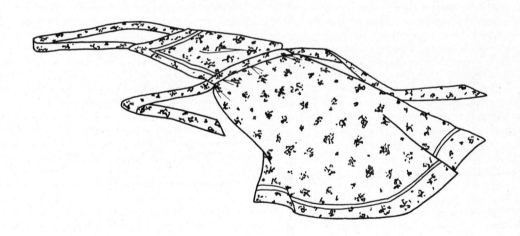

The roots of American cooking lie deep within the progress of a developing nation. American cooking is very simple, down-to-earth, and yet at the same time imaginative. It's flavored with fresh taste, lots of butter, cream, eggs and often herbs or pungent spices, adapting to the foods of a particular region, not to be confused with ethnic cooking in America. Admittedly, a fine line. However, ethnic cooking is based upon food prepared in an undiluted manner, retaining its national identity in the purest form. American heritage cooking can be either regional or ethnic, and is considered to be a cooking style passed down from preceding generations.

Modern food writers generally categorize New England, Pennsylvania Dutch, Southern, Creole and Cajun, Tex-Mex and West Coast as the six distinct styles of cookery in America. Some food historians disagree and claim American cooking began in either New England or the Tidewater, while others maintain the only true American cooking was on the frontier, keeping its originality in the Ozark Mountain homestyle cookery of today. Perhaps the latter is partially true because it took the Scotch-Irish in the Shenandoah Valley to learn how to make potatoes grow in the temperate North American climes. What would an authentic New England clam chowder be without potatoes?

Americans have always been a mobile people. How they cook depends largely upon where their ancestors came from and how they adapted the foods at hand. A case in point: It has been four generations since my ancestors emigrated from their homes in the South to central Indiana, and yet I remain basically a Southern cook. I recently recognized some very old recipes in a newly-published West Coast cookbook. The recipes undoubtedly crossed the Plains by covered wagon.

Distinct American cooking did not begin to develop until the cookstove was invented in the mid-1800s. By the end of the Civil War it was in general use with dampers to regulate the heat flow which, of course, improved the ability of the cook to control cooking temperatures.

A strong middle-class society began to emerge in the aftermath of the Civil War. Both the whites and the blacks, with their natural talent for cooking, started to put their indelible mark on a home style of cooking which has come to be known as American. A hired girl may have served as a helper in the kitchen of a white family, but the lady of the house maintained full control over all food preparation. Recipes were copied and passed about the community, each cook changing ingredients along the way. This accounts for the many variations in a recipe even within a local area. Daughter learned to cook at mother's elbow. Therefore, many recipes were not recorded because it was assumed one already knew how to prepare the basics. Only recipes requiring strict measuring were recorded for posterity, so that when people research old journals they are led to believe that American cooking is composed of a heavy dose of cured hams, cakes, puddings, cookies, candy and pickles. Mother continued to teach daughter the subtleties of American cooking up until World War II.

World War II, with the advent of can-of-soup cookery and ready-mixes, almost caused the demise of good American cookery. "By the end of the century," reads one 1941 food magazine, "Americans will be preparing food electronically by merely pushing a button for recipe selection." Thus, a whole generation of young cooks were denied their culinary heritage.

It remained for the flower children of the sixties, and their back-to-basics movement, to steer us forward to an appreciation of good food prepared with natural ingredients.

The word "natural" took on a lot of meaning in the seventies. Most of us were trying to establish a more basic, natural way of both eating and living. "Natural" is what American cookery is all about, and who needs additives and chemicals? Women, joined by the men, have returned to the kitchen in force. As a result, the careful preparation of food can now be considered a national pastime.

Progress in the development of fine American wines has unquestionably contributed to the refinement of American cooking. In the recent words of a noted Frenchman, "First you had to build a nation. Then you had to show your power. Now, at last, you are learning how to live."

Good appetite!

KITCHEN
BASICS

Cooking begins with planning. Your kitchen should be organized with the necessary equipment and staple ingredients basic to your cooking ability and style of entertaining. If you are a beginning cook you may find this advice overwhelming but do not be discouraged. If you start with simple recipes and the basic pots and pans and other kitchen aids, you will soon find you are developing a kitchen work pattern without giving the matter further thought.

Utensils

More than ever before, American cooks look for a combination of quality, function and design when purchasing cookware. The difference in the style and price of utensils and kitchen aids can be staggering, and it is worthwhile spending time making comparisons.

   Before making any purchase, one should carefully consider how often the piece of equipment will be used. If it is used frequently and serves many purposes, the expense will, of course, be justified. However, in many kitchens space is at a premium, and it makes sense to improvise. For example, a covered roasting pan and rack can be converted to a fish poacher. The top part of a double boiler turned upside down over the bottom half can substitute as an expensive asparagus steamer. A fine mesh sieve can double as a flour sifter. Metal coffee cans are utilized for making round loaves of bread and for steaming puddings.

   BASIC KNIVES   Buy sturdy high-carbon stainless steel with riveted wooden handles and a sharpening steel or stone.

TYPE:	RECOMMENDED SIZE
Chef's knife	8″, 10″ or 12″
Paring Knife	3″ or 4″
Boning Knife	6″ flexible
Slicing Knife	10″ or 12″
Serrated Slicing Knife	8″

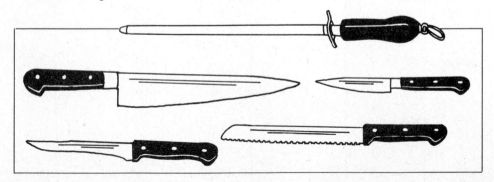

CHOPPING BOARD   Buy one made of wood or polyethelene and made so there are no joints or cracks for food to lodge in.

Recommended Size

24″ × 18″

POTS AND PANS   It is better to have a few quality utensils than a complete set of matching pots and pans that conduct heat poorly.

Always purchase pots and pans with matching cover—except for omelet pans and griddles. It is recommended for convenience to have utensils which can be used both on the stove top and in the oven. These dual purpose pots and pans are often referred to as "flameproof" cookware. Recommended metals are: cast iron, enameled cast iron, lined copper, stainless steel and aluminum combinations, heavy lined aluminum and heavy duty nonstick aluminum.

TYPE	RECOMMENDED SIZE(S)
Saucepans	1 to 1½ quart, 2 to 2½ quart, 3 to 4 quart and 5 to 6 quart
Double Boiler	1½ to 2 quart
Skillets	8″ to 9″ and 10″ to 12″
Dutch Oven	4 to 5 quart with tight-fitting lid
Omelet Pan	8″
Griddle	10″
Vegetable Steamer Insert	Adjustable
Kettle	6 to 8 quart with tight-fitting lid

COOKING AND BAKING UTENSILS   These can be of metal, oven-proof pottery or glass.

TYPE	RECOMMENDED SIZE(S)
Baking Pans	8″ × 8″, 9″ × 9″, 11″ × 7″, 12″ × 7½″ and 13″ × 9″
Loaf Pans	8″ × 4″ and 9″ × 5″
Roasting Pan	17″ × 12″ × 2½″
Casseroles	1 quart, 1½ quart and 2 quart
Ramekins or Custard Cups	1 cup
Baking Sheets	18″ × 12″ × 1″
Tube Pan	10″
Springform Pan	10″
Round Baking Pans	9″
Pie Pans	9″ and 10″
Tart Pans	5″ to 6″
Ring Mold	4 to 6 cup

Muffin Pans	2½"
Sifter	1 quart
Wire Whisk	Small and large
Cooling Rack	Large
All-purpose Metal Grater	Medium-size

MEASURING AND MIXING UTENSILS

TYPE	RECOMMENDED SIZE(S)
Measuring Spoons	¼ teaspoon, ½ teaspoon, 1 teaspoon and 1 tablespoon
Glass Liquid Measuring Cups	1 cup, 2 cup and 4 cup
Dry Measuring Cups	¼ cup, ⅓ cup, ½ cup and 1 cup
Mixing Bowls	Small, medium and large
Rubber Scraper	10"
Spatula	7" blade
Wooden Spoon	10"

PREPARATION UTENSILS

TYPE	RECOMMENDED SIZE(S)
Colander	10"
Can Opener	Optional
Bottle and Jar Opener	Optional
Funnel	Optional
Juice Squeezer	Optional
Long-handled Fork	12"
Pancake Turner	10"
Slotted Spoon	10"
Pastry Blender	Optional
Pastry Cloth	24" × 18"
Rolling Pin and Cover	12" to 14"
Fine Mesh Sieve	1 quart
Tongs	10"
Vegetable Brush	6"
Vegetable Peeler	6"
Kitchen Scissors	8" to 9"

MISCELLANEOUS

TYPE	RECOMMENDED SIZE(S)
Skewers, Poultry Pins and Toothpicks	Optional
Kitchen String	Optional

TYPE	RECOMMENDED SIZE(S)
Cheesecloth	3 yards
Wooden or Metal Mallet	Optional
Pepper Grinder	Optional
Corkscrew	Optional
Baster with Bulb	Optional
Meat Thermometer	Optional
Potato Ricer	2 cup
Ice Cream Freezer	Optional
Mesh Skimmer	10"
Pastry Brush	6"
Gelatin Molds	1 cup and 1 quart
Broiler Pan and Rack	Optional

ELECTRICAL APPLIANCES

Rotary Hand Beater
Toaster
Blender and/or Food Processor
10- to 12-inch Skillet

Staples/Shelf Life

Staples are basic items used in the preparation of food. It is a convenience to have staples such as flour, sugar, salt, baking powder, baking soda, certain herbs and spices, etc. handy on the kitchen shelf to be used as needed.

Even though most food items are dated or coded by food companies for market shelf life, very few are dated for consumer shelf life after the package or container has been opened. It is the latter that is of vital concern to those of us who consider a nutritious diet important to our lives. (It is helpful to make it a habit to pen the date of purchase on all staple ingredients.)

The following is a list of the basic staples ordinarly stocked in the home kitchen and their recommended shelf life.

NOTE: Perishable items should be stored in airtight containers.

COOKING AND BAKING ITEMS	ROOM TEMPERATURE	REFRIGERATED
All-purpose White Flour (Bleached and Unbleached)	2 to 3 months	Up to 9 months*
Untreated Grain Flours (Wheat and Rye)	—	4 to 6 weeks

Untreated Cornmeal	——	6 weeks
Untreated Bran and Oatmeal	——	6 weeks
Untreated Buckwheat	——	4 weeks
Untreated Wheatgerm	——	1 month
Baking Powder	8 months	——
Baking Soda	Unlimited	——
Cream of Tartar	4 to 5 months	——
Sugar	Unlimited	——
Salt	Unlimited	——
Unsalted Butter	——	Until exp. date on pkg.
Margarine	——	Until exp. date on pkg.
Solid White Shortening (Crisco)	6 months (or as long as not discolored)	——
Fresh Lard	——	2 weeks
Chocolate	1 year	——
Cocoa	Unlimited	——
Dried Milk	——	6 months
Yeast (Dry)	Until exp. date on pkg.	——
Yeast (Fresh)	——	Until exp. date on pkg.
Honey	3 to 4 months	——
Molasses	——	2 months
Corn Syrup	Until exp. date on bottle	——
Unflavored Gelatin	Unlimited	——
Beans	1 year	——
Rice	Unlimited	——
Peanut Oil	2 months	——
Vegetable and Corn Oil	2 months	——
Olive Oil	1 month	——
Canned Products (Unopened)	1 year from coded date†	——
Canned Products (Opened)		
Evaporated Milk	——	10 days
Chicken and Beef Broth	——	3 to 4 days
Tomato Sauce	——	1 week
Tomato Paste	——	1 week
Tomato Catsup	6 months	——
Chili Sauce	6 months	——
Prepared Mustard	1 year	——
Coffee (vacuum-packed)	2 weeks	——
Coffee (instant)	6 months	——
Tea	6 months	——
Tabasco Sauce	Unlimited	——
Worcestershire Sauce	Unlimited	——
Vinegars	Unlimited or until cloudy	——
Pickles	——	As long as firm

Olives	—	As long as firm
Flavorings (Opened)		
Almond	1 year	—
Lemon	1 year	—
Orange	1 year	—
Vanilla	1 year	—

NOTE: Refrigeration and freezing increase the shelf life of all-purpose flour by two to three times the room temperature shelf life. It is recommended to bring the flour to room temperature for at least 24 hours to allow any excess moisture time to evaporate in order to ensure successful baking results.

†*NOTE: Large food chains have freshness codes on their canned produce. These are usually a set of numbers including dates. The dates mean one of three things—the date the item was packaged, the date after which it should not be used or the date when it should be removed from the market shelf. Other numbers may indicate information of storage time for buyer. Check with the market manager for information relative to decoding these numbers.*

HERBS AND SPICES   Replace all herbs and spices as soon as they have lost their scent and color. It is almost impossible to judge the shelf life of either by any other means. You can prolong their shelf life by storing both herbs and spices in metal or colored glass containers away from direct heat and sunlight. *Caution*: Never store herbs and spices near the stove top.

Essential oils are the beginnings which furnish the aroma and flavor characteristic of herbs and spices. These oils are released by either chopping or grinding. For this reason whole leaves, berries and seeds keep longer than those purchased already powdered or ground.

HERBS	**SPICES**	
Basil	Allspice	Black Pepper
Bay Leaves	Cinnamon	White Pepper
Celery Seed	Cloves	Red Pepper (crushed)
Coriander	Chili Powder	Cayenne Pepper
Dill	Cumin	Turmeric
Oregano	Curry Powder	
Rosemary	Ginger	
Sage	Dry Mustard	
Savory	Mace	
Tarragon	Nutmeg	
Thyme	Paprika	

CHOWDERS,
SOUPS,
STEWS,
GUMBOS

Chowders

Years before the English settled at Jamestown, French and English fishermen were squabbling over territorial fishing rights off the coast of Maine. It must have been during a temporarily declared truce ashore that the first Yankees learned to make chowder. These chowders were made without milk, for there couldn't have been a milk cow within 2,000 miles, and the white potato had not yet traveled to North America via Europe from South America. But ship's biscuit, salt pork and onions, being shipboard staples, undoubtedly were available to make a clam or fish soup, which the French fishermen made in heavy iron pots called "*chaudières.*" The word was freely translated by the English fishermen as "chowder." Thus the first distinctive American word in the development of native American dishes.

An authentic American chowder is a thick, hearty soup that usually contains shellfish, fish, salt pork, vegetables and milk or broth. There are also turkey and all-vegetable chowders, which are inland adaptations, far away from a ready supply of fresh coastal ingredients.

Chowder-making Basics

SALT PORK   The quality of salt pork generally sold at the supermarket has fallen into a sorry state. (A good ethnic meat market can be relied upon for top-quality salt pork.) Coated with heavy salt and cured for long storage, it is apt to give off a rancid odor when being fried. Therefore, it is advisable to buy salt pork in small quantities. *To help freshen supermarket salt pork,* place the solid piece in a pan. Cover

with cold water and bring to a boil over high heat. Immediately rinse under cold water and slice, dice, or cube, as the recipe specifies. After this, if you detect a rancid odor when frying the pork, discard and use bacon or butter. No cook, no matter how capable, can disguise this objectionable taste.

POTATOES   Use Maine, Eastern or any waxy potato that will hold its shape during cooking. In old recipes these were called "Irish" potatoes, to distinguish them from the sweet potato. Do not use a baking potato, because its texture is too mealy to make a proper chowder.

Good New England home cooks deplore the use of flour or cornstarch to thicken a milk chowder. Rather, they cook the potatoes uncovered. This method will release enough starch from the potato to thicken the chowder.

MILK CHOWDERS   New England milk chowders originally were made with whole milk, ultrarich and unpasteurized. Homogenized milk tends to curdle during the heating process. Maine home cooks fortify homogenized milk with a small amount of undiluted evaporated milk. "Oh, not enough for the taste to come through," says a cooking companion of mine from Ellsworth, and that is just about as far Down East as you can go. For those finicky about using evaporated milk, either half-and-half or light cream can be substituted.

NOTE: 1 13-ounce can undiluted evaporated milk = 1⅔ cups
1 5.33-ounce can undiluted evaporated milk = ⅔ cup

BROTH CHOWDERS   Fresh or bottled clam juice is used to make seafood and fish chowders that call for a liquid other than milk. Turkey, chicken or ham broth is used most often in making other types of chowders.

CLAMS   These are bivalves known as quahogs, the American Indian name for clams. Large quahogs are known as "chowders," medium-sized are called "cherrystones" and small quahogs are "littlenecks." The large quahog, or chowder clam, is chopped or minced and used in preparing clam chowder. The "cherrystones" and "littlenecks" are delicacies traditionally served raw on the half shell.

CANNED CHOPPED CLAMS   There is nothing better than a New England chowder made with fresh soft-shelled clams. However, even New Englanders are using canned clams because commercial clammers have leased the harvesting grounds and the source of fresh clams has been reduced. Never cook fresh clams more than three minutes, for this toughens the clams. Add canned chopped clams just before heating and serving.

TO PREPARE FRESH CLAMS   (See illustration, page 102.) Scrub clams with a stiff brush and wash thoroughly to remove all traces of sand and grit. If fresh clams must be kept overnight, place them in the refrigerator in a bowl but do not cover them with water. They must have air to breathe. Discard any of the clams with opened shells. Open the clams just before preparing the chowder. After the clams have been taken from the shells, using a cutting board and a sharp knife cut the head of each clam in two or three pieces. Do the same with the firm part of the clam and the soft part also. Discard the black neck. Save all the juice for the chowder.

SEASONINGS FOR CHOWDERS   The delicate taste of a fish or shellfish chowder should not be overpowered by the use of strong herbs or spices. Salt, pepper and sometimes thyme is usually seasoning enough. Resist the temptation to add anything more.

FREEZING   This is not recommended for fish and shellfish chowders, because the texture tends to break down in the reheating. Better to make the chowder ahead of time and let it ripen in the refrigerator for several hours, or up to a day or so. Old recipes always advised this ripening period to develop flavor.

Maine Clam Chowder

This is a home-style clam chowder with an old-fashioned flavor. Way Down East it is traditionally served with corn bread or a local cracker known as Sea Toast. (Uneeda brand crackers may be used if Sea Toast is unavailable.) In other parts of Maine the chowder is often served with blueberry muffins.

At-home cooks slice the potatoes for the chowder, but in restaurants they are more likely to be cubed.

2 cups fresh soft-shelled chopped clams or 2 7½-ounce cans chopped clams and juice

3 slices (¼ pound) salt pork

1 medium-sized to large onion, chopped

1 cup (8 ounces) clam juice

3 cups sliced or cubed Maine, Eastern or any waxy potato

3 cups milk and ½ cup undiluted evaporated milk; or 3½ cups half-and-half

4 tablespoons unsalted butter

Salt and freshly-ground black pepper to taste

1. If using fresh clams, clean and chop, reserving the juice. Set aside.
2. In a small, heavy pan fry out salt pork over low heat. Remove pork, cool and chop for garnish. Add onion to the fat and cook until translucent but not brown.
3. In a separate heavy, 4-quart saucepan add the 1 cup clam juice to potatoes; cook gently, uncovered, until just tender. Do not allow the potatoes to become mushy. Add the cooked onion to the clam juice

and potato mixture. *If using fresh clams,* add these along with their juice and simmer 3 minutes. *If using canned clams,* add these along with their juice, but do not simmer. Add milk or half-and-half and the butter. Season to taste with salt and pepper. Note: May be prepared to this point several hours before serving.
4. Reheat slowly to serving temperature but do not boil. Pour into individual bowls or mugs and garnish with chopped salt pork.
Serves 4. The recipe may be doubled.

Rhode Island Clam Chowder

One bright and early morning, the captain of my flight introduced himself with the remark, "I understand you are writing a cookbook on American cooking. I hope you are going to include an authentic Rhode Island clam chowder recipe." Not being a New Englander, I was unaware of a regional controversy. It seems that no self-respecting Rhode Islander will eat either a New England milk-based clam chowder or a Manhattan-style clam chowder. A few days later I received the following carefully written recipe from the captain's wife. The clam chowder has been given a three-star rating by my kitchen tasters, which proves the captain's wife has a very good recipe.

2 cups fresh chopped clams or 2 7½-ounce cans chopped clams and juice
2 cups fresh or 2 8-ounce bottles clam juice
18 or 19 ¾-inch cubes salt pork (¼ pound)
1½ cups chopped onion

1 16-ounce can solid-pack tomatoes
½ cup water
1 tablespoon sugar
5 large Maine, Eastern or any waxy potato, cut into ⅓-inch cubes
2 tablespoons unsalted butter
Salt and freshly ground black pepper to taste

1. If using fresh clams, clean and chop, reserving the juice. Set aside.
2. In a heavy, 5-to-6-quart saucepan fry salt pork over low heat; cook until enough fat has been rendered to cook the onion.
3. Add the onion and cook until translucent but not brown. Add tomatoes, water and sugar. Simmer uncovered about 30 minutes. Stir occasionally with a wooden spoon. If tomatoes are drying out, add a bit more water.
4. Add potatoes and add water to just cover the potatoes. Cook uncovered until potatoes are just tender. Do not allow the potatoes to become mushy. Add clam juice and boil rapidly 5 minutes, uncovered. Turn heat down to medium and boil gently 20 minutes.
5. Discard salt pork. *If using fresh clams,* add these along with remainder of their juice and simmer 3 minutes. *If using canned clams,*

add these along with their juice, but do not simmer. Season to taste with salt and pepper. Heat to serving temperature but do not boil. Serve in bowls or mugs.
Serves 10 to 12. Recipe may be halved to serve 5 or 6.

Maryland Seafood Chowder

In testing this recipe, the gift of a friend from Maryland, it was unanimously voted one of the outstanding chowder recipes in American cooking by my students.

¼ cup unsalted butter
¼ cup chopped onion
½ cup chopped leeks, white part only
2 cups chicken broth, preferably homemade
3 medium-sized carrots, chopped
1 cup chopped celery
1 teaspoon salt, or to taste
⅛ teaspoon freshly ground black pepper, or to taste

2 bay leaves
¼ teaspoon ground thyme
1 cup cooked flaked striped bass or other whitefish
2 cups heavy cream
1½ cups crabmeat, preferably fresh, picked over to remove cartilage and shell
1 cup minced clams with juice
Parsley for garnish

1. In a heavy, 3-quart saucepan melt the butter. Add the onion and leeks and cook until tender but not brown. Add chicken broth, carrots, celery, salt, pepper, bay leaves, thyme and cooked fish. Simmer uncovered 30 minutes. Remove bay leaves.
2. Slowly add the cream and stir well to blend. Add crabmeat and clams and reheat to serving temperature. Refrigerate 24 hours, if desired, to ripen flavors.
3. Reheat slowly to serving temperature. Serve in bowls garnished with parsley.
Serves 6.

New England Fish Chowder

Fish chowder is traditionally made with fresh haddock, cod or cusk, and is served as a simple supper dish with Sea Toast or Uneeda brand crackers. Any white nonoily fish may be substituted. In areas where fresh fish is not readily available, this chowder can be made with frozen fish fillets.

5 pounds fresh cod, haddock or cusk;
  or substitute 3 12- to 16-ounce
  packages frozen fish fillets
1 cup (8 ounces) clam juice
1 cup (¼ pound) diced salt pork
¾ cup thinly sliced onion

4 cups Maine, Eastern or any waxy
  potato, sliced or diced
3 cups milk and 1⅔ cups undiluted
  evaporated milk; or 4⅔ cups half-
  and-half
Salt and freshly ground black pepper
  to taste

1. Place fish in large pan and add clam juice. Cover and simmer until fish flakes and falls from the bone when touched with a fork. Remove from heat; remove fish and discard skin and bones. Strain and save broth.
2. In a heavy, 5-to-6-quart saucepan fry out salt pork over low heat. Remove pork and save for garnish. Add onions to the fat and cook until translucent but not brown. Set this mixture aside.
3. Place the onion mixture and potatoes in the pan used to cook the fish. Add enough lightly salted water to barely cover the potatoes. Cook uncovered about 15 minutes. Do not allow the potatoes to become soft and mushy. Add fish broth and stir well.
4. Break the cooled fish into large pieces and place in the pan with the onions, potatoes and broth. Pour the milk over this and stir gently with a wooden spoon until mixed. Fish should remain in large pieces and not be flaked, which would cause the consistency to be mushy. Add salt and pepper to taste. Cool.
5. Place chowder in the refrigerator for 1 hour to a day to allow time to ripen and blend the flavors.
6. Reheat slowly to serving temperature but do not boil. Serve in large bowls.

Serves 4 to 6.

Turkey Chowder

Just-tender vegetables, a flavorful, homemade turkey broth and the blend of delicate herbs enhance the taste of an American country-style dish.

1 large onion, minced
3 cups Maine, Eastern or waxy
  potatoes, cut into ½-inch cubes
3 cups turkey broth, preferably
  homemade
1 cup carrots, cut into ¼-inch dice
1 cup fresh or frozen green peas
2 tablespoons unsalted butter

1 cup light cream, or half-and-half
⅛ teaspoon ground thyme
⅛ teaspoon ground sage
Salt and freshly ground black pepper
  to taste
2 cups finely diced cooked turkey
Paprika and chopped parsley for
  garnish

1. In 4-quart, heavy saucepan cook the onion, potatoes and turkey broth uncovered until the potatoes are just tender. Do not allow the potatoes to become mushy. Add carrots and peas and cook no more than 4 minutes.
2. Add butter, cream, thyme and sage. Stir well. Add salt and pepper to taste. Add turkey and heat to serving temperature. Serve in bowls garnished with paprika and chopped parsley.

Serves 6.

Fresh Corn Chowder

This chowder must be made with fresh corn on the cob. The scoring of the kernels will release enough starch to thicken the chowder properly.

6 large ears fresh corn	1 cup heavy cream
2 tablespoons unsalted butter	Salt and freshly ground black pepper
1 small onion, diced fine	to taste
2 cups half-and-half	Chopped parsley for garnish

1. With a sharp knife score each row of kernels down the middle, starting at the top of the ear. Then carefully scrape the kernels and the "milk" from the ears.
2. Melt the butter in a heavy, 3-quart saucepan. Add the onion and cook until translucent but not brown. Add the corn and cook no more than 5 minutes.
3. Remove mixture from the heat. Combine the half-and-half with the cream. Gradually stir into the corn mixture. Season to taste with salt and pepper. Reheat to serving temperature and serve in bowls or mugs garnished with chopped parsley.

Serves 4 to 6.

Maine Corn Chowder

An authentic Main corn chowder is always made with canned cream-style corn. The canning industry began in that state around the time of the Civil War, when Isaac Winslow perfected the steam retort, which made possible the commercial canning of fresh foods. In the long, cold winters, it would have been only natural for cooks to have concocted a variation of their favorite regional dish from canned corn. There is no reason that today's cooks cannot use fresh corn, but then it is not an authentic Maine corn chowder.

This recipe is one used in Ellsworth by cooks who combine the canned cream-style corn with whole kernels to contrast the texture for better flavor. A gelatin fruit and vegetable salad of celery, grated carrots and crushed pineapple, accompanied by hot baking powder biscuits, is often served with corn chowder.

NOTE: The cooking time for the corn may seem abnormally long by today's standards, but that's the way they still do it in Maine.

½ cup (⅛ pound) diced salt pork
1 cup thinly sliced onion
4 to 5 cups thinly sliced Maine, Eastern or any waxy potato
2 cups whole-kernel corn
2 cups cream-style corn

3 cups homogenized milk and ⅔ cup undiluted evaporated milk; or 3⅔ cups half-and-half
Salt and freshly ground black pepper to taste

1. In a heavy, 4-quart saucepan fry out salt pork over low heat. Remove pork and set aside for garnish. Add onion to the fat and cook until translucent but not brown. Add potatoes, at least 3 cups of water and the whole-kernel corn. Cook uncovered until the potatoes are very tender. Add cream-style corn and milk. Season to taste with salt and pepper. Stir carefully to mix the ingredients. Let rest at room temperature at least one hour to allow flavors to blend.
2. Reheat to serving temperature but do not boil. Pour into individual bowls or mugs and garnish with the chopped salt pork.
Serves 6.

Soups

Unlike the clear, thin soups of other cuisines, American soups fall basically into two groups: (1) Light and delicate soups, such as thin cream soups and vegetable broth; (2) Heavy and thick soups that include meat, poultry, fish, shellfish or perhaps game.

Thin, light soup can be the first course of a substantial meal or can be served with a sandwich or salad. Hearty soups are filling enough to be served as the main course for dinner. With the modern trend toward eating less and enjoying it more, hearty soups have taken on a stylish connotation when served at informal dinner parties.

Unlike French soup-making, in which ingredients often past their prime are puréed into a creamed soup, American soups must be made with the freshest ingredients, prepared in a manner that not only enhances their appearance but also their flavor. Each ingredient stands on its own merit. Using leftovers is not recommended for making a good American soup.

Soup-making Basics

BROTH   A good soup needs a firm foundation. Start with a good, strong broth. This can be made of meat, poultry, fish, shellfish or vegetables.

PREPARING INGREDIENTS   Soup cookery requires meticulous perfection, even in small details. Perhaps you have noticed in fine restaurants how evenly the vegetables are sliced, diced and cubed. With the invention of the food processor, and with the dexterity of modern cooks in using a chef's knife, even pieces are not hard to achieve. Aside from the fact that a hodgepodge of uneven pieces is not attractive, uneven pieces cook unevenly.

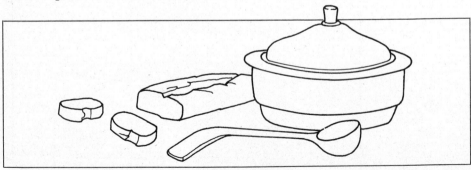

CUTTING AND CHOPPING INGREDIENTS   A basic rule to remember in cutting and chopping food is that you cannot do a proper job unless the cutting surface is flat. When the ingredient being cut slips and rolls under the hand, the knife will do to your fingers what it does to the food being cut. If you watch an accomplished cook, you will see that the hand is held in such a way that the ends of the fingers curve under slightly and the blade of the knife is angled ever so slightly away from the hand. With a little practice, anyone can dice, chop and julienne ingredients with lightning speed.

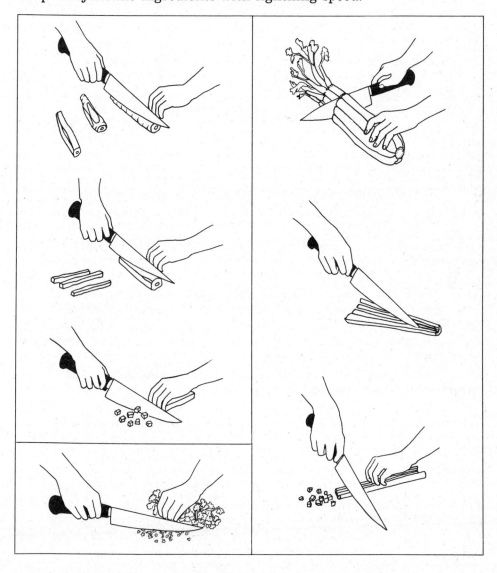

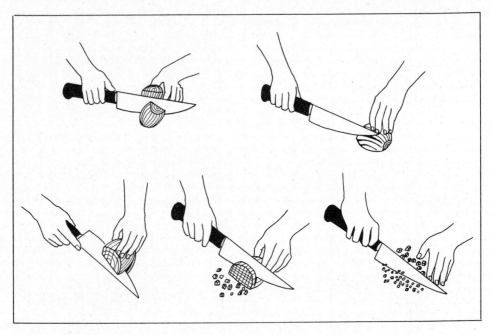

REHEATING SOUPS   Most soups reheat beautifully, actually improving the flavor.

FREEZING SOUPS   Soups other than those containing fish and shellfish can be frozen successfully. Freezing in small portions and thawing before reheating are recommended.

BASIC BROTHS

In American cooking a soup stock is commonly referred to as broth. The three most-used broths in soup-making are chicken, meat and fish. Some vegetable soups create their own flavorful broth as the vegetables cook in water or cream.

Among my younger students the most misunderstood of all the basics of cooking is the ability to make a good, strong broth.

Not so long ago all American soup broths were made at home. Methods change, and we all have to admit there are some very good quality broths and concentrated beef and chicken bouillon cubes on the market. These should be kept on the shelf for ready use, to enrich a homemade broth that is thin and lacking in flavor.

The three following basic broth recipes can be made in quantity. Meat and chicken broth can be made in 1-cup portions and frozen for ready use.

NOTE: Refrain from using too many herbs or spices in making soup broth. These can overwhelm the flavor of the finished soup.

Beef Broth

5 pounds beef bones with ample meat and marrow
About 3 quarts cold water
2 medium-sized onions, sliced
1 carrot, sliced
1 small white turnip, sliced
1 rib celery with leaves, sliced
1 bay leaf
½ teaspoon ground thyme or few sprigs of fresh thyme
3 sprigs parsley
Salt and freshly ground black pepper

1. Have the butcher saw or crack beef bones. This is done to increase the surface exposed to the action of hot water.
2. Brown from one-fourth to one-half the beef bones in a large frying pan over high heat. This gives added color and improves the flavor.
3. Place the meat and bones in a large, 5-to-6-quart kettle. Cover with the cold water for 30 minutes or more before cooking. This helps to extract the juices of the meat.
4. Heat gradually to the simmering point. If the broth is to be used to make a clear soup, skim at this time. Cover and continue to simmer 3 to 4 hours to insure the complete extraction of juices and flavor of the meat. Remove meat and bones from the kettle and discard.
5. Add the onion, carrot, turnip, celery, bay leaf and thyme; season very lightly with salt and pepper. Continue simmering for 45 minutes.
6. Strain the hot broth through several layers of cheesecloth into a large bowl.
7. Cool the broth quickly—rapid cooling improves the keeping quality of the broth. Broth should, if possible, always be cold before being used, since the fat hardens and collects in a cake on top and can be removed easily. Do not remove fat from the top of broth until it is to be used. It helps protect the stock against spoilage. *Caution:* Either keep broth chilled in the refrigerator about 3–4 days or freeze for future use. Spoiled broth, like spoiled meat, is dangerous food.

Makes 2 quarts. Recipe may be doubled or tripled.

Chicken Broth

4 pounds chicken necks, backs, wings and giblets (do not use livers)
1 large onion, sliced
1 carrot, sliced
1 rib celery with leaves, sliced
1 small bay leaf
2 sprigs parsley
¼ teaspoon ground thyme
Salt and freshly ground black pepper
2 quarts cold water

1. Place all the ingredients in a 5-to-6-quart heavy kettle and cover. Simmer gently about 2 hours. Skim occasionally to remove foam from top.
2. Strain the hot broth through several layers of cheesecloth into a large bowl.
3. Cool the broth quickly—rapid cooling improves the keeping quality of the broth. Broth should, if possible, always be cold before being used, since the fat hardens and collects in a cake on top and can be removed easily. Do not remove fat from the top of broth until it is to be used. It helps protect the stock against spoilage. *Caution:* Either keep broth chilled in the refrigerator or freeze for future use. Keeps in the refrigerator for about 3 to 4 days.

Makes about 1¾ quarts. Recipe may be doubled or tripled.

Variation: Double-Strength Chicken Broth

In Step 3, after the broth has been strained, return to high heat and boil until reduced in half.

Fish Broth

2 pounds whitefish or 2 pounds head and trimmings (from fish market)
1½ quarts cold water
2 peppercorns
3 tablespoons lemon juice

1 clove
2 sprigs parsley
1 bay leaf
2 tablespoons each, finely chopped carrot, celery and onion

1. Place all the ingredients in a 4-quart kettle and cover. Simmer gently about 40 minutes.
2. Strain the hot broth through several layers of cheesecloth into a medium-sized bowl.
3. Use as soon as possible, because fish broth does not keep well.

Makes approximately 1½ quarts. Recipe may be doubled or tripled.

Beef-Vegetable Soup

Every section of the country has its own version of vegetable soup. Some are as thick and heavy as stews, others are as thin as a French consommé.

A carefully prepared vegetable soup takes time. First you make a basic beef broth. This can be done ahead of time. Then you carefully slice, dice and chop the vegetables, not only for attractive presentation but also to ensure even cooking for tenderness. Serve with homemade bread or garlic bread and red wine.

This is a recipe I have used for many years. The soup freezes very well if the vegetables are not overcooked.

1 recipe Beef Broth (page 25)
2 cups peeled, seeded and chopped tomatoes, or 2 cups canned tomatoes
1 cup finely sliced cabbage
3 large carrots, diced
1 large white turnip, diced

2 ribs celery, chopped
½ to 1 cup chopped onion
1 cup cubed Maine, Eastern or any waxy potato
½ cup minced parsley
Salt and freshly ground black pepper to taste

1. Prepare one recipe for Beef Broth (page 25), to measure 2 quarts of liquid.
2. In a 4-to-5-quart kettle combine beef broth, tomatoes, cabbage, carrots, turnip, celery, onion and potatoes. Cover and cook until the vegetables are tender. During the last 5 minutes of cooking add the parsley and season to taste with salt and pepper. Serve steaming-hot in large bowls.

Serves 6. Recipe may be doubled.

Harvesttime Cabbage Soup

This is a tasty soup to make when inundated with a surplus of fall vegetables at their peak of flavor. Can be frozen in quantity and reheated for informal winter meals.

3 cups chicken broth, preferably homemade
3 cups water
½ cup grated carrots
½ cup thinly sliced celery
2 large Maine, Eastern or any waxy potatoes, diced
½ cup chopped onion
2 cups fresh tomatoes, peeled seeded and chopped

1½ teaspoons salt
1 bay leaf
4 peppercorns
3 cups shredded cabbage
¼ cup lemon juice
1 tablespoon sugar
Salt and freshly ground black pepper to taste

1. In a 4-quart, heavy kettle combine chicken broth, water, carrots, celery, potatoes, onion, tomatoes, salt, bay leaf and peppercorns. Bring to a boil, lower heat, cover and simmer until vegetables are tender.

2. Add cabbage and simmer 5 minutes or until tender. Add lemon juice and sugar. Stir well to blend. Season with additional salt and pepper to taste. Heat to serving temperature.

Serves 6.

Navy Bean Soup

I feel that no one has been properly introduced to American cooking who has not sampled an authentic navy bean soup (not to be compared with restaurant fare, which are usually bean chowders). Strictly speaking, it is a soup of the frontier, made from sugar-cured ham, navy pea beans, onion, seasoning and nothing more. There is an old saying among the devotees of this delicious soup: "Navy bean soup made with the shank end of a country ham has a flavor as unforgettable as a feud." It is a soup so hearty and filling that it gave the frontiersmen the true grit necessary to face whatever hardships might be in store.

Both my grandmothers, who lived almost a century each, in their later years were much given to reminiscing about the hardships of their childhoods. My grandmother Heavin's favorite pitiful tale was that her family often lived all winter long on a daily diet of navy bean soup and corn bread spread with sorghum. Not from necessity but from an inborn Scottish thriftiness she in turn brought up her own hungry brood of nine on navy bean soup, but without the corn bread and sorghum. My mother never served this soup, and she was of little help in reconstructing the old-fashioned flavor of my grandmother's. When I finally reconstructed the recipe with the addition of a small dried red pepper and a small amount of brown sugar, my mother recalled that both ingredients had been used in curing ham.

It has become the rage in southern Indiana and Kentucky to serve navy bean soup at local fund-raising functions. However, it also can be served in an elegant style with Indian puffs (rather than the heavier corn bread), hot butter and a chilled white wine.

2 cups navy pea beans, presoaked
2 quarts hot water
1 large onion, diced
1 tablespoon brown sugar, firmly packed

1 small red pepper or ⅛ teaspoon crushed red pepper
1 shank end of country ham or 4 smoked ham hocks
Salt and freshly ground black pepper to taste

1. Presoak beans. *Quick method*: Measure cold water to cover 2 inches over the beans. Bring to a boil. Cover pot and cook 2 minutes; remove from heat. Let stand 1 hour. Drain. Proceed with recipe. *Overnight method*: Measure water 2 inches over the beans and let stand overnight. Drain. Proceed with recipe.

2. In a heavy, 5-to-6-quart kettle combine drained beans, hot water, onion, sugar, red pepper and ham. Cover and simmer about 2½ hours, or until beans are soft and the skins start to burst.
3. Remove ham bone or hocks. Cut away fat and dice the remaining ham. Skim any fat from the surface of the cooked beans. Remove the red pepper and season to taste with salt and pepper. Return the diced ham to the soup and reheat to serving temperature.

Serves 6.

New Jersey Lima Bean Soup

In the past, when New Jersey was principally an agricultural state, farmers grew lima beans of superior quality, which were dried and sold nationwide.

This hearty soup should be made with country-flavored ham.

2 cups dried lima beans, presoaked	1 ham bone with ample meat
2 quarts hot water	½ cup diced celery (optional)
½ cup chopped onion	½ teaspoon ground thyme
2 cups diced Maine, Eastern or any waxy potato	Salt and freshly ground black pepper to taste
2 cups canned tomatoes	Chopped parsley for garnish

1. Presoak beans. *Quick method*: Measure cold water to cover 2 inches over the beans. Bring to a boil. Cover pot and cook for 2 minutes; remove from heat. Let stand 1 hour. Drain. Proceed with recipe. *Overnight method*: Measure water 2 inches over the beans and let stand overnight. Drain. Proceed with recipe.
2. In a heavy, 5-to-6-quart kettle combine drained beans, hot water, onion, potatoes, tomatoes, ham bone and optional celery. Cover and simmer about 2½ hours, or until beans are soft and the skins start to burst. Add the thyme during the last 30 minutes.
3. Remove ham bone and cut away fat. Dice the lean ham. Skim any fat from the surface of the cooked beans. Return the diced ham to the soup and add salt and pepper to taste. Reheat and serve in large bowls garnished with chopped parsley.

Serves 6 to 8.

Lentil Soup

The Bible often mentions lentils; the most famous reference is to Esau, who sold his birthright for bread and "pottage of lentils" (Genesis 25:29-34). In American cooking lentils are most generally eaten in soup.

For full flavor this soup should be made a day ahead and refrigerated overnight. Serve with whole-wheat bread and unsalted butter.

1 cup dried lentils
6 cups water
1 ham bone with ample meat
1 large carrot, coarsely chopped

2 ribs celery with leaves, chopped
1 small bay leaf
Salt and freshly ground black pepper
  to taste

1. In a heavy, 4-quart saucepan soak the lentils in the water 3 hours.
2. Add the ham bone, carrot, celery and bay leaf to the soaked lentils. Cover and simmer 2 hours.
3. Remove ham bone from soup; remove meat and dice. Discard bay leaf. Add diced meat to soup. Add salt and pepper to taste and reheat. Refrigerate overnight. Reheat and serve in bowls or mugs.

Serves 6.

Dried Pea Soup

Pea soup, probably of New Amsterdam origin, has always been a very popular winter dish with my students. This recipe has the old-fashioned flavor of a hearty soup. With fresh bread, who needs anything more? For this recipe you will need an extra-large soup kettle.

1 pound dried green split peas
4 quarts water
1-pound piece salt pork, with ample
  lean streaks
1 cup finely chopped onion
1 cup finely diced celery
1 cup finely diced carrots

½ teaspoon ground thyme
2 potatoes, cooked
Salt and freshly ground black pepper
  to taste
2 small sausages, cooked and sliced
  thinly for garnish (optional)

1. Combine the peas, water, salt pork and onion in a 6-quart soup kettle. Simmer 2 hours.
2. Remove the salt pork and cut into fine dice, discarding the fat. Return lean salt pork to the broth. Add the celery, carrots and thyme. Simmer 30 minutes.
3. Rice or mash the potatoes and add to the broth mixture. Add salt and pepper to taste. Reheat to serving temperature and serve in large bowls. Garnish with optional sausages.

Makes 3 quarts.

Chicken Corn Soup

This is a classic dish in Pennsylvania Dutch cooking. Canned chicken broth and commercially-made noodles may be substituted, but the true flavor of this rich main-course soup is enhanced when both are home-made.

6 cups double-strength chicken broth (page 26)
2 cups water
2 cups cooked chicken, cut into bite-size pieces
2 cups freshly cut corn from the cob
1½ cups Pennsylvania Dutch brand or homemade egg noodles, cut into 2-inch pieces

1 cup finely chopped celery
2 tablespoons minced parsley
Salt and freshly ground black pepper to taste
2 hard-cooked eggs for garnish

1. To prepare double-strength chicken broth, first make Chicken Broth recipe (page 25). Add 3½ pounds chicken and 2 cups water to broth. Cover and cook until tender. Remove chicken from broth and cool slightly. Remove skin from chicken and debone. Cut the meat into bite-size pieces. Measure 2 cups and reserve the rest for another use. Remove fat from surface of cooled chicken broth and measure 6 cups. Any remaining broth can be frozen.
2. Bring the chicken broth to a boil in a heavy, 4-quart kettle. Add the corn, noodles, celery and parsley. Boil uncovered until noodles show a slight resistance to the bite. The cooking time will depend on whether the noodles are store-bought or homemade. Add the chicken and salt and pepper to taste. Cook until the chicken is heated through and the noodles are tender. Serve at once in soup bowls garnished with the sliced eggs.

Serves 4 to 6.

Home-Style Cream of Chicken Soup

The strong flavor of onion has been eliminated from this refined chicken soup, often served in America's finest hotels. Either chicken or turkey can be used in this recipe.

½ cup unsalted butter
1 rib celery (no leaves), chopped
4 scallions (white part only), chopped
4 tablespoons flour
6 cups chicken broth, preferably homemade, hot but not boiling

1 cup heavy cream
1 cup cooked diced chicken
½ cup cooked white rice
¼ cup finely chopped celery
Salt and freshly ground black pepper to taste

1. Melt ¼ cup of the butter in a heavy, 3-quart saucepan. Add chopped celery and scallions. Cook, stirring constantly, until the celery is tender. Stir in the flour and cook 3 minutes, but do not allow the flour to brown.
2. Remove mixture from heat and use a wire whisk to blend in the hot chicken broth. When mixture is smooth return to low heat and simmer gently 20 minutes, stirring often. Remove from heat. Cool slightly and strain through a sieve.
3. Off the heat, blend in the heavy cream with a whisk. Add chicken, rice, finely chopped celery and salt and pepper to taste.
4. Reheat to serving temperature but do not boil. Enrich the soup with the remaining ¼ cup butter, if desired. (It may be omitted.) Stir well to blend. Serve in cream soup bowls.

Serves 8.

Fresh Cream of Tomato Soup

No canned soup can possibly equal the flavor of a made-from-scratch cream of tomato soup. For full flavor this soup should be made with tomatoes that are fully ripe—almost too ripe for slicing. It can be made throughout the year with high-quality canned tomatoes. This soup is popular in New Jersey and Indiana, states known for their exceptionally well-flavored tomatoes. In our family it was served with oyster crackers.

3 tablespoons unsalted butter
3 tablespoons flour
¼ cup finely chopped onion
½ teaspoon sugar

3½ cups peeled, seeded and chopped tomatoes
3 cups milk or half-and-half
Salt and freshly ground black pepper to taste

1. In a heavy, 3-quart saucepan melt the butter. Add the flour and cook 3 minutes, stirring constantly. Add the onion and cook until tender but not brown. Add the sugar and tomatoes. Simmer uncovered 20 minutes. Stir occasionally to keep mixture from sticking to bottom of pan.
2. Remove mixture from heat and cool slightly. Process in blender or food processor until smooth. (If container is large enough, tomato mixture and milk can be blended together.)
3. Return mixture to saucepan and gradually add the milk, stirring constantly to blend.
4. Return to low heat and cook 10 minutes, stirring constantly. *Caution:* Do not boil, or the mixture will curdle. Serve in bowls or mugs.
Serves 6.

Cream of Celery Soup

Never make celery soup with the white hearts of celery; it is much more sensible to eat them raw. The outer stalks and the well-scrubbed root make an excellent soup. In milk soups it is always wise to eliminate the celery leaves, since these tend to make the milk curdle.

The potatoes in this soup serve as a thickener—much easier than making a *roux*-based white sauce.

Cream of celery soup has always been considered a holiday treat at Thanksgiving or Christmas time.

Outer ribs of 2 bunches of celery, chopped
2 medium-sized potatoes, sliced thin
2 medium-sized onions, sliced thin
1½ tablespoons unsalted butter
1 small bay leaf

2 cups chicken broth, preferably homemade
Salt and freshly ground black pepper to taste
2 cups half-and-half
1 cup heavy cream
Grated nutmeg (optional)

1. In a 3-quart, heavy saucepan combine the celery, potatoes, onions and butter. Stir well over low heat. Cover the pan and steam the mixture until the vegetables are soft.
2. Add the bay leaf, broth and salt and pepper to taste. Simmer uncovered 30 minutes. Discard the bay leaf.
3. Put mixture through a sieve or food processor. Return to saucepan and add the half-and-half, stirring well to blend. Reheat to serving temperature.
4. Divide the 1 cup of heavy cream evenly into 6 soup bowls or mugs. Pour in the heated soup and garnish with the optional nutmeg.
Serves 6.

Cream of Potato Soup

Potato soup was a family favorite when I was growing up in central Indiana. This soup can be made in less than 40 minutes, and when served with homemade rolls and a green salad, it makes a fine repast for guests.

¾ cup finely chopped onion
½ cup finely diced celery
4 tablespoons unsalted butter
3 cups diced Maine, Eastern or any waxy potato
1 cup water

3 cups milk or half-and-half
Salt and freshly ground white pepper to taste
2 tablespoons minced parsley for garnish

1. In a heavy, 3-quart saucepan cook the onion, celery and butter until onion is translucent but not brown. Add water and potatoes. Cover and cook until tender.
2. Put mixture through a sieve or food processor, if desired, and return to saucepan. Add milk and season to taste with salt and pepper. Reheat to serving temperature. Serve in bowls or mugs, garnished with minced parsley.

Serves 4 to 6.

Variation: Turnip Soup

Substitute 3 cups diced white turnips for the potatoes.

Cream of Mushroom Soup

Serve in small ramekins as a first course at dinner or in large bowls as a luncheon main course. Serve with toasted croutons.

One-fourth pound of America's famous moral mushrooms can be substituted for the one-half pound of the commercial variety.

6 tablespoons unsalted butter
½ cup finely chopped onion
½ pound fresh mushrooms, chopped finely
3 tablespoons flour

3 cups chicken broth, preferably homemade
1 small bay leaf
Salt and freshly ground white pepper to taste
¾ cup light cream

1. Melt the butter in a 2-quart, heavy saucepan; add the onion and cook until transparent but not brown. Add mushrooms and cook about 4 minutes, stirring constantly.

2. Remove saucepan from heat and blend in the flour. Add the broth slowly, stirring constantly. Add the bay leaf and salt and pepper to taste. Bring to a simmer and then cook 5 minutes, stirring constantly. Remove bay leaf and slowly stir in the cream. Reheat to serving temperature but do not boil. Serve in ramekins or larger bowls.

Serves 6.

Apple and Squash Soup

This is a very old recipe for a delicious cream soup. The blender or food processor makes quick work of the old method of sieving the ingredients.

1 cup thinly sliced onion
4 large cooking apples, peeled and sliced thin
3 tablespoons unsalted butter or bacon fat
¼ cup flour
2½ cups chicken broth

2 cooked and peeled acorn squash, cubed
Salt and freshly ground black pepper to taste
½ cup heavy cream
2 tablespoons chopped chives for garnish

1. In a 3-quart saucepan cook the onion, apples and butter or fat over low heat until mushy. Sprinkle flour over mixture and blend well. Add the chicken broth and stir again until well mixed. Bring mixture to a boil and boil at least 3 minutes, stirring constantly. Add the cooked squash and stir to blend. Season to taste with salt and pepper.
2. Process the mixture in a blender or food processor until smooth and return to saucepan. Add cream. Reheat to serving temperature but do not boil. Serve in bowls or mugs garnished with chopped chives.

Serves 6.

New England Cream of Pumpkin Soup

Pumpkin and squash were only two of the numerous Indian foods used by the early settlers. The following soups are refined variations of the original recipes and are suitable as a first course or as a light luncheon main meal.

1 small pumpkin (about 2 pounds)
3 tablespoons unsalted butter
½ cup finely chopped onion
Salt and freshly ground black pepper to taste
⅛ teaspoon ground allspice

½ teaspoon sugar
3 cups chicken broth, preferably homemade
½ cup light cream
Finely chopped parsley for garnish

1. Peel the pumpkin and cut into inch-thick slices. Remove and discard the seeds. Put the slices in a steamer over boiling water and steam until tender, about 20 minutes.
2. Sieve the pumpkin or process the mixture in a blender or food processor until smooth. There should be 2 cups of cooked puree.
3. Heat the butter in a 2-to-3-quart, heavy saucepan and add the onion. Cook until the onion is translucent but not brown. Add the pumpkin and salt and pepper to taste. Then add the allspice, sugar and broth. Bring to a boil. Add the cream and reheat to serving temperature, but do not boil. Serve in bowls garnished with chopped parsley.
Serves 6 to 8.

Variation: Cream of Squash Soup

Use puree of squash instead of pumpkin. Omit allspice and use ¼ teaspoon ground nutmeg.

Deep-South Cheese Soup

Unlike the French-Canadian cheese soups of New England, the Deep South prefers a more highly flavored dish.

6 tablespoons plus 2 tablespoons unsalted butter
6 tablespoons flour
1 quart half-and-half
2 cups grated Cheddar cheese
½ cup finely chopped celery
½ cup finely chopped green pepper

½ cup chopped onion
½ cup grated carrot
2 cups chicken broth
Several dashes of Tabasco sauce, or to taste
Salt to taste

1. In a heavy, 3-quart saucepan melt the 6 tablespoons butter. Blend in flour and cook 3 minutes, stirring constantly.
2. Remove mixture from heat and slowly add the half-and-half, stirring constantly to blend.
3. Return the mixture to heat and cook until mixture thickens. Stir in cheese and remove from heat but keep in a warm place.

4. In a heavy, medium-sized skillet melt the 2 tablespoons butter. Add celery, green pepper, onion and carrots. Cook until onion is translucent but do not brown.
5. Process the mixture in a blender or food processor until smooth. Return to saucepan and add chicken broth. Stir to blend and add to cheese mixture.
6. Add Tabasco sauce and salt to taste. Reheat but do not boil. Serve hot in bowls or mugs.
Serves 6 to 8.

Southern Peanut Soup

Peanut soup is to a Southerner what clam chowder is to a New Englander. This recipe is an adaptation of a delicious soup served at the Hotel Roanoke, a Virginia establishment with a national reputation for serving fine Southern Food. Serve as an appetizer.

¼ cup unsalted butter
¼ cup finely chopped onion
1 rib celery, chopped fine
1½ tablespoons flour
4 cups chicken broth, preferably homemade

1 cup creamy peanut butter
1½ teaspoons lemon juice
Salt to taste
Finely chopped peanuts for garnish

1. In a heavy, 2-quart saucepan melt the butter over low heat. Add the onion and celery. Cook, stirring constantly, until tender but not brown. Add the flour and stir constantly for 3 minutes over low heat. Do not let the mixture brown.
2. Remove mixture from heat and slowly add the chicken broth, stirring constantly to blend.
3. Return to heat and simmer 30 minutes, stirring occasionally to prevent mixture from sticking to bottom of saucepan.
4. Remove mixture from heat and strain through a sieve or process in a blender or food processor until smooth. Add peanut butter, lemon juice and salt. Stir to blend. Serve very hot, garnished with chopped peanuts.
Serves 6.

Charleston She-Crab Soup

There are many versions of this soup in and around Charleston, South Carolina. There it is made with meat from the female crab, identifiable by the wide apron on the underside of the shell. This soup can be made with any fresh, frozen or canned crabmeat of good quality.

2 cups milk
¼ teaspoon ground mace
½ teaspoon finely grated lemon peel
¼ cup unsalted butter
¼ cup finely chopped onion
1 pound fresh, frozen or canned crabmeat, picked over to remove cartilage and shell

2 cups light cream
¼ cup finely ground cracker crumbs
Salt and freshly ground white pepper to taste
6 teaspoons dry sherry

1. Combine the milk, mace and lemon peel in the top of a 2-quart double boiler and heat over simmering water for 3 minutes but do not boil. Set aside.
2. In a small, heavy pan melt the butter and cook the onion until translucent, but not brown.
3. Add the cooked onion, the crabmeat and cream to the hot milk mixture. Return to cook over simmering water. Cook 15 minutes, stirring constantly, but do not boil. Add cracker crumbs and stir to thicken. Add salt and pepper to taste. Remove mixture from heat and let stand over the hot water for several minutes to develop flavor. Add 1 teaspoon sherry to each bowl just before serving. In elegant Charleston restaurants the waiter usually pours the sherry with a flourish from a large brandy snifter after the soup has been served.

Serves 6.

Seafood Bisque
(Basic Recipe)

Bisques are thick cream soups. In American cooking they are made with shellfish and are heavily spiced in the Southern manner. They may be served hot or chilled.

1 pound fresh raw shrimp, without heads
½ cup chopped onion
½ cup chopped celery, with a few leaves
1 cup thinly sliced carrots
2 cups water
½ cup dry white wine

2 cups light cream; or 1 cup heavy cream and 1 cup milk
1 tablespoon unsalted butter
Salt to taste
⅛ teaspoon Tabasco sauce, or to taste
A few sprinklings of grated nutmeg
2 tablespoons chopped chives for garnish

1. Wash shrimp and combine with onion, celery, carrots, water and wine in a 3-quart, heavy saucepan. Bring to a boil and cook a few minutes, until shrimp turn pink.

2. Remove the shrimp from the boiling liquid. Peel and devein, reserving the shells. Set the shrimp aside.
3. Return the shrimp shells to the liquid in the pan. Cover and simmer 25 minutes. Discard shells.
4. Process the chopped shrimp, liquid and vegetables in a blender or food processor until smooth.
5. Return the mixture to the saucepan and gradually add the cream, stirring constantly to blend.
6. Return the mixture to low heat and cook 5 minutes, stirring constantly, to blend flavors. *Caution:* Do not let this mixture come to a boil, or it will curdle. During the reheating, gradually add the butter bit by bit, stirring constantly to blend. Add the salt, Tabasco and nutmeg to taste. Serve hot or chilled, garnished with chives.

Serves 6.

Variation: Crab Bisque

Substitute 2 cups crabmeat for the shrimp.

Maryland Oyster Bisque

This is a very rich bisque. Small servings are recommended.

½ cup chopped onion
½ cup chopped celery
3 tablespoons unsalted butter
2 cups half-and-half
2 cups heavy cream
½ teaspoon ground mace

Salt and freshly ground black pepper to taste
⅛ teaspoon Tabasco sauce, or to taste
2 cups oysters with liquor
¼ cup chopped chives for garnish

1. In a 2-quart, heavy saucepan combine the onion, celery and butter. Cook over low heat until the vegetables are tender but not brown.
2. Combine the half-and-half and heavy cream; gradually add to the cooked vegetables, stirring constantly to blend. Add the mace, salt, pepper and Tabasco sauce. Cook over low heat 5 minutes, stirring constantly. *Caution:* Do not let this mixture come to a boil, or it will curdle.
3. Process the mixture in a blender or food processor to a smooth puree. Return mixture to saucepan and place pot over hot, but not boiling, water for 30 minutes. Refrigerate 12 hours.
5. Slowly reheat the cream mixture and gradually blend in the oyster puree. Heat to serving temperature but do not boil. Reseason with salt, pepper and Tabasco sauce, if desired. Serve hot or chilled, garnished with chopped chives.

Serves 8.

Stews

It is said that the ingredients of a stew, more than any other foods, reflect the personality of a nation.

The technique for making a flavorful stew is almost as old as man. European colonists found our first countrymen eating stews of wild game that were flavored with dried plants and mixed either with honey or water. The Iroquois even used the berries of the sumac tree to flavor their stews.

Meat cooked with vegetables has been the standard dish of the European masses for centuries. It is only natural that colonial housewives would use this cooking method to add balance and nutrition to family meals when supplies were often meager and meat was unavailable.

Even though our early American stews would be considered primitive and unrefined by cooking standards of today, these main-dish meals are just as adaptable to the problems of food shortages and inflation that face the modern cook who uses the latest kitchen equipment. Fortunately the open fireplace has been replaced by the modern range and the heavy iron kettle has given way to the cast-iron casserole with a tight-fitting lid. However, we all strive to reproduce the old-fashioned flavor of a hearty stew, made with the finest ingredients.

One of the most relaxed and gratifying ways to entertain, for both the cook and the guests, is to serve a satisfying one-dish stew with homemade bread and wine or beer, and a simple dessert. Most stews can be prepared completely in advance, and because the flavors intensify with time, they offer an ideal combination of ease in preparation and fine flavor.

Usually stews are made of beef, lamb, pork or veal. However, they can be made from poultry, fish or seafood. Chili dishes and gumbos also are considered stews.

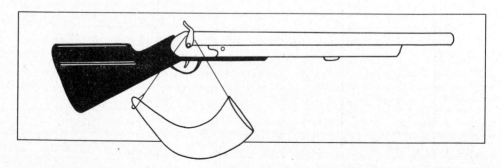

Stew-making Basics

UTENSILS   You will need a large, heavy skillet for browning the meat and cooking the aromatic pot vegetables (chopped onion, carrots, celery, etc.), and it must be large enough to hold the amount of liquid specified in the recipe. You will also need a large, heavy, flame-proof casserole with a tight-fitting lid to cook the stew. Most professional cooks recommend a 10-to-12-inch cast-iron Dutch oven. They claim the iron helps flavor a slow-simmering stew. A large electric skillet or a slow-cooker also may be used. Follow the manufacturer's instructions if using either of the latter two.

PREPARATION   To prepare meat stews, buy less-expensive cuts of meat. These meats will be tough because they contain very little internal fat. Trim the gristle and any large tendons running through the meat. Reserve these bits and pieces and freeze for making broth. Cut the meat into 1-inch cubes. Two and a half pounds of meat will serve six to eight people.

SEASONING WITH HERBS   A good stew is only as flavorful as the ingredients and seasonings used to prepare it. Dried herbs should be added before the stew is cooked. Fresh herbs are more delicate and should be added approximately 5 minutes before the cooking time is over. 1 tablespoon fresh herbs = 1 teaspoon dried. Remember, bay leaf always should be discarded as soon as the stew is cooked.

VEGETABLES FOR STEW   Vegetables should not be added to a stew more than 1 hour before serving time. They should be as fresh as possible. Vegetables past their prime do not add flavor to a stew. If freshness is in question, use frozen vegetables. Fresh vegetables should be parboiled or steamed separately before they are added to the stew, with the exception of tomatoes or other vegetables with high water content, which can be added raw to the stew. Frozen vegetables do not need to be precooked because they were blanched before they were frozen. Mushrooms should be sautéed, so that they will retain their shape and flavor before they are added to a stew.

COOKING STEWS
Stovetop method: Cover casserole tightly and let meat simmer until tender, but do not boil. (Veal, pork, and lamb require about 1½ hours;

beef, about 2 hours.) Follow cooking times in individual recipes for poultry, fish and seafood.

Oven method: Preheat oven to 325°F. Cover casserole tightly and cook 1½ hours, or until meat is tender.

REHEATING STEWS   To develop full flavor, any stew can be refrigerated 24 hours. Add precooked vegetables. Reheat on stovetop until serving temperature, being careful not to let the stew boil; or reheat in preheated 350°F. oven 30 minutes.

Old-Fashioned Beef Stew
(Basic Recipe)

This is an honest, back-to-basics beef stew, flavored with fresh garden vegetables and seasonings. Those of us whose careers include extensive travel and dining on restaurant fare find that American beef stew seldom appears on any menu. Traditionally, this dish is served to the kitchen help.

This recipe has been in my collection as long as I have been entertaining. If I want to glamorize this simple main course, I make small round loaves of bread in individual casseroles. I slice off the top of the loaf to use as a lid. Then I carefully scoop out the inside of the loaf to form a bowl. (This bread can be reserved for making crumbs.) The stew is served piping-hot in the bread bowl, covered with the top slice to form its own little serving pot. This never fails to impress my guests. Serve with a green salad, beer or wine and a fruit dessert.

2½ pounds boneless chuck, trimmed
    of all fat
3 tablespoons peanut oil
1½ cups finely chopped onion
1 clove garlic, minced
1 cup thinly sliced carrots
1 cup finely chopped celery
2 tablespoons unsalted butter
3 tablespoons flour
1 tablespoon tomato paste
3 cups water

1 tablespoon lemon juice
1 bay leaf
1 teaspoon ground thyme
Salt and freshly ground black pepper
    to taste
6 small carrots, sliced on the diag-
    onal into ½-inch pieces, parboiled
12 small white onions, parboiled
6 small potatoes, parboiled
¼ cup chopped parsley for garnish

Preheated oven temperature 325°F., or use stovetop method

1. Trim the gristle and any large tendons that run through the meat. Cut meat into 1-inch cubes.
2. Heat the oil in a heavy, 10-to-12-inch skillet. When the oil is sizzling, add a few pieces of the meat and quickly brown on all sides. As

pieces brown, remove and place in a heavy, 5-quart casserole with a tight-fitting lid. Do not crowd the skillet, or the meat will steam and become gray and limp. Continue until all the meat has been browned.

3. After all the meat has been removed to the casserole, add the chopped onion, garlic, thinly sliced carrots and celery to the skillet. Cover and cook, stirring occasionally. Brown the vegetables over medium heat but do not burn; then add the butter. Stir well to blend. If the vegetables have been thinly and evenly cut, the mixture should be the consistency of a thick puree.

4. Add the flour and cook about 2 to 3 minutes, stirring constantly, until the vegetables are reddish-brown. Add the tomato paste and cook an additional 5 minutes. Stir in the water, lemon juice, bay leaf and thyme. Season to taste with salt and pepper.

5. Transfer all these ingredients to the casserole with the beef. Cover and simmer in a preheated oven or on top of the stove for 1½ hours, or until the meat is almost tender. Remove bay leaf. At this point the stew can be refrigerated for 24 hours, if desired.

6. Reheat and add the parboiled carrots, small whole onions and potatoes. Cover and cook 30 minutes, or until vegetables and meat are tender. Add salt and pepper to taste. Serve hot, garnished with chopped parsley.

Serves 6.

Variations: Lamb Stew

Omit beef and substitute 2½ pounds lamb shoulder, trimmed of all fat and cut into 1-inch cubes. Omit potatoes and substitute 1½ cups parboiled baby lima beans. *Caution:* Remove all fat from lamb. The fat will cause the stew to develop a strong flavor in the reheating process.

Venison Stew

Omit beef and substitute venison. The cooking time, depending upon the tenderness of the venison, will be approximately 2½ hours.
NOTE: In step 3 the stew must be refrigerated for 24 hours. This eliminates the need to marinate the venison prior to step 2.

Beef Stew in a Baked Pumpkin

Baking a stew in a pumpkin is an American Indian custom. For today's food stylist it makes an interesting presentation.

3 pounds boneless chuck trimmed of all fat and cut into 1-inch cubes
2 cups chopped onion
2 cups chopped green pepper
1 cup diced celery
2 cloves garlic, minced
1 tablespoon tomato paste
2 tablespoons light olive oil
1 tablespoon salt
½ teaspoon freshly ground black pepper
1 bay leaf
1 teaspoon ground thyme

½ cup dry red wine (optional)
2 cups beef broth, preferably home-made
2 cups sliced yellow squash, such as butternut
2 cups cooked fresh green beans
2 cups canned solid-pack tomatoes, drained
1 short pumpkin, 6 to 8 pounds
½ cup milk
2 teaspoons salt, or to taste
½ teaspoon freshly ground black pepper

Preheated oven temperature— 325°F.

1. In a heavy, 10-to-12-inch skillet brown the beef, onion, green pepper, celery, garlic and tomato paste in the oil over medium heat for about 5 minutes. Pour off excess oil. Stir in salt, pepper, bay leaf, thyme, optional red wine and the beef broth. Place stew in a covered casserole or kettle and bake in a preheated 325°F. oven 1½ hours. Add the squash, green beans and tomatoes. Return to oven for 20 to 30 minutes, or until beef is tender and squash is cooked.
2. The pumpkin can be baked at the same time as the stew. To prepare pumpkin, slice off top and clean out inside. Sprinkle inside with milk, salt and pepper. Bake in preheated 325°F. oven for 1 to 1½ hours, or until the meat of the pumpkin is tender. Ladle hot stew into pumpkin for serving. Scoop out a little pumpkin with each serving.

Serves 10.

Veal Stew

Blanquette de Veau is a classic white veal stew in French bourgeois cooking. French home cooks pride themselves on keeping it as white, or *blonde*, as possible by blanching the veal and bleaching the whitest mushrooms in lemon juice to keep them from turning dark. American veal stew is put through the *roux* process of browning the pot vegetables with the flour to add more flavor and color, which is more in keeping with the personality of American cooking.

In this dish the mushrooms may be left whole or, if they are different sizes, they may be sliced before they are sautéed and added to the stew.

2½ pounds boneless veal shoulder
4 slices (¼ pound) salt pork
1½ cups finely chopped onion
1 clove garlic, minced
1 cup thinly sliced carrots
1 cup finely chopped celery
2 tablespoons unsalted butter
3 tablespoons flour
1 tablespoon tomato paste
3 cups chicken broth, preferably homemade

1 tablespoon lemon juice
1 bay leaf
1 teaspoon ground thyme
Salt and freshly ground black pepper to taste
½ pound whole or sliced mushrooms, sautéed
2 cups frozen green peas
Grated nutmeg and thinly sliced lemon for garnish

Preheated oven temperature 325°F., or use stovetop method

1. Trim away the gristle or tendons that run through the meat. Cut into 1-inch cubes.
2. Fry out the salt pork in a heavy, 10-to-12-inch skillet. Discard the salt pork, reserving the fat, and heat until sizzling. Add a few pieces of the veal and quickly brown on all sides. As pieces brown, remove and place in a heavy, 5-quart casserole with a tight-fitting lid. Do not crowd the skillet, or the meat will not brown. (Add peanut oil if meat appears to be sticking to the pan.) Continue until all the meat has been browned.
3. After all the meat has been removed to the casserole, add the onion, garlic, carrots and celery to the skillet. Cover and cook, stirring occasionally. Brown the vegetables over medium heat but do not burn; then add the butter. Stir well to blend. If the vegetables have been thinly and evenly cut, the mixture should be the consistency of a thick puree.
4. Add the flour and cook the mixture 2 to 3 minutes, stirring constantly, until the vegetables are reddish-brown. Add tomato paste and cook an additional 5 minutes. Stir in the chicken broth, lemon juice, bay leaf and thyme. Season to taste with salt and pepper.
5. Transfer all these ingredients to the casserole with the veal. Cover and simmer in a preheated oven or on top of the stove for 1 to 1¼ hours, or until meat is tender. Remove bay leaf. At this point the stew can be refrigerated 24 hours, if desired.
6. Reheat and add sautéed mushrooms and green peas. Cover and cook 5 minutes, or until the peas are tender. Add salt and pepper to taste. Garnish with a light sprinkling of nutmeg and very thin slices of lemon.

Serves 6.

Pork Stew

A hearty pork stew is a typical Midwestern dish, suitable for serving after any active winter sport.

2½ pounds boneless pork shoulder
4 slices (¼ pound) salt pork
1½ cups finely chopped onion
2 cloves garlic, minced
1 cup thinly sliced carrots
1 cup finely chopped celery
2 tablespoons unsalted butter
3 tablespoons flour
1 tablespoon tomato paste
1½ cups tomato juice
1½ cups water

1 tablespoon lemon juice
1 bay leaf
1 teaspoon ground thyme
Salt and freshly ground black pepper to taste
6 small carrots, sliced on the diagonal into ½-inch pieces, parboiled
6 small turnips, parboiled
1½ cups fresh green beans, parboiled

Preheated oven temperature 325°F., or use stovetop method
1. Trim away as much fat as possible from the meat. Cut into 1-inch cubes.
2. Fry out the salt pork in a heavy, 10-to-12-inch skillet. Discard the salt pork, reserving the fat, and heat until sizzling. Add a few pieces of the meat and quickly brown on all sides. As pieces brown, remove and place in a heavy, 5-quart casserole with a tight-fitting lid. Do not crowd the skillet, or the meat will not brown. Continue until all the meat has been browned.
3. After all the meat has been removed to the casserole, add the onion, garlic, thinly sliced carrots and celery to the skillet. Cover and cook, stirring occasionally. Brown the vegetables over medium heat but do not burn; then add the butter. Stir well to blend. If the vegetables have been thinly and evenly cut, the mixture should be the consistency of a thick puree.
4. Add the flour and cook 2 to 3 minutes, stirring constantly, until the vegetables are reddish-brown. Add tomato paste and cook an additional 5 minutes. Stir in the tomato juice, water, lemon juice, bay leaf and thyme. Season to taste with salt and pepper.
5. Transfer all these ingredients to the casserole with the pork. Cover and simmer in a preheated oven or on top of the stove for 1 to 1¼ hours, or until meat is tender. Remove bay leaf. At this point the stew can be refrigerated for 24 hours, if desired.
6. Reheat and add the parboiled carrots and turnips. Cover and cook 15 minutes. Add green beans and cook an additional 10 to 12 minutes, or until vegetables are tender. Add salt and pepper to taste.

Serves 8.

North Carolina Brunswick Stew

There are just about as many ways to prepare Brunswick Stew as there are cooks in the state. Originally this dish was made with young, tender squirrels, whose meat is similar to the dark meat of chicken, and with garden-fresh vegetables cooked down to a thick puree. Modern taste dictates cooking the vegetables less for better flavor. Naturally, serve with buttered corn bread.

NOTE: If using squirrels, clean, draw and soak in cold salted water for 3 hours. Parboil and then proceed with the recipe.

1½ cups chopped onion
2 tablespoons vegetable oil or bacon fat
1 3½-pound frying chicken, quartered
4 cups water
4 cups fresh tomatoes, peeled and seeded
1½ cups fresh lima beans
2 cups Maine or Eastern potatoes, cut into ½-inch cubes

1½ cups freshly cut corn with milk scrapings
Salt and freshly ground black pepper to taste
1 tablespoon unsalted butter
½ cup diced carrots
½ cup diced celery
½ cup grated cabbage (optional)

1. In a heavy, 4-quart casserole or Dutch oven cook onion in oil or bacon fat until translucent but not brown. Remove and set aside.
2. Place chicken in casserole, add water, cover and simmer about 1 hour, until chicken is tender. Remove chicken from broth and set aside.
3. Add cooked onion, the tomatoes, beans and salt to taste to the broth and cook until beans are tender. Add potatoes and cook uncovered approximately 20 minutes, or until almost tender. Add corn, additional salt to taste and pepper, butter, carrots, celery and optional cabbage. Cook until all vegetables are tender.
4. Remove bones from chicken and cut into bite-size pieces. Return to vegetables and broth. Heat to serving temperature.

Serves 6.

Chili

A Tex-Mex dish, chili has become one of the ecumenical dishes of American cooking. "Chilihead" is an affectionate term used to describe a devotee of this highly seasoned dish.

Most chili cooks guard their recipes like fine jewels. Some even grind their own special blend of chili powder, though others admit to using Gebhardt's.

Chili can be made with or without beans—even in Texas, it is made both ways. This recipe is a compromise, geared to the busy lifestyle of today's cooks, who lack the time to soak pinto beans overnight and then cook the ingredients 5 to 6 hours, as older, traditional recipes specified.

Canned pinto beans are available in any well-stocked market. If unavailable, red kidney beans may be substituted. Serve this dish with a salad of avocado, rings of purple onion and fresh tomatoes, to counteract the flavor of the hot spices in the chili. A side dish of grated cheese can be passed around as a topping for the chili. Serve with ice-cold beer.

2½ pounds very lean beef, ground or coarsely chopped
1 pound very lean pork, ground or coarsely chopped
⅓ cup chili powder, or to taste
1½ teaspoons ground cumin
2 cloves garlic, minced
1½ tablespoons vegetable oil or bacon fat

3 cups finely chopped onion
2 cups finely chopped green pepper
½ cup chopped parsley
5 cups canned tomatoes with juice
Salt and freshly ground black pepper to taste
4 cups drained pinto beans or red kidney beans

1. Lightly mix the beef, pork, chili powder, cumin and garlic.
2. Heat the oil in a large, 6-quart, heavy kettle and add the meat. Cook, chopping with the side of a large metal kitchen spoon to break up the lumps. Cook 15 minutes, or until the meat is browned.
3. Add the onion, green pepper, parsley and tomatoes. Season lightly with salt and pepper. Stir well to blend. Cover and simmer 1 hour. Add more chili powder, if desired. Add the beans and cook uncovered 30 minutes. Serve piping-hot in bowls. Makes 4 quarts. Extra portions freeze very well.

Serves 8 to 10.

Chili con Carne

This is a recipe from an exceptional and locally famous restaurant in Clearwater, Florida. They serve several types of chili, but this one is made with shredded beef and without beans. Frijoles, a puree of pinto beans, is served on the side.

2 pounds boneless chuck, trimmed of all fat and cut into 1½-inch cubes

3 medium-sized tomatoes, peeled, seeded and diced

1½ cups water

1 cup chopped onion

2 cloves garlic, crushed

1 teaspoon salt, or to taste

1½ cups tomato sauce, preferably homemade

1 4-ounce can chopped green chilis

1 tablespoon chili powder, or to taste

1 tablespoon ground cumin

1. Combine meat, tomatoes, water, onion, and garlic in a 6-quart, heavy kettle with a cover, and bring to a boil over high heat. Reduce heat, cover and simmer, adding water as necessary so that meat is always partially covered, until beef is tender enough to shred, about 2 hours.
2. Add tomato sauce, chilis, chili powder and cumin. Cover and simmer 30 minutes, stirring often to prevent sticking. Serve hot.

Serves 6 to 8.

Oyster Stew

Oysters were about the only fresh seafood available to Midwesterners prior to World War II. Needless to say, they were considered a great delicacy. So much so, that my grandmother Prichard, a legendary local cook, served oyster stew at my parents' wedding supper.

1 pint oysters and their liquid

4 cups half-and-half

¼ cup unsalted butter

Salt and cayenne pepper to taste

1. Strain the liquid from the oysters through three thicknesses of cheesecloth into the top of a 1½-quart double boiler and bring to a boil over simmering water.
2. In a 2-quart, heavy saucepan heat the half-and-half and stir in the butter. Pour this mixture into the oyster liquid. Stir well to blend. Add the oysters; season with salt and cayenne pepper to taste. Cook over simmering water until the soup is hot but not boiling. The oysters will rise to the top. Serve at once with oyster crackers.

Serves 4. Recipe may be doubled.

New England Seafood Stew

This is a seafood stew that matches anything the Mediterranean has to offer. Rich and satisfying, this dish is a complete meal in itself. Serve with a good white wine.

4 slices (¼ pound) salt pork, diced
¼ cup unsalted butter
½ teaspoon salt
½ teaspoon paprika
2 teaspoons Worcestershire sauce
⅛ teaspoon Tabasco sauce
2 cups fish broth or 2 8-ounce bottles
      clam juice

1 pound cod fillets, cut into 2-inch
      pieces
2 cups shrimp, shelled and deveined
2 cups lobster meat, diced
2 tablespoons chopped chives
½ cup finely diced celery
3 cups milk
1 cup light cream

1. In a heavy 3-quart saucepan fry out salt pork over low heat. Reserve the pork. Add the butter, salt, paprika, Worcestershire sauce, Tabasco sauce and clam juice to the fat. Boil 3 minutes.
2. Add the fish, seafood, chives and celery. Cover and simmer until tender and the codfish flakes—this should take no more than 12 to 14 minutes. Add the reserved pork, the milk and cream and heat to serving temperature.

Serves 6.

Maine Lobster Stew

A private-collection recipe based on New England thrift, this is one of the taste treats in the repertory of shellfish stews. Not many years ago lobster was so plentiful in Maine that people considered it too much bother to "pick out" all the meat, so there often was much left untouched in the shells. The next morning the cook made her family a stew from the leftover shells and meat, and served it the second day.

Stirring is the most important step in the preparation of this culinary masterpiece. In addition, the milk, cream and half-and-half should be combined and heated before being added to the lobster mixture. Lobster stew should be "aged" in the refrigerator at least 6 hours—overnight is better; this develops the taste considerably. A light sprinkling of salt and cayenne pepper is all the seasoning needed to "lift" the flavor of this rich lobster stew. Serve with toasted crackers or warm Uneeda brand crackers.

NOTE: In New England restaurants the cook often garnishes lobster stew with a sprinkling of paprika and sometimes with chopped fresh dill.

2 2-pound boiled lobsters (2 2-pound lobsters have sweeter meat than 1 4-pounder)
½ cup unsalted butter
4 cups milk
2 cups heavy cream
3 cups half-and-half
Salt and cayenne pepper to taste

1. Remove meat from lobster shells, reserving the tomalley, the coral and thick white substance from inside the shell. Cube the meat. Reserve a few of the legs for garnish.
2. In a heavy, 4-quart kettle melt the butter. Add the cubed lobster, tomalley, the coral and the thick white substance from inside the shell. Sauté 3 to 4 minutes—*no longer!* This adds flavor and color to the stew.
3. In a separate saucepan heat the milk, cream and half-and-half just to the boiling point; if the mixture boils, it will curdle.
4. Remove the lobster mixture from the heat and slowly add the hot liquid.
5. Return the stew to low heat and reheat just to boiling temperature, stirring very gently a few times so as not to shred the cubes of lobster. Remove from heat and cool to room temperature. Refrigerate 6 hours.
6. Reheat to serving temperature but do not boil; season with a few sprinklings of salt and cayenne pepper. Stew will be a delicate pink color with a pale yellow topping. Garnish with the reserved lobster legs. Serve very hot.

Serves 6.

East Coast Scallop Stew

In the United States sea scallops are available fresh and frozen all year round. Bay scallops are available fresh only in the early fall. All scallops have a slightly sweet taste; a delicious stew can be a rare flavor treat. Overcooking toughens all fish and shellfish, but particularly scallops. Cook only until the meat turns white.

1 pound sea or bay scallops
2 tablespoons unsalted butter
3 cups milk
1 cup heavy cream
1 teaspoon Worcestershire sauce
Salt and freshly ground black pepper to taste
Paprika for garnish
¼ cup chopped parsley for garnish

1. If using sea scallops, cut into bite-size pieces.
2. In a heavy, 3-quart saucepan melt butter. Add scallops and cook slowly until they turn white—this will take less than 5 minutes.

3. Combine milk and cream and add slowly to the scallops, stirring constantly. Add Worcestershire sauce and salt and pepper to taste. Stir to blend. Reheat and serve in bowls garnished with a sprinkling of paprika and chopped parsley.

Serves 4 to 6.

Cioppino

Pronounced "cho-PEEN-o," this is a fish stew popular in California, particularly in the San Francisco Bay area. No one knows when or how it became an American dish. However, it is thought that during the gold-rush days, visiting Mediterranean fishermen adapted their bouillabaisse to the local varieties of fish and shellfish.

Cioppino is a rather loosely organized dish, dependent upon the catch of the day, and its preparation is really a matter of taste. Some cooks use red wine, others use a dry white. Some cooks use all shellfish, others use a combination of fish and shellfish.

Cioppino can be served with garlic bread or it can be served in deep bowls over grilled buttered squares of sour-dough bread. Either way, the sauce is heavenly. For dessert, serve a variety of fruits and cheeses.

This dish is prepared in two steps. First you prepare the fish and shellfish, and then you prepare the sauce.

3 pounds any variety of firm white fish (halibut, flounder, tilefish, etc.)
1 large live Dungeness (hardshell crab; or 1 pound crabmeat, fresh or frozen

1 pound large shrimp
1 pint oysters or mussels

Sauce

¼ cup light olive oil
1 cup finely chopped onion
3 cloves garlic, crushed with 1 teaspoon salt
1 cup finely chopped green pepper
2 teaspoons finely chopped parsley
½ cup chopped green onions, with tops
1 bay leaf
½ teaspoon basil
¼ teaspoon oregano

3½ cups solid-pack tomatoes
Liquid from oysters or mussels
2 cups dry red wine
2 cups tomato juice
2 cups fish broth made from fish trimmings; or use bottled clam juice
Salt and freshly ground black pepper to taste
½ cup minced parsley for garnish

To prepare the fish:
1. Cut fish into 2-inch serving pieces. Crack the crab; remove top shell but keep it for making broth. Split shrimp shells down the back and remove the black vein. Steam the oysters or mussels in a small amount of water just until they open. Remove the top shells and save the juice.

To prepare the sauce:
1. In a heavy, 10-to-12-inch skillet combine the oil, onion, garlic and green pepper. Cook, stirring constantly, until onion is just soft but not brown. Add the parsley, green onions, bay leaf, basil, oregano, tomatoes, oyster or mussel juice, wine, tomato juice and fish broth. Cook uncovered over medium heat 10 minutes. Remove bay leaf and season to taste with salt and pepper.
2. Layer the fish, crab and shrimp in a heavy, 6-quart kettle or casserole with a lid. Pour sauce over all and cover pan. Simmer over low heat 10 minutes, or until fish is done. Three minutes before removing from the heat, add the oysters or mussels.
3. Serve in deep bowls, shells and all. Garnish with chopped parsley.
Serves 6 generously.

Cajun Crab Stew

This rich stew is a fine example of good Louisiana cooking. Serve with garlic bread.

1 pound crabmeat, fresh or frozen
6 slices lean bacon, blanched
¾ cup finely chopped onion
1 clove garlic, minced
4 tablespoons tomato paste
2 cups julienne strips lean cooked ham

⅓ cup dark rum, heated
2 cups white wine
1 tablespoon finely chopped parsley
¼ teaspoon sugar
¼ cup heavy cream
3 cups cooked rice

1. Pick over the crabmeat well for bits of shells and cartilage.
2. In a heavy, 4-quart saucepan fry the bacon until crisp. Remove bacon, cool and crumble for garnish. To the bacon fat add the onion and garlic and cook until onion is translucent but not brown. Add the tomato paste and ham. Stir well to blend.
3. In a separate small pan heat the rum and pour hot over the ham mixture. Ignite with a match. When the flame subsides, cook 3 to 4 minutes, stirring constantly to prevent sticking. Stir in the crabmeat. Add the wine, parsley and sugar. Stir well to blend and simmer 15 minutes. Stir in the heavy cream and blend well. Serve hot over steamed or boiled rice. Garnish with crumbled bacon.

Serves 6.

Jambalaya
(Basic Recipe)

This is a classic Louisiana Cajun dish with many variations. Jambalaya is considered a stew and most resembles a Spanish paella—a mixture of rice, meat and seafood.

Jambalaya makes an excellent party dish, since it can be prepared ahead of time by partially cooking until almost done and then refrigerating it. The cooking can be finished just before serving. Serve with garlic bread, a green salad and a bland, custard-type dessert.

1 tablespoon light olive oil
1 tablespoon unsalted butter
1 clove garlic, minced
1/3 cup chopped onion
2 tablespoons chopped green pepper
3 ripe tomatoes, peeled, seeded and chopped
2 cups double-strength chicken broth, preferably homemade
3/4 cup uncooked rice
1 small bay leaf
1/2 teaspoon chili powder

1/8 teaspoon ground cloves
1/8 teaspoon ground thyme
Scant 1/8 teaspoon cayenne pepper
1 teaspoon salt, or to taste
2 cups cooked diced ham
3 small, highly seasoned cooked pork sausages, sliced thin (optional)
2 cups raw shrimp, shelled and deveined
Salt and freshly ground black pepper to taste

In a 4-quart Dutch oven heat the oil and butter. Add the garlic, onion and green pepper. Cook until the onion is translucent but not brown. Add the tomatoes, chicken broth, rice, bay leaf, chili powder, cloves, thyme, cayenne pepper and salt. Cover and simmer 20 minutes. Add the ham and optional sausage slices and cook 5 minutes. Add the shrimp and cook until pink. Add salt and pepper to taste.

Serves 6.

Variations: Crayfish Jambalaya

Omit ham and sausage slices and shrimp. Substitute 4 cups peeled crayfish or small frozen rock lobster tails. Cover and cook 12 minutes, or until crayfish is tender.

Oyster or Shrimp Jambalaya

Omit ham and sausage slices. In step 1 heat 2 cups drained oysters in the olive oil and butter; cook over low heat until edges begin to curl. Remove oysters from pan and refrigerate. Add the liquor from the oysters to the liquid mixture in the recipe. Add oysters to the mixture at the same time as the shrimp.

Chicken and Shrimp Jambalaya

Omit ham and sausage slices. Substitute 2 cups cubed cooked chicken.

Red Beans and Rice

"Red and White," one of the most popular dishes of everyday Louisiana cooking, is red beans and rice. For many decades it has been the staple dish of the region—inexpensive and delicious. Admittedly a peasant dish, this stew can be made either with salt pork, ham or beef. Serve with pungent toasted garlic bread and ice-cold beer.

2 cups dried red or kidney beans, presoaked
1 pound lightly smoked ham hocks
2 tablespoons bacon drippings
2 tablespoons flour
1 cup chopped onion
2 cloves garlic, minced
1 cup thinly sliced carrot
2 ribs celery, chopped
1 cup chopped green pepper
1 bay leaf
⅛ teaspoon ground thyme
1 small dried red pepper
3 sprigs parsley, chopped
6 cups beef broth
1 teaspoon salt, or to taste
¼ teaspoon freshly ground black pepper, or to taste
3 cups boiled or steamed long-grain white rice
¼ cup finely chopped parsley for garnish

1. *Prepare beans. Quick method:* Measure water to cover the beans 2 inches and bring to a boil. Cover pot and cook 2 minutes; remove from heat. Let stand 1 hour and then follow recipe instructions. *Overnight method:* Measure water to cover the beans 2 inches and let stand 6 to 8 hours or overnight.

2. In a large, heavy, 5-to-6-quart kettle, preferably an iron pot with a tight-fitting lid, brown the ham hocks in the bacon drippings on all sides.
3. Remove ham hocks and set aside. Add the flour to the fat in the kettle and cook over low heat 3 minutes, stirring constantly. Add the onion, garlic, carrot, celery and green pepper; cook until tender.
4. Drain the beans. Add the browned ham hocks, beans, bay leaf, thyme, red pepper, sprigs of parsley and beef broth to the kettle. Cover and simmer over low heat 1½ hours.
5. Remove ham hocks and cool enough to handle. Discard all fat and bone and cut the meat into small pieces.
6. Return the ham to the kettle. Cover and cook 30 additional minutes, or until the beans are tender. Discard bay leaf.

NOTE: If a thicker sauce is desired, process 1 cup of the mixture in a blender or food processor until smooth and return to the kettle. Reheat and serve over hot rice. Garnish with chopped parsley.
Serves 6.

Variation: Red Bean Soup

Traditionally the leftover beans are placed in a blender or food processor with enough water to make a thick soup, depending upon the quantity of beans. Add Tabasco sauce to taste. Pour into a saucepan and simmer 5 minutes to blend flavors. Serve with thin slices of toasted French bread for garnish.

Creole Courtbouillon

In classic French cooking, a courtbouillon can be a number of different mixtures. However, in Louisiana it is made with redfish, a favorite of hostesses and often a house specialty in the finest restaurants. The channel bass, known in Southern waters as redfish, ranges from Delaware, around the coast of Florida and into the Gulf Coast.

Serve as a stew over bowls of cooked rice, accompanied by thick slices of toasted garlic bread.

This is a home-style recipe from the kitchen of friends, natives of New Iberia, Louisiana. Enjoy!

4 to 5 pounds redfish
Salt and freshly ground black pepper
  to taste
1 cup water
¼ cup vegetable oil
¼ cup unsalted butter
2 tablespoons flour
3 cups finely chopped onion
1 cup chopped green pepper
4 cups solid-pack canned tomatoes
1 cup finely chopped celery

3 cloves garlic, minced
3 cups hot water
1 teaspoon Worcestershire sauce
Salt and freshly ground black pepper
  to taste
⅓ cup minced parsley
1 cup dry white wine
1 lemon, sliced thin
3 cups boiled or steamed long-grain
  white rice

1. Cut the thick, meaty part of the fish into 2-inch squares and set aside. Put the remainder of the fish (head, bones and small bits of fish) in a saucepan. Add salt and pepper and 1 cup water. Cover and simmer 20 minutes. Discard head and bones; reserve broth with fish bits.
2. Make a *roux* by the following method: In a 6-quart, heavy kettle heat the oil, butter and flour. Cook over low heat, stirring constantly, until mixture is medium brown (about the color of peanut butter).
3. Add onions and cook until tender but not burned. Add green pepper, tomatoes, celery and garlic. Cover and simmer 25 minutes, stirring occasionally to keep mixture from sticking to the bottom of the kettle.
4. Add 1 cup of the hot water and cook mixture down until it is very thick. Add the remaining 2 cups of hot water, the fish, broth, Worcestershire sauce, salt, pepper and parsley.
5. Cover and simmer about 20 minutes, or until the fish is cooked. Five minutes before the end of the cooking period add the wine and sliced lemon. Serve hot over bowls of rice.

Serves 6.

Gumbos

When I lived in New Orleans during the early fifties, I was introduced to the flavorful gumbos of the region—an entirely new field of cookery for me. Gumbo, a dish that defies classification, is something like a soup, a stew or a chowder. Gumbos may be based on many different foods—chicken, game birds, shrimp, crabs, oysters, crayfish, vegetables—the list is endless. Such freedom in ingredients is not allowed in classical cookery. New Orleans folks are apt to use this pert sally when bidding each other adieu: "Au revoir, meet you in the gumbo."

A good gumbo is a luscious blend of the best traditional cookery of France and Spain, interpreted by Black cooks who have given it a subtle and exotic touch to make it a distinctive American dish. Somehow, these African natives have managed to hand down an extraordinary instinct for cooking; and their knowledge of culinary herbs is probably responsible for the use of herbs in the making of a fine gumbo.

Standard recipes for gumbos exist in almost every all-purpose cookbook, but nearly every New Orleans family has its own variation, which may contain ingredients and cooking techniques whose secrecy is carefully guarded. One is born to making a delicious gumbo; it is a matter of family pride and tradition.

The basic recipe for seafood gumbo that follows is the specialty of a native of New Orleans. She is known as a superb cook and gracious hostess among her social and political friends.

Gumbos are a delicious example of what can be done with simple ingredients. Serve with garlic bread, a green salad and a fruit dessert.

Gumbo-making Basics

Before you begin the preparation of a seafood gumbo, a word of advice. Like the famous Marseilles bouillabaisse in French cooking, seafood gumbo has more flavor if made with fresh seafood. Even Louisianians who live a mere 60 miles from the sea call themselves "land cooks," and make their gumbos with poultry and game birds. Fresh-frozen seafood can be used, but more seasoning will be needed to flavor the gumbo.

ABOUT OKRA AND FILÉ POWDER   Both are used to thicken gumbos. Okra is distinctively American and grows prolifically in the South. It is used as a vegetable and as an essential ingredient in making gumbo. Okra can be purchased fresh in all seasons in most Northern markets. Frozen okra is always available. *Caution:* Never cook okra in a cast-iron skillet or kettle. The iron will cause the okra to darken and, in the words of one old cookbook, "turn black with rage." Okra is called the "lazy man's filé," since the latter requires considerably more cooking expertise when added during the final preparation of a gumbo.

NOTE: Precook okra until slices separate and cease to be "ropey" before adding to gumbo. This will keep the gumbo from being slimy.

TOP

OKRA

TAIL

It is generally agreed among cooks born to gumbo-making that both okra and filé powder should be used in a well-flavored gumbo. The New Orleans Import Co., Ltd. lists filé powder as a mixture of sassafras leaves and thyme. It was first prepared by the Choctaw Indians who lived in the woods around New Orleans. The leaves were gathered by the squaws and sold in the French market to the early French and Spanish settlers. This condiment is quite perishable. When fresh, it has a distinctive flavor, but must be used with discretion, because it can overthicken a gumbo and make it "tacky." Gumbos made with filé powder cannot be reheated. Natives of New Orleans use okra to thicken their gumbo, and then they pass around a bowl of filé powder to be sprinkled over each serving individually and then stirred into the gumbo to taste.

UTENSILS   You will need a medium-sized, heavy skillet— do not use cast-iron to cook the okra. You will need a 5-to-6-quart, heavy kettle with a tight-fitting lid. A porcelain-lined cast-iron or stainless-steel kettle is recommended for the *roux* and to make the gumbo. An authentic Creole seafood gumbo is always made with a *roux* base.

New Orleans Seafood Gumbo

1 pound fresh raw shrimp, without heads

2 quarts water, with a few celery tops

1 dozen hard-shell crabs or ½ pound fresh or frozen crabmeat

1 pound fresh or 2 10-ounce packages frozen okra, sliced into ½-inch pieces

2 tablespoons vegetable oil

2 tablespoons unsalted butter

2 tablespoons flour

1 cup chopped onion

¾ cup chopped green onions, with tops

½ cup finely chopped celery

1 cup canned solid-pack tomatoes

2 sprigs parsley, chopped

1 bay leaf

¼ teaspoon ground thyme

¼ teaspoon cayenne pepper, or to taste

Salt and freshly ground black pepper to taste

2 cups boiled or steamed long-grain white rice

Filé powder (optional)

1. Peel and devein the shrimp, reserving the shells.
2. Place the shrimp shells, water and celery tops in a pan. Cover and simmer 25 minutes. Discard shells and celery tops. Strain liquid and set aside.
3. If using fresh hard-shell crabs, prepare as in Basic Instructions, page 109. Whether using fresh or frozen, pick over crabmeat well for bits of shells and cartilage. Set aside.
4. Top and tail fresh okra and slice into ½-inch pieces. Melt 1 table-spoon of the oil and 1 tablespoon of the butter in a medium-sized skillet—do not use cast iron—and add the okra. Cook, stirring occasionally, until okra ceases to be "ropey" and the slices separate. Set aside.
5. In a 5-to-6-quart, heavy kettle mix remaining tablespoons of oil and butter and the flour before placing over heat.
6. Place over low heat and stir constantly. Continue cooking and stir-ring until the *roux* turns a rich, light brown, the color of peanut butter. Do not brown the *roux* too fast—30 minutes should be the minimum time—or it will be too hot and burn. Discard and start over if this happens.
7. When *roux* has been cooked to proper color and consistency, remove from the heat immediately. Stirring constantly, add the chopped onion to lower the temperature of the *roux*. Stir until the onion is coated with the *roux*.
8. Return to the heat and add the green onions and celery. Cook, stirring constantly, until onion and celery are tender—about 5 minutes. Add okra, tomatoes, parsley, bay leaf, thyme and shrimp liquid. Stir well to blend. Cover and simmer 30 minutes. Add cay-enne pepper, salt and black pepper to taste.

9. Add the shrimp and crabmeat. Simmer very slowly, uncovered, for an additional 20 minutes. At this point the gumbo can be cooled and refrigerated for 24 hours, if desired.

10. Reheat over low heat to serving temperature. Serve in heated bowls, topped with a scoop of boiled or steamed long-grain white rice. Pass around a bowl of optional filé powder, to be sprinkled over gumbo to taste. Makes 4 quarts. Freezing is not recommended. **Serves 8.**

Variation: Shrimp and Oyster Gumbo

Omit crabmeat. Substitute 2 cups oysters and liquor. Drain oysters and strain liquor. Reserve oysters and add liquor to the water. Add oysters at end of cooking and bring mixture to full boil before serving.

Catfish Gumbo

This recipe is from Des Allemands, Louisiana, preclaimed the "Catfish Capital of the World" through the efforts of an enterprising parish priest. In South Carolina this dish is known as "catfish stew."

Throughout the South, catfish farming is flourishing as a commercial venture. Formerly a game fish, catfish is rapidly becoming not only America's most popular fish but economical too.

NOTE: Any firm white-fleshed fish can be substituted for the catfish fillets in this recipe.

1 pound fresh or 2 10-ounce packages frozen okra, sliced into ½-inch pieces
2 tablespoons vegetable oil
2 tablespoons unsalted butter
2 tablespoons flour
1 cup chopped onion
½ cup finely chopped celery
½ cup chopped green pepper
1 clove garlic, chopped fine
2 quarts chicken broth, preferably homemade

2 cups canned solid-pack tomatoes
2 sprigs parsley, chopped
1 bay leaf
¼ teaspoon ground thyme
¼ teaspoon cayenne pepper, or to taste
Salt and freshly ground black pepper to taste
2 pounds skinned catfish fillets, cut into 2-inch pieces
2 cups boiled or steamed long-grain white rice

1. Top and tail fresh okra and slice into ½-inch pieces. Melt 1 tablespoon of the oil and 1 tablespoon of the butter in medium-sized skillet—do not use cast iron—and add the okra. Cook, stirring occasionally, until okra ceases to be "ropey" and the slices separate. Set aside.

2. In a 5-to-6-quart, heavy kettle, mix remaining tablespoons of oil and butter and the flour before placing over heat.
3. Place over low heat and stir constantly. Continue cooking and stirring until the *roux* turns a rich, light brown, the color of peanut butter. Do not brown the *roux* too fast—30 minutes should be the minimum time—or it will burn. Discard and start over if this happens.
4. When *roux* has been cooked to proper color and consistency, remove from heat immediately. Stirring constantly, add the chopped onion to lower the temperature of the *roux*. Stir until the onion is coated with the *roux*.
5. Return to the heat and add the celery, green pepper and garlic. Cook, stirring constantly, until vegetables are tender—about 5 minutes. Add chicken broth, tomatoes, parsley, bay leaf and thyme. Cover and simmer 30 minutes. Add cayenne pepper, salt and black pepper to taste. At this point the gumbo can be refrigerated for 24 hours, if desired.
6. Simmer, uncovered, 15 minutes. Add the catfish but do not stir during the cooking. Turn heat to medium and cook an additional 10 to 15 minutes, depending upon the thickness of the fillets.
7. Place a serving of rice in each bowl. With a spatula lift the fish and place over the rice. Then ladle the gumbo over the fish.

Serves 6.

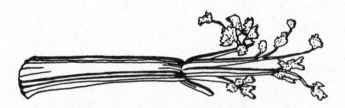

Main-Dish Pies
With Stews

American main-dish pies made with stews are stylish enough to appear on the menus of the most sophisticated New York City restaurants. Made of meat, poultry and fish, these pies can be made with one or two crusts or baked in individual dishes and covered with pastry. They also may be dressed up with latticed tops or diamonds of rich pastry or biscuit topping.

    A main-dish pie made with simple ingredients is the perfect entrée for light entertaining and is quick and easy to prepare. It is practically foolproof. And if necessary, it can be made in advance and reheated. Serve with a salad and a nice wine. Follow with a special fruit dessert, and you have a perfect lunch or supper menu.

The basis for a tasty main-dish pie is good, flaky pastry or rich biscuit topping made from your favorite recipe. My grandmother Prichard, a farm-style cook and pastry maker, used the recipe below. The handling of this pastry is in the manner of rolling the classic French *pâté feuilletée*, a pastry my pioneer-bred grandmother could not possibly have known. The pastry freezes beautifully and will keep up to a year, if securely wrapped.

Rich Pastry

3 cups sifted all-purpose unbleached flour
½ teaspoon baking powder
½ teaspoon salt

1½ cups (3 sticks) cold unsalted butter
½ cup ice water
Egg wash: 1 egg yolk lightly beaten with 2 tablespoons milk

1. Sift the flour and measure 3 cups onto a sheet of wax paper. Add the baking powder and salt. Sift this mixture into a medium-sized bowl.
2. Shave the cold butter in slivers into the flour mixture. If butter starts to melt from too much handling, place in refrigerator a few minutes to firm.
3. With the hands, mix the cold butter in the flour until the butter is lightly coated. Do not overhandle, or the butter will melt.
4. With an electric hand mixer or pastry blender, blend the butter into flour until the mixture looks like coarse cornmeal.
5. With a fork stir in the ice water. Continue stirring until the dough starts to form a ball. Then, with the hands, gather up and shape the dough into a 5-x-7-inch rectangle. Wrap in wax paper, put into a plastic bag and refrigerate 1 hour.
6. Lightly flour surface and roll the dough gently into a 16-x-8-inch rectangle—cut a wax-paper pattern, if necessary.
7. Fold both ends of the rectangle to the middle, to meet in the center. Then fold again, as in closing a book. Refrigerate 1 hour.
8. Remove the pastry from the refrigerator and, with open end facing up and down, roll the pastry into another 16-x-8-inch rectangle and repeat the folding process in step 7. This must be done 3 times so that the layers will separate and become a light and desirable, tender, flaky pastry.

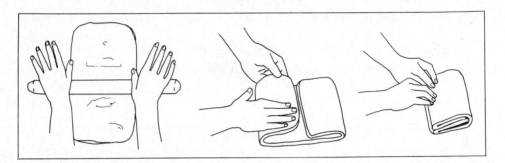

NOTE: It will take a total of 3 hours in the refrigerator to make this pastry. Makes 3 generous 12-inch pastry crusts.

9. Remove the pastry from the refrigerator and divide into thirds. Place one third of the pastry on floured marble or Formica. Reserve the rest, since it is only practical to roll out one crust at a time. Follow individual recipe instructions for rolling out dough.
10. To prevent soggy pastry, brush the underneath side of the pastry topping with an egg wash made with 1 egg yolk lightly beaten with 2 tablespoons of milk. This technique also will seal the crust to the edge of the baking pan.

Rich Biscuit Topping For Main-Dish Pies

Biscuits, plain or with herbs and special flavors, are used mostly in making New England potpies. Southerners are more apt to make potpies with a rich pastry.

2 cups sifted unbleached white flour
2½ teaspoons baking powder
¾ teaspoon salt

6 tablespoons cold unsalted butter
⅔ cup milk

1. Sift the flour and measure 2 cups onto a sheet of wax paper. Add the baking powder and salt. Sift this mixture into a medium-sized bowl.
2. Shave the cold butter in slivers into the flour mixture. If butter starts to melt from too much handling, place in refrigerator a few minutes to firm.
3. With the hands, mix the cold butter in the flour until the butter is lightly coated. Do not overhandle, or the butter will melt.
4. With an electric hand mixer or pastry blender, blend the butter into the flour until the mixture looks like coarse cornmeal. With a fork stir in the milk. Continue stirring until the dough starts to form a

ball. Then, with the hands, gather up and place on lightly floured surface. Knead gently for 30 seconds to shape into a ball. (Takes about 15 turns.)

5. Roll or pat the dough to 1/3-inch thickness. Follow individual recipe instructions for cutting shapes. Enough dough for 6 individual pies.

Variations: Parsley Biscuits

Add 1 tablespoon minced fresh parsley to flour mixture.

Celery-Seed Biscuits

Add 1 teaspoon celery seed to flour mixture.

Cheese Biscuits

Add 1 cup finely grated or shredded Vermont Cheddar cheese to flour mixture.

Individual Potpies

The real, old-fashioned American potpie, made of chicken, veal or a combination of meats and fowl, was made in a large, black iron kettle, using leftover stew. Strips of dough were placed in the greased kettle, the cooked meat and uncooked vegetables were put in with broth around them, biscuits were placed on top, the cover weighted down and the whole mass simmered for an undetermined length of time. Thankfully, our taste buds have come of age. Individual potpies with a savory top crust are not only more appealing to the eye, but also are more appetizing to the palate.

This recipe for chicken potpie was served at the elegant Palmer House in Chicago during World War II.

Chicken Potpie

3 cups cooked chicken, cut into bite-size pieces (poach chicken in strong, flavorful broth)

1 cup diced carrots, parboiled

12 small white onions, parboiled

2 cups cubed potatoes, parboiled

1 cup sliced mushrooms, sauteed

4 tablespoons vegetable shortening or chicken fat

4 tablespoons flour

1½ cups chicken broth, preferably homemade

1 cup light cream or half-and-half

Salt and freshly ground black pepper to taste

Rich Pastry for a 2-crust 10-inch pie; or 1 recipe Rich Biscuit Topping (see page 65)

1. Arrange the chicken and the cooked vegetables in 6 individual, lightly buttered ovenproof casseroles.
2. In a heavy, 1-quart saucepan melt the shortening, blend in the flour and cook 3 minutes, stirring constantly.
3. Remove mixture from heat and slowly add the chicken broth and cream, stirring constantly to blend. Add salt and pepper to taste.
4. Return the mixture to heat and boil, stirring constantly, until mixture thickens. Pour over chicken and vegetables. Top with Rich Pastry or Biscuit Topping.

Serves 6.

To form Rich Pastry Topping   Preheated oven temperature: 425° F. Use two thirds of the recipe. Roll out two 12-inch crusts. Roll each piece to form a rough circle 1/8-inch thick; roll from the center to the edges of the dough, not back and forth—this stretches the dough. Cut 3 circles from each 12-inch crust, allowing 1-inch overlap of dough to be trimmed and tucked under. Brush the underneath side of the crust with the egg wash before placing the crust over the pie. Flute or crimp the pastry to the edge of the casseroles. Prick a design with a fork or a skewer all over each crust, and cut a small center hole in each to allow steam to escape. If you like, decorate the tops with shapes of leaves or other designs, and affix them with the egg wash. Bake in preheated oven 25 to 30 minutes, until crust is nicely browned.

To form Rich Biscuit Topping   Preheated oven temperature: 425° F. Pat or roll dough to 1/3-inch thickness. Cut dough to fit top of pan or cut into individual rounds or diamond shapes, slitting a design in the large crust to allow steam to escape. Bake in preheated oven about 25 minutes, until browned and heated through. Do not immerse rounds or diamonds in the liquid, or they will not brown well.

Variations: Turkey Potpie

Substitute turkey for chicken. Omit mushrooms and substitute 1 cup cooked green peas.

Beef Potpie

Omit chicken and substitute 3 cups 1/2-inch cubes cooked beef. Substitute beef broth for chicken broth.

Frozen Beef Potpies

Those who shun frozen potpies should know that they can be prepared successfully from scratch at home and frozen and baked as needed. These are particularly popular with the career woman who must provide nutritious meals for her family while she is away from home. These pies *must* be frozen before baking, or the sauce will not thicken at all. Do *not* defrost before baking.

5 tablespoons vegetable oil
2 pounds boneless chuck, trimmed of all fat and cut into 1/2-inch cubes
2 tablespoons flour
¾ cup finely chopped onion
1 clove garlic, minced
4 beef bouillon cubes
6 cups water
¾ teaspoon salt, or to taste
¼ teaspoon freshly ground black pepper, or to taste

1 teaspoon Worcestershire sauce
1 bay leaf
1½ cups diced baking potatoes, cut into ¼-inch pieces
1 cup cubed carrots, cut into ½-inch pieces
1 cup frozen green peas
3 12-inch Rich Pastry crusts, unbaked (see page 67)

Preheated oven temperature: 425°F.

1. Heat the oil in a heavy, 10-to-12-inch skillet. Dredge the beef in the flour and brown, a few pieces of meat at a time. As pieces brown, remove and set aside.
2. After all the meat has been browned, add the chopped onion and garlic to oil. Cook until onion is translucent but not brown.
3. Stir in the bouillon cubes, water, salt, pepper and Worcestershire sauce. Add the bay leaf and browned meat. Heat to boiling. Cover and simmer 1½ hours, stirring occasionally. The meat should be almost tender at this point; if not, cook longer.
4. Add the potatoes and carrots. Simmer, covered, 30 minutes. Add the frozen peas and cook, covered, an additional 7 minutes. Season to taste with additional salt and pepper, if desired. Cool slightly. Remove bay leaf.
5. Fill eight 5-x-1¼-inch aluminum foil pans with ¾ cup each of the meat mixture.
6. Roll out three 12-inch crusts of Rich Pastry. Cut a total of 8 rounds to fit the tops of the pans, allowing 1-inch overlap of dough to be trimmed and tucked under. Dampen edges of pans before affixing the crust. This will help keep the pastry from shrinking during baking. Prick a design with a fork or a skewer all over each crust, and cut a small center hole in each crust to allow steam to escape.

7. Freeze the pies on trays; then transfer to individual freezer bags.
8. Bake frozen pies in preheated oven 40 minutes, or until crust is golden brown.

Serves 8. This recipe can be doubled or tripled.

Variation: Frozen Chicken Potpies

Substitute chicken for the beef and substitute chicken bouillon cubes for beef bouillon cubes.

Deep-Dish Ham Pie With Cheese Biscuits

More Southern than New England, this tasty pie is popular at church suppers and other community affairs. Three cups of any cooked meat, fish or seafood may be used in place of ham.

¼ cup unsalted butter
2 tablespoons finely chopped onion
¼ cup flour
¼ teaspoon dry mustard
2 cups milk
1 cup fresh mushroom slices sautéed

3 cups cubed cooked ham
1 cup peas, cooked
Salt and freshly ground black pepper to taste
1 recipe Cheese Biscuits (see page 66)

Preheated oven temperature: 425° F.
1. In a heavy, 2-quart saucepan melt the butter. Add the onion and cook until barely tender. Add the flour and cook 3 minutes, stirring constantly. Stir in the mustard.
2. Remove from the heat and slowly add the milk, stirring constantly to blend.
3. Return to the heat and boil, stirring constantly, until mixture thickens. Add mushrooms, ham and peas. Add salt and pepper to taste and pour into a lightly buttered 1½-quart casserole.
4. For Cheese Biscuit topping, see instructions on page 66. Roll or pat the dough to ⅓-inch thickness. Cut into diamonds or rounds and place on top of ham mixture. Bake in preheated oven 20 minutes, or until biscuits are nicely browned and the mixture is bubbly.

Serves 6. Recipe may be doubled.

Tamale Pie

A trendy dish of the fifties generation, tamale pie has its roots in Tex-Mex cooking. "Serve with green salad and toasted garlic bread at both indoor and outdoor parties, when friends gather informally to eat and drink," says one food writer of that era.

1 cup chopped onion
1 clove garlic, minced
½ cup chopped green pepper
2 tablespoons light olive oil
1 pound round steak, ground or coarsely chopped
1 to 2 tablespoons chili powder
1 teaspoon ground coriander

3⅓ cups solid-pack canned tomatoes
Salt to taste
12 pitted black olives, halved
1 cup yellow cornmeal
1 cup water
4 cups double-strength chicken or beef broth (See page 26)
Unsalted butter

Preheated oven temperature: 350°F.

1. In a heavy, 10-to-12-inch skillet cook the onion, garlic and pepper in the oil until onion is tender but not brown.
2. Lightly mix the beef, chili powder and coriander. Add to the onion mixture. Cook 15 minutes, chopping up and down with the side of a large metal kitchen spoon to break up the lumps, or until the meat is browned.
3. Add tomatoes, salt and olives. Cook slowly, uncovered, 20 minutes, stirring occasionally.
4. Mix cornmeal and water in the top of a 1-quart double boiler.
5. Heat chicken or beef broth and slowly add to the cornmeal mixture. Place mixture over boiling water. Stir constantly until mixture thickens. Lower heat and cook 20 to 25 minutes, stirring occasionally.
6. Lightly oil or butter a 2-quart casserole and line with half the cornmeal mixture. Pour meat mixture over the cornmeal mixture. Spread remaining cornmeal mixture over meat. Cool slightly and crisscross top with knife identations. Dot with butter. Bake in preheated oven 45 minutes.

Serves 6.

FISH
AND
SHELLFISH

Fish

Because the United States is surrounded by vast expanses of water and is the possessor of many inland lakes and streams, Americans always have prepared a great variety of fish dishes, both plain and fancy.

Only recently have we begun to appreciate nature's bounty. And this is due in large part to the culinary influences of the great James Beard, who first introduced American cooks to the Canadian Cooking Theory. This is a method that takes the timing guesswork out of fish cookery, regardless of the kind of fish or the method of preparation—whether you bake, broil, steam, poach, pan-fry or charcoal-broil whole fish, steaks, or fillets. I was introduced to this theory as a student in Mr. Beard's Greenwich Village classes during the early seventies, and throughout this section my recipes will reflect his influence.

Fish Cooking Basics

Fish will give off a strong odor during cooking if it is not fresh or if it is being overcooked. The best cook in the world cannot disguise the former, but a good cook can control the latter.

HOW TO PURCHASE FISH   Purchase fish in season, when the supply is plentiful and the price is apt to be lower. Like fruits and vegetables, fish has its season. Even though almost any variety of fish can be purchased throughout the year, it will have a better flavor in season. Seasons vary from fish to fish and from coast to coast. Check with your local source of supply as to availability.

NOTE: Professional chefs advise aspiring young cooks not to take fish-cooking courses during January, February or March.

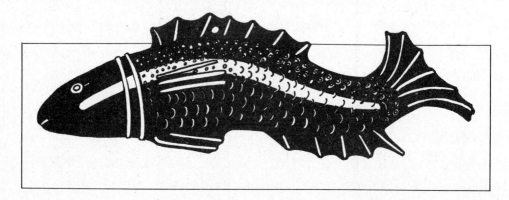

HOW TO SELECT FRESH FISH   Fresh fish or fish that has been frozen fresh has full or bulging bright eyes, bright-red gills, scales that are tight to the skin, and firm and elastic flesh, which should spring back when pressed. Fresh fish should have a lemonlike scent. If the freshness of the fish is in question, ask to smell the backbone—fish starts to spoil there first.

Obtaining fresh saltwater fish is not a problem along America's coastal regions or in large cities. However, it can be for the rural areas of Middle America. In these areas cooks must depend upon air express and ground transportation to supply the local markets. Usually there is a special fish section at the market. Here is an old, but tried and true, method for testing the freshness of a whole fish, and one I grew up with in rural Indiana: Submerge a whole fish in water. If the fish shows any bounce whatsoever, the fish is of questionable freshness. To restore freshness, professional chefs recommend soaking the fish in a solution of lemon juice and water. Since good cooking depends on fresh ingredients, in my opinion it is wiser to use solid frozen fish or to cook something else, rather than prepare a dish of inferior quality.

AMOUNT OF FISH TO BUY

Whole and drawn fish: the whole fish with only the entrails removed: allow 1 pound per serving.

Dressed and pan-dressed fish: scaled, with entrails, head, tail and fins removed. This is ready to cook as purchased—allow ½ pound per serving.

NOTE: Fish that weighs less than 1 pound is referred to as pan-dressed; fish larger than this as dressed.

Steaks and fillets: steaks are a cross-section slice from a large, dressed fish; fillets are the sides of the fish, sliced lengthwise from head to tail—allow ½ pound per serving.

TRANSPORTING AND STORING FISH   After purchasing fish, if traveling any distance or if additional stops are to be made, ask the market to place the fish in a plastic bag with plenty of ice. Fresh fish is very perishable and should be placed in the coldest part of the refrigerator as soon as possible, wrapped in moistureproof paper or placed in a tightly covered plastic container.

FROZEN FISH   Frozen fish is sometimes packaged whole, but more often is available as steaks and fillets. These may be cooked while frozen if the cooking time is *doubled*, or they may be thawed first. *Caution*: Never refreeze frozen fish.

COOKING FISH   In the past, whole or dressed fish was cooked 10 to 15 minutes per pound at a low temperature. Fillets and steaks were cooked until the texture could be flaked easily with a fork. Both methods very often resulted in the fish being overcooked and tasteless. Use the following method for perfectly cooked fish.

The Canadian Cooking Theory

The fish is measured by thickness, regardless of the intended manner of preparation, and cooked 10 minutes per inch at a very high temperature.

HOW TO MEASURE FISH   Whole fish, steaks and fillets: Place whole fish on its side, resting it on a flat surface. Place a straight-edged knife across the fish at the thickest part. Using a small ruler, measure the distance from the knife to the surface of the table. If this is 2½ inches, for example, the fish should be cooked 25 minutes. If a large fish such as salmon measures 5 inches, then the fish should be cooked 50 minutes, and so on, according to the thickness of the fish.

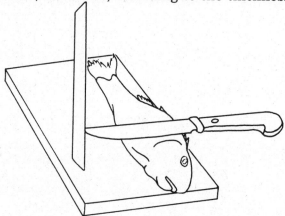

How to Cook Fish

BAKING   Preheat oven to 450°F. Measure whole fish, steaks or fillets and bake 10 minutes per inch of thickness or fraction thereof. Start timing as soon as the surface starts to cook and the skin begins to crisp and shrink.

STUFFED FISH   Stuff fish and then measure as for whole fish. Bake 10 minutes per inch of thickness or fraction thereof. Start timing as soon as the surface starts to cook and the skin begins to crisp and shrink.

BROILING   Preheat broiler. Measure thickness of fish. Brush top with unsalted butter, oil or other fat and place on a lightly oiled broiler pan, approximately 3 inches from the source of heat. Broil 10 minutes per inch of thickness. Start timing as soon as the surface starts to cook and the fat starts to bubble. Halfway through broiling time, turn fish and brush other side with melted fat. Very thin fish under ½-inch need not be turned.

STEAMING   Use a lightly oiled steamer rack and place in a kettle with a tight-fitting lid. Add 1 teaspoon salt and 1 tablespoon lemon juice or vinegar for every 2 quarts of water used. (Make certain the liquid will not touch the rack.) The acid in the lemon juice or vinegar helps keep the flesh firm and white. Heat to simmering. Measure thickness of fish, place on rack and start timing as soon as kettle is covered. Cook 10 minutes per inch of thickness or fraction thereof.

POACHING   Measure thickness of fish. Prepare poaching liquid following recipe instructions. Boil poaching liquid for 10 minutes. Add fish and cook 10 minutes per inch of thickness or fraction thereof. Start timing as soon as the liquid is simmering.

PAN-FRYING   This method is recommended for small game fish and for fish cut in serving pieces. Coat fish following recipe instructions. Measure thickness of fish. Heat ¼-inch of a combination of vegetable oil and unsalted butter in a skillet until the fat is sizzling hot but not smoking. Fry the fish until golden brown on one side; turn and brown the other side. Frying time should be about 10 minutes per inch of thickness or fraction thereof.

CHARCOAL BROILING   A well-oiled, hinged rack is a great help in charcoal-broiling fish; it will be much easier to turn the fish. Measure thickness of fish and brush with unsalted butter, marinade or a light sauce. Place over glowing coals, brushing the fish a few times as it cooks. Turn to cook on both sides. Cook 10 minutes per inch of thickness or fraction thereof. Start timing as soon as the surface starts to cook and the fat starts to bubble.

TO COOK SOLID FROZEN FISH   Use any of the above methods and *double* the cooking time, to 20 minutes per inch of thickness or fraction thereof.

Recommended Fish for Baking

SALTWATER

Barracuda	Hake	Sea Trout
Black Drum	Halibut	Shad
Bluefish	Ling Cod	Sheepshead
California Black Sea Bass	Mackerel	Smelt
California Kingfish	Mullet	Sole
California Whitefish	Ocean Perch	Spanish Mackerel
Cod	Pollack	Striped Bass
Cusk	Pompano	Swordfish
Flounder	Redfish	Tautog
Fluke	Red Snapper	Tuna
Grunion	Sablefish	Yellowtail
Haddock	Salmon	

FRESHWATER

Bass	Sheepshead
Catfish	Trout
Pike	Whitefish
Perch	

Baked Whole Fish
(Basic Recipe)

In American cooking baked fish is either served with an accompanying sauce or stuffed. Sometimes both a sauce and stuffing are used to prepare a particularly fancy specialty. Recipes vary widely, depending upon the cook, the region and the availability of the fish. Fish that weighs from 3 to 5 pounds is considered ideal for baking. Any type of fish, lean or fatty, can be baked, using this method.

NOTE: It is not necessary to brush fatty fish such as salmon, mackerel, trout, tuna, pike, carp, bluefish, bass, whitefish, etc. with butter.

3-5-pound fish (or larger), cleaned and dressed; head and tail may be left on

Salt and freshly ground black pepper to taste

Lemon juice to taste

Melted butter for lean fish—cod, scrod, flounder, halibut, ocean perch, pollack, sole, whiting, etc.

Paprika to taste

Vegetable oil for coating fish and oiling pan

Preheated oven temperature: 450°F.

1. Wash fish and wipe dry. Sprinkle inside with salt, pepper and lemon juice. Brush with butter if necessary or desired and sprinkle with paprika.
2. Measure thickness of fish and coat with vegetable oil. Cover head and tail with aluminum foil. Place in a lightly oiled pan and bake 10 minutes per inch of thickness or fraction thereof. Remove skin and serve with recommended sauce. See page 146.

Baked Fish Steaks and Fillets

Preheated oven temperature: 450°F.

Arrange steaks or fillets in a lightly oiled shallow baking dish. Sprinkle with salt and pepper. Combine melted butter and lemon juice and brush over fish. Sprinkle with paprika. Start timing as soon as surface of fish begins to cook and fat starts to bubble. Bake 10 minutes per inch of thickness or fraction thereof. Serve with recommended sauce. See page 146.

Fish Baked in Tomato Sauce

This is a simple and uncomplicated all-purpose sauce, used in American cooking to bake whole fish, steaks or fillets. Recommended fish—salmon, mackerel, trout, tuna, pike, catfish, carp, bluefish, bass and whitefish, all of which are considered fatty fish.

Tomato Sauce for Baked Fish

¼ cup chopped onion
2 tablespoons unsalted butter
2 cups peeled and seeded chopped tomatoes, fresh or canned
¼ teaspoon ground thyme or marjoram

3 tablespoons chopped parsley
Salt and freshly ground black pepper to taste
Tomato juice, if necessary

Preheated oven temperature: 450°F.

1. Prepare fish as in Baked Whole Fish, Basic Recipe (see page 76), Step 1. Proceed to Step 2. Place the fish in the lightly oiled pan.
2. In a medium-sized skillet cook the onion in the butter until translucent but not brown. Add the tomatoes, thyme or marjoram and parsley. Season lightly with salt and pepper. Cook for a few minutes to blend flavors.
3. Spoon sauce over fish and bake 10 minutes per inch of thickness or fraction thereof. Baste a few times during the baking with the sauce. Add a little *tomato juice* if the sauce seems to be drying out during the baking.

Variation: Fish Steaks and Fillets Baked in Tomato Sauce

Preheated oven temperature: 450°F.

Arrange steaks or fillets in a lightly oiled shallow baking dish. Spoon tomato sauce over steaks or fillets. Bake 10 minutes per inch of thickness or fraction thereof. Start timing as soon as surface of fish starts to cook and the liquid in the bottom of the pan is hot. Baste with the sauce a few times during the baking.

Recommended Fish for Stuffing

SALTWATER

Bluefish	Grouper	Salmon
Cod	Haddock	Shad
Cusk	Halibut	Spanish Mackerel
Flounder	Pollack	Striped Bass
Fluke	Red Snapper	

FRESH WATER

Catfish   Trout
Pike   Whitefish

Baked Stuffed Fish
(Basic Recipe)

Baked stuffed fish dishes range from New England, down the coast to Florida, around the Gulf of Mexico and along the entire West Coast. Stuffing ingredients are as varied as the flavor of the fish along this vast expanse of shoreline. Normally the milder fishes of Northern waters are filled with oyster, herbed bread or sage stuffing and the more highly densely flavored fishes of Southern waters are blended with a stuffing of very spicy bread, crabmeat, shrimp and sometimes a combination of all three.

The preparation of a fish for stuffing is basic to all types of fish.

3-to-5 pound fish (or larger), cleaned and dressed; head and tail may be left on

Salt to taste

Lemon juice to taste

Melted butter for basting during baking

Preheated oven temperature: 450°F.
1. Wash fish and wipe dry. Sprinkle inside with salt and lemon juice. Set aside.
2. Prepare stuffing appropriate to type of fish being baked. See recommended stuffings (page 79).
3. Stuff the fish lightly. Caution: Do not pack the stuffing in the fish, because the ingredients will expand during the baking. Use skewers to close the cavity.
4. Measure thickness of stuffed fish and coat with melted butter. Cover head and tail with foil. Place in a lightly oiled pan and bake 10 minutes per inch of thickness or fraction thereof. Brush occasionally with melted butter. Remove skin and serve.

A 5-pound stuffed fish will serve 6.

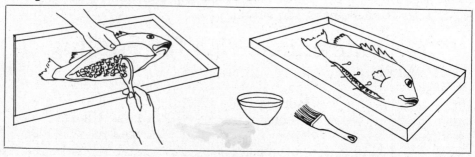

American Fish Stuffings

These include a representative collection of stuffing recipes commonly used in American fish cookery.

Eastern Shore Crabmeat Stuffing

Recommended Fish: Striped bass or rockfish, flounder

¼ cup unsalted butter
2 tablespoons chopped onion
¼ cup chopped celery
¼ cup chopped green pepper
2 cups fresh bread crumbs

1 cup crabmeat, fresh or frozen, picked over to remove cartilage and shell
1 tablespoon chopped parsley
Cayenne pepper to taste
Salt and freshly ground black pepper to taste

Melt butter in a medium-sized, heavy skillet. Add onion, celery and green pepper and cook until vegetables are tender. Stir in bread crumbs, crabmeat and parsley; season to taste with cayenne pepper, salt and black pepper. Enough stuffing for a 5-pound fish. Bake following Baked Stuffed Fish Basic Recipe instructions, page 78.

Variation: *Eastern Shore Shrimp Stuffing*

Substitute 1 cup chopped cooked shrimp for crabmeat.

New Orleans Seafood Stuffing

Recommended fish: Flounder, bass, red snapper

¼ cup unsalted butter
½ cup chopped celery
½ cup chopped green onion with tops
1 clove garlic, chopped fine
1 cup fresh bread crumbs
1 tablespoon lemon juice
1 cup chopped cooked shrimp

1 cup crabmeat, fresh or frozen, picked over to remove cartilage and shell
2 tablespoons chopped parsley
1 large egg, lightly beaten
Cayenne pepper to taste
Salt and freshly ground black pepper to taste

1. Melt butter in 10-inch, heavy skillet; add celery, onion and garlic. Cook over low heat until vegetables are tender but not brown.
2. Gently stir in bread crumbs, lemon juice, shrimp, crabmeat, parsley and egg. Stir well to blend just until egg is incorporated into stuffing.

Caution: Do not overstir, or the mixture will be soggy and heavy. Season to taste with cayenne pepper, salt and black pepper. Enough stuffing for a 5-pound fish. Bake following Baked Stuffed Fish Basic Recipe instructions, page 78.

New England Herb-Bread Stuffing for Fish

Recommended Fish: All types, both saltwater and freshwater

¼ cup unsalted butter
½ cup chopped onion
¼ cup chopped celery
2 cups dry bread crumbs
2 tablespoons chopped parsley

¼ teaspoon dried tarragon
A pinch of ground thyme
Salt and freshly ground black pepper to taste
1 tablespoon clam juice or milk

Melt butter in a medium-sized, heavy skillet. Add onion and celery. Cook until tender but not brown. Stir in bread crumbs, parsley, tarragon and thyme. Season to taste with salt and pepper. Blend in clam juice or milk. Enough stuffing for 4 pounds of fish. Bake following Baked Stuffed Fish Basic Recipe instructions, page 78.

New England Sage Stuffing for Fish

Recommended Fish: Trout, shad, salmon

¼ cup unsalted butter or bacon fat
¼ cup chopped onion
2 cups fresh bread crumbs

½ teaspoon ground sage or to taste
Salt and freshly ground black pepper to taste

Melt butter in a medium-sized, heavy skillet. Add onion and cook until translucent but not brown. Stir in bread crumbs and sage. Season to taste with salt and pepper. Enough stuffing for 4 pounds of fish. Bake following Basic Recipe instructions, page 78.

Oyster Stuffing for Fish

This is a delicately flavored, all-purpose stuffing for lean fish such as cod, scrod, flounder, sole and halibut; it also complements the less-lean flavor of the Atlantic striped bass.

6 tablespoons unsalted butter
2 ribs celery, chopped
½ cup chopped onion
8 slices day-old white bread, crusts removed and cut into ½-inch cubes
½ teaspoon ground thyme

¼ teaspoon dried crumbled sage
2 cups oysters, drained (reserve oyster liquor)
2 tablespoons lemon juice
Salt and freshly ground black pepper to taste

1. Melt the butter in 10-to-12-inch, heavy skillet. Add the celery and chopped onion and cook until tender but not brown. Remove vegetables and set aside.
2. Add the bread crumbs to the butter in the skillet and fry until cubes are golden.
3. Remove mixture from heat and stir in the vegetables, thyme and sage. Sprinkle oysters with lemon juice and fold into bread mixture. Season to taste with salt and pepper. If mixture seems dry, add a small amount of the liquor from the oysters. Enough stuffing for 5-to-6-pound fish. Any remaining stuffing can be baked in a lightly buttered casserole. Bake following Basic Recipe instructions, page 78.

Red Snapper with Shrimp Stuffing

From Florida to Texas, this is a favorite method of baking this delicate and lean-fleshed fish.

1 5-to-6-pound red snapper, cleaned and dressed; head and tail may be left on

Salt and freshly ground black pepper to taste

Stuffing

¼ cup unsalted butter
3 tablespoons finely chopped onion
1 tablespoon flour
½ teaspoon ground thyme
1 tablespoon minced parsley
½ cup milk

1 cup cooked chopped shrimp
1 cup boiled or steamed white rice
3 tablespoons lemon juice
Salt and freshly ground black pepper to taste
Unsalted butter for coating
Lemon slices and parsley for garnish

Preheated oven temperature: 450°F.
1. Wash fish and wipe dry. Sprinkle inside with salt and pepper. Set aside.

2. Prepare stuffing: In a medium-sized heavy skillet melt the butter. Add the onion, and cook until translucent but not brown. Stir in the flour and cook 3 minutes, stirring constantly.
3. Remove mixture from heat. Stir in the thyme and parsley. Slowly add the milk, stirring constantly to blend.
4. Return mixture to heat and cook over low heat 5 minutes, stirring constantly. Stir in the shrimp, rice and lemon juice. Season to taste with salt and pepper. Remove from heat and set aside.
5. Stuff the fish lightly with the stuffing mixture. Use skewers to close the cavity.
6. Melt butter and brush over fish on both sides. Measure thickness of fish. Place in a lightly oiled pan and bake 10 minutes per inch of thickness or fraction thereof. Baste occasionally with more melted butter. Remove skewers and serve garnished with lemon slices and parsley.

Serves 6.

Stuffed Fillets of Flounder Creole

Flounders are caught along the sandy bottom of coastal waters from Cape Cod to Florida. Imaginative regional cooks on the East Coast devised a recipe for stuffing the fish and baking it with a Creole sauce—thus, the suggestion it is of Creole origin, which it is not.

The early colonists believed the flounder to be the same fish as sole from their European homeland. Therefore, the Old World name of sole still lingers on in American cooking terminology.

8 thin flounder or sole fillets
1 recipe New Orleans Seafood
    Stuffing (see page 79)
Oil or melted unsalted butter for
    coating

1 recipe Creole Sauce (see
    page 242)
½ cup chopped parsley for garnish

Preheated oven temperature: 450°F.
1. Wipe fillets dry and sprinkle with salt. Set aside.
2. Prepare seafood stuffing and set aside.
3. Prepare Creole sauce and set aside.
4. Spread the stuffing mixture evenly over each of the 8 fillets to within ¼-inch of the edge. (The stuffing will spread during the rolling.) Roll each fillet and secure end with a toothpick. Measure fillets for thickness. They should be no more than 2½ inches thick after they are rolled.

5. Lightly brush the tops of the rolls with oil or melted butter, place in lightly-oiled pan and place in preheated oven. As soon as the surface of the fish begins to bake, pour heated Creole sauce over fish and start the timing. Bake 10 minutes per inch of thickness or fraction thereof, basting with more sauce if necessary. Remove toothpicks. Serve garnished with chopped parsley.

Serves 8.

Baked Catfish, Southern Style

Not so long ago catfish was considered a freshwater fish of dubious reputation from the wrong side of the tracks. But recently a visiting French chef said he considers it one of the finest freshwater fishes in America. Food writers are now taking a new look at the catfish, which lends itself to many different forms of preparation. Fortunately, we are beginning to see small shipments of this fish on the East Coast and it is plentiful in Southern and Midwestern markets the year around.

The channel catfish, which is larger than the bullhead, is considered ideal for baking, and takes readily to spicy saucing.

1 large (4-to-5-pound) catfish, cleaned, skinned and head removed

Stuffing

2 tablespoons unsalted butter
2 teaspoons finely chopped onion
1 cup fresh bread crumbs
1 teaspoon sweet pickle relish
2 teaspoons finely chopped parsley
½ teaspoon salt, or to taste
¼ teaspoon freshly ground black pepper, or to taste

1 large egg, well beaten
1 recipe Tomato Sauce for Baked Fish (page 77)
6 thin strips salt pork
Melted unsalted butter for coating fish
Flour for coating fish

Preheated oven temperature: 450°F.
1. Catfish must be skinned before baking. If the market has not skinned the fish, draw a very sharp knife around the fish just in back of the gills and pull off the skin by hand. Discard the head, because it does not make an attractive presentation. Wash the fish and wipe dry. Set aside.
2. *Prepare stuffing:* Melt butter in medium-sized skillet. Add onion and cook until translucent but not brown. Stir in bread crumbs, pickle

relish, parsley, salt and pepper. Cool slightly and blend in beaten egg. Set aside.

3. Prepare one recipe for Tomato Sauce for Baked Fish (page 77).
4. Stuff the fish lightly with bread mixture. Use skewers to close the cavity.
5. With a sharp knife, make 6 S-shaped curves on the top side of the fish to accommodate the 6 strips of salt pork. Brush fish with melted butter and roll in flour to coat.
6. Measure thickness of fish and place in a lightly oiled pan. Bake in preheated oven 10 minutes per inch of thickness or fraction thereof. Baste frequently with the tomato sauce. While the fish is baking, continue to simmer the remaining tomato sauce over low heat to serve with the fish.

Serves 6.

Pompano en Papillote

Beloved by connoisseurs of fine food the world over, the pompano is an important fish in American cookery.

Pompano en Papillote (pompano in a paper bag) has been made internationally famous by New Orleans restaurants. The paper is made of heavy parchment and can be cut in the shape of hearts or squares; it is folded to enclose the pompano fillets. Home cooks often use small heavy paper bags, just as the recipe suggests. *Caution*: Do not use foil for making the bags. This will cause the fish to steam rather than brown lightly through the parchment, as is desired in the presentation of the finished dish.

If pompano is unavailable, substitute fillets of flounder or sole. The first two parts of this recipe may be prepared several hours in advance and refrigerated until the dish is ready to be assembled.

Sauce

1 cup finely chopped fresh mushrooms
¼ cup finely chopped green onion, with tops
1 tablespoon unsalted butter

2 tablespoons flour
2 cups Fish Broth (see page 26)
Salt and freshly ground black pepper to taste
¼ cup dry white wine

Stuffing

1 cup crabmeat, fresh or frozen, picked over to remove cartilage and shell
2 tablespoons unsalted butter

1 tablespoon dry white wine
½ teaspoon salt, or to taste
1 large egg yolk, lightly beaten

Pompano

6 pompano fillets
2 tablespoons unsalted butter

6 12-inch parchment hearts or squares, brushed with oil on both sides
thin slices of lemon for garnish

Sauce
1. In a medium-sized, heavy skillet cook the mushrooms and onion in the butter over low heat until the liquid from the mushrooms evaporates. Stir in the flour and cook over low heat 3 minutes, stirring constantly.
2. Remove from the heat and slowly stir in the fish broth. Add salt and pepper to taste.
3. Return mixture to heat and bring to a boil. Reduce heat and cook 5 minutes, stirring constantly. Stir in ¼ cup wine and set aside.

Stuffing
In a medium-sized, heavy skillet sauté the crabmeat in butter for 5 minutes. Add wine, salt and egg yolk. Stir well to blend and cook, stirring constantly, until mixture thickens and binds together. Set aside.

Pompano
In a 10-to-12-inch, heavy skillet sauté the fillets very lightly on both sides. Do not overcook, because they will finish cooking in the paper bag. Place on a platter and set aside.

To Assemble
Preheated oven temperature: 450°F.
Spread the stuffing mixture lengthwise on one half of each fillet to within ¼ inch of the edge. Fold other half of each fillet over the stuffing.

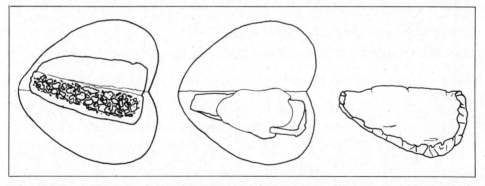

Place the stuffed and folded fillets on one side of the heart-shaped papers or squares. Spoon the prepared sauce over the fillets. Fold the edges of the paper together to seal the fillets. Place on a lightly oiled baking

sheet and place in preheated oven. Bake 10 to 12 minutes, or until the
bags are puffed and brown. Remove sealed bags to serving places and
slit open. Garnish with lemon slices and serve immediately.
Serves 6.

Halibut Loaf

This is an old, prize-winning New England recipe with a mousse-like
texture. Served hot or cold with an appropriate sauce, this American
dish can vie with the best of French cooking. The modern food processor
makes light work of the laborious task of hand grinding or chopping
the fish to the desired consistency.

     Any firm-fleshed white or pink-toned fish may be substituted for
the halibut. Avoid using fish with very dark flesh, because the dark
color will come through in the unmolded loaf and will spoil the appearance of an otherwise appetizing presentation.

     If mixed in the order of recipe instructions, the bread crumbs
will absorb not only the flavor but also the texture of the ground fish;
thus, 1 pound of fish will serve 6 to 8, depending upon whether the loaf
is to be served as an appetizer or an entrée. Do not use ready-mix bread
crumbs—they will be too dry. Use homemade or home-style bakery
bread, with crust removed.

2 cups finely ground fresh bread crumbs, with crust removed	1 teaspoon salt, or to taste
1 cup heavy cream	Cayenne pepper to taste
2 tablespoons finely chopped celery	Whites of 4 large eggs
1 pound boned uncooked halibut, cod, flounder, haddock or salmon, coarsely ground or chopped	Parsley or watercress for garnish

Preheated oven temperature: 350°F.
1. Line the bottom of a 9-x-5-inch loaf pan with well-oiled wax paper
   or parchment. Set aside.
2. Combine the bread crumbs and heavy cream and let stand 15 minutes.
3. Grind the celery in the food processor until chopped fine. Cut the
   fish into 1-inch cubes and add to celery. Process until fish is coarsely
   chopped or chop with chef's knife (see note). Using the food processor, quickly add the bread crumb mixture, but do not overprocess.
   Turn mixture out into a large mixing bowl.
4. Beat the egg whites in another mixing bowl until stiff peaks form.
   Add about one fourth of the egg whites to the fish mixture. Stir well
   to blend. Gently fold in the remainder of the egg whites, an over-

and-under motion, using a wide spatula, until just a few traces of the egg white remain visible. Do not overblend.

5. Pour mixture into loaf pan. Place in a shallow pan and pour boiling water to measure 1 inch up the sides of the loaf pan. Bake in preheated oven 45 minutes, or until mixture is firm. Remove from oven and let stand about 10 minutes before unmolding.

6. Release sides of loaf with a spatula and turn out onto platter. Remove wax paper or parchment. Garnish with parsley or watercress. Slice and serve warm or cold with recommended sauce.

Serves 6 to 8.

Recommended warm sauces: Almond Sauce, Caper Sauce, Lobster Sauce, Shrimp Sauce, Egg Sauce or New England Tomato Sauce (see page 146)

Recommended cold sauces: Rémoulade Sauce, Aurora Sauce, Cold Cucumber Sauce or Tartar Sauce (see Index)

NOTE: If not using a food processor, chop the celery and fish with a chef's knife and combine the mixture in a large mixing bowl. Proceed with beating and folding of egg whites as in recipe instructions.

Ethel's New England Salmon Loaf

Ethel was a wonderful cook. She had to be, because her husband had a very discriminating palate. One day she found herself with an extra egg white while preparing a salmon loaf. Born to the old-fashioned school of "waste not, want not," she incorporated it into the salmon mixture. The result was a much appreciated lighter variation of an ordinary dish.

Salmon loaf is served with a tomato sauce in the South and Midwest, but in New England it is traditionally served with egg sauce laced with green peas.

2 cups flaked, cooked salmon or 1 1-pound can salmon

2 tablespoons liquid from canned salmon; or use 2 tablespoons clam juice

½ cup hot milk

1 cup soft bread crumbs, preferably homemade

2 large eggs, lightly beaten

1½ tablespoons fresh lemon juice

1 tablespoon finely chopped onion

¼ cup melted unsalted butter

½ teaspoon salt, or to taste

¼ teaspoon freshly ground black pepper, or to taste

White of 1 large egg

1 recipe Egg Sauce (see page 148)

1 cup fresh or frozen cooked green peas

Preheated oven temperature: 350°F.

1. If using canned salmon, drain, bone, skin and flake, reserving 2 tablespoons of liquid. If using cooked salmon and liquid is not available, substitute clam juice. Place in a large mixing bowl.
2. In a small mixing bowl combine the hot milk and bread crumbs. Stir to mix. Set aside for a few minutes to allow crumbs to absorb the milk; then add to the salmon.
3. Lightly stir the eggs, lemon juice, onion, butter, salt and pepper into salmon mixture.
4. In a small bowl beat the egg white until stiff peaks form. With a rubber spatula, gently fold into salmon mixture until the egg white is barely visible.
5. Spoon mixture into a well-buttered 9-x-5-inch loaf pan. Smooth top with spatula and bake in preheated oven 40 minutes, or until firm to the touch.
6. Prepare recipe for egg sauce. Just before serving, fold 1 cup fresh or frozen cooked peas into the sauce. Reheat to serving temperature.
7. Unmold loaf onto a platter and spoon sauce over it. Serve immediately with additional sauce.

Serves 6.

Recommended Fish for Broiling

SALTWATER

Black Drum	Hake	Sheepshead
Blowfish	Halibut	Smelt
Bluefish	Ling Cod	Sole
Butterfish	Mackerel	Spanish Mackerel
California Kingfish	Mullet	Striped Bass
California Whitefish	Ocean Perch	Surf Perch
Cod	Pollack	Swordfish
Croaker	Pompano	Tautog
Cusk	Redfish	Tuna
Flounder	Sablefish	Whiting
Fluke	Salmon	Yellowtail
Grunions	Sea Trout	
Haddock	Shad	

FRESHWATER

Bass	Sucker
Bluegill	Trout
Crappies	Whitefish

Broiled Whole Fish
(Basic Recipe)

Start with a 3-to-5-pound fish. Smaller or larger fish also can be broiled.
Preheated broiler
1. Wash fish and wipe dry. If frozen fish is to be broiled, thawing first is recommended in order for the fish to absorb the basting sauce.
2. Place on oiled broiler rack and brush lightly with melted unsalted butter or other fat. Sprinkle with salt and freshly ground black pepper.
3. Prepare basting sauce (see page 91).
4. Measure thickness of fish and broil about 4 inches from source of heat for 10 minutes per inch of thickness or fraction thereof. Start timing as soon as the surface of the fish starts to cook and fat starts to bubble. Brush frequently with basting sauce. Turn fish with a wide spatula halfway through broiling time. Serve hot on heated serving plates.

Broiled Fish Steaks and Fillets
(Basic Recipe)

Steaks and fillets less than ½-inch thick need not be turned during broiling.
1. Thaw frozen steaks and fillets before broiling, if time permits; otherwise, double the broiling time of 10 minutes per inch of thickness.
2. Proceed as in steps 2, 3 and 4 above for broiling whole fish.
    Use sauces recommended here for basting all types of broiled whole fish, steaks and fillets.

Lemon Butter Sauce
(Basic Recipe)

Salt and freshly ground black pepper to taste

1 teaspoon lemon juice per pound of fish

1 tablespoon unsalted butter per pound of fish

Preheated broiler
1. Score fish at 2-inch intervals, if desired, so fish will absorb more sauce. Rub with salt and pepper to taste. Sprinkle with lemon juice and dot with butter.
2. Measure thickness of fish and broil as in Basic Recipe.

Variations: Fish Broiled with Onions

Turn fish halfway through broiling time. Cover with very thin slices of onion and continue to baste with additional lemon juice combined with melted butter.

Fish Broiled with Fresh Tomato Slices

Turn fish halfway through broiling time. Cover with thin slices of fresh tomatoes and continue to baste with additional lemon juice combined with melted butter.

Fish Broiled with Parsley-Worcestershire Sauce

Combine ¼ cup finely chopped onion, 2 teaspoons finely chopped parsley, 1 clove finely chopped garlic, 1 tablespoon Worcestershire sauce and ¼ cup melted unsalted butter. Baste both sides of the fish with this mixture during broiling.

Broiled Red Snapper Steaks Flamingo

This is an adaptation of a recipe developed by the Florida Board of Conservation.

6 1-inch-thick red snapper steaks or other fish steaks

Salt and freshly ground black pepper to taste

1 cup grated Swiss cheese

1 tablespoon Dijon-style prepared mustard

2 tablespoons prepared horseradish

2 tablespoons chili sauce

¼ cup melted unsalted butter

Preheated broiler
1. Wipe and dry fish steaks. Sprinkle both sides with salt and pepper and place on well-oiled broiler pan.
2. Combine cheese, mustard, horseradish and chili sauce.
3. Brush fish with melted butter and broil 5 minutes, or until lightly browned. Turn and brush again with melted butter and broil 5 minutes, or until lightly browned.
4. Remove steaks from oven and spread cheese mixture evenly on top of each steak.
5. Return to oven and broil not more than 1 to 2 minutes, or until cheese melts and starts to brown. Serve immediately.
Serves 6.

Recommended Fish for Charcoal Broiling or Barbecuing

SALTWATER
Barracuda
California Black Sea Bass
Flounder
Sole
Swordfish
Tuna

FRESHWATER
Bass
Bluegill
Crappie
Sucker
Trout
Whitefish

Charcoal-Broiled Fish
(Basic Recipe)

Charcoal broiling has been made popular around the world by American troops and their families stationed abroad. Actually, this is an old and primitive method of fish cookery. Any whole fish, steak or fillet may be charcoal broiled by simply coating it with oil and then placing the fish over hot coals. Basting sauces are popular with American cooks who charcoal broil fish, meats and poultry. (See page 146 for recommended sauces.) You should have a brush to spread the basting sauce, and a hinged rack is of great help in turning the fish.

1. Make a fire with charcoal briquets. When coals are white-hot, spread them evenly over bottom of grill.
2. Wipe fish dry. Place on a well-oiled rack. Brush generously with basting sauce. Cook about 10 minutes per inch of thickness or fraction thereof. (Cooking time has to be approximate. Every fire behaves differently, depending on the wind, air temperature, humidity, and the density of the coals.) Turn fish halfway through cooking time. If the fire flames up, remove fish from the coals until flames die down.

Spicy Basting Sauce

This is a favorite Southern barbecue sauce for broiled fish.

½ cup strained honey
½ cup prepared horseradish mustard
½ cup cider vinegar
¼ cup Worcestershire sauce
1 tablespoon chopped parsley

2 teaspoons Tabasco or red pepper sauce
1 teaspoon salt, or to taste
1 teaspoon cornstarch, dissolved in 1 tablespoon cold water

In heavy, 1-quart saucepan blend together honey and mustard over low heat. Add vinegar, Worcestershire sauce, parsley, Tabasco or pepper sauce and salt. Stir well to blend. Add cornstarch mixture and cook over medium heat, stirring constantly, until mixture comes to a boil and thickens.
Yield: About 1½ cups sauce.

Recommended Fish for Poaching

SALTWATER

Cod

Cusk

Flounder

Fluke

Grouper

Haddock

Hake

Halibut

Ling Cod

Mackerel

Pollack

Redfish

Red Snapper

Sablefish

Salmon

Sole

Striped Bass

Tuna

Whiting

FRESHWATER

Catfish

Crappie

Pike

Sucker

Trout

Whitefish

Poached Whole Fish
(Basic Recipe)

Poaching can be a quick and easy method of cooking fish; many fish recipes for salads, fish cakes and casseroles are prepared in this manner. The poaching liquid is called a "court bouillon" in French cuisine and a "broth" in American cooking; the difference being that wine is not used in an authentic recipe for broth. The obvious reason for the deletion is that until recent years American wines were not considered refined enough for cooking purposes.

Cod, haddock, halibut, red snapper, channel bass, tilefish, salmon, trout, pike and sole are varieties of fish particularly suited to poaching.

3-to-5-pound fish or larger, cleaned and dressed; head and tail may be left on
1 tablespoon unsalted butter
1 cup chopped onion
2 tablespoons chopped green pepper
¼ cup chopped celery

5 cups water or 4 cups water and 1 cup of dry white wine
1 tablespoon chopped parsley
2 teaspoons salt
4 black peppercorns
2 whole cloves
1 small bay leaf
2 tablespoons lemon juice

1. Melt butter in a 2½-quart saucepan. Add onion, green pepper and celery. Cook 10 minutes, stirring often, or until vegetables are tender.
2. Add water, parsley, salt, peppercorns, cloves, bay leaf and lemon juice. Bring to a boil. Cover, reduce heat and simmer 30 minutes. Strain. Discard the vegetables and reserve the broth for poaching fish.

Yield: About 5 cups.

3. *To Poach Fish*: Wrap the cleaned fish securely in a piece of cheesecloth, leaving long ends to make it easier to remove from the broth after it is cooked. Measure thickness of fish.
4. Bring poaching liquid to a boil. Lower the fish into the liquid. Tie the ends of the cheesecloth to the handles of the poaching pan, making certain that the wrapped fish does not touch the bottom of the pan. Return the liquid to a boil; then cover and reduce heat to barely a simmer. Cook 10 minutes per inch of thickness or fraction thereof. Take care not to overcook; the fish will continue to cook after it is taken from the broth.
5. Lift the fish from the broth and remove the cheesecloth. Place on a hot serving platter and remove skin very carefully. Garnish with lemon and parsley. Serve with a sauce (see page 146).

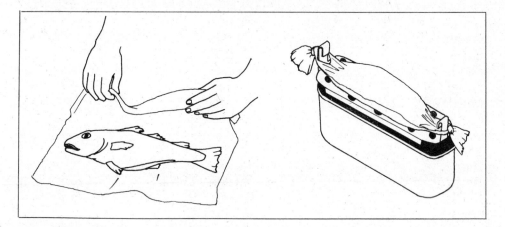

Variations: Cold Poached Whole Fish

In step 4 let the fish cool in the broth; then chill, skin and bone. Serve with a cold sauce.

Poached Fish Steaks and Fillets

Pour about 2 cups of fish broth into a 10-to-12-inch skillet. Add fish steaks or fillets and bring broth to a boil. Cover, reduce heat to a bare simmer and cook 10 minutes per inch of thickness or fraction thereof. Serve immediately with a sauce.

Cold Poached Fish Steaks and Fillets

Prepare as for poached fish steaks and fillets. Let the fish cool in the broth; then chill and serve with a cold sauce.

Recommended Fish for Pan-Frying

SALTWATER

Barracuda	Pollack
Blowfish	Porgy
Bluefish	Redfish
Butterfish	Red Snapper
Cod	Sablefish
Croaker	Salmon
Cusk	Sand Dabs
Flounder	Sea Bass
Fluke	Sea Trout
Grunion	Shad
Haddock	Smelt
Hake	Surf Perch
Halibut	Tautog
Kingfish	Tuna
Mackerel	Whitebait
Mullet	Whiting
Ocean Perch	

FRESHWATER

Bass	Perch
Bluegill	Sucker
Catfish	Trout
Crappie	Whitefish

Pan-Fried Fish
(Basic Recipe)

This is a favorite method that Southern and Midwestern cooks use to prepare catfish and other small freshwater fish such as perch, black bass and crappie. Little is needed in the way of equipment except a 10-to-12-inch skillet, preferably made of cast iron.

Catfish are first skinned, but other fish must be scaled. Remove the front fins, head and viscera by cutting fish from back of head down to vent.

Traditionally, crisp pan-fried fish is served with tartar sauce, hush puppies and coleslaw.

Fresh-caught small fish are often just cleaned, wiped with a damp paper towel, sprinkled with salt and pepper, pan-fried in butter and nothing more. Home cooks usually first dip the fish in evaporated milk or half-and-half and then coat it with seasoned flour, fine bread crumbs or cornmeal. Some cooks favor a combination of seasoned flour and cornmeal, either white or yellow.

The coating for pan-fried fish varies depending on the region of preparation, ranging from the lightly seasoned flour coating of New England to the very hot and spicy, cayenne-flavored cornmeal coating of Cajun cooks.

Allow 1 pound of fish per serving.

Pan-frying: The right amount of oil or combination of oil and butter is important for good frying results. Follow this chart:

Pan size	8-inch skillet (2 to 3 tablespoons)	9-inch skillet (¼ cup)
	10-inch skillet (⅓ cup)	12-inch skillet (½ cup)

See Pan-frying basic instructions p. 75.

NOTE: For fish floured, breaded or coated with batter before pan-frying, increase the above amounts by 2 tablespoons.

1. In a heavy skillet heat a combination of oil and butter not more than ½ inch deep to 375°F.
2. Dredge fish in coating and place in the pan immediately. Keep the fish well separated during the frying so that they will brown evenly.
3. Fry fish until golden on one side and then turn and brown the other side. This should take about 10 minutes—5 minutes for each side, depending upon the thickness of the fish. Serve immediately, garnished with lemon and parsley or watercress.

Seasoned Flour Coating   Mix 2 cups all-purpose unbleached flour, 2 teaspoons salt and ½ teaspoon freshly ground black pepper.

Cornmeal Coating　　　Mix 2 cups white or yellow cornmeal, 2 teaspoons salt and ½ teaspoon freshly ground black pepper or a good pinch of cayenne pepper.

Flour and Cornmeal Coating　　　Mix 1 cup all-purpose unbleached flour, 1 cup white or yellow cornmeal, 2 teaspoons salt and ½ teaspoon freshly ground black pepper.

Bread-Crumb Coating

Salt and freshly ground black pepper to coat fish	1 large egg, well beaten, mixed with 1 tablespoon water
1 cup very fine fresh bread crumbs	

1. Sprinkle 2 pounds of fish with salt and pepper.
2. Coat the fish with bread crumbs. Then dip the coated fish in the beaten egg mixture. Again coat the fish with bread crumbs. Place in the hot skillet immediately.

Spicy Cajun Cornmeal Coating　　　Spread 1 pound of white or yellow cornmeal in 9-x-9-inch shallow baking pan. Sprinkle red pepper or cayenne pepper over cornmeal to cover completely. Sprinkle salt over red pepper. Stir mixture well to blend. Dredge the fish in the mixture and place in the hot skillet immediately. Cook as in Basic Recipe (page 76).

Oven-Fried Fish Fillets

This is a quick and easy method for preparing fish fillets. Oven frying is a lower-calorie method and it eliminates the messy clean-up of stove-top frying.

2 pounds fish fillets—flounder, sole, cod, grouper or any fresh- or salt-water fish suitable for frying	1 cup finely ground home-style bread crumbs, without crusts
2 teaspoons salt, or to taste	4 tablespoons melted unsalted butter
1 cup milk	Lemon wedges

Preheated oven temperature: 500°F.
1. Wipe fillets dry and cut into serving portions. Place in well-oiled baking dish.
2. Combine the salt, milk and bread crumbs. Cover the fish evenly with this mixture and then brush with butter. Measure thickness of fish.
3. Place in preheated oven about 3 inches from the heating element. Bake 10 minutes per inch of thickness or fraction thereof. Serve immediately on a hot platter with a squeeze of lemon juice.

Serves 4 to 6.

Trout Amandine

This is the traditional American method for preparing trout fillets. Any delicately flavored fish may be substituted for the trout.

4 6-to-8-ounce trout fillets
Salt and freshly ground black pepper
  to taste
⅓ cup peanut oil or more
½ cup flour

½ cup unsalted butter
½ cup thinly slivered almonds
1 lemon, sliced thin, for garnish
2 teaspoons chopped parsley for garnish

1. Sprinkle the fillets with salt and pepper and set aside.
2. In a heavy skillet heat not more than ¼ inch of oil to 375°F. The amount of oil will depend upon the size of the skillet; follow chart for pan-fried fish (page 95).
3. Dredge the fillets in the flour and place in the pan immediately. Keep the fillets separated during the frying so that they will brown evenly.
4. Fry fish until golden on one side and then turn and brown the other side. This should take about 10 minutes—5 minutes for each side, depending upon the thickness of the fish. Remove fish and place on a heated platter.
5. Discard the oil and wipe the skillet with a paper towel. Add butter and stir in almonds. Stirring constantly, lightly brown the almonds; then pour over the warm trout. Garnish with lemon slices and parsley. Serve immediately.

Serves 4.

Fresh Codfish Cakes

In early American cooking, codfish cakes were made with dried and salted cod, a mainstay of the New England economy. Unfortunately, this product is no longer widely available; it has been replaced by a dehydrated product found among the canned fish and seafood items at the market. Repeated testing of this new product has failed to produce the desired old-fashioned flavor of traditional New England codfish cakes. Fresh codfish has been used in the following recipe with excellent results. Serve hot with Lemon Butter Sauce and New England Baked Beans (see page 304). Accompany with gherkins or green tomato pickles.

1 codfish steak, about 2 inches thick
     (about 1¼ pounds)
1½ cups water
1 rib celery with leaves
1 small onion, chopped
5 medium-sized potatoes, peeled and
     quartered
2 tablespoons minced onion

1½ teaspoons salt, or to taste
1 large egg
Salt and freshly ground black pepper
     to taste
Flour for coating
2 tablespoons vegetable oil
2 tablespoons unsalted butter
Parsley for garnish

1. Place codfish in a medium-sized saucepan and just cover with water;
   add celery and chopped onion. Bring water to a boil. Cover, reduce
   heat to a simmer and cook until fish flakes easily. This should take
   20 to 25 minutes, depending upon the thickness of the fish. Remove
   fish and strain the broth.
2. Add potatoes, minced onion and salt to the fish broth. Bring to a
   boil. Cover, reduce heat and simmer about 25 minutes, or until
   potatoes are tender. Drain potatoes and dry them slightly over
   heat—about 2 minutes.
3. Mash or rice the potatoes in a medium-sized mixing bowl. (Do not
   add cream.) Flake the codfish with the fingers into the potatoes,
   being careful to discard fine bones and skin.
4. With a fork, blend in the egg and add salt and pepper to taste. Form
   mixture into twelve 2-inch cakes. Dust cakes with flour and refrigerate 30 minutes.
5. In a 10-to-12-inch, heavy skillet melt the oil and butter until hot
   but not smoking. Fry the cakes 5 minutes on each side, turning them
   and adding more butter if needed, until they are golden. Serve immediately, garnished with parsley.

Serves 6.

Salmon Cakes

Before the days of iodized salt, air transportation and frozen saltwater
fish, canned salmon was used in American cooking between the Al-
leghenies and the Rockies as a dietary supplement. This recipe was
widely used in rural Indiana. These fish cakes can be prepared with
either canned or cooked fresh salmon. Serve with lemon wedges and
tartar sauce.

¼ cup finely chopped onion
4 tablespoons unsalted butter
2 cups flaked, cooked salmon or 1
  1-pound can
2 large eggs, lightly beaten
1 cup soft bread crumbs
1 teaspoon Worcestershire sauce

¼ cup finely chopped parsley
Salt and freshly ground white pepper
  to taste
Flour for coating
3 tablespoons vegetable oil
Parsley for garnish

1. In a heavy, medium-sized skillet cook the onion in 1 tablespoon of butter until translucent but not brown.
2. If using canned salmon, drain, bone, skin and flake.
3. In a large mixing bowl combine the onion, salmon, eggs, bread crumbs, Worcestershire sauce, chopped parsley, and salt and pepper. Stir gently to blend.
4. Form the salmon mixture into 4 large or 8 small cakes. Dust cakes with flour and refrigerate 30 minutes.
5. In a large, heavy skillet melt the oil and 3 tablespoons of butter until hot but not smoking. Sauté the cakes 5 minutes on each side, turning them and adding more butter if needed until they are golden. Serve immediately, garnished with parsley.

Serves 4.

Variation: West Coast Salmon Cakes

Cook 1 tablespoon finely chopped green pepper and ¼ cup finely chopped celery with the onion. Add more butter if needed. Add ½ teaspoon ground sage to the salmon mixture.

Sauced Frogs' Legs, Southern Style

Frogs' legs can be broiled, smothered in a sauce or fried in the same way as chicken, which they resemble in flavor and texture.

Frogs' legs are available both fresh and frozen in fish stores. Allow 6 small pairs or 3 very large pairs per serving.

12 large pairs frogs' legs
1 tablespoon finely chopped parsley
1 tablespoon finely chopped onion
3 or 4 black peppercorns
2 tablespoons peanut oil, combined
  with 2 tablespoons unsalted butter

2 tablespoons unsalted butter
Salt to taste
½ cup dry white wine
1 tablespoon lemon juice
Watercress for garnish

1. Cover frogs' legs with ice water and refrigerate 2 hours. Drain and dry thoroughly.
2. In a 12-inch, heavy skillet cook the parsley, onion and peppercorns very slowly in the oil and butter until well flavored. Do not over-brown.
3. Strain the mixture through a fine sieve, returning the flavored oil and butter to the skillet. Discard the vegetables and peppercorns. Add the 2 tablespoons butter to the skillet. Heat until hot but not smoking.
4. Place the frogs' legs in the skillet and fry on both sides until lightly browned. Season to taste with salt. Add wine and lemon juice, cover and simmer 15 to 30 minutes, or until tender: the timing will depend upon the size of the frogs' legs. Transfer to heated platter and cover with sauce from the skillet. Garnish with watercress.

Serves 4.

Shellfish

Modern Americans are particularly fond of shellfish, which belong roughly in two very large groups, the mollusks and the crustaceans.

Mollusks have a soft anatomy and are classed as either "univalve," which includes abalone and conch, or "bivalve," which includes the clam, oyster and scallop.

Crustaceans are covered with hard shells. Among those used extensively in American cooking are the crab, Louisiana crayfish, lobster and shrimp.

Within the memory of many senior citizens living along the coastal regions of this country, shellfish were so plentiful that home cooks stretched their imaginations to the limit in order to disguise this monotonous and inexpensive protein substitute for meat and poultry. Thus, an extensive list of innovative and creative recipes have become American classics.

Clams

The American Indians, who often took themselves to the beach for a clambake, taught the early New England colonists the importance of utilizing this bivalve as a staple of their diet. Clams were for the taking, and the colonists relied upon them to see them through hard times, leaving a legacy of fine New England recipes. Later, as the West Coast was settled, home cooks contributed sophisticated recipes using the Pacific clams.

Clams are classified as "hard shell" or "soft shell." Fresh clams generally are available in limited supply near the source, or clams can be purchased in cans.

Hard Shell (Quahog)
Chowder, large
Chowder, medium
Cherrystone
Littleneck

Soft Shell
Large steamers

4 quarts (1 gallon) clams in the shell = 2 cups shucked
One 7½-ounce can, minced or chopped clams = about ½ cup clams and
about ½ cup juice

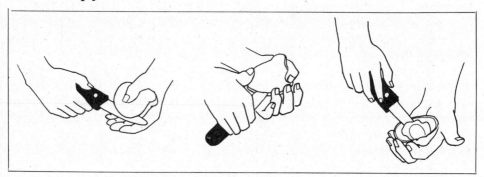

Steamed Clams

Freshly dug clams, which are steamed in a combination of beer and
water and then dipped in clarified butter, are a Down East tradition.
The quantity for this method of cookery is variable, depending upon
the appetites of the people to be served. Allow 1 quart of steamer clams
for an average serving, and serve very hot.

1. Prepare clarified butter: Put desired quantity of unsalted butter in
   small, deep saucepan. Melt over low heat and leave on low heat
   until foam appears on top and the sediment rests on the bottom of
   the pan. The liquid should be golden. Remove from heat and skim
   off foam from top. Pour off the clear butter, leaving the sediment on
   the bottom. Pour into individual dipping dishes.
2. Scrub clam shells thoroughly, through several changes of water,
   until there is no trace of sand left.
3. Place clams in a deep kettle; cover the bottom with a combination
   of half beer and half water to a depth of ¼ inch. Cover tightly and
   cook over low heat until shells open. *Caution:* Do not overcook.
4. Remove clams from broth to large soup plates. Strain broth and pour
   over the clams.
5. Lift each clam from the shell by the black neck. Dip into the broth
   and then into the clarified butter, eating all but the neck.

Eastern Shore Deviled Clams

Hot and spicy, this dish can be served either as an appetizer or as a light luncheon entrée.

2 tablespoons finely chopped onion
¼ cup finely chopped celery
2 tablespoons finely chopped green pepper
4 tablespoons unsalted butter
2 cups fresh or 4 7½-ounce cans minced or chopped clams, drained
½ cup clam juice

½ teaspoon salt, or to taste
Freshly ground black pepper to taste
⅛ teaspoon Tabasco sauce, or more to taste
½ teaspoon dry mustard
1 large egg, lightly beaten
½ cup finely ground cracker crumbs

Preheated oven temperature: 350°F.
1. In a large, heavy skillet cook the onion, celery and green pepper in the butter until tender but not brown. Add the drained clams and juice.
2. Stir the salt, black pepper, Tabasco sauce and dry mustard into the lightly beaten egg. Stir into the clam mixture; add cracker crumbs and mix lightly but thoroughly to blend ingredients.
3. Spoon the mixture into 6 well-buttered ramekins or scallop shells, allowing about ¾ cup per serving. Bake in preheated oven 20 minutes, or until the mixture is hot and bubbly.
Serves 6.

New England Clam Cakes

In early American recipes clam cakes were made with fresh clams, cracker crumbs, eggs and nothing more than a little salt and pepper for seasoning. With the loss of a ready supply of fresh clams, canned clams are being used by both home and restaurant cooks. The result is a clam cake made in the manner of a crab cake and served with tartar sauce.

2 tablespoons finely chopped green onion, white part only
2 tablespoons unsalted butter
1¼ cups finely ground fresh bread crumbs, crusts removed
2 large eggs, lightly beaten
½ cup heavy cream
1 cup fresh or 2 7½-ounce cans minced clams, drained
¼ cup finely chopped celery
2 teaspoons lemon juice

2 tablespoons finely chopped parsley
½ teaspoon salt, or to taste
⅛ teaspoon cayenne pepper, or to taste
1 large egg, beaten and combined with 1 tablespoon clam juice
¼ cup peanut oil
¼ cup unsalted butter
Parsley for garnish

1. In a large skillet cook onion in the butter until translucent but not brown. Add ½ cup of the bread crumbs, the 2 lightly beaten eggs, and cream, clams, celery, lemon juice, parsley, salt and cayenne pepper. Stir with a fork to blend and refrigerate mixture several hours to blend flavors.
2. Form mixture into eight 2-inch cakes. Dip the cakes in the egg and clam juice mixture and then in the remainder of the bread crumbs. This may be done a second time if a heavier, crisper coating is desired. Refrigerate 30 minutes.
3. In a 12-inch, heavy skillet melt the oil and butter until hot but not smoking. Sauté the cakes 4 minutes on each side, or until they are golden, adding more butter if necessary. Serve immediately, garnished with parsley.

Serves 4.

New England Fried Clams
(Cape Cod Fannie Daddies)

Generally associated with fast-food, roadside restaurants, fried clams can be prepared successfully at home. Fresh-shucked clams are a must to bring out the true flavor of this traditional repast. Serve with tartar sauce, sour pickles and potato salad or coleslaw.

2 cups fresh-shucked soft-shell clams, drained
1 large egg, separated
½ cup milk, or ¼ cup milk and ¼ cup light beer

¼ teaspoon salt
1 tablespoon melted unsalted butter
½ cup sifted unbleached all-purpose flour
Peanut oil for deep-frying

1. See page 102 for preparing clams.
2. Combine the egg yolk, milk, salt, melted butter and flour in a blender or food processor and blend until smooth. Pour mixture into a medium-sized bowl.
3. Beat egg white until stiff peaks form and gently fold into the egg yolk mixture.
4. Pour the peanut oil into a deep-fryer or an electric skillet to about half the capacity. Heat to 375°F.
5. Dip each clam individually into the batter mixture and fry until golden. This will take a very few minutes. Transfer clams with a slotted spoon onto paper towels to drain. Serve immediately.

Serves 3 or 4.

Crabs

Americans lead the world in the consumption of crabs. Only shrimp is a more popular shellfish than crabmeat in this country.

There are several types of crabs available along the coastal waters of the United States. The hard-shell, or blue, crab of the Atlantic, the Dungeness of the West Coast and the giant Alaskan, or king, crab are the most readily available.

Of all the varieties the Atlantic hard-shell crab is the most prized for its delectable meat and it accounts for about 50 percent of the commercial crabmeat sold.

The hard-shell crab is abundant from Long Island, down the Atlantic Coast, around the tip of Florida and along the entire Gulf Coast. When the hard-shell crab is in its soft-shell state (meaning that it has just molted and lost its shell, at which stage the entire crab is edible), it is considered one of the special pleasures of the table by many Americans.

Hard-shell and Dungeness crabs are available live in the shell all through the year. The soft-shell crab begins to appear in markets about the beginning of April. The hard-shell crab sheds its shell several times during the summer, so soft-shell crabs remain in season until September.

All live crabs should be vigorous and squirming around when purchased. *Caution:* If the crabs are not lively, do not purchase them; the meat will not be good. Cook live crabs immediately, pick out the meat, refrigerate and use as soon as possible.

Pasteurized fresh crabmeat, frozen crabmeat and canned crabmeat are available in all parts of the country and can be used interchangeably in recipes calling for freshly cooked crabmeat. All are available in the following forms:

Lump meat (back fin)—solid lumps of white meat used in recipes where appearance is important.

Flake meat—small pieces of white meat.

Claw meat—the outer surface of the meat has a brownish tinge, which in no way affects the flavor.

Frozen legs—Alaskan crab legs, frozen with the meat in the shell.

How to Freshen Canned Crabmeat

Recommended shelf life: 1 year
1. Drain crabmeat in a sieve.
2. Place the sieve holding the crabmeat in a bowl of ice water and let soak 2 minutes. This helps rid the crabmeat of preservatives and gives it a fresher taste.

3. Drain again but do not rinse.
4. Remove any cartilage and bits of shell. *Caution:* Canned crabmeat has a more crumbly texture than fresh or frozen meat. Handle very gently. Use in any recipe where the crabmeat is flaked.

Boiled Hard-Shell Crabs or Crayfish

This is the Cajun method used all along the Gulf Coast for boiling fresh crabs and crayfish.

According to the Cajun theory, both fresh crabs and crayfish should be purged of their impurities before they are boiled. This is an optional step for preparing crabs—crayfish are always "purged" first. Cover the live crabs or crayfish with cold water and add about 1 cup of salt to 4 quarts of water. Soak 2 hours. Rinse well before dropping in the boiling water.

Serve boiled hard-shell crabs and crayfish hot with Lemon Butter Sauce (see page 89), garlic bread and cold beer. The cold meat can also be used for appetizers and salads.

NOTE: One 5-ounce hard-shell crab should yield about 1½ ounces of picked-out meat.

To Prepare For 1 dozen hard-shell crabs or 5 pounds of crayfish add the following ingredients to each quart of boiling water:

¼ cup coarse salt	1 bay leaf
2 slices of lemon	1 small dried red pepper
2 whole allspice	¾ teaspoon celery seed
1 large onion, sliced	¼ teaspoon freshly ground black pepper
¼ teaspoon ground thyme	

1. Pour water into a large kettle to a depth of 6 inches and bring to a boil. Add salt, lemon slices, allspice, onion, thyme, bay leaf, red pepper, celery seed and black pepper. Cover and boil 20 minutes.
2. Add the crabs or crayfish and boil until the shells are bright red. Remove from heat and allow crabs or crayfish to remain in water 10 minutes. Drain. Serve hot or cold.

How to Steam Hard-Shell Crabs

1. Fit a large kettle with a rack for steaming. Place in the kettle 1 sliced large onion, 1 sliced lemon, 2 cloves mashed garlic, 1 bay leaf and ¼ cup salt. Pour in water to measure just below the rack.
2. Place the crabs in layers on the rack. Cover tightly and steam the crabs just until the top layer has turned bright red. (Do not overcook.) Remove and cool on paper towels.

How to Pick the Meat Out of a Cooked Hard-Shell Crab

1. Remove legs and claws.
2. Take the body of the crab in both hands. With one thumb, pull off the apron.
3. Remove all the orange waxy material and white substance between the halves of the body and at the sides.

NOTE: *The edible part of the crab lies in the two compact masses remaining and the meat from the large claws.*

4. Crack claws with a mallet. Remove the body and claw meat with the fingers or a seafood cocktail fork.
5. Pick over meat well to remove bits of shell and cartilage. Refrigerate until ready to use.
6. If desired, rinse crab shells, drain and use to make stuffed crabs.

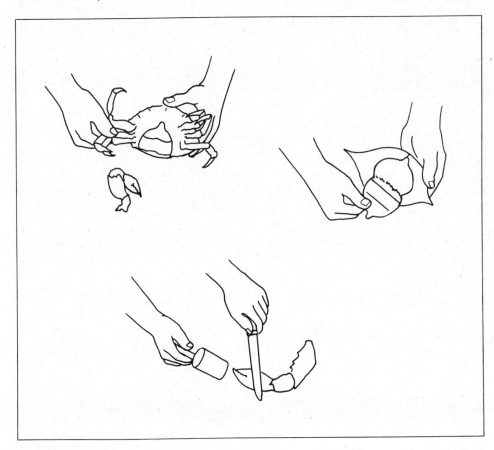

How to Clean a Soft-Shell Crab

1. Place live crab on a cutting board.
2. Stick the point of a sharp knife into the body between the eyes to kill it.
3. Remove the eyes and "dead men's fingers" under the points. Lift up the pointed ends of the soft shell and remove the white substance.
4. Turn the crab over on its back and remove the apron from the underneath part of the body.

NOTE: All the rest of the crab is edible, including the small legs and fins.

5. Wash crabs under running water and drain on paper towels. Cook immediately, following recipe instructions.

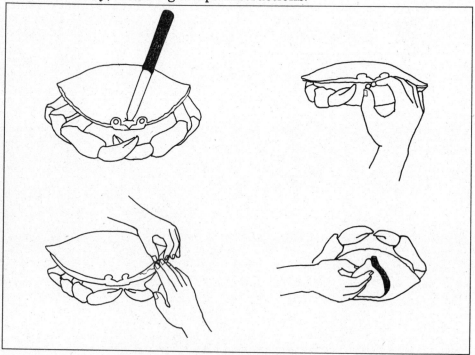

How to Prepare Frozen Crabmeat

1. Defrost and drain well.
2. Remove any cartilage and bits of shell. Cook as soon as possible, following recipe instructions.

NOTE: Three 6-ounce packages frozen Alaskan king crabmeat, thawed and drained, can be substituted for 1 pound of fresh lump crabmeat.

Soft-Shell Crabs
(Basic Recipe)

This is the old-fashioned Southern method of broiling or sautéing soft-shell crabs. Crabs come in various sizes. Use the small ones for sautéing and broil the larger ones. If you are buying live crabs, have them killed and cleaned at the market, just before you are ready to cook them. If you clean them yourself, see basic instructions, page 108. If you buy soft-shell crabs frozen, they have been cleaned and only need to be thawed before they are cooked. Allow two small or medium-sized crabs per person. Serve with Lemon Butter Sauce or Tartar Sauce (pages 89, 153).

12 soft-shell crabs
2 cups milk, combined with 2 teaspoons salt and ¼ teaspoon freshly ground black pepper

½ cup flour
1 cup unsalted butter
Chopped parsley and lemon slices for garnish

1. Wipe the crabs with paper towels.
2. In a large, shallow pan soak the crabs in the combined milk, salt and pepper for 10 minutes on each side.
3. Drain the crabs and discard the seasoned milk.
4. Dredge the crabs in the flour and either sauté or broil them, according to the instructions below.

Sautéed Soft-Shell Crabs

1. Prepare crabs through Step 4, above.
2. Either use two large skillets or prepare the crabs in two batches. If using two skillets, heat ½ cup butter in each skillet until hot but not smoking. Place the crabs in the skillets, shell side down. Sauté 4 minutes on each side. *Caution:* Do not crowd the crabs in the skillets and do not overcook. If the crabs begin to pop and spatter during the cooking, puncture legs and claws with a sharp fork. Drain the crabs on paper towels. Garnish with parsley and lemon slices. Serve hot with sauce.

Serves 6.

Broiled Soft-Shell Crabs

1. Prepare crabs through Step 4, above.
2. Place the crabs, shell side down, on broiler pan in a single layer. Brush with ½ cup melted butter.

3. Broil 3 to 4 inches from the source of heat about 4 minutes, or until nicely browned. Turn, brush with the remaining ½ cup melted butter and broil 4 more minutes, or until brown. Drain the crabs on paper towels. Garnish with parsley and lemon slices. Serve hot with sauce.
Serves 6.

Batter-Fried Soft-Shell Crabs

12 soft-shell crabs
1 recipe All-Purpose Dipping Batter (see page 145)

1 cup unsalted butter
Chopped parsley and lemon slices for garnish

1. Wipe the crabs with paper towels.
2. Prepare the Dipping Batter and pour into a medium-sized bowl.
3. Either use two large skillets or prepare the crabs in two batches. If using two skillets, heat ½ cup butter in each skillet until hot but not smoking. Add more butter if necessary, depending upon the size of the skillet.
4. Submerge each crab in the Dipping Batter, shake off excess and place in the skillet, shell side down. Fry until golden brown on each side. Drain the crabs on paper towels. Serve at once with tartar sauce.
Serves 6.

Crab Imperial

Both Louisiana and Maryland cookery include recipes for Crab Imperial. Both regions prepare the dish in basically the same manner, using either a base of cream sauce or mayonnaise. Crab Imperial can be prepared in a casserole or in individual shells.

3 tablespoons unsalted butter
1½ tablespoons flour
1 cup half-and-half
1 large egg yolk, lightly beaten
¼ cup finely chopped chives
2 tablespoons lemon juice
1 teaspoon Dijon-style mustard
⅛ teaspoon Tabasco sauce
½ teaspoon salt, or to taste

¼ teaspoon freshly ground white pepper, or to taste
⅛ teaspoon ground mace
1 pound fresh crabmeat or 3 6-ounce packages frozen Alaskan king crabmeat, thawed and drained
1 cup fresh bread crumbs, without crusts, combined with 2 tablespoons unsalted butter

Preheated oven temperature: 350°F.

1. In a heavy, 2-quart saucepan melt the butter, blend in flour and cook 3 minutes, stirring constantly.
2. Remove mixture from heat. Slowly add the half-and-half, stirring constantly to blend.
3. Return mixture to heat and cook slowly for at least 5 minutes, stirring constantly, until the mixture has thickened. Remove from heat and cool slightly.
4. Add a few tablespoons of the heated sauce to the egg yolk, 1 tablespoon at a time, stirring constantly to blend.
5. Slowly add the egg mixture to the sauce, stirring constantly to keep the egg mixture from separating. Add the chives, lemon juice, mustard, Tabasco sauce, salt, pepper and ground mace.
6. Return the mixture to low heat and cook 5 minutes, stirring constantly to blend flavors.
7. Pick over drained crabmeat to remove cartilage and shell; fold into the sauce and pour into a well-buttered 1-quart casserole.
8. Sauté the buttered crumbs in a small skillet until very lightly browned; sprinkle evenly over the crab mixture. Bake in preheated oven until hot and bubbly—about 25 minutes.

Serves 6.

Maryland Crab Cakes

Crab cakes have been a specialty of Maryland—and all the other areas bordering the seafood-rich Chesapeake Bay—since early Colonial times. But very often the crab cakes served in local restaurants are overflavored with onion and a combination of hot spices. Many recipes were tested for this book, and this one was rated "excellent" by the testers.

The secret of making good crab cakes is to handle the mixture gently when shaping the cakes and to use Uneeda brand crackers to bind the ingredients together.

⅓ cup finely crushed cracker crumbs
1 large egg, lightly beaten
½ cup finely chopped parsley
1 teaspoon dry mustard or 1 tablespoon Dijon-style mustard
⅛ teaspoon cayenne pepper
A few drops of Tabasco sauce, to taste

2 tablespoons mayonnaise, preferably homemade
1 pound fresh lump crabmeat, drained
Salt to taste
2 tablespoons vegetable oil
2 tablespoons unsalted butter

1. In a large bowl combine the cracker crumbs, egg, parsley, mustard, cayenne pepper, Tabasco sauce and mayonnaise. Stir to blend.
2. Pick over crabmeat to remove cartilage and shell. *Caution:* Handle the crabmeat gently to keep the pieces as large as possible.
3. Add the crabmeat to the ingredients in the bowl. Toss the mixture together very lightly with a fork. Add salt to taste.
4. With a light touch, shape the mixture into 8 cakes about 1 inch thick. Place the cakes in the refrigerator to chill at least 1 hour.
5. In a large, heavy skillet add the vegetable oil and butter. Heat until hot but not smoking. Cook the cakes over medium heat 3 minutes on each side, or until nicely browned. Garnish with lemon wedges and parsley. Serve immediately.

Serves 4.

Maryland Crabmeat Balls

Almost as popular as crabmeat cakes, this is a treasure that can be served as a party appetizer or used to garnish a baked fish platter. These can be made in advance and reheated in a 325°F. oven.

¼ cup unsalted butter
½ cup finely ground fresh bread crumbs, without crusts
2 tablespoons finely chopped onion (optional)
¼ teaspoon cayenne pepper, or more to taste
⅛ teaspoon ground mace

⅛ teaspoon grated nutmeg
1 teaspoon dry mustard
½ teaspoon salt, or to taste
1 pound flaked crabmeat, drained
Yolks of 2 large eggs, lightly beaten
⅓ cup flour for coating
Peanut oil for frying

1. In a medium-sized heavy skillet melt the butter and add bread crumbs, optional onion, cayenne, mace, nutmeg, mustard and salt. Cook over low heat until the onions are tender but not brown.
2. Pick over crabmeat to remove cartilage and shell.
3. Add the crabmeat and egg yolks to the bread mixture. Stir to blend. *NOTE: All the ingredients may be placed in a food processor. Process 1 to 2 seconds, or until the mixture is smooth. Do not overprocess. Place the mixture in the refrigerator to chill at least 1 hour.*
4. With the fingertips, gently form the crabmeat mixture into 1-inch balls and lightly coat with flour. Return to refrigerator for 15 minutes.
5. Pour the peanut oil into a heavy skillet to a depth of 1 inch. Heat until oil is hot but not smoking, or 375°F.
6. Drop the balls into the hot oil and fry until golden. Transfer them with a slotted spoon onto paper towels to drain. Serve hot.

Makes 36 1-inch balls.

Boothbay Harbor Crab Cakes With Lobster Sauce

New England cooking can be very refined, and this recipe is a case in point.

1 recipe Lobster Sauce (see page 148)
½ cup unsalted butter
1 tablespoon finely chopped green pepper
1 tablespoon finely chopped celery
1 cup finely ground cracker crumbs
1 cup finely ground fresh bread crumbs, without crusts

4 teaspoons fresh lemon juice
Yolks of 7 large eggs, well beaten
½ teaspoon salt, or to taste
¼ teaspoon freshly ground black pepper
3 cups fresh or frozen crabmeat, drained
Whites of 6 eggs, stiffly beaten

Preheated oven temperature: 375°F.

1. Prepare Lobster Sauce and set aside.
2. In a small, heavy skillet melt the butter. Add the green pepper and celery. Cook until tender but not brown. Place mixture in a large mixing bowl.
3. Add cracker crumbs, bread crumbs, lemon juice, egg yolks, salt and pepper. Stir gently to blend.
4. Pick over crabmeat to remove cartilage and shell. Gently stir the crabmeat into the mixture in the mixing bowl.
5. Stir about one fourth of the stiffly beaten egg whites into the crab mixture. With a rubber spatula gently fold in the remainder of the egg whites. *Caution:* Do not overstir—a few traces of egg white should be visible.
6. Spoon the mixture into 8 well-buttered 1-cup custard cups. Set cups in a large, shallow pan and add boiling water to measure halfway up the sides of the cups. Bake in preheated oven 25 minutes, or until the centers are firm. Unmold and coat lightly with the Lobster Sauce. Serve extra sauce on the side.

Serves 8.

Lobster

There are two varieties of lobster used in preparing American dishes: the Maine lobster of the colder northern waters and the spiny, or rock, lobster of the southern waters. Both are delicious eating, but the sweet and tender meat of the Maine lobster is considered the superior of the two. Until the early sixties Maine lobsters were comparatively inexpensive in season, selling in East Coast markets for as little as 89 cents per pound. Lobsters are in season from June through September.

Lobsters were so plentiful in former times that home cooks prepared them in every conceivable manner. Today the effects of conservation laws and the elements of Nature and Mankind have reduced the supply to the extent that lobsters have become one of our most expensive luxury foods.

Americans born to the taste of fresh-caught lobster generally prefer them boiled or steamed, served with hot melted butter and nothing more. Corn pudding—corn being in season at the same time as the lobsters—often is served as the accompanying vegetable, the theory being that this mild dish will not overwhelm the succulent taste of the fresh lobster.

Lobster meat can be purchased live in the shell, cooked in the shell, frozen or canned in all parts of the country. Often the meat can be used interchangeably in recipes that call for cooked lobster.

LIVE IN THE SHELL   A fresh live lobster will curl its tail under the back part of the body when picked up; this indicates it is freshly caught. *Caution:* Never cook a dead lobster.

COOKED IN THE SHELL   Lobster cooked in the shell should be bright red and have a pleasant odor. To test for freshness, straighten the tail of the cooked lobster. If it springs back into place, the lobster was alive when placed in the kettle. Cooked lobster meat should be firm and reddish-white or pale pink.

FROZEN LOBSTER MEAT   This is meat already picked out of the shell—a convenience when making casserole dishes and salads. However, the delicious tomalley and the roe of the female lobster will be missing.

FROZEN ROCK LOBSTER TAILS   These are sold uncooked in plastic packages in the frozen-food section of markets. Thaw before cooking.

CANNED LOBSTER   This is picked-out meat and usually is sold in 5-ounce tins. One 5-ounce tin is equal to 1 cup of picked-out lobster.

A 1-pound lobster in the shell will yield about ¼ pound of cooked meat. Lobster are sold in the following sizes:

Jumbo—lobsters weighing over 2 pounds
Large—lobsters weighing from 1½ to 2 pounds
Quarters—lobsters weighing 1¼ pounds
Eighths—lobsters weighing 1⅛ pounds
"Chicken"—lobsters weighing 1 pound or less

How to Freshen Canned Lobster

The recommended shelf life of canned lobster is one year.
1. Drain lobster in a sieve.
2. Place the sieve holding the lobster in a bowl of ice water and let soak 2 minutes. This helps rid the lobster meat of preservatives and gives it a fresher taste.
3. Drain again but do not rinse.

How to Dress a Cooked Lobster

1. To split the lobster in half, place it on its back, shell side down, on a cutting board. Cross the large claws over the head and hold firmly with your left hand. With a sharp, pointed, heavy knife, make an incision down the entire length of the body and tail of the lobster, deep enough to release the meat from the shell.
2. Spread the lobster out flat.
3. With a teaspoon remove the tomalley and the roe of a female lobster. (See below.)
4. With two fingers, pull out the stomach, a small sac just behind the head. The intestinal vein should pull out with the sac. If it does not, use a fork to remove it. The spongy particles between the meat and shell should be discarded.
5. Rinse the cleaned lobster under cold, running water, meat side down, and place on paper towels to drain.
6. Crack the claws and remove the meat. If the lobster is not to be served whole, take out the meat from the body. Use as in recipe instructions. Save the lobster shell to use in serving, if desired.

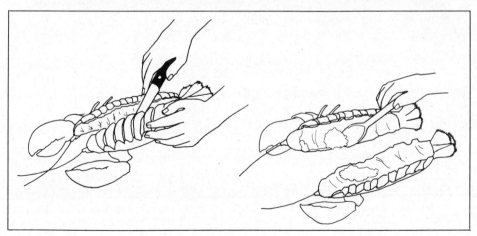

About Tomalley

The tomalley is the soft, greenish-gray liver found in the "head" or upper part of the lobster. Do not discard. It is a prized part of the lobster and has a rich, creamy flavor. Eat it straight from the lobster or use it as a thickener in making a sauce.

About Roe

The roe is the pink eggs found in female lobsters. Mix with a little sour cream and serve as a cocktail spread.

Steamed Maine Lobsters

This is the cooking method most New Englanders prefer. Steaming ensures tender meat, and eliminates handling a large kettle of boiling water.

To Prepare Four 1½-pound Lobsters

1. Measure 2 inches of boiling water into a large kettle; add 2 table-spoons salt. Fit kettle with a rack.
2. Place lobsters on rack, head first. Cover kettle with a tight-fitting lid. Bring water quickly back to steaming point and start timing. Allow about 12 minutes total cooking time for all of the lobsters, or cook until the shells are bright red. *Caution:* Do not overcook, or the meat will be tough.
3. Quickly remove the lobsters one by one and lay them on their backs.
4. Dress lobsters—see basic instructions (page 115).
5. Serve hot with melted unsalted butter, or cold with homemade mayonnaise made with lemon juice.

Serves 4.

Boiled Lobsters

To Prepare Four 1½-pound Lobsters

For each quart of boiling water add 1 tablespoon salt.

1. Measure enough water into a large kettle to cover the lobsters and bring to a boil; add salt.
2. Plunge live lobsters in, head down. Cover kettle with a tight-fitting lid. Reduce the heat to simmer and start timing. Allow 5 minutes cooking time for the first pound and about 4 minutes for each additional pound, per lobster. Allow 7 minutes for 1½-pound lobsters. *Caution:* Do not overcook, or the meat will be tough.

3. Quickly remove the lobsters one by one and lay them on their backs to drain.
4. Dress lobsters—see basic instructions (page 115).
5. Serve hot with melted unsalted butter, or cold with homemade mayonnaise made with lemon juice.

Serves 4.

Broiled Lobsters

Broiled lobsters are usually served in restaurants. Home cooks prefer the juicier, tenderer flavor of boiled or steamed lobsters.

To Prepare Four 1½-pound Lobsters
Preheated broiler
1. Prepare as in How to Dress a Cooked Lobster, Steps 1 through 5 (page 115).
2. Brush each lobster generously with melted unsalted butter. Place the lobster halves, shell side down, about 5 to 6 inches from heating element in preheated broiler. Brush the lobsters with more melted butter during the cooking because they have a tendency to be very dry from the direct heat of the broiler. The shells should be bright red, the meat translucent and the surfaces lightly browned. Serve a small dish of Lemon-Butter Sauce (page 89) with each lobster.

Serves 4.

New England Stuffed Lobster

This is a typical Maine recipe for stuffed lobster. Both the tomalley and the roe of the female are used to make a flavorful stuffing. Serve with crisp corn oysters and whole freshly peeled and seeded tomatoes filled with marinated cucumber slices.

4 1½-pound live lobsters
Tomalley and roe of lobsters
1 cup melted unsalted butter
2¼ cups finely ground dry bread crumbs, without crusts

½ teaspoon salt, or to taste
2 teaspoons Worcestershire sauce, or to taste

Preheated oven temperature: 350°F.
1. Prepare as in How to Dress a Cooked Lobster, Steps 1 through 5 (page 115).
2. Spread the lobster halves out on a cutting board. Remove the tomalley and roe and reserve for the stuffing.

3. With two fingers, pull out the stomach, a small sac just behind the head. The intestinal vein should pull out with the sac. If it does not, use a fork to remove it. The spongy particles between the meat and shell should be discarded.
4. Rinse the cleaned lobsters under cold, running water and place on paper towels to drain, meat side down.
5. In a medium-sized bowl mix the tomalley and roe with the melted butter. With the fingertips, lightly blend in the bread crumbs, salt and Worcestershire sauce.
6. Lightly stuff the cavities of the lobsters with the bread mixture. Divide the remainder evenly and spread over the tops of the lobsters.
7. Line a baking pan large enough to hold the lobsters with foil, alternating heads and tails to fit into the pan. Bake in preheated oven 15 to 20 minutes, or until the stuffing is golden brown. Serve hot.

Serves 8, allowing ½ lobster per serving.

Lobster Au Gratin
(Lobster Pie)

This traditional New England recipe has always been known as lobster pie. Perhaps this is because the ingredients are baked in individual deep-dish pie plates.

1 cup unsalted butter
4 cups cooked lobster meat fresh or frozen, cut into bite-size pieces
¾ cup dry sherry
4 tablespoons flour
3 cups half-and-half
Yolks of 8 large eggs, lightly beaten
Salt (optional)

1½ cups finely ground Uneeda brand cracker crumbs
4 tablespoons coarsely ground toast crumbs, lightly browned
1 teaspoon paprika
4 tablespoons freshly grated Parmesan cheese
6 tablespoons melted unsalted butter

Preheated oven temperature: 350°F.
1. In a heavy, medium-sized skillet melt ½ cup of the butter. Add lobster and cook over medium heat 2 minutes, stirring constantly. Remove lobster and set aside.
2. Add the sherry to the butter remaining in the skillet and boil over high heat 1 minute. Set aside.
3. In a heavy, 2½-quart saucepan melt the remaining ½ cup of butter. Blend in flour and cook 3 minutes, stirring constantly.
4. Remove mixture from heat. Slowly add half-and-half and the sherry mixture, stirring constantly to blend.

5. Return mixture to heat and cook at least 5 minutes, stirring constantly, until the mixture has thickened slightly. Remove from heat and cool a few minutes.
6. Slowly add the sauce to the egg yolks, stirring constantly to blend.
7. Return mixture to heat and cook slowly, stirring constantly, until mixture has thickened. *Caution:* Do not boil the mixture after the eggs have been added. Add optional salt. Stir in lobster.
8. Spoon the lobster mixture into 8 lightly buttered 1-cup, deep-dish pie plates, or use casserole dishes.
9. Combine the cracker crumbs, toast crumbs, paprika, Parmesan cheese and the 6 tablespoons of melted butter. Sprinkle evenly over the lobster mixture. Bake in preheated oven 15 minutes, or until mixture is bubbling and the topping golden brown. Serve at once.

Serves 8.

Rock Lobster Cutlets

These are also known as lobster cakes or chops in New England cookery.

2 large eggs
½ cup heavy cream
2 tablespoons melted unsalted butter
1½ teaspoons flour
1 tablespoon finely chopped parsley
⅛ teaspoon freshly grated nutmeg
A few sprinklings of cayenne pepper
½ teaspoon salt, or to taste

2 cups cooked lobster meat, chopped fine
1 cup ¼-inch dry bread cubes, without crusts
1¼ cups finely ground cracker crumbs for coating
Peanut oil for frying
Parsley for garnish

1. In a large mixing bowl beat 1 egg; add the cream and stir to blend. Add the butter, flour, chopped parsley, nutmeg, cayenne pepper and salt. Stir well to blend.
2. Drain the lobster meat well and add to mixture in the bowl but do not stir. Add bread cubes and gently stir to blend all the ingredients together.
3. Gently form the mixture into 8 cutlets about ½ inch thick. Place the cutlets in the refrigerator to chill at least 2 hours.
4. Lightly beat remaining egg and dip the chilled cutlets in it and then coat with cracker crumbs. Return the cutlets to the refrigerator for 15 minutes.
5. Add the peanut oil to a large, heavy skillet. Heat until hot but not smoking. Cook the cakes over medium heat a few minutes on each side, until they are golden brown. Garnish with parsley.

Serves 4.

In 1908, a practical guide to housekeeping, titled *Household Discoveries and Mrs. Curtis's Cook Book,* was published by the Success Company. The book was sold door to door all through the rural Midwest, and gained wide acceptance among the housebound farm women as the last word in the preparation of good food. The recipes were so well written that surprisingly they did not have to be adjusted to our modern cooking techniques.

How Mrs. Curtis arrived at her collection is a mystery. She either copied outrageously or she was an exceptionally fine cook. The three lobster recipes that follow are from her 257-page book of outstanding American recipes.

Mrs. Curtis's Curry of Lobster

Use rock lobster tails to make this three-star Southern specialty. Serve over toast points or hot, cooked rice.

4 cups water
Salt
1 bay leaf
6 3-to-5-ounce fresh or frozen rock
    lobster tails
3 tablespoons unsalted butter
2 tablespoons finely chopped onion
3 tablespoons flour

2 teaspoons curry powder, or to taste
1 chicken bouillon cube
⅛ teaspoon Tabasco sauce
Freshly ground white pepper to taste
Strips of canned pimiento for garnish
Chutney

1. In a large kettle bring water to boil. Add 1 teaspoon of salt, the bay leaf and lobster tails. Boil 6 minutes.
2. Remove tails. Reserve the boiling water. Rinse the tails under cold, running water and set aside to cool a few minutes.
3. Reduce the liquid in which the tails were boiled to 1½ cups. Discard the bay leaf and set liquid aside.
4. Remove lobster meat from shells and cut into bite-sized pieces.
5. Melt the butter in a medium-sized heavy saucepan. Add the onion and cook until very lightly colored but not brown. Blend in flour and curry powder. Cook 3 minutes, stirring constantly.
6. Remove mixture from heat. Slowly add the 1½ cups of reduced liquid and the bouillon cube, stirring constantly to blend. Add Tabasco sauce and salt and pepper to taste.
7. Return mixture to heat and cook slowly at least 5 minutes, stirring constantly, until the mixture has thickened. Stir the lobster into the hot sauce. Serve hot over toast points or hot, cooked rice. Garnish with strips of pimiento and serve a spoonful of chutney on the side.

Serves 6.

Mrs. Curtis's Creamed Lobster

This is a very old New England recipe that for some reason has become known as "Lobster Newburg." True Down Easters use lemon juice rather than sherry to keep from masking the flavor of fresh lobster meat.

This is a very rich dish. Small portions are recommended.

2 cups fresh or frozen lobster meat	Salt to taste
4 tablespoons unsalted butter	½ cup heavy cream
2 tablespoons finely chopped onion	Yolks of 2 large eggs
2 tablespoons flour	Toast points
2 cups half-and-half	Paprika for garnish
1 tablespoon lemon juice	

1. Cut lobster into bite-size pieces and set aside.
2. Melt the butter in a heavy, 2-quart saucepan. Add the onion and cook until tender but not brown. Blend in the flour and cook 3 minutes, stirring constantly.
3. Remove mixture from heat. Slowly add the half-and-half, stirring constantly to blend. Add lemon juice and salt.
4. Return mixture to heat and cook slowly at least 5 minutes, stirring constantly, until the mixture has thickened. Remove from heat and cool slightly. Stir in the cream.
5. In a small bowl lightly beat the egg yolks. Add a few tablespoons of the heated sauce to the egg yolks, 1 tablespoon at a time, stirring constantly to blend.
6. Slowly add the egg mixture to the sauce, stirring constantly to keep the egg mixture from separating. *Caution:* Do not boil the mixture after the eggs have been added.
7. Add the lobster to the sauce while it is still hot. Serve hot over toast points. Garnish with a sprinkling of paprika.

Serves 4 to 6.

Mrs. Curtis's Scalloped Lobster

Scalloped lobster is a dish popular from Maine to the Carolinas. Please resist the temptation to "Frenchify" the dish by adding garlic, shallots and sophisticated herbs to the sauce.

4　1 ¼-pound cooked lobsters; or use
　　2 cups frozen cooked lobster meat
3　tablespoons unsalted butter
3　tablespoons flour
1　cup chicken broth, preferably
　　homemade
Salt to taste
A few sprinklings of cayenne pepper

¼　teaspoon paprika
½　cup heavy cream
2　large egg yolks, lightly beaten
2　to 4 tablespoons dry sherry
½　cup freshly ground bread crumbs,
　　without crusts, combined with 1 ta-
　　blespoon melted unsalted butter

Preheated oven temperature: 400°F.

1. Steam live lobsters following basic recipe instructions, page 116. Clean and cut into bite-size pieces. Reserve shells for stuffing. If using frozen cooked lobster meat, cut into bite-size pieces. May be baked in buttered scallop shells or small ramekins.
2. Melt the butter in a medium-sized, heavy saucepan. Blend in flour and cook 3 minutes, stirring constantly.
3. Remove mixture from heat. Slowly add the chicken broth, stirring constantly to blend. Add salt, cayenne and paprika.
4. Return mixture to heat and cook at least 5 minutes, stirring constantly, until the mixture has thickened. Remove from heat and cool slightly. Stir in the cream.
5. Add a few tablespoons of the heated sauce to the egg yolks, 1 tablespoon at a time, stirring constantly to blend.
6. Slowly add the egg mixture to the sauce, stirring constantly to keep the egg mixture from separating.
7. Return mixture to low heat and cook, stirring constantly, until thickened. *Caution:* Do not boil the mixture after the eggs have been added.
8. Add the lobster to the sauce while it is still hot. Then stir in the sherry to taste.
9. Spoon the mixture into the reserved lobster shells, scallop shells or ramekins. Sprinkle with buttered crumbs. Bake in preheated oven 8 to 10 minutes, or until the bread crumbs are golden brown. Serve hot.

Serves 4.

Variation: Deviled Lobster

In Step 3 add ½ teaspoon dry mustard, or more to taste. In Step 7 omit sherry.

Crayfish (Crawfish) Etouffée

Obtaining fresh crayfish is the difficult part of assembling this simple-to-prepare dish. Capturing the small creature, which is found in sloughs, swamps, roadside ditches and along the banks of small streams, is a local sport in rural Louisiana where it is commonly known as the *crawfish*. In season, crayfish are sold along the roadsides near New Orleans by the bucketful. Large shrimp may be substituted for the elusive crayfish in this recipe.

This dish is surprisingly mild in flavor. Not quite a stew, Crayfish Etouffée usually is served as a dinner entrée, accompanied by French bread and a good white wine.

1 pound shelled crayfish tails, or large shrimp
½ cup unsalted butter
1 cup finely chopped onion
1 cup finely chopped green pepper
½ cup finely chopped celery
1 teaspoon finely chopped garlic
2 tablespoons flour
1 large tomato, peeled, seeded and chopped (optional)

2 cups fish or chicken broth
Salt to taste
Freshly ground black pepper to taste
A few sprinklings of cayenne pepper
1 tablespoon Worcestershire sauce
½ cup finely chopped green onion tops
6 cups boiled or steamed white rice

1. If using fresh crayfish, clean following basic instructions. See page 136. Use only the tails for this recipe. If using shrimp, peel and devein.
2. Melt the butter in a large, heavy, 10-to-12-inch skillet. Add the onion, green pepper and celery. Cook over medium-low heat, stirring constantly, until tender. Add the garlic and cook 1 minute. Add the flour and cook at least 3 minutes, stirring constantly, until the mixture is golden brown. Add the optional tomato and cook at least 5 minutes to remove the raw flour and tomato flavor of the *roux*-based mixture.
3. Remove from heat and slowly add the fish or chicken broth, stirring constantly to blend.
4. Return the mixture to medium-low heat and simmer uncovered 10 minutes.
5. Add salt, pepper, cayenne pepper, Worcestershire sauce, green onion tops and crayfish, or shrimp. Cover and simmer over low heat 12 to 15 minutes, stirring occasionally. Serve hot over cooked rice.
Serves 4.

Oysters

Since the days of the early colonists, Americans have been immoderately fond of oysters. Purists claim that the only proper way to eat them is American Indian fashion—directly from the shell. Be this as it may, home cooks have devised numerous tasty recipes to enhance the flavor of this bivalve mollusk, which is found between the tidal levels or in shallow waters from Maine, down the East Coast, around the Gulf of Mexico and along the Pacific Coast.

Fortunately, with careful harvesting and the cooperation of nature, oysters are becoming more plentiful; I hope we will have an ample supply for future generations to enjoy. Considering the price of other shellfish, oysters are currently comparatively inexpensive.

Patrons of the famous Grand Central Oyster Bar, in New York City, are treated to a large selection of oysters, among them the Caraquet, Blue Points, Belon (from Maine), Box, Chincoteague, Malpeques, Wellfleet and Golden Mantle, all of which are from separate specific regions. However, to those of us who purchase our oysters at the local fish market, Blue Point means any oyster from 2 to 4 inches long and 2 to 2½ inches wide, regardless of where it's from. There are three sizes of oysters in the oyster trade. They are the "half-shells," the smallest, preferred for eating raw; "culls," of medium size, for eating raw and for stews, chowders and gumbos; and "box," the largest, generally used for frying.

I grew up with the culinary old wives' tale that fresh oysters could be safely eaten only in the "R" months. As a child this led me to believe that they were poisonous if eaten at any other time. Considering the distance they had to be shipped to central Indiana and the primitive refrigeration conditions of that era, they probably were deadly. However, the real reason for eating oysters in the "R" months only is that in the months of April through August oysters are not as tasty—they are milky, because those months comprise the breeding season. During these months use fresh-frozen oysters, since they will be of better flavor than those that are strictly fresh.

Oysters are sold by the gallon, by the quart, by the pint and in the shell. My fish market sells shucked oysters by the dozen. Since the size of oysters varies considerably, in the interest of consistency, the recipes that follow specify numbers or cups.

NOTE: *Unlike European cooks, American cooks in the past often were disdainful of mussels, considering them the trash of the sea. However, tastes change, and now that mussels are more often available in fish markets they can be substituted in most oyster recipes.*

How to Clean and Open Oysters

Oysters in the shell should be alive when purchased and the shell tightly closed.

1. Scrub the shells thoroughly in water with a stiff brush. Rinse well in cold water.
2. To open an oyster, hold it firmly, with the thick part of the shell toward the palm of the hand.
3. Push a strong, thin knife between the halves of the shells near the back and run it along until it cuts the strong muscle that holds the shell together.
4. Drop the shucked oysters into a sieve, set over a bowl and reserve the liquor that drains through to use in cooking the oysters; or freeze the liquor for making soups, stews and chowders.
5. Thoroughly examine each oyster by passing it through the fingers to remove any remaining particles of shell. Use following recipe instructions.

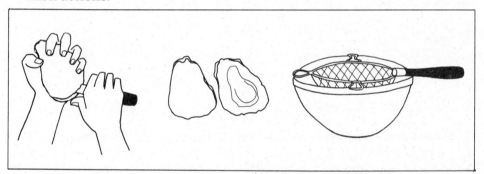

How to Purchase Shucked Oysters

Shucked oysters should be plump with no sunken areas or evidence of shrinkage, with no shell particles and with clear liquor. Shucked oysters also should be of grayish color with the fresh scent of the sea. Prepare as soon as possible after purchasing. Do not refrigerate more than 1 or 2 days.

General Cooking Instructions

Shucked oysters should be cooked gently or poached until the edges begin to curl. This should take about 3 minutes. *Caution:* Overcooking will toughen the oysters, diminishing their delicate flavor.

Long Island Baked Oysters in the Shell

Considering the large number of oyster shells found in archaeological digs along the Eastern Shore and other areas, this early method of preparing oysters must have originated with the American Indian. The Lemon, Butter and Chive Sauce is an added refinement of the white man. Serve as a quick and easy first course.

36 large oysters in the shell

6 tablespoons melted unsalted butter or 1 recipe Lemon, Butter and Chive Sauce (see page 148)

Preheated oven temperature: 450°F.
1. Scrub oysters following basic instructions.
2. Place oysters on a baking sheet and roast in preheated oven about 15 minutes, or until shells begin to open. Spoon melted butter over the oysters and serve immediately. If desired, remove the top shells when the oysters begin to open, spoon the Lemon, Butter and Chive Sauce over the oysters and bake another 2 to 3 minutes. Serve immediately.

Serves 6.

Escalloped Oysters

New England cooks created this dish, which later followed the covered wagon migration to the frontier. It is generally associated with Thanksgiving and church suppers. The ingredients in this dish vary greatly from region to region, the only stipulation being that it must contain oysters. This recipe is from the private collection of an outstanding cook in the Midwest, who annually takes many of the blue ribbons at the county and state fair.

This is a two-part recipe. First you prepare a thin white sauce and then you layer the ingredients in the casserole. Serve with roast turkey or baked ham.

Sauce

2 tablespoons unsalted butter
2 tablespoons flour
1¾ cups half-and-half
¼ cup oyster liquor

⅛ teaspoon ground mace
½ teaspoon salt, or to taste
¼ teaspoon freshly ground black pepper

Casserole Ingredients

1 cup chopped celery, white part only

1 cup finely ground day-old bread crumbs, combined with 1 tablespoon melted butter

2 cups shucked oysters, drained

½ teaspoon salt, or to taste

¼ teaspoon freshly ground black pepper

Sprinkling of cayenne pepper

1 tablespoon unsalted butter for center of casserole

Parsley for garnish

Sauce

1. In a heavy, 2-quart saucepan melt the butter and blend in the flour. Cook 3 minutes, stirring constantly.
2. Remove mixture from heat. Slowly add the half-and-half and oyster liquor, stirring constantly to blend. Add the mace, salt and pepper.
3. Return mixture to heat and cook over low heat 5 minutes, stirring constantly. Set aside.

Casserole

Preheated oven temperature: 350°F.

1. Steam the celery until barely tender. Set aside.
2. Butter a 1-quart, shallow casserole and spread half the bread crumb mixture on the bottom. Cover the bread crumb mixture with half the drained oysters and then cover with half the celery. Sprinkle with salt, pepper and a small amount of cayenne pepper. Dot with the 1 tablespoon of butter and then pour half the sauce evenly over the surface.
3. Add a second layer of oysters and celery. Season again with salt, pepper and cayenne pepper. *Caution:* No more than 2 layers of oysters should be used; otherwise the top and bottom layers will be overcooked and tough before those in the middle are heated through. Pour the remaining sauce evenly over the surface. Top with the remainder of the bread crumbs and bake in preheated oven 30 minutes, or until the crumbs are a rich golden brown. Garnish with parsley.

Serves 4 to 6.

Creole Baked Oysters

(Oysters Johnny Reb)

This is a tangy variation of escalloped oysters from Vicksburg, Mississippi, an area remembered in history for its devotion to the Southern cause.

4 cups shucked oysters, drained
2 tablespoons chopped parsley
4 tablespoons finely chopped green
  onions with tops
¼ teaspoon Tabasco sauce, or more
  to taste
2 teaspoons Worcestershire sauce
1 tablespoon lemon juice

Salt and freshly ground pepper to
  taste
4 tablespoons unsalted butter
1½ cups coarsely ground cracker
  crumbs
½ cup heavy cream
Parsley for garnish

Preheated oven temperature: 350°F.

1. Spread half the oysters in a well-buttered 1-quart, shallow casserole. Cover the oysters with half the parsley, half the green onion, half the Tabasco sauce, half the Worcestershire sauce, half the lemon juice, half the salt and pepper and half the butter; cover with half the cracker crumbs. *Caution:* No more than 2 layers of oysters should be used; otherwise the top and bottom layers will be overcooked and tough before those in the middle are heated through. Pour half the cream evenly over the surface.

2. Add a second layer of oysters, parsley, green onion, Tabasco sauce, Worcestershire sauce, lemon juice, salt and pepper; cover surface with the remaining cream. Add a little of the oyster liquor if the mixture seems dry. Top with the remaining cracker crumbs and dot surface with the remaining butter. Bake in preheated oven 30 minutes, or until the crumbs are a rich golden brown. Garnish with parsley.

Serves 6 to 8.

Deviled Oysters

This is a very popular, garlicky and spicy Cajun dish, which can be served as an appetizer or as a light entrée.

2 cups finely chopped celery, white
  part only
1 cup finely chopped onion
4 cloves garlic, chopped fine
½ cup unsalted butter
2 cups shucked oysters, drained and
  chopped
¼ cup oyster liquor
½ cup chopped green onion with
  tops
½ cup finely chopped parsley

½ teaspoon Worcestershire sauce
Salt and freshly ground black pepper
  to taste
¼ teaspoon cayenne pepper, or more
  to taste
4 hard-cooked eggs, chopped fine
1 cup finely ground day-old bread
  crumbs
4 tablespoons unsalted butter
Lemon slices for garnish
Parsley for garnish

Preheated oven temperature: 350°F.
1. In a large, heavy skillet cook the celery, onion and garlic in the ½ cup butter until tender but not brown. Add the chopped oysters, oyster liquor, green onion, parsley and Worcestershire sauce. Stir well to blend and season to taste with salt and black pepper. Add cayenne pepper and stir thoroughly. Gently stir in the hard-cooked eggs.
2. Spoon mixture into 8 well-buttered small ramekins and top with bread crumbs. Dot the 4 tablespoons of unsalted butter evenly over the bread crumbs, allowing ½ teaspoon for each ramekin. Bake in preheated oven 25 minutes, or until the crumbs are a rich golden brown and the mixture is firm. Garnish with lemon slices and parsley.

Serves 8.

Oysters Bienville

This is one of the classic first courses in Louisiana cooking. Allow six stuffed oysters per serving. Originally this dish was made with imported truffles.

Rock salt
4½ cups shucked oysters, with liquor (3 dozen large oysters in the shell)
⅛ teaspoon cayenne pepper
1 cup finely chopped fresh mushrooms
3 tablespoons unsalted butter
2 tablespoons flour
2 cups chopped green onion with tops
1 cup oyster liquor

1 tablespoon finely chopped parsley
¾ cup dry white wine
Yolks of 2 large eggs, lightly beaten
2 cups cooked shrimp, chopped fine
Salt and freshly ground black pepper to taste
2 tablespoons freshly grated Parmesan cheese, combined with 1 cup dry bread crumbs, without crusts
Unsalted butter for topping bread crumbs

Preheated oven temperature: 350°F.
1. Fill a large baking pan with rock salt and place in oven to preheat the salt. Use 2 pans, if necessary, to hold 36 oyster shells.
2. In a separate pan, sprinkle the oysters with cayenne pepper and cook gently in their own liquor a few minutes, until the edges curl. Do not overcook. Place in a sieve over a bowl to drain and reserve liquor.
3. In a heavy, 2-quart saucepan cook the mushrooms in the butter 5 minutes. Remove mushrooms and set aside. Add the flour to the pan and cook 3 minutes, stirring constantly. Add the onion and cook, stirring constantly, until tender but not brown. Add more butter if necessary. Remove from heat.

4. Measure 1 cup of oyster liquor; if necessary add chicken broth to measure 1 cup. Slowly add the liquor to the butter-flour mixture, stirring constantly to blend. Add the mushrooms, parsley and wine. Stir to blend.
5. Return to low heat and simmer 10 minutes. Remove from heat.
6. Slowly stir the sauce into the lightly beaten egg yolks, 1 tablespoon at a time, until eggs are heated. Then add the egg mixture to the sauce, stirring constantly.
7. Return to low heat and cook gently 10 minutes, stirring often. Add shrimp and season to taste with salt and black pepper. Cook a few minutes to blend flavors.
8. Place 36 oyster shells on the heated rock salt, or use small scallop shells. Place an oyster in each shell.
9. Use either a pastry bag or a spoon to cover each oyster with sauce. Top with a light sprinkling of the cheese and bread crumb mixture. Dot each lightly with butter. Bake in preheated oven until crumbs are golden brown.

Serves 6.

Fried Oysters
(Batter-Fried)

Light, puffy and wonderful, fried oysters are as popular in the Midwest and South as fried clams are in New England. They are considered informal fare for light entertaining. Traditionally, they are served with tomato catsup or chili sauce and cold beer. My preference is tartar sauce or a squeeze of fresh lemon juice to contrast with the rich flavor of the oysters.

2 cups finely ground cracker crumbs
2 teaspoons baking powder
½ teaspoon salt, or to taste
Cayenne pepper to taste
4 cups large shucked oysters, drained

Flour for coating oysters
2 large eggs, lightly beaten with 2 tablespoons water
Peanut oil for deep-frying

1. Grind the cracker crumbs in the blender or food processor until the consistency of cornmeal.
2. Measure the cracker crumbs into a shallow bowl and combine with the baking powder, salt and cayenne pepper. Stir well to blend.
3. Coat the oysters with flour. Dip each oyster in the egg mixture and then roll each oyster in the cracker-crumb mixture. Arrange the coated oysters on a wax-paper-lined tray, making sure they do not touch. Refrigerate 30 minutes. This will set the coating so that it

will be less likely to come off during frying.
4. In a large skillet (electric preferred), pour the oil to a depth of ½ inch. Heat to 375°F. or until the oil is hot but not smoking. Fry the oysters until golden—this should take about 5 minutes. Transfer with a slotted spoon onto paper towels to drain.
Serves 4 to 6.

Hangtown Fry

Many stories have circulated regarding the origin of this distinctive northern California method of preparing oysters with scrambled eggs.

According to culinary reference books, Hangtown Fry was created during the Gold Rush of 1849. A successful miner from Shirttail Bend blew into Hangtown with a bag of nuggets, plunked his newfound fortune down on the counter of Cary House and ordered the finest, most expensive meal they could serve. When he was told that oysters and eggs were the most expensive items on the menu, he ordered the cook to put them together and serve his food. This dish originally was made with small Pacific Olympia oysters.

This is a wonderful entrée to serve for a Sunday champagne brunch. Accompany with crisply fried lean bacon and whole-wheat toast.
NOTE: To double recipe, prepare twice.

12 fried oysters
2 tablespoons unsalted butter
8 large eggs

Salt and freshly ground white pepper to taste

1. Prepare oysters as in recipe for Fried Oysters (page 130). Drain on paper towels and keep warm in oven at low temperature.
2. Melt the butter in a heavy, medium-sized skillet. Add the oysters.
3. Beat the eggs with the salt and pepper and pour over the oysters. Cook until firm on the bottom. Turn with a large spatula and cook the other side 1 to 2 minutes longer. Roll onto platter. Serve immediately.
Serves 4.

Scallops

There are two varieties of this bivalve mollusk with its lovely shaped shell, the small bay scallop and the larger deep-sea scallop. The bay scallop is the tenderer and more delicately flavored of the two. Unfortunately, the bay scallop has a much shorter season than the sea scallop.

The peak period for the bay scallop is the early fall. Sea scallops can be purchased fresh the year round, but they are most flavorful from November to April. *Caution:* Unscrupulous fish markets have been accused of passing off the tender part of the baby shark as sea scallops. If in doubt, ask to see the shells. Frozen sea scallops are generally available 12 months of the year.

Many cooks consider the meat of the scallop the sweetest of all the shellfish. As a result, scallops are never embellished with elaborate sauces or overseasoned with condiments. Rather, they are prepared simply and served sautéed in butter, broiled, baked or lightly coated with bread crumbs and fried to a golden brown. I am told that die-hard Down Easters actually prefer scallops *au naturel*, straight from the shell, without any sauce or condiment.

How to Prepare Scallops

If fresh and in the shell, open the shell and remove meat. Discard all but the muscle; the remaining bits and pieces are bitter and rather tough. Wash the scallops to remove shell fragments. Drain on paper towels and pat dry. Use as soon as possible. Prepare as in recipe instructions.

If purchased by the pound. 1 pound will measure 2 cups of scallops. Wash the scallops to remove shell fragments. Drain on paper towels and pat dry. Use as soon as possible. Prepare as in recipe instructions.

If frozen, thaw first. Drain on paper towels and pat dry. Use as soon as possible. Prepare as in recipe instructions.

General Cooking Instructions

Generally speaking, 1 pound of scallops will serve four people as an entrée. *Caution:* Cook scallops until they are just done and lose their translucency. If they are overcooked, they will be dry and tasteless; 5 to 6 minutes should be ample cooking for the largest scallops. Tiny bay scallops will cook in less time.

Sautéed Bay Scallops

The secret to the success of this dish is to use as little butter as possible to sauté the scallops. Sea scallops may be used if bay scallops are not available. Slice sea scallops across the grain to a thickness of about ⅝ inch.

1 pound (2 cups) fresh bay scallops
Salt and freshly ground black pepper
  to taste
Flour for coating scallops

¼ cup unsalted butter for sautéeing,
  plus 2 tablespoons unsalted butter
  for sauce
2 teaspoons lemon juice
1 tablespoon chopped parsley

1. Wash scallops, drain on paper towels and pat dry.
2. Sprinkle scallops with salt and pepper; coat lightly with flour. Set aside.
3. In a large, heavy skillet melt 2 tablespoons of the ¼ cup butter until hot but not smoking. Add the scallops and sauté quickly over medium-high heat until tender and lightly browned. Shake the skillet to turn to scallops. Add more butter if necessary. Remove scallops to a heated platter.
4. In a small, heavy skillet melt the 2 tablespoons butter for sauce and brown lightly. Stir in the lemon juice and chopped parsley and pour over the scallops. Serve immediately.

Serves 4.

Broiled Scallops

Broiling scallops is a very simple affair; it is a cooking method that is becoming increasingly popular as Americans try to slim down. Scallops have a low fat content, plus they contain some calcium, traces of riboflavin, niacin and a larger amount of phosphorus. Allow ⅓ pound of scallops per serving.

2 pounds (4 cups) fresh or frozen
  sea scallops
About ¼ cup melted unsalted butter

Salt and freshly ground black pepper
  (optional)
6 thick lemon wedges

Preheated broiler
1. If using fresh scallops, wash them first. Drain on paper towels and pat dry.
2. Line broiler pan with well-oiled foil. Arrange scallops in pan. Brush with melted butter. Sprinkle with optional salt and pepper.
3. Place broiler pan 3 to 4 inches from source of heat. Broil scallops 4 to 6 minutes, depending on the size. If the scallops are not too large, they will not need to be turned. Broil until lightly browned. Serve immediately with a few squeezes of lemon juice.

Serves 6.

New England Baked Scallops

Traditionally, this dish is served with baked potatoes, scalloped tomatoes and a relish tray of celery, carrot sticks, olives and pickles.

1 pound (2 cups) sea scallops   About 1½ cups half-and-half
Salt and freshly ground black pepper
   to taste

Preheated oven temperature: 400°F.
1. Wash the scallops, drain on paper towels and pat dry. If the scallops
   are large, slice across the grain to a thickness of about ⅝ inch.
2. Sprinkle the scallops with salt and pepper and place in a well-buttered shallow, 1-quart casserole. Pour half-and-half into the baking
   dish to a depth of ½ inch.
3. Bake in a preheated oven 20 minutes. Serve immediately.
Serves 2-3.

Fried Scallops

Frozen scallops already breaded for frying can be purchased in most
markets. However, the coating is so heavy and soggy that one is hard
put to find the scallop underneath the miserable-tasting mass.

    The breading technique in this recipe guarantees the cook a juicy
and tender scallop with a light and crispy coating. Fried to an appetizing
golden brown, the succulent morsel has no equal. Serve with homemade
tartar sauce. Allow ⅓ pound of scallops per serving.

2 pounds (4 cups) fresh or frozen   1 cup flour
   sea scallops   Peanut oil for frying
1 large egg, lightly beaten   Salt and freshly ground pepper (op-
1 cup milk   tional)
1 cup finely ground dry bread crumbs,
   without crusts

1. If using fresh scallops, wash them first. Drain on paper towels and
   pat dry.
2. Combine the egg and milk in a small bowl.
3. Combine the bread crumbs and flour in another bowl. First dip the
   dry scallop in the egg and milk mixture. Then immediately coat the
   scallop well with the bread crumb and flour mixture. Place on wax-
   paper-lined tray. Continue until all scallops have been dipped and
   coated, making sure that the scallops do not touch each other on the
   tray.

4. Place the coated scallops in the refrigerator at least 30 minutes. This will bind the coating to the scallop so the bread crumbs will not fall off during the frying process. Do not remove until the oil is hot for frying.
5. Pour the oil into a heavy skillet (preferably electric) to a depth of about 1½ inches. Heat to 375°F.
6. Gently drop the scallops into the hot oil and fry, turning them once, until they are golden brown. This will take no more than 2 to 3 minutes on each side. Transfer with a slotted spoon onto paper towels to drain. Sprinkle with the optional salt and pepper. Serve immediately.

Serves 6.

Shrimp

Shrimp is the runaway favorite shellfish in America. Many varieties abound in American coastal waters, from the tiny Maine, Pacific and river shrimps to the large Gulf shrimps.

Gulf shrimp are particularly prized for their size and flavor, and they provide the largest commercial supply. In this country the largest Gulf shrimp are called jumbos, and are also sold as prawns.

Shrimp are available the year round, fresh, fresh-frozen and canned.

I feel strongly that preservative-laden canned shrimp should not be used. In my opinion, they detract from the honest, fresh flavor of any shrimp dish.

Shrimp are sold by the pound. Generally speaking, 1 pound of shrimp in the shell, without the heads, will yield 2 cups of peeled, deveined shrimp when cooked. Allow 1 cup per person for salads and ½ cup per person if the shrimp is to be combined with other ingredients.

First-quality fresh shrimp are firm to the touch and have a fresh, slightly sweet scent of the sea.

Shrimp are sold in the following sizes:
  Prawns (jumbo)—6 to 8 per pound
  Large—12 to 16 per pound
  Medium—18 to 25 per pound
  Small—25 or more per pound

How to Peel Fresh Shrimp

For best flavor, the modern theory leans toward peeling the shrimp before cooking. However, in many traditional American dishes, shrimp are cooked in the shell. Follow recipe instructions.

1. Wash shrimp under water to remove as much grit as possible.
2. Hold the tail end of the shrimp firmly in the left hand, slip the thumb of the right hand under the shell between the feelers and push the shell back to the tail. Then carefully lift the shell from around the tail. Certain recipes will call for leaving the tail on the shrimp. Reserve shells if a recipe calls for them to be boiled separately, which will add more flavor if the recipe calls for liquid.
3. To devein, use a sharp knife or serrated kitchen shears and cut about ⅛ inch deep along the entire outside curve of the shrimp. Then with the fingers lift out the vein—often there will not be one—and wash under running water.

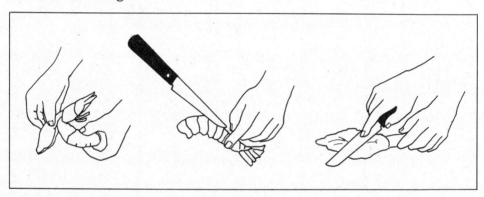

General Cooking Instructions

Boiling. Peel and devein 5 pounds of fresh shrimp in the shell. Measure enough water into a large kettle so that it will cover shrimp when they are added. Add salt to taste, ½ sliced lemon, 2 ribs of celery with leaves, 1 medium-sized sliced onion, 1 bay leaf and cayenne pepper to taste. Cover and boil 15 minutes. Drop shrimp into the kettle. Cover, reduce heat and simmer 2 to 5 minutes, or until the shrimp are pink. The timing will depend upon the size of the shrimp. If a large amount of shrimp is being cooked in this manner, stir at least once to keep the ones on the bottom of the kettle from being overcooked. Drain and refrigerate until needed.

Yield: Approximately 10 cups shrimp.

Specific Cooking Instructions

"If I were to name the one ingredient that is often elaborately over-cooked in American kitchens, it would certainly be shrimp," writes one highly respected French chef, who recommends only the briefest sim-mering—a minute or two. In most cases the writer is correct in saying that Americans overcook shrimp. However, a minute or two is cooking mighty "short" in the opinion of the fine traditional cooks of my ac-quaintance. Shrimp dishes that contain tomatoes, which act as a ten-derizer, should be simmered very slowly about 20 to 30 minutes, depending upon the size of the shrimp, to impart the proper flavor to the finished dish.

The recipes in this book were tested using both the short and the long of the debate. For certain dishes such as gumbos and stews, the longer period won hands down.

Steamed Gulf Shrimp

This is the preferred method of cooking fresh shrimp along the Gulf Coast. Home cooks believe that shrimp steamed in their own juices are much more tender and flavorful than those boiled in a large amount of water.

4 pounds any size shrimp in the shell   2 lemons, quartered
2 ribs celery with leaves   Salt and cayenne pepper
2 medium-sized onions, quartered

1. Wash the shrimp well under cold, running water to remove as much grit as possible.
2. Place the celery, onions and lemons in a large, heavy kettle with a tight-fitting cover. Add the shrimp and spread evenly around the kettle. Sprinkle generously with salt and cayenne pepper.
3. Cover the kettle and cook over medium heat. With a large wooden spoon stir gently from the bottom so that the shrimp will cook evenly. Cooking time will depend upon the size of the shrimp. Taste for tenderness when the shrimp start to turn bright pink. This may take as little as 2 minutes after the shrimp begin to cook. Remove from heat immediately and drain. There will be a surprising amount of broth in the kettle when the steaming is finished. This probably will be too hot and spicy for any other use and should be discarded. After the shrimp have cooled, peel, devein and refrigerate until needed.

Yield: Approximately 8 cups shrimp.

South Carolina Shrimp Pilau

This is the Charleston, South Carolina, version of Turkish pilaf. Charleston's being a port city may account for this regional adaptation of an international dish.

This dish can be extended with okra or tomatoes, and more rice may be added to accommodate unexpected guests.

4 to 5 slices bacon	3 cups cooked long-grain white rice
1 cup chopped onion	Salt to taste
1 cup chopped green pepper	Freshly ground black pepper to taste
4 cups cooked shrimp	A sprinkling of cayenne pepper

1. In a large, heavy skillet—cast iron is ideal—fry the bacon until crisp. Drain on paper towels and crumble. Set aside.
2. Add the onion and green pepper to the bacon drippings and cook about 10 minutes, stirring constantly.
3. In a heavy, 2-quart saucepan combine the onion and green pepper mixture, the crumbled bacon and the shrimp with the cooked rice. Add salt, black pepper and cayenne pepper to taste. Cover and cook over low heat until heated through.

NOTE: This mixture should be rather dry; if it seems too dry, add a little chicken broth or tomato juice.

Serves 4 to 6. Recipe may be doubled or tripled.

Broiled Stuffed Shrimp Baltimore

This is one of the traditional American dishes that has been updated to appeal to the changing preference of Americans for broiled rather than deep-fried foods. In the original recipe the shrimp were stuffed and the halves pressed together; then the filled shrimp were coated with seasoned flour, dipped in beaten egg, rolled in finely ground cracker crumbs and finally deep-fried to a golden brown. A tartar sauce was served with the shrimp. A much lighter method of preparing the dish is to butterfly the shrimp, open them up and spread the stuffing on top; then the shrimp are sprinkled with bread crumbs, a little butter is dotted on top and shrimp are broiled. No sauce is needed because the stuffing will still be moist and flavorful.

24 large shrimp
5 tablespoons unsalted butter
½ cup finely chopped onion
¼ cup finely chopped green pepper
1 tablespoon finely chopped celery
½ teaspoon finely chopped garlic
Salt and freshly ground black pepper
  to taste

A few drops of Tabasco sauce (optional)
½ cup fresh or frozen crabmeat, shredded
1 cup fresh bread crumbs
1 large egg, lightly beaten
¼ cup finely chopped parsley
3 tablespoons unsalted butter for topping

Preheat broiler.

1. If using shrimp in the shell, wash under cold, running water to remove as much grit as possible. Peel and devein but do not remove the tails. Wash again under cold, running water. To butterfly the shrimp, split them down the back almost but not all the way through, using a very sharp knife. Open the shrimp and place on a flat surface on paper towels to drain, cut side down.

2. In a medium-sized, heavy skillet melt 2 tablespoons of the butter and add the onion, green pepper, celery and garlic; season to taste with salt and pepper and the optional Tabasco sauce. Cook over low heat, stirring constantly, until the vegetables are tender but not brown.

3. Remove mixture from heat and add the crabmeat. Gently stir in ¾ cup of the bread crumbs, the egg and parsley. *Caution:* Stir only until mixture is blended; overstirring will cause the mixture to be soggy.

4. Use a broilerproof baking dish large enough to hold the shrimp in one layer and butter the bottom well. Place the shrimp cut side up in the baking dish and spoon equal portions of the crabmeat mixture on top of each shrimp as "stuffing."

5. Sprinkle each shrimp with about ½ teaspoon of remaining bread crumbs and dot with about ½ teaspoon butter for each shrimp. At this point the shrimp may be refrigerated several hours.

6. Place the shrimp under the preheated broiler about 5 inches from the source of heat. Broil about 5 minutes, or until the "stuffing" is golden brown. Serve immediately.

Serves 4.

Broiled Barbecued Shrimp

This is a favorite Southern way of preparing shrimp. The shrimp are marinated in a highly flavored, spicy sauce, sometimes called Hell-Bent Sauce, and broiled or grilled over charcoal. The cooked shrimp are served in soup bowls with French bread to dip in the extra sauce. Allow 1 pound of shrimp in the shell per serving, and have plenty of paper napkins handy—this is strictly informal entertaining.

8 pounds large shrimp in the shell
1 cup unsalted butter
1 cup light olive oil or vegetable oil
1 cup chili sauce
3 tablespoons Worcestershire sauce
2 lemons, sliced thin
4 cloves garlic, chopped fine
3 tablespoons lemon juice

1 tablespoon finely chopped parsley
2 teaspoons paprika
2 teaspoons ground marjoram
1 teaspoon crushed red pepper, or to taste
1 teaspoon Tabasco sauce, or to taste
Salt to taste

1. Wash the shrimp under cold, running water to remove as much grit as possible. Place on paper towels to drain.
2. In a heavy, 2-quart saucepan combine remaining ingredients, except salt and cook over low heat 20 minutes, stirring often. Add salt to taste.
3. Arrange the shrimp in a large, shallow, broilerproof pan. (The broiler drip pan may be used.) Pour the hot marinade over the shrimp and turn to coat. Refrigerate 2 hours. Turn the shrimp in the marinade every 30 minutes. Either broil the shrimp or charcoal grill them over an open fire.

Serves 8.

Broiler Method

　　Preheat broiler. Place the shrimp in the marinade under the broiler about 5 inches from the source of heat. Broil 9 to 10 minutes, depending upon the size of the shrimp. Test for tenderness. If using jumbo shrimp, turn them halfway through cooking time. Serve with the sauce.

Charcoal-Grilled Method

1. Drain shrimp and arrange on skewers. Pour the marinade into a small saucepan and cook separately. Use as a dipping sauce.
2. Place the skewered shrimp over glowing coals. Grill 8 to 9 minutes, depending upon the size of the shrimp. Test for tenderness. Turn shrimp halfway through cooking period. Serve with dipping sauce.

Shrimp Creole

If properly prepared, this dish bears no resemblance to the tomato-based vegetable mixture with too few shrimp that is served over a bed of poorly cooked rice and is passed off in many restaurants as "Shrimp Creole."

　　This recipe is from the private collection of a family of exceptional New Orleans Black cooks, who prepare and serve it as a special-occasion dish to celebrate birthdays and anniversaries.

NOTE: Shrimp Creole may be served in a molded rice ring and garnished with chopped parsley. (See page 267 for rice ring.)

1 cup finely chopped onion
1 tablespoon vegetable oil, combined with 1 tablespoon unsalted butter
1 clove garlic, chopped fine
2 tablespoons finely chopped green pepper
1 tablespoon flour
1 cup tomato sauce, canned or homemade
1 cup water

⅛ teaspoon ground thyme
2 tablespoons finely chopped parsley
2 cups fresh shrimp, peeled and deveined
1 teaspoon salt, or to taste
½ teaspoon freshly ground black pepper
A sprinkling of cayenne pepper
3 cups cooked long-grain white rice
Chopped parsley for garnish

1. In a large, heavy, 2-quart saucepan—a large iron skillet is ideal—cook the onion in the oil and butter 6 to 8 minutes, stirring constantly, until tender but not brown. Add garlic and green pepper and cook 2 minutes longer. Add flour and stir well to blend. Add tomato sauce and simmer uncovered 5 minutes.
2. Add water, thyme, parsley, shrimp, salt, black pepper and cayenne pepper. Cover and simmer slowly 25 to 30 minutes.

NOTE: If using large Gulf shrimp, they will not be overcooked and tough. If using smaller shrimp, adjust the cooking time by adding shrimp after the sauce is partially cooked. At this point the sauce may be cooled and refrigerated several hours or overnight. Reheat slowly to serving temperature and serve over rice. Allow about ¾ cup cooked rice per serving.
Serves 4. Recipe may be doubled.

Shrimp Fricassee

A fricassee usually is an extremely thrifty dish composed of less-than-tender fowl simmered for a long period in a seasoned broth and served as a stew. In this case the shrimp are simmered in a well-seasoned sauce for a much shorter period, garnished with chopped parsley and served on a platter surrounded by a ring of fluffy white rice. This is a fine Southern dish!

6 tablespoons unsalted butter
6 tablespoons flour
2 tablespoons finely chopped onion
2 tablespoons finely chopped green pepper
1 tablespoon finely chopped celery
½ teaspoon finely chopped garlic
1 cup tomatoes, peeled, seeded and chopped
4 cups fresh large shrimp, peeled and deveined

½ cup dry white wine
1½ cups clam juice
2 small bay leaves
¼ teaspoon ground thyme
2 sprigs parsley
Salt and freshly ground black pepper to taste
3 to 4 cups boiled or steamed long-grain white rice
½ cup chopped parsley for garnish

1. In a heavy, 3-quart saucepan melt the butter, blend in the flour and cook 3 minutes, stirring constantly. Add the onion, green pepper, celery and garlic. Cook over very low heat until the vegetables are tender, stirring often to keep from overbrowning.
2. Add tomatoes and cook 5 minutes. Add shrimp, wine, clam juice, bay leaves, thyme, parsley and season to taste with salt and pepper. Simmer uncovered 20 minutes. Remove bay leaves and parsley.
3. Arrange the rice in a ring on a large serving platter deep enough to hold the shrimp and sauce. Spoon the sauced shrimp in the middle and garnish with chopped parsley.

Serves 6.

About Shrimp de Jonghe

Both Louisiana and Chicago claim this American regional dish. It has always been my understanding that Shrimp de Jonghe was the creation of a chef at a famous Chicago restaurant. Recently I participated in a cooking course in New York, under the direction of a fellow member of the International Association of Cooking Schools. One of the dishes prepared in class was Shrimp de Jonghe from a recipe obtained by the instructor's parents on a visit to New Orleans many years ago.

Shrimp de Jonghe
(New Orleans Style)

4 cups fresh large shrimp, peeled and veined

4 tablespoons unsalted butter

1 clove garlic, minced

¾ cup cold unsalted butter (keep refrigerated)

3 cloves garlic, chopped fine

1 teaspoon salt or to taste

1 cup dry white wine

1½ cups toasted bread crumbs

½ cup chopped parsley

¼ cup freshly grated Parmesan cheese

4 tablespoons unsalted butter, melted

Preheated oven temperature: 350°F.
1. In a medium-size heavy skillet, melt the 4 tablespoons of butter. Add the 1 clove of minced garlic and the shrimp. Cook lightly for a minute or two, depending on the size of the shrimp, until shrimp are barely tender. Remove from skillet and spread evenly on the bottom of a 6-cup gratin dish.
2. With an electric mixer, beat the cold butter until light and fluffy. While the mixer is still running slowly add the 3 cloves of finely

chopped garlic, salt, wine, bread crumbs and parsley. Spread this mixture evenly over the shrimp. Sprinkle with the grated cheese and drizzle the surface with the 4 tablespoons of melted butter.

3. Bake 30 minutes in preheated oven.

4. Turn oven to broil and brown the topping for 2 minutes.

Serves 4, or, if used as a first course, serves 8.

Variation: Oysters de Jonghe

Substitute 2 cups well-drained oysters for the shrimp. Sprinkle oysters with about ⅛ teaspoon cayenne pepper or to taste.

Shellfish Casserole

This versatile recipe was first published in the Ellsworth *Maine American*, and was written by a food editor who thoroughly understands the home cooking of the area. "A recipe that everyone can use right now has a simple title—Fish Casserole. Food styles come and go—but this is a dish that will not go out of fashion, no matter what you call it. This is a Maine recipe easily adjusted to your own taste and budget," writes the knowledgeable editor.

In my kitchen a recipe is only as good as it tests out with ingredients normally available to the cook in local markets. Seafood on the coast of Maine is not only plentiful but also is only a few hours away from the home kitchen. Regional cooks use no seasonings or spices, allowing the fresh flavor of the seafood to predominate. This recipe is an adaptation of the original, using frozen crabmeat and a little salt, pepper and paprika for seasoning. My testers and I found this to be one of the best ways to use packaged frozen crabmeat—the original flavor seems to return. Serve with hot buttered biscuits or French bread, white rice, peas and salad as an accompaniment and top off the meal with a light fruit dessert.

The fish casserole is a two-part recipe. First you prepare a thick white sauce and then you combine the ingredients in the casserole.

Sauce

3 tablespoons unsalted butter
3 tablespoons flour
1 cup cup milk

½ teaspoon salt, or to taste
⅛ teaspoon freshly ground white pepper, or to taste

Casserole Ingredients

1 6-ounce package frozen crab-meat, thawed and drained; or 1 cup fresh crabmeat

½ pound fresh or frozen bay or sea scallops

½ pound firm whitefish—use cod, haddock, halibut, flounder or scrod—cut into 1-inch cubes

1 cup fresh shrimp, peeled and de-veined; or use 1 cup cooked lob-ster, cut into bite-size pieces

½ cup unsalted butter

½ cup fresh bread crumbs, without crusts, combined with 1 table-spoon melted unsalted butter

⅛ teaspoon paprika

Sauce

1. In a heavy, 1-quart saucepan melt the butter and blend in the flour. Cook 3 minutes, stirring constantly.
2. Remove mixture from heat. Slowly add the milk, stirring constantly to blend. Add the salt and pepper.
3. Return mixture to heat and cook over low heat 5 minutes, stirring constantly. Set aside.

Casserole Ingredients
Preheated oven temperature: 375°F.
1. Pick over the crabmeat to remove cartilage and shell.
2. In a heavy, 10-to-12-inch skillet, sauté the crabmeat, scallops, fish and shrimp in the butter over medium-high heat a few minutes, or until the shrimp turn pink. Remove cooked seafood with a slotted spoon.
3. Combine the white sauce with the seafood and spoon into a well-buttered 1½-quart shallow casserole. Top with buttered crumbs and a sprinkling of paprika. Bake in preheated oven 20 minutes, until crumbs are golden brown and the mixture is bubbles.
Serves 4 to 6.

Deep-Fried Seafood Platter

The types of fish and shellfish used to prepare a platter can be varied to accomodate the supply at hand. Often these platters are composed of all fish or of all shellfish. Allow about ½ pound of any combination per serving. Serve with traditional tartar sauce or any desired cold seafood sauce, and coleslaw.

Suggested Fish and Shellfish:

Shrimp, peeled and deveined, butterflied if large
Clams, scallops or oysters, without shells but whole
Rock lobster tails, cut into slices across the grain
Fillet of fish, cut with the grain into finger-size strips
1 recipe All-Purpose Dipping Batter, below
Peanut oil for deep-frying

1. Prepare fish and shellfish. Drain and pat dry with paper towels. *Caution:* Do not eliminate this step. Otherwise the batter will not adhere during the frying process. Set aside.
2. Pour the peanut oil into a deep-fryer or an electric skillet to about half its capacity. Heat to 375°F.
3. Dip each piece individually into the batter and fry until golden. This will take a very few minutes. Transfer with a slotted spoon onto paper towels to drain. Serve immediately.

All-Purpose Dipping Batter
(Basic Recipe)

Deep-fried, batter-coated foods and the current public penchant for foods prepared without fat or sodium are very much at odds. However, deep-fried, batter-coated foods still remain very popular specialties in both home and restaurant cooking.

Restaurant cooks and frozen-food companies, who dip foods in heavy, doughy batter to increase the size of portions, have unquestionably given this method of cooking a low mark. But if the following tempura-like batter recipe is used, this will not be the result. The batter can be used to coat not only fish and seafood but onion rings and thin slices of fresh vegetables as well.

NOTE: Ice water, rather than baking powder or beer, is the secret ingredient that keeps the fried batter thin, light as air and crispy.

1 large egg
1 cup ice water
½ teaspoon sugar
½ teaspoon salt

1 cup unsifted unbleached flour
A few drops of Tabasco sauce (optional)
2 tablespoons vegetable oil

Place all ingredients in a blender or food processor. Blend until smooth. Use immediately or refrigerate until ready to use.

Yield: About 2 cups.

Fish Sauces

Sauces, both hot and cold, are an important part of regional fish dishes in this country. Generally speaking, the lighter sauces match the milder flavored fish and shellfish and more pungent sauces complement fish of deeper flavor.

Almond Sauce

This is a New England home-style sauce traditionally served with halibut, a firm whitefish of delicate flavor. This sauce should not be overly thickened.

1¼ cups almonds, slivered or chopped
1½ tablespoons unsalted butter
1½ tablespoons flour
2 cups light cream or 2 cups half-and-half

2 teaspoons dry sherry
⅛ teaspoon freshly ground nutmeg
1 teaspoon salt, or to taste
½ teaspoon freshly ground white pepper, or to taste

1. In a heavy, 2-quart saucepan lightly brown the almonds in the butter. Blend in the flour and cook 3 minutes, stirring constantly.
2. Remove mixture from heat. Slowly add the cream and sherry, stirring constantly to blend. Add nutmeg and season to taste with salt and pepper.
3. Return mixture to heat and cook gently 5 minutes, stirring constantly, until slightly thickened.

Yield: About 2½ cups.

Anchovy Sauce

This is a sauce popular in Maryland cooking, and is served with both fish and shellfish.

¼ cup unsalted butter
4 tablespoons flour
2 cups milk
½ cup heavy cream
½ cup dry white wine
2 tablespoons dry sherry

1 tablespoon anchovy paste, or to taste
½ teaspoon Worcestershire sauce
1 teaspoon salt, or to taste
¼ teaspoon freshly ground black pepper, or to taste
2 tablespoons chopped parsley

1. In a heavy, 2-quart saucepan melt the butter, blend in flour and cook 3 minutes, stirring constantly.
2. Remove mixture from heat. Combine the milk and cream. Slowly add to the flour mixture, stirring constantly to blend. Add wine, sherry, anchovy paste, Worcestershire sauce, salt, pepper and parsley. Stir to blend.
3. Return mixture to heat and simmer 10 to 15 minutes, stirring constantly. This should not be an overly thick sauce; rather it should be just thick enough to coat the food lightly.

Yield: About 2½ cups.

Caper Sauce

This is an excellent sauce to serve with mild-flavored fish such as cod, scrod, tilefish, flounder and halibut.

⅓ cup unsalted butter
2 tablespoons flour
2 cups boiling water
1 tablespoon lemon juice

3 tablespoons capers
Yolks of 2 eggs, lightly beaten
Salt and freshly ground black pepper
  to taste

1. In a heavy, 2-quart saucepan melt the butter, blend in flour and cook 3 minutes, stirring constantly.
2. Remove mixture from heat. Slowly add the boiling water, stirring constantly to blend. Add lemon juice and capers. Stir to blend.
3. Return mixture to heat and cook gently at least 5 minutes, stirring constantly, until the mixture has thickened. Remove from heat and cool slightly.
4. Add a few tablespoons of the heated sauce to the egg yolks, 1 tablespoon at a time, stirring constantly to blend. Then slowly add the egg mixture to the sauce, stirring constantly to keep the egg mixture from separating. Season to taste with salt and pepper.
5. Return mixture to low heat and cook until thickened, stirring constantly. *Caution:* Do not boil the mixture after the eggs have been added. Serve hot.

Yield: About 2½ cups.

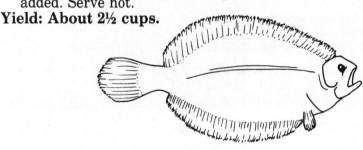

Egg Sauce

In New England cooking, salmon, cod and halibut traditionally are served with this egg sauce.

1 cup milk	3 tablespoons unsalted butter
1 cup light cream; or 2 cups half-and-half in place of milk and cream	3 tablespoons flour
	1 teaspoon salt, or to taste
2 small onions, sliced thin	Freshly ground white pepper to taste
1 small bay leaf	2 hard-cooked eggs, coarsely chopped
1 whole clove	

1. In a 1-quart saucepan combine the milk, cream, onions, bay leaf and clove. Heat slowly until skim forms on top but do not boil. Set aside.
2. In a heavy, 2-quart saucepan melt the butter, blend in flour and cook 3 minutes, stirring constantly.
3. Remove mixture from heat. Strain the milk mixture and slowly add to the butter mixture, stirring constantly to blend. Add salt and pepper to taste.
4. Return mixture to heat and cook gently 5 minutes, stirring constantly. This sauce should be quite thick; however, if it seems overly so, add a little more cream. Add eggs and heat through but do not boil.
5. Remove from heat and serve immediately from a heated sauceboat.
Yield: About 2½ cups.

Lemon, Chive and Butter Sauce

This is a classic heated sauce to serve with baked and broiled fish. In New England the sauce is made without chives; in other regions they are included.

½ cup unsalted butter	3 tablespoons chopped chives (optional)
Grated rind and juice of 1 lemon	

1. Melt the butter over low heat. Add the lemon rind, juice and optional chives. Heat slowly to serving temperature to blend flavors. Serve immediately.
Yield: A little over ½ cup.

Lobster Sauce

This is an inexpensive way to add the delicate flavor of lobster to a fish dish. The firm, white-fleshed fish of New England waters go nicely with this sauce. For a more colorful presentation, garnish the dish with parsley and lemon slices.

2 tablespoons unsalted butter
2 tablespoons flour
2 cups half-and-half
Salt and cayenne pepper to taste

A few gratings of nutmeg
1 cup cubed cooked lobster
¼ cup dry sherry (optional)

1. In a heavy, 2-quart saucepan melt the butter, blend in flour and cook 3 minutes, stirring constantly.
2. Remove mixture from heat. Slowly add the half-and-half, stirring constantly to blend. Add salt, cayenne pepper and nutmeg.
3. Return mixture to heat and cook gently at least 5 minutes, stirring constantly, until the mixture has thickened. Stir in the lobster. To develop flavor, reduce heat to lowest setting or place over hot water 20 minutes.
4. Reheat to serving temperature and stir in optional sherry.
Yield: About 3 cups.

Variations: Shrimp Sauce

Substitute 1 cup cooked shrimp for the lobster.

Oyster Sauce

Omit lobster, nutmeg and sherry. Substitute small oysters and their liquor. Heat mixture to the boiling point and cook ½ minute. Add oysters and liquor. Season to taste with a generous pinch of cayenne pepper.

New England Tomato Sauce

This is a lightly thickened sauce with a nice tomato color and flavor. Serve with baked fish made with the milder-flavored New England fishes such as halibut and cod.

2 cups canned solid-pack tomatoes with juice; or use peeled and seeded fresh tomatoes
2 tablespoons chopped onion
1 teaspoon salt, or to taste

½ teaspoon sugar (do not omit)
¼ teaspoon freshly ground black pepper, or to taste
3 tablespoons unsalted butter
1½ tablespoons flour

1. In a heavy, 2-quart saucepan combine the tomatoes, onion, salt, sugar and pepper. Cover and simmer 15 minutes. Puree in a blender or food processor and set aside to cool.
2. In a heavy, 2-quart saucepan melt the butter and blend in the flour. Cook 3 minutes, stirring constantly.

3. Remove mixture from heat. Strain the tomato mixture and slowly add to the butter mixture, stirring constantly to blend.
4. Return mixture to heat and cook gently 5 to 7 minutes, stirring constantly, or until slightly thickened. Serve hot.
Yield: 1½ cups.

Mustard Sauce

The zesty flavor of this heated sauce contrasts nicely with salmon, mackerel, trout, tuna, pike, bluefish, bass, whitefish and all shellfish. The consistency of the sauce will be rather thick, much like that of hollandaise sauce.

3 tablespoons unsalted butter
2 tablespoons flour
1 to 1¼ cups clam juice

2 teaspoons Dijon-style mustard
Freshly ground black pepper to taste

1. Melt the butter in a 1-quart, heavy saucepan. Add the flour and cook 3 minutes, stirring constantly.
2. Remove mixture from heat. Stir in 1 cup of the clam juice, stirring constantly to blend. Add mustard and pepper and stir again.
3. Return mixture to heat and cook gently at least 5 minutes, stirring constantly. If the mixture seems too thick, add the remainder of the clam juice. Serve hot.
Yield: About 1¼ cups.

Aurora Sauce

An Eastern Shore interpretation of the classic *sauce Aurore* of French cooking. Serve chilled with cold fish or seafood.

1½ cups mayonnaise, preferably homemade
⅓ cup chili sauce

2 teaspoons Worcestershire sauce
1 teaspoon lemon juice
½ cup heavy cream, whipped

1. Combine the mayonnaise, chili sauce, Worcestershire sauce and lemon juice in medium-sized bowl. Stir well to blend.
2. Gently fold in whipped cream and refrigerate several hours. Serve well-chilled.
Yield: About 2½ cups.

Cold Butter Dressing

These small butter balls are traditionally served with pan-fried fish.

½ cup unsalted butter
¼ teaspoon salt
Freshly ground black pepper to taste

2 teaspoons lemon juice
1 teaspoon minced parsley or watercress

1. Cream the butter until fluffy; gradually add the salt, pepper, lemon juice and parsley or watercress.
2. Form balls about ¾ inch in diameter and place on wax paper. Refrigerate until firm. Place one ball atop each serving of fish.

Yield: 6 to 8 balls.

Cold Cucumber Sauce

This sauce is probably of New England origin. It is traditionally served with cold poached salmon.

¼ cup mayonnaise, preferably homemade
¼ cup sour cream
1 cup peeled, seeded and thinly sliced or grated cucumbers, drained

1 tablespoon finely chopped onion
1 tablespoon finely chopped parsley
½ teaspoon salt, or to taste
¼ teaspoon paprika

Combine all the ingredients in small mixing bowl. Cover tightly and refrigerate several hours to blend flavors. Serve cold.

Yield: 1½ cups.

Remoulade Sauce

This is a Southern seafood sauce that is served with cold shrimp, crabmeat, fried fish and shellfish. Homemade mayonnaise should be used to prepare this sauce. Refrigerate at least 24 hours to blend flavors.

1 cup mayonnaise, preferably homemade
1 tablespoon minced onion
1 clove garlic, minced
1 teaspoon finely chopped anchovies

½ teaspoon dry mustard
2 tablespoons tarragon wine vinegar
1 tablespoon dry sherry
1 tablespoon capers
½ cup finely chopped parsley

Blend all ingredients in a medium-sized bowl or use a mixer. Do not use the blender or food processor unless care is taken not to overprocess the ingredients. Serve well-chilled.

Yield: About 1½ cups.

Sauce Suzee

This is a New Orleans remoulade sauce, often referred to as Arnaud's sauce in regional cookbooks. Arnaud's, a famous restaurant in the French Quarter, serves a similar sauce, which can be purchased in many specialty-food stores throughout the country.

This recipe was first brought to my attention many years ago by a friend, born and bred to Louisiana cooking, who found it in a fish and game magazine. The recipe has withstood the test of time and remains one of my favorite spicy seafood sauces. *Caution:* This sauce has a rather unpleasant taste until refrigerated at least 2 to 3 days to blend the pungent flavors. However, it can be made in quantity and it keeps indefinitely. If Creole mustard is not available, substitute a Dijon-style French mustard.

½ cup light olive oil
½ cup vegetable oil
½ cup diced fresh horseradish
1 teaspoon white vinegar
¼ cup lemon juice
2 tablespoons Worcestershire sauce
¼ cup Creole mustard; or use Dijon-style mustard
¼ cup chopped green onion with tops
¼ cup chopped celery

2 teaspoons chopped parsley
¼ cup paprika
1 teaspoon whole cloves
1 teaspoon crushed bay leaves
1 clove garlic
½ teaspoon ground thyme
1½ teaspoons salt
⅛ teaspoon each freshly ground black pepper and cayenne pepper, or to taste

Place the oils, horseradish, vinegar, lemon juice, Worcestershire sauce and mustard in blender or food processor. Process until a thick purée. Add the green onion, celery, parsley, paprika, cloves, bay leaves, garlic, thyme, salt and peppers. Continue to process until smooth. Refrigerate 2 to 3 days.
Yield: About 3 cups.

Seafood Cocktail Sauce

This all-purpose, hot and spicy tomato-horseradish sauce came to favor in American restaurant cooking because, I strongly suspect, it is quick, easy and inexpensive to prepare. It is not a favorite of mine, and in my opinion it smothers the delicate flavor of seafood. For those who remain dedicated to the pungent flavor, I warn you that the following recipe is especially zesty.

1 cup tomato catsup
2 tablespoons cider vinegar
¼ cup diced fresh horseradish
2 tablespoons finely chopped onion
½ teaspoon very hot prepared mustard

1 cup chili sauce
¼ teaspoon Tabasco sauce
2 tablespoons finely chopped celery
1 tablespoon Worcestershire sauce

Combine all the ingredients in a blender or food processor. Process until smooth. Refrigerate several hours or overnight to blend flavors.
Yield: About 2½ cups.

Tartar Sauce

This is an all-purpose cold sauce to serve with fried fish cakes or fillets and with chilled fish and seafood salads.

1 cup mayonnaise, preferably
   homemade
2 tablespoons lemon juice
1 tablespoon finely chopped sweet
   pickle
1 tablespoon chopped fresh chives

1 tablespoon drained capers,
   chopped, or 1 tablespoon chopped
   green olives
½ teaspoon dry mustard or 1½ teaspoons Dijon-style mustard

Combine all the ingredients in a medium-sized bowl. Stir well to blend. Cover tightly and refrigerate several hours. Serve cold.
Yield: About 1¼ cups.

POULTRY

Poultry is a word used to identify all domesticated birds bred and raised for human consumption. The commonest are chickens, turkeys, guinea fowls, ducks and geese.

Most poultry sold in this country already has been fully drawn, pin-feathered and cleaned inside and out.

Poultry can be bought whole, with the neck and giblets wrapped and tucked inside the body. Chicken and turkey parts, such as breasts, thighs, legs, wings and backs can be purchased by the pound.

In the recipes that follow it is assumed that the reader has purchased ready-to-cook fresh or frozen poultry.

Caution: Always keep frozen poultry frozen until ready to use; allow sufficient time for thawing completely before cooking.

Chicken

Chicken wasn't always as available as it is today. Down on the farm in Indiana when I was growing up, chicken was a special treat reserved for Sunday dinner, which was served in midafternoon. Not every Sunday, either! Only for special occasions and when company was expected.

Not that we didn't have plenty of chickens. We did, and they scratched around the fenced-in chicken yard all day and feasted on an ample supply of home-grown corn. My mother, grandmothers and aunts had one thing in mind—eggs. Young, tender female chickens grew into hens and laid eggs. The marketing of the eggs provided an independent income for these hard-working farm women, and was referred to in our family as "pin-money." Only young roosters were chosen for the ever-

popular summer treat of a platter heaped with tender, crispy fried chicken. Once the roosters were culled out of the flock, the fried chicken season was over. The young female chickens, called poulets, grew into hens and were left to their business of laying eggs. After a hen had outlived her marketing usefulness, into the pot she went, to be simmered slowly until tender. Then we had a hearty dish of chicken and dumplings or homemade egg noodles, and sometimes scalloped chicken. For church suppers the meat was made into chicken salad or pressed chicken loaf.

As late as 1934 a city cook paid, pound for pound, more for chicken than for prime aged steaks, lobster or loin of pork. Is it any wonder that chicken dishes are so highly regarded in American cooking? Since the 1930s we have become a chicken-producing nation. We produce a tender, plump, meaty hybrid bird that is reared indoors on high-energy feed laced with vitamin supplements. This accelerated feeding process means the bird can be rushed from chick to chicken to market in eight weeks. Unfortunately the haste in "feeding out" the young chickens for profit results in the chicken not having time to develop maximum flavor. When people of my generation complain that chicken just doesn't taste like it used to, they mean it just doesn't have that honest-to-goodness, down-on-the-farm flavor of a bird left to wander at will around the chicken yard for a full twelve weeks.

Classic Fried Chicken

Nowadays, chicken fried in the classic American manner is unavailable in restaurants and rarely is served at the family table. The poor quality of preservative-laden processed lard has encouraged food writers to substitute butter for frying chicken—a well-meant but lamentable practice because lard not only crisps the skin but also imparts a delicate flavor. Freshly rendered lard can be purchased in ethnic markets. Those uneasy about using lard may substitute peanut oil, which is about 90 percent as satisfactory.

Chicken should not be deep-fried or coated with an egg batter. Chicken should be pan-fried in no more than ½ inch of bubbling hot fat in a large cast-iron or electric skillet. Unless applied sparingly, flour tends to leave a pasty, sticky coating on the surface of the fried chicken. Water-ground cornmeal may be used instead of flour; it lends a delicate flavor and crisp touch of its own.

When buying chicken for frying, you should allow about ¾ pound per person from a chicken with bone in. Plan on 2 drumsticks or 2 thighs per serving; 1 breast, split, for 2 servings.

Fried chicken should be served at room temperature.

1 3-pound chicken, cut into serving
pieces
1 cup flour
1½ teaspoons salt, or to taste

2 teaspoons freshly ground black
pepper
Peanut oil or freshly rendered lard for
frying chicken

1. Wipe excess moisture from chicken pieces and set aside.
2. Combine the flour, salt and pepper in a plastic bag (the flavor of freshly ground pepper is important). Shake well to blend and empty out onto a flat baking dish.
3. Coat the chicken pieces all over with the flour mixture and place on a tray; pieces should not be touching. Refrigerate at least 30 minutes.
4. Pour peanut oil to a depth of ½ inch in a 10-to-12-inch cast-iron or electric skillet, or melt enough lard to measure the same depth. The skillet should be large enough to hold the chicken pieces in one layer without touching. Heat the fat over medium-high heat until hot but not smoking. Carefully place the chicken pieces in the hot fat, skin side down; cook, without turning, until golden brown on one side. Turn the pieces and reduce the heat to medium-low. *Caution:* Lowering the temperature is an important step to prevent the chicken from cooking too fast, which will dry out the meat. Cook the pieces until tender, removing them one by one, since the cooking time varies according to thickness. Drain on paper towels.

Serves 4.

Variation: Southern Fried Chicken

In Step 1 place the chicken pieces in a bowl and add milk, buttermilk or half water and half undiluted evaporated milk to cover. Turn pieces to coat. Refrigerate 1 hour or longer. In Step 3 coat the chicken pieces well all over with the flour mixture.
NOTE: You may need additional flour, salt and pepper. Do not refrigerate. Proceed to Step 4.

Maryland Fried Chicken with Cream Gravy

Pan-frying, braising and sauce-making are the three cooking techniques used in preparing this classic regional dish, which traditionally is served with a generous portion of fluffy mashed potatoes.

3 whole chicken breasts, boned and
split
1 cup flour
1 teaspoon salt, or to taste
1½ teaspoons freshly ground black
pepper

Peanut oil or freshly rendered lard for
frying chicken
Boiling water
2 tablespoons unsalted butter
1¼ cups half-and-half

1. Wipe excess moisture from chicken and set aside.
2. Combine the flour, salt and pepper in a plastic bag (the flavor of freshly ground pepper is important). Shake well to blend and empty out onto a flat baking dish.
3. Coat the chicken pieces all over with the flour mixture and place on a tray; pieces should not touch. Refrigerate at least 30 minutes. Reserve 2 tablespoons of the flour mixture.
4. Pour peanut oil to a depth of ½ inch in a 10-to-12-inch cast-iron or electric skillet with a tight-fitting lid, or melt enough lard to measure the same depth. The skillet should be large enough to hold the chicken pieces in one layer without touching. Heat the fat over medium-high heat (350°F.) until hot but not smoking. Carefully place the chicken in the hot fat, with skin side down; cover and cook 7 minutes. Turn chicken and cook, covered, an additional 7 minutes. Turn each piece and continue to pan-fry until golden on both sides.
5. Reduce heat to medium-low. Pour off excess fat from skillet and add boiling water to a depth of ¼ inch. Cook, covered, until chicken is tender and juicy—this should take no more than 15 minutes. Remove chicken to a heated platter.
6. Pour off and discard all the fat in the skillet, leaving the brown crumbs. With a wooden spoon scrape the crumbs from the sides and bottom of the skillet.
7. Add the butter to the crumbs and melt over medium heat. Add the 2 tablespoons of reserved flour mixture and cook 3 minutes, stirring constantly.
8. Remove from heat and slowly add the half-and-half, stirring constantly to blend.
9. Return the mixture to low heat and cook for 5 minutes, stirring constantly. The gravy, or sauce, should not be thicker than medium white sauce. Add more salt and pepper to taste. If desired, the gravy may be strained through a coarse sieve. Spoon the gravy over the chicken or serve separately from a sauce boat.

Serves 6.

Chicken Fricassee
(Chicken Stew)

This is a very old American dish. The flavor should be simple and pure chicken. Any temptation to add wine or strong spices should be resisted. Serve with egg noodles or rice.

3 whole chicken breasts, boned and
  split
1 cup flour
1 teaspoon salt, or to taste
½ teaspoon freshly ground black
  pepper
1 tablespoon unsalted butter, combined with 1 tablespoon peanut oil

½ cup finely chopped onion
1 sprig fresh thyme or ¼ teaspoon
  ground thyme
1 tablespoon finely chopped parsley
1 small bay leaf
3 cups boiling water

1. Skin may be removed from chicken if desired, but the dish will have
   more flavor if not removed. If breasts are large, flatten them with
   a mallet to a thickness of 1 inch; this also makes a better presentation of the finished dish. Wipe excess moisture from chicken and
   set aside.
2. Combine the flour, salt and pepper in a plastic bag. Shake well to
   blend and empty out onto a flat baking dish.
3. Coat the chicken pieces all over with the flour mixture and place on
   a tray; pieces should not touch. Refrigerate at least 30 minutes.
4. In a heavy, 3-quart skillet or flameproof casserole with a tight-fitting
   lid, heat the butter and peanut oil until hot but not smoking. Carefully place the chicken in the hot fat, skin side down, and fry on both
   sides until golden. Add the chopped onion, thyme, parsley, bay leaf
   and water. Bring to a boil; cover and reduce heat. Simmer slowly
   until chicken is tender, about 45 minutes. It will take longer if the
   chicken breasts are thicker than 1 inch. Discard bay leaf. Place
   chicken on a heated platter and cover with the pan sauce. Serve hot.
Serves 6.

Variation: Chicken and Batter Dumplings

1 cup sifted unbleached flour (sift
  before measuring)
2 teaspoons baking powder

½ teaspoon salt
1 tablespoon finely chopped parsley
½ cup milk

Mix all ingredients together to form a thick batter. Drop a tablespoon
at a time into simmering Chicken Fricassee 20 minutes before chicken
is cooked. Cover tightly and cook chicken and dumplings an additional
20 minutes *without* removing cover. Do not peek! Serve immediately.

Southern-Style Chicken and Flat Dumplings

⅓ cup unsalted butter; or use half butter and half solid white shortening

2 cups sifted unbleached flour (sift before measuring)

1 teaspoon salt

2 teaspoons baking powder

½ cup milk

1. Place the butter, flour, baking powder and salt in a medium-sized mixing bowl. With a pastry blender or electric mixer cut the butter into the mixture until the consistency of cornmeal.
2. Add milk and stir with a fork until flour is incorporated but do *not* overmix. Gather dough into a ball.
3. Roll out on a lightly floured, smooth surface to ⅛-inch thickness. *Caution*: Care should be taken to keep the dough thin. This is the secret of a good flat dumpling. Cut the dough into 1½-inch strips. Cut the strips on the diagonal to make diamonds. Dust with additional flour if the dough begins to stick to the cutting surface. Keep the diamonds separated.
4. Drop the diamonds one by one into the simmering Chicken Fricassee 20 minutes before chicken is done. Cover tightly and cook chicken and dumplings an additional 20 minutes *without* removing cover. Do not peek! Serve immediately.

Smothered Chicken

"Smothered" is an Elizabethan culinary term meaning "covered" that was brought over by the early colonists. The term is used in authentic New England and Southern dishes. In this recipe a rich chicken broth "covers" the savory chicken.

3 pounds chicken parts, including boned breasts, legs and thighs

1 teaspoon salt, or to taste

½ teaspoon freshly ground black pepper

¼ cup unsalted butter or peanut oil

⅔ cup finely chopped onion

1 cup thinly sliced mushrooms

1 tablespoon flour

¼ cup chopped parsley

½ teaspoon rosemary

½ teaspoon thyme

2 cups double-strength chicken broth (page 26)

1½ tablespoons lemon juice

Thin lemon slices for garnish

Finely chopped parsley for garnish

1. Wipe excess moisture from chicken and sprinkle with salt and pepper.
2. Heat the butter or peanut oil in a 10-to-12-inch, heavy skillet until hot but not smoking. Carefully place the chicken in the hot fat and

fry approximately 7 minutes on each side, or until nicely browned. Remove the chicken and set aside.

3. Add the onion, mushrooms and flour to the fat in the skillet. Cook over low heat 3 minutes, stirring constantly until the onions are tender. Stir in the parsley, rosemary, thyme and chicken broth. Return the chicken to the broth, cover and cook at a very slow simmer 40 minutes, or until chicken is tender. Add lemon juice and stir to blend. Cook an additional 2 minutes. Transfer chicken and sauce to a heated platter. Dip half of each lemon slice in chopped parsley and arrange around the edge of the platter.

Serves 6.

Chicken Breasts with Ham and Oyster Sauce

This dish is a medley of a Virginian's favorite foods—chicken, ham and oysters. Classically speaking, the ham should be Smithfield.

16 oysters, with liquor	2 cups half-and-half
2 large whole chicken breasts, boned and split	1 teaspoon Worcestershire sauce
¼ cup unsalted butter	1 teaspoon salt, or to taste
8 thin slices cooked Smithfield ham	⅛ teaspoon cayenne pepper, or more to taste
3 tablespoons flour	1 teaspoon freshly ground white pepper
1 tablespoon unsalted butter	
1 tablespoon chopped green pepper	8 thin slices toast, crusts removed
¼ cup finely chopped celery	Parsley or watercress for garnish

1. Drain oysters in a sieve over a bowl. Reserve ½ cup of the liquor. Set oysters and liquor aside.
2. Remove skin from chicken breasts. Place each piece of chicken between two pieces of clear plastic wrap; pound to ¼-inch thickness, working from center. Remove plastic wrap, trim and cut each piece of chicken in half, to make a total of 8 pieces.

NOTE: This is a very rich dish; 1 whole piece would make too large a portion for a single serving.

3. In a 10-to-12-inch, heavy skillet melt the ¼ cup butter until hot. Cook the chicken pieces about 3 minutes on each side, or until tender but do not brown. Transfer the cooked chicken to a warm platter and keep warm.
4. Place the ham slices in the same skillet and heat 1 minute on each side. Transfer to same platter with chicken.
5. Add the flour, 1 tablespoon butter, the green pepper and celery to the skillet. Cook, stirring constantly, until the vegetables are tender but not brown.

6. Remove from heat and slowly add the half-and-half, reserved oyster liquor, Worcestershire sauce, salt, cayenne pepper and white pepper.
7. Return to heat and cook until thickened. Add the oysters and heat until the edges just begin to curl.
8. Place a slice of ham on each piece of toast. Place a piece of chicken over each piece of ham. Spoon the hot oyster sauce and oysters over the chicken (allow 2 oysters per serving). Garnish with parsley or watercress. Serve immediately.

Serves 8.

Country Captain

This is a highly seasoned dish that first gained popularity in Georgia. The late Mrs. W. L. Bullard of Columbia, Georgia, is credited with serving Franklin D. Roosevelt his first Country Captain at her summer home in Warm Springs, Georgia. This was long before Mr. Roosevelt became President.

The dish also has been enjoyed by a star-studded list, including Generals Pershing, Patton, Eisenhower and Marshall. The story goes that General Patton once wired a friend when he was to spend only a few hours in Columbus, "If you can't give me a party and have Country Captain, put some in a tin bucket and bring it to the train."

This curry-flavored dish is of East Indian origin, and it's thought to have found its way to this country via spice shipments to Savannah. In any case, it is a festive dinner-party dish.

4 pounds chicken thighs, legs and boned breasts
1 cup flour
1 teaspoon salt
¼ teaspoon freshly ground black pepper
1 cup peanut oil
1 cup finely chopped onion
1 cup finely chopped green pepper
1 clove garlic, minced
1½ teaspoons salt, or to taste
½ teaspoon freshly ground white pepper

1 tablespoon curry powder, or to taste
2 16-ounce cans crushed tomatoes, undrained
½ teaspoon finely chopped parsley
½ teaspoon ground thyme
3 heaping tablespoons dried currants or raisins
4 cups boiled or steamed long-grain white rice
1 cup slivered almonds, toasted
Parsley for garnish

Preheated oven temperature: 350°F.
1. Remove skin from chicken and wipe excess moisture from pieces.
2. Combine the flour, salt and pepper in a plastic bag. Shake well to blend and empty out onto a flat baking dish.

3. Coat the chicken pieces lightly all over with the flour mixture and place on a tray; pieces should not touch. Refrigerate at least 30 minutes.
4. Pour peanut oil into a 10-to-12-inch cast-iron or electric skillet. The skillet should be large enough to hold the chicken pieces in one layer without touching. Heat the oil over medium-high heat until hot but not smoking. Carefully place the chicken pieces in the hot oil and cook, without turning, until golden brown on one side. Turn the pieces and continue cooking until golden brown all over.
5. Remove chicken to an ovenproof platter and keep warm. *Caution:* This is an important step for the success of this dish.
6. Pour off all but ¼ cup of the drippings from the skillet. Add the onion, green pepper and garlic. Cook until tender but not brown. Add salt, pepper and curry powder. Stir to blend. Add tomatoes, chopped parsley, thyme and currants or raisins. Stir gently to mix.
7. Transfer the warm chicken to a 4-quart flameproof casserole with a tight-fitting lid. Pour the sauce mixture over the chicken—it should cover the chicken. If it does not, rinse out the skillet in which the sauce has been cooked and pour water mixture over the chicken to cover. Cover and bake in preheated oven about 45 minutes, or until chicken is tender.
8. Place chicken in the center of a large platter and pile rice around it to form a ring. Spoon sauce over the rice and sprinkle almonds on top. Garnish with parsley. Serve hot.

Serves 8.

Curried Chicken and Fruit

This is a West Coast party recipe with international overtones. Serve with boiled or steamed long-grain white rice.

3 whole chicken breasts, boned, split and skinned
⅓ cup flour
½ teaspoon ground ginger
1 tablespoon curry powder, or to taste
1 teaspoon salt, or to taste
½ cup unsalted butter
1 9-ounce can sliced pineapple
1 11-ounce can mandarin orange sections
1 large tart apple, cored and sliced into ¼-inch sections
½ cup heavy cream
1 tablespoon lemon juice
2 tablespoons canned sliced pimiento

Preheated oven temperature: 350°F.
1. Wipe excess moisture from chicken and set aside.
2. Combine the flour, ginger, curry powder and salt in a plastic bag. Shake well to blend and empty out onto a flat baking dish.

3. Coat the chicken pieces lightly all over with the flour mixture and place on a tray; pieces should not touch. Refrigerate at least 30 minutes. Reserve any of the remaining flour mixture.
4. Melt the butter in a 10-to-12-inch heavy skillet until hot but not smoking. Carefully place the chicken in the hot fat. Sprinkle reserved flour mixture over the chicken. Fry on medium-high heat on both sides until golden.
5. Transfer the chicken to a 2½-quart flameproof casserole with a tight-fitting lid.
6. Drain pineapple and oranges, reserving juice. Cut pineapple slices in half. Arrange the pineapple, orange and apple slices on the chicken.
7. Add the fruit juices to the pan drippings in the skillet and bring to a boil. With a wooden spoon scrape the crumbs from the bottom and sides of the skillet. Quickly stir in the cream and lemon juice and cook, stirring constantly, until the mixture has thickened slightly. Add the pimiento and pour over the chicken in the casserole. Cover and bake in a preheated oven about 45 minutes, or until the chicken is tender. Serve hot.

Serves 6.

Scalloped Chicken

This is a dish dear to the hearts of those born to American cooking. Served at room temperature unadorned, it always has been associated with covered-dish church suppers. Hot and dressed with Lemon Gravy (page 166), it is fancy enough to serve as a glamorous dinner-party dish.

4 cups cooked chicken, sliced or cubed into bite-size pieces
Salt and freshly ground black pepper to taste
½ cup unsalted butter
1 cup thinly sliced fresh mushrooms
½ cup flour
2 cups chicken broth, combined with 1½ cups milk

Yolks of 2 large eggs, lightly beaten
½ teaspoon salt, or to taste
⅛ teaspoon freshly ground black pepper, or to taste
2 cups freshly ground dry bread crumbs
½ cup chicken broth
Whites of 2 large eggs, stiffly beaten

Preheated oven temperature: 350°F.
1. Prepare chicken following Basic Recipe for Stewed Chicken (page 169) and reserve broth (see page 25).
2. Place the sliced or cubed chicken in a well-oiled 12-x-7½-x-2-inch baking dish. Sprinkle lightly with salt and pepper to taste. Set aside.

3. Melt the butter in a 2½-quart, heavy saucepan. Add the mushrooms and cook over medium heat 5 minutes. Remove with a slotted spoon and set aside.
4. Add the flour to the butter remaining in the saucepan and cook 3 minutes, stirring constantly.
5. Remove from heat and slowly add the chicken broth and milk mixture, stirring constantly to blend.
6. Return to medium-high heat and cook at least 5 minutes, stirring constantly, until the mixture has thickened. Remove from heat and cool slightly.
7. Add a few tablespoons of the heated sauce to the egg yolks, stirring constantly to keep the mixture from separating. Slowly stir the egg mixture back into the heated sauce. Add the ½ teaspoon salt, ⅛ teaspoon pepper, bread crumbs, ½ cup chicken broth and cooked mushrooms. Stir well to blend.
8. With a rubber spatula gently fold the egg whites into the sauce. *Caution:* Do not overblend.
9. Pour the sauce carefully over the chicken, place in preheated oven and bake 45 minutes, or until firm in the center. Cut into squares and serve hot or at room temperature.

Serves 8 to 10.

Variation: Scalloped Turkey

Substitute turkey and turkey broth for chicken and chicken broth.

Lemon Gravy for Scalloped Chicken

3 tablespoons unsalted butter
3 tablespoons flour
1½ cups chicken broth
½ teaspoon salt, or to taste
¼ teaspoon freshly ground black pepper
3 tablespoons lemon juice
Parsley for garnish

1. In a heavy, 1-quart saucepan melt the butter, blend in flour and cook 3 minutes, stirring constantly.
2. Remove mixture from heat. Slowly add the chicken broth, stirring constantly to blend. Add salt, pepper and lemon juice. Stir well to blend.
3. Return mixture to heat and cook gently 5 minutes, stirring constantly, until the mixture has thickened. Spoon sauce over scalloped chicken squares and garnish with parsley.

Yield: About 1½ cups.

Chicken with Cranberry Sauce

The contrast of the red sauce, white rice and parsley garnish makes this a festive holiday dish.

3 pounds chicken thighs, legs and boned breasts
½ cup flour
1 teaspoon salt
¼ cup chopped onion
1 tablespoon unsalted butter
1½ cups fresh cranberries
½ cup strained honey
1 teaspoon grated orange rind

¼ teaspoon ground ginger
¾ cup orange juice
2 tablespoons unsalted butter, combined with 2 tablespoons peanut oil
3 cups boiled or steamed long-grain white rice
¼ cup finely chopped parsley for garnish

1. Wipe excess moisture from chicken pieces and set aside.
2. Combine the flour and salt in a plastic bag. Shake well to mix and empty out onto a flat baking dish.
3. Coat the chicken pieces lightly all over with the flour mixture and place on a tray; pieces should not touch. Refrigerate at least 30 minutes.
4. Prepare the cranberry sauce: In a medium-sized, heavy saucepan cook the onion in the 1 tablespoon of butter over low heat until tender but not brown. Add the cranberries, honey, orange rind, ginger and orange juice. Bring to a boil and cook 2 minutes. Set aside.
5. Melt the 2 tablespoons of butter and the peanut oil in a large, 10-to-12-inch skillet with a tight-fitting lid until hot but not smoking. Carefully place the chicken pieces in the hot fat, skin side down, and cook until golden on both sides, turning only once.
6. Pour off all the excess fat in the skillet. Add the cranberry sauce and cover. Simmer over low heat, basting the chicken occasionally with the sauce, about 35 to 40 minutes, or until the chicken is tender.
7. Place the chicken and sauce in the center of a large platter and pile rice around it to form a ring. Garnish with parsley. Serve hot.

Serves 6.

Country-Style Roast Chicken with Stuffing
(Basic Recipe)

Do not use skinny broilers or frying chickens for this dish—only a plump, old-fashioned, 5-pound roaster with plenty of meat on its bones will do justice to the savory stuffing. It is tradition to serve giblet gravy with this dish.

1 whole 5-pound, ready-to-cook roasting chicken

⅓ cup melted unsalted butter or rendered chicken fat

Stuffing

½ cup unsalted butter

½ cup chopped celery with a few leaves

½ cup finely chopped onion

4 cups ½-inch cubes day-old white bread; or use 3 cups of white bread cubes and 1 cup of coarsely crumbled corn bread

2 tablespoons chopped parsley

½ teaspoon salt, or to taste

¼ teaspoon freshly ground black pepper, or to taste

½ teaspoon ground sage, thyme or poultry seasoning, or more to taste

Giblet Gravy

Neck, heart and gizzard of chicken

1 medium-sized onion, peeled and halved

1 cup celery leaves

1 cup water

½ teaspoon salt, or to taste

¼ teaspoon freshly ground black pepper

1⅓ cups double-strength chicken broth (page 25)

Preheated oven temperature: 400°F.

1. Remove giblets from chicken. Reserve liver for stuffing. Wipe chicken inside and out with a damp cloth and set aside.
2. *Prepare stuffing:* Melt the ½ cup butter in a small, heavy skillet. Add the celery, onion and chicken liver and cook until tender but not brown. Remove from the heat and transfer to a large mixing bowl. Chop liver and add bread cubes, parsley, salt, pepper and sage, thyme or poultry seasoning. Stir gently to blend ingredients.
3. *To stuff chicken:* First stuff the neck cavity with a thin layer of stuffing. Fold the neck skin over to the back of the chicken. Then place the remainder of the stuffing in the body cavity lightly, allowing room for expansion during roasting.

4. Tuck wings under. Close body cavity with poultry pins at regular intervals. Loop twine around pins, crisscrossing to lace the cavity together; then loop the twine under one leg, up around the other leg, and bring together. Bring twine up under wings; tie over back.

5. Place the stuffed chicken on a lightly oiled rack in a shallow roasting pan. Brush well with melted butter or chicken fat. Place in preheated oven and bake uncovered about 1¾ hours, or until tender, brushing every 20 minutes or so with the butter or chicken fat to seal in the juices and brown the chicken. *Caution:* Do not overcook the chicken, or it will be dry and tasteless. To test for doneness: If the leg and thigh move easily, the chicken is done.

6. While the chicken is baking prepare the giblet gravy. Place the neck, heart and gizzard in a medium-sized saucepan. Add the onion, celery leaves, water, salt and pepper; cover and simmer 1½ hours. Remove neck and discard skin and bones. Chop the neck meat, heart and gizzard fine and set aside. Strain the broth and discard the onion and celery leaves. Set aside.

7. When chicken is done, remove pins and twine; let stand 15 minutes before carving.

8. Pour off the pan drippings from the roasting pan. Return ¼ cup of the drippings to the pan. Add chopped meat, giblets, giblet broth and chicken broth to the pan. Bring mixture to a boil. Lower the heat and simmer uncovered a few minutes, stirring with a wooden spoon to loosen the bits that cling to the sides and bottom of the roasting pan. Turn the heat up high and boil until the sauce is reduced and thickened.

NOTE: The older method is to thicken the gravy with a mixture of flour and water, or roux. Add salt and pepper to taste. Pour into a sauceboat and serve with the chicken and stuffing.
Serves 6.

Stewed Chicken
(Basic Recipe)

Chicken parts may be used in this recipe, but a stewing hen or roaster simmered slowly until tender has more flavor. This is important in the preparation of many dishes such as scalloped chicken, pressed chicken, chicken and noodles or chicken salad.

I buy chickens in quantity when they are on special sale and freeze the cooked meat in 2-cup portions. I strain the broth, reduce it to double strength and freeze 1-cup portions.

NOTE: This recipe makes about 5 cups cooked chicken and about 3 cups double-strength broth. By precooking the basic ingredients most traditional chicken dishes can be prepared in less than an hour.

1 5-to-6-pound stewing hen or roaster, quartered; or 6 pounds chicken parts
Water
4 ribs celery with leaves, cut into 2-inch pieces
1 large carrot, cut into 1-inch pieces

1 medium-sized onion, quartered
2 sprigs parsley
1 bay leaf
2 teaspoons salt, or to taste
¼ teaspoon freshly ground black pepper

1. Place the chicken in a large kettle or a flameproof casserole with a tight-fitting lid; add enough water to cover. Add remaining ingredients.
2. Cover and bring to a rolling boil. Reduce and simmer 1 hour for chicken parts or 2 to 2½ hours for stewing hen or roaster. Chicken is cooked when it is easily pierced with a fork. Remove chicken from heat and cool in the broth.
3 Remove the meat from the bones; discard skin and bones. Cut meat into bite-size pieces or slice it, depending upon the dish to be prepared. Use following recipe instructions or store in airtight containers for freezing.
4. Strain the broth; discard vegetables and bay leaf. Return the broth to heat and bring to a rolling boil. Reduce heat and continue at a low boil, uncovered, until broth is reduced by about half. Cool. Measure into 1-cup portions for immediate use or freeze in airtight containers.

Cajun-Style Chicken Breasts with Oyster Stuffing

This is one of the most highly spiced chicken dishes in all of American cooking. Pungent with the taste of oysters, garlic and cayenne pepper, it is not recommended for those faint of palate.

Serve with rice and cranberry-gelatin salad.

4 whole chicken breasts, boned, split and skinned
Salt and freshly ground black pepper to taste

4 teaspoons melted unsalted butter

Stuffing

5 tablespoons unsalted butter
2 tablespoons finely chopped onion
3 tablespoons finely chopped green pepper
2 tablespoons finely chopped celery
1 clove garlic, minced

1 cup oysters, drained and chopped
¼ teaspoon cayenne pepper
1 cup coarsely ground fresh bread crumbs
½ cup oyster liquor

Coating

½ cup finely ground dry bread crumbs, without crusts

3 tablespoons peanut oil, combined with 3 tablespoons unsalted butter

Preheated oven temperature: 400°F.

1. Place each piece of chicken between two pieces of clear plastic wrap; pound to ⅛-inch thickness, working from center. Remove plastic wrap and brush each piece of chicken with ½ teaspoon of the melted butter, using a total of 4 teaspoons. Sprinkle each piece to taste with salt and pepper. Refrigerate until ready to use.
2. *Prepare stuffing:* Melt the 5 tablespoons butter in a medium-sized skillet. Add the onion, green pepper, celery and garlic. Cook, stirring constantly, until the vegetables are tender but *not* brown. Add the oysters and cook 4 minutes. Add the cayenne pepper, 1 cup bread crumbs and oyster liquor. Season to taste with salt and pepper.

NOTE: This mixture should be of a pâté-like consistency.

3. Remove the chicken pieces from the refrigerator. Divide the stuffing mixture evenly and spread with a spatula down the center of each piece of chicken but not to the edge. Fold in the sides of the pieces of chicken; roll up jelly-roll style, pressing ends to seal. Coat the chicken rolls with the ½ cup finely ground bread crumbs. Chill in the refrigerator at least 1 hour.
4. Heat the peanut oil and butter in a 10-to-12-inch, heavy skillet until hot but not smoking. Fry chicken rolls all over until lightly browned. Transfer to a 12-x-7½-x-2-inch baking dish. Bake in preheated oven 15 to 18 minutes. Serve immediately.

Serves 8.

Pressed Chicken

This is a molded loaf of boned chicken in jellied broth. It should be prepared with chicken, seasonings and very little broth. To press the loaf, a weight is placed on top of the chicken; hence, pressed chicken. Unmold onto lettuce leaves and serve with homemade mayonnaise.

NOTE: Pressed chicken must be prepared at least 24 hours prior to serving.

1 5-pound stewing hen or roaster
1 large hard-cooked egg, sliced for garnish
Stuffed green olives, sliced for garnish

Salt and freshly ground black pepper to taste
Lettuce for garnish

1. Prepare chicken as in Basic Recipe for Stewed Chicken (page 169). Cook the chicken until meat almost falls from the bones. Cool chicken in broth. Remove chicken and reserve broth.
2. Remove the meat from the bones with the fingers and shred into bite-size pieces. *Caution:* This is important—cubed meat seems to change the flavor of the dish. Discard the skin. Crack the chicken bones with a mallet and return them to the broth. Boil uncovered until the broth is reduced to 2 cups. Cool to room temperature.
3. Oil a 9-x-5-x-3-inch loaf pan; the pressed chicken should come out easily if the loaf pan is well oiled. Arrange egg and olive slices in a decorative pattern on the bottom of the loaf pan. Place the shredded chicken evenly over the eggs and olives. Sprinkle with salt and pepper to taste. Refrigerate.
4. Strain the chicken broth over a bowl. Refrigerate strained broth until the mixture begins to jell. Carefully spoon the mixture over the chicken.
5. *To press the chicken:* Oil the underside of the bottom of another 9-x-5-x-3-inch loaf pan and set this pan on top of the chicken mixture. Weight down—a 1-pound can of tomatoes is good for this. Refrigerate 24 hours. Unmold onto lettuce leaves. Slice and serve.
Serves 6 to 8.

Chicken Barbecue

"Barbecue" is an American term for the cooking technique of grilling over hot coals in the open air. Since World War II, chicken barbecue parties have become popular summertime entertainments.

1. Prepare fire and, when briquets are gray (a medium-hot fire), you have the proper temperature for barbecuing chicken. To test the temperature, hold your hand over the grill approximately where the chicken will be. *Caution:* Don't touch the grill. If you can hold your hand over the fire for just 3 seconds without pulling away, the coals are ready for grilling.
2. Remove the hot grill and brush well with oil to prevent the chicken from sticking during the cooking and turning.
3. *To prepare chicken:* Have each broiler-size chicken cut in two—split down back and through breast. One half is one serving. However, if the chicken is large, it may be quartered. Wipe excess moisture from chicken.
4. Brush chicken well with sauce (see recipes below) and place chicken on grill, bone side down. Turn every 5 to 10 minutes, brushing with sauce each time; the hotter the fire, the more often the chicken will

have to be turned. Most of the grilling should be done bone side down to prevent blistering of the skin. Cooking time should be about 1 hour. The leg will twist out of the thigh joint easily when the bird is done.

Chicken Barbecue Sauce

This is a mild sauce that brings out the fine flavor of a perfectly barbecued chicken.

1 cup water
1 cup cider vinegar
½ cup peanut oil
1 teaspoon Worcestershire sauce

⅛ teaspoon Tabasco sauce (optional)
Salt to taste

Combine all the ingredients and heat to boiling. Brush on chicken before and during grilling. Enough for 4 broiler halves.

All-Purpose Southern Barbecue Sauce

½ cup cider vinegar
1 cup water
2 tablespoons brown sugar, or more to taste
2 tablespoons Dijon-style mustard
1½ teaspoons salt, or to taste
½ teaspoon freshly ground black pepper, or to taste

¼ teaspoon cayenne pepper
6 tablespoons lemon juice
1 large onion, chopped fine
½ cup unsalted butter
1 cup tomato catsup
4 tablespoons Worcestershire sauce

Combine the vinegar, water, brown sugar, mustard, salt, black pepper and cayenne pepper, lemon juice, onion and butter in a heavy, 2-quart saucepan. Bring to a boil over high heat and cook at a low boil 20 minutes, stirring occasionally. Add catsup and Worcestershire sauce. Brush on chicken before and during grilling. Enough for 4 broiler halves.

Variation: Texas Barbecue Sauce for Chicken

Omit cayenne pepper and substitute 2 teaspoons chili powder, or to taste. Add 1 large garlic clove, chopped fine, to the mixture before cooking.

Tex-Mex Chicken Enchiladas
(Enchiladas de Pollo)

Here is an easy recipe for enchiladas that has been adapted for the home kitchen, using ingredients ordinarily available on any well-stocked market's shelves.

This makes a beautiful presentation to serve at informal parties. Serve with rice and Fried Beans (Frijoles Fritos , page 306).

¾ cup Chili Salsa (see below); or use 1 7-ounce can

2 tablespoons light olive oil or corn oil

1 cup chopped onion

1 clove garlic, chopped fine

2 cups tomato sauce, preferably homemade

2 cups finely cubed cooked chicken or turkey

½ teaspoon salt, or to taste

Cooking oil or lard for frying tortillas

1 dozen fresh or frozen tortillas

1½ cups light cream, combined with 1 cup double-strength chicken broth, or use ¾ cup milk and ¾ cup heavy cream

½ pound Monterey Jack cheese, grated or shredded

Preheated oven temperature: 350°F.
1. Prepare Chili Salsa and set aside.
2. In a heavy, 2-quart saucepan heat the oil and cook the onion and garlic until onion is translucent but not brown. Add tomato sauce, chicken or turkey, Chili Salsa and salt. Simmer uncovered 10 minutes. Add more salt if necessary. Set aside.
3. Heat 1 inch of oil or lard in a small, heavy skillet until hot but not smoking. Fry each tortilla a few seconds but not until crisp. Immediately dip in the cream and chicken broth mixture. Remove and stack. Reserve liquid after all the tortillas have been dipped.
4. Spread chicken mixture on tortillas, roll and place, seam side down, in a well-oiled baking pan large enough to hold the 12 filled tortillas, or use two 12-x-7½-x-2½-inch 2-quart oblong baking dishes. Pour reserved liquid over tortillas. Sprinkle cheese evenly over the tortillas and bake in preheated oven 25 minutes, or until the cheese is lightly browned and bubbling-hot.

Serves 6.

Chili Salsa
(Basic Recipe)

This is a quick and easy, all-purpose chili sauce to use with Tex-Mex cooking.

2 tablespoons light olive oil or corn oil
1 tablespoon flour
½ cup chopped onion
1 teaspoon finely chopped garlic
3 tablespoons chili powder, or to taste

½ teaspoon dried oregano
¼ teaspoon ground cumin
1 teaspoon salt, or to taste
1 cup tomato purée
1 cup chicken or beef broth

Heat the oil in a heavy, medium-sized skillet. Add the flour and cook 3 minutes, stirring constantly. Stir in the onion and garlic and cook, stirring constantly, until onion is translucent but not brown. Add the chili powder, oregano, cumin, salt, tomato purée and broth. Simmer uncovered 10 minutes, stirring occasionally.
Yield: 2 cups.

Turkey

Originally the turkey was a native American game bird closely related to the pheasant. The Indians domesticated turkeys long before the white man arrived in the Western Hemisphere. It is reported that Spanish *conquistadores* took domesticated turkeys back to Spain as early as 1519. Later some of the strains of these birds were brought back across the Atlantic and cross-bred with American wild turkeys. All the interbreeding of superior strains has produced a much tenderer and juicier bird, which requires far less cooking time than his tough ancestors.

In American cooking, turkey is stuffed, roasted and served with giblet gravy as a traditional Thanksgiving or Christmas dinner. The "leavings" from the turkey are used to make chowder, soup, scalloped or creamed dishes, salad and sandwiches.

NOTE: One 12-pound turkey will yield about 11 cups of cooked meat.

How to Prepare Turkey for Roasting

1. Rinse the bird inside and out under running water, drain well and pat dry with paper towels.
2. Rub salt lightly into the breast and body cavities. *Caution:* Do not rub salt on the outside, or the skin will be tough when cooked.
3. Insert stuffing. See recipes below. Always stuff the turkey loosely because the ingredients will expand during roasting. Any extra stuffing can be placed in a well-oiled pan and baked with the turkey. The baking time will depend upon the amount of leftover stuffing.
4. Close the body cavities with poultry pins and lace together with twine. Fold wings and bring wing tips onto the back. Push drumsticks under the narrow band of skin at the tail or tie them to the tail with twine.
5. Rub the outside of the bird with melted unsalted butter or vegetable oil.

Tips for Roasting the Perfect Stuffed Turkey

Caution: Differences in the size, shape and breed of the bird may necessitate increasing or decreasing the cooking time slightly.

1. Preheat oven to 325°F. The low oven temperature assures a higher yield of edible meat and better flavor.
2. Place the stuffed turkey, breast up, on a rack at least ½ inch high in a shallow, open pan. If a meat thermometer is used, insert so that the bulb rests in the center of the inside thigh muscle adjoining the body cavity.
3. If desired, cover the bird loosely with foil. *Caution:* Do not wrap the bird in foil; this will cause the meat to steam rather than roast. The real purpose of the foil is to keep the breast meat from overbrowning and drying out.
4. Brush with melted unsalted butter at 1 hour intervals.
5. The turkey is done when the meat thermometer registers 185°F. If no thermometer is used, there are two other tests that can be used to determine doneness. Press fleshy part of drumstick with fingers; when the meat feels soft, the turkey is done. Another indication of doneness is the looseness of the drumstick in the joint. Grasp the drumstick and rotate it; if it feels slightly loose, the turkey is cooked.
6. *Chart of Cooking Times.* Remember, do not overcook. The turkey must rest 30 minutes before carving, and it will continue to cook during this period.

Weight	*Time*
8 to 12 pounds	4 to 5 hours
12 to 16 pounds	4½ to 6 hours
16 to 20 pounds	5½ to 7 hours
20 to 24 pounds	6½ to 7 hours

7. Remove turkey to platter and prepare Giblet Gravy.

How to Prepare Giblet Gravy

1. Wash the giblets. Place neck, heart and gizzard in a medium-sized saucepan and cover with water. Add 1 bay leaf, 1 onion and a handful of celery tops. Add salt to taste. Boil until the gizzard is tender. Drain, reserve broth and discard vegetables and bay leaf. Remove meat from neck and chop with the gizzard and heart. Set aside.
2. To make 6 cups of gravy, pour drippings from roasting pan into a bowl. Skim off the fat and measure ½ cup of the drippings back into the roasting pan. Add ½ cup of flour and cook 3 minutes, stirring

constantly, to remove the raw taste of flour. Remove from heat.

3. Combine the reserved giblet broth and water to measure 6 cups. Slowly stir this liquid into the flour mixture, stirring constantly to blend.

4. Return the mixture to heat and boil a few minutes, stirring constantly with a wooden spoon to loosen the bits that cling to the sides and bottom of the roasting pan. Reduce heat and cook until gravy has thickened—this should take about 10 minutes. Add chopped giblets and salt and pepper to taste. Serve hot over stuffing or on the side from a sauceboat.

Yield: 6 cups.

Traditional Stuffings for Roast Turkey

Turkey stuffings vary widely according to region. New Englanders prefer a bread stuffing lightly flavored with herbs, nutmeg and onion. Southerners, myself included, favor a traditional corn bread stuffing pungent with sage. Cooks in New Jersey and Massachusetts often make cranberry stuffing, and Farm-Style Oyster Stuffing seems to be a universal favorite.

Stuffings can be made in advance. It is advisable to add the liquid in the recipe to the stuffing just before it is placed in the turkey. Otherwise, particularly if it is refrigerated overnight, the stuffing tends to become soggy. *Caution: Never* stuff the turkey until just before it is to be placed in the oven for roasting.

The following recipes make enough stuffing to fill a 10-to-12-pound turkey with enough left over to bake in a separate pan along with the turkey.

New England Bread Stuffing

1 cup chopped onion
2 cups finely chopped celery
1½ cups unsalted butter
10 cups cubed dry white bread
1½ teaspoons salt, or to taste
½ teaspoon freshly ground black pepper

½ teaspoon ground thyme
½ teaspoon ground marjoram
½ tablespoon ground sage
¾ teaspoon freshly grated nutmeg (optional)

1. In a heavy saucepan cook the onion and celery in the butter until tender but not brown. Set aside.

2. In a very large mixing bowl blend bread cubes, salt, pepper, thyme, marjoram, sage and optional nutmeg. Add the onion and celery mixture and stir lightly to blend.
3. To test for seasoning, return a spoonful to the saucepan the onion and celery were cooked in and cook 3 to 4 minutes. Taste and add more seasoning to the stuffing if desired.

Southern Cornbread Stuffing

1 cup chopped onion
4 cups chopped celery
1 cup unsalted butter
5 cups crumbled corn bread
7 cups cubed dry white bread
1 tablespoon salt, or to taste

½ teaspoon freshly ground black pepper
½ teaspoon ground marjoram
½ teaspoon ground thyme
1 teaspoon ground sage
4 large eggs, well beaten
1½ to 2 cups chicken or turkey broth

1. In a heavy saucepan cook the onion and celery in the butter until tender but not brown. Set aside.
2. In a very large mixing bowl blend the corn bread, bread cubes, salt, pepper, marjoram, thyme and sage. Add onion and celery mixture. Blend in eggs and add 1½ cups of the broth. If the mixture seems dry, add the remaining ½ cup broth. Stir lightly to blend.
3. To test for seasoning, return a spoonful to the saucepan the onion and celery were cooked in and cook 3 to 4 minutes. Taste and add more seasoning to the stuffing if desired.

My Mother's Old-Fashioned Oyster Stuffing

¼ cup finely chopped onion
1½ cups finely chopped celery
¼ cup chopped parsley
¾ cup unsalted butter
2 cups oysters, drained and liquor reserved

6 cups cubed dry white bread
1 teaspoon ground savory or sage
¼ teaspoon freshly grated nutmeg
1½ teaspoons salt, or to taste
1 teaspoon paprika
About 1 cup of milk

1. In a heavy, medium-sized saucepan cook the onion, celery and parsley in the butter until the vegetables are tender but not brown.
2. Add the oysters to the mixture in the saucepan and cook a few minutes, until the edges curl. (If the oysters are large they may be chopped).

3. In a very large mixing bowl blend together the bread cubes, savory, nutmeg, salt and paprika. Add the oyster mixture and oyster liquor' with enough milk to moisten the stuffing slightly.
4. Taste and add more seasoning to the stuffing if desired.

Cranberry-Nut Stuffing

1 cup chopped onion
1 cup chopped pecans or walnuts
½ cup unsalted butter
8 cups cubed dry white bread
2 cups coarsely chopped cranberries, with juice, combined with 6 tablespoons sugar

1 small red apple, unpeeled, cored and chopped
¼ teaspoon ground thyme
¼ teaspoon ground marjoram
¼ teaspoon ground sage
½ cup chopped parsley

1. In a heavy saucepan cook the onion and pecans or walnuts in the butter on low heat 5 minutes, taking care that the onion does not brown.
2. In a very large mixing bowl blend together the bread cubes, cranberry mixture, apple, thyme, marjoram, sage and parsley. Add the onion and nut mixture and stir lightly to blend. Add a little water if stuffing seems dry.
3. To test for seasoning, return a spoonful to the saucepan the onion and nuts were cooked in and cook 3 to 4 minutes. Taste and add more seasoning to the stuffing if desired.

Guinea Fowl

In my family, guinea hen was prepared much in the same manner as chicken, the meat of the female being preferred to that of the male. Young, tender hens were disjointed and fried. Older hens were made into fricassee or stuffed and roasted.

The meat of the guinea fowl is darker than chicken and has a slightly gamey taste. The meat also is drier and must be cooked slightly longer than chicken.

A guinea hen weighs from 2 to 4 pounds. A farmer's market or specialty meat market is the best source of supply.

How to Roast Guinea Hen

Two average-size guinea hens will serve 4 to 6 people.
Preheated oven temperature: 350°F.
1. Prepare any desired recipe for chicken or turkey stuffing.
2. Place stuffed birds, breast down, in a shallow roasting pan and cover with thin strips of blanched bacon or salt pork.
3. Roast in preheated oven, allowing 35 to 45 minutes per pound cooking time. Turn the breast side up halfway through the cooking time. Baste frequently with pan drippings and continue roasting until the meat is tender and the juices run clear when the thigh is pierced with a fork.

Goose

Roast goose with stuffing was the traditional Christmas bird of the upper-class English colonists in the Tidewater area of Virginia. (The Puritans did not celebrate the holiday). The yeomen and refugees from debtors' prison had to be content with rabbits, squirrels or other wild game. All their descendants for the most part prefer roast stuffed turkey with all the trimmings.

Even though roast goose never has been popular in this country, Catherine Beecher, an early cookbook writer, published a Pennsylvania Dutch recipe for roast goose with potato stuffing. Traditionally, this dish is served with applesauce.

Potato Stuffing

3 cups hot mashed potatoes, unseasoned

2¼ cups coarse dry white bread crumbs

¾ cup finely chopped onion

3 large eggs, lightly beaten

1½ teaspoons salt, or to taste

Freshly ground black pepper to taste

1½ teaspoons ground sage

¾ cup chopped celery leaves

⅓ cup chopped parsley

In a large mixing bowl combine the potatoes, bread crumbs, onion, eggs, salt, pepper, sage, celery leaves and parsley. Stir to blend.
Yield: Stuffing for 8-to-9-pound goose.

Roast Goose

1 8-to-9-pound goose
Salt and freshly ground black pepper
  to taste
1 lemon

Potato Stuffing
1 garlic clove
1 rib celery with leaves
Watercress for garnish

Preheated oven temperature: 350°F.

1. Scrub the goose inside and out under hot running water; drain well and pat dry with paper towels.
2. Rub salt lightly into cavity and sprinkle cavity with freshly ground black pepper. Rub cavity and outside skin with cut lemon halves to crisp the skin during roasting.
3. Insert the stuffing. Any extra stuffing can be placed in a small, well-oiled pan and baked with the goose; the baking time will depend upon the amount of leftover stuffing.
4. Close the body cavity with poultry pins and lace together with twine as for Roast Chicken (page 168).
5. Place on a rack in a shallow roasting pan, breast side up. Place 1 split garlic clove and 1 rib celery with leaves, chopped into 1-inch pieces, in the bottom of the roasting pan; put a small amount of water in the roasting pan; this will keep the vegetables from burning and also will control the splattering of grease from the roasting goose.
6. Prick the skin on the breast and around the legs and wings in a few places with a fork to release the fat. Bake in preheated oven 18 to 20 minutes per pound. Baste occasionally with pan drippings. When the goose is tender and the skin brown and crisp, place on a heated platter garnished with watercress.

Serves 8.

Duck

Farmers in America have been breeding ducks to sell to city markets for the restaurant trade since the 1880s. As prized as the domestic duck is in Europe and China as a great table delicacy, it is not highly regarded by American cooks, the reason being that until the invention of the rotisserie for home use, it was almost impossible to remove the excessive grease from a domestic duck.

Allow 1½ pounds of drawn duck per serving.

Rotisserie Roasted Duck

1 4-to-5-pound duckling
1 teaspoon salt
¼ teaspoon ground ginger, or more to taste

⅛ teaspoon freshly ground black pepper
1 orange or 1 apple, quartered

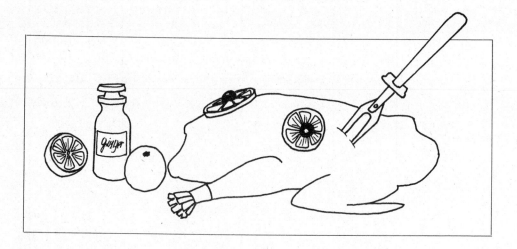

1. Rinse the duck inside and out under hot running water; drain well and pat dry with paper towels.
2. With the pointed end of a sharp knife, prick the skin all over at 1-inch intervals.
3. Combine the salt, ginger and pepper. Rub the mixture all around the cavity and on the skin. Place the orange or apple in the cavity.
4. Skewer neck skin to back with a poultry pin. Wrap duck by criss-crossing twine, starting at the neck and ending with the legs. Insert spit rod through the center of body cavity. Insert prong holders firmly at both ends of the duck and tighten screws. Duck should be perfectly balanced over the heat to roast evenly.
5. Follow manufacturer's instructions for using electric or charcoal rotisserie. Roast about 1¾ hours, or until duck is tender and the leg joint moves easily. Remove duck from spit, discard orange or apple and serve hot.

Serves 2 or 3.

Variation: Barbecued Duck

Prepare one-half recipe All-Purpose Southern Barbecue Sauce (page 173). Omit orange or apple. Substitute 1 rib celery with leaves and 1 medium-sized onion, quartered, to be placed in the cavity. During the last half of roasting time, brush the duck about every 20 minutes with sauce.

MEATS

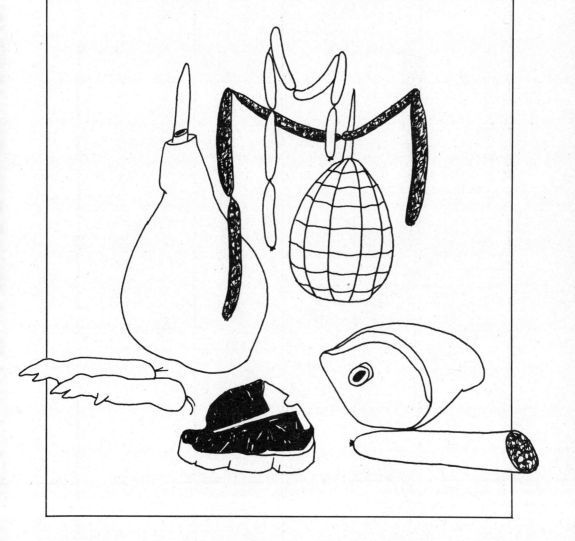

Pork

Since the first time Indians and swine met as the Chickasaws stole hogs from the herd that de Soto's men drove along as a self-supporting commissary, pork has been at the heart of American cooking.

These runty beasts were able to pick out a living unattended in alien wilds for almost seventy years. The prolific pig so flourished on pine seeds, acorns and other nuts of the forest that by the time the first Jamestown settlers arrived, the descendants of the original razorbacks were abundant. Southerners have been eating pork in all forms since.

I regret that the colorful communal butchering days of my rural youth have become folklore, and the fine roasts, chops, tenderloin strips, savory hams and other by-products of the pig must be purchased retail. But I'm thankful that we have been left a fine collection of American regional recipes. As my European friends often point out, "Only the Americans really know how to cook pork."

The progressive hog farmer of modern times usually has a degree from a state college of agriculture and heads a family corporation that is geared for corporationlike profits. . . . Porkers, or young hogs, are scientifically bred and readied for market in record time. Meat from these force-fed animals often lacks the taste of a corn-fed porker. The only reliable method to test pork for flavor is to cook it.

TESTING METHOD: Take a small slice of the pork to be cooked and sprinkle it lightly with salt and pepper. Fry it until thoroughly cooked. If the cooking pork gives off a savory scent, the porker probably was corn-fed. Cooked pork dishes should be served with stuffing or sauce to enhance the flavor.

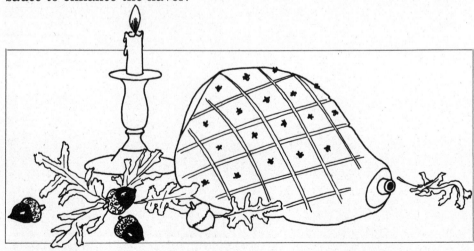

The Southern Way to Roast Pork

The roast may be purchased boned and tied or left with the bone in. If bone-in, have the butcher remove the bones or have him cut through the bones to facilitate carving.

Maryland Pork Loin Roast with Gravy

1 5-pound pork loin, trimmed and tied if boned
Salt and freshly ground black pepper to taste
About ¼ cup flour
1 cup chopped onion
2 medium-sized carrots, diced

1 rib celery with leaves
2 sprigs parsley
¼ teaspoon dried marjoram
1 bay leaf
1½ cups boiling chicken broth or water
About ¼ cup brown sugar

Preheated oven temperature: 325°F.

1. Rub the roast lightly with salt and pepper. Then sprinkle the roast well with flour, rubbing it into the meat with the hands.
NOTE: Pork needs more salt than most meats to point up the flavor.
2. In a shallow roasting pan make a bed of the onion and carrots. Tie the celery and parsley together for easy removal and place in the pan; add the marjoram and bay leaf.
3. Place the loin, fat side up, and the bone if it is detached, over the vegetables. Pour the chicken broth or water into the bottom of the pan but not over the roast. Roast in preheated oven about 25 to 30 minutes per pound—about 2¼ to 2½ hours—or until a meat thermometer registers an internal temperature of 165°F.; baste often with the pan juices. Add more chicken broth or water if the roast seems to be drying out.

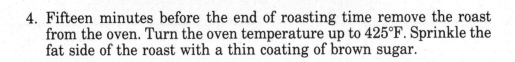

4. Fifteen minutes before the end of roasting time remove the roast from the oven. Turn the oven temperature up to 425°F. Sprinkle the fat side of the roast with a thin coating of brown sugar.

5. Return the roast to the oven and continue roasting until the sugar has carmelized to a nice golden brown.
6. Remove the roast to a heated platter and let rest about 15 minutes before carving.
7. Meanwhile, prepare the gravy. Remove the celery, parsley and bay leaf from the pan droppings, leave the onion and carrot. Skim off excess fat and heat the gravy, or sauce, to boiling. The gravy should be thick enough without further reduction. Spoon over individual servings or serve on the side from a sauce boat.

Serves 6.

Stuffed Fresh Leg of Pork with Pan Gravy
(Cajun-Style)

This cut is known as fresh leg of pork in the South and fresh ham north of the Mason-Dixon Line. This recipe comes from a great cook in Alexandria, Louisiana. The pork and gravy customarily are served with long-grain white rice.

Fresh leg of pork should be cooked thoroughly to bring out its full flavor as well as to kill any *trichinae* organisms present.

1 6-to-8-pound fresh leg of pork
2 tablespoons salt, combined with 1 teaspoon freshly ground black pepper and ½ teaspoon cayenne pepper
3 to 4 cloves garlic, cut into slivers

1 large green pepper, cut into ¼-inch strips
1 medium-sized onion, cut lengthwise into thin slices
¼ cup flour
2 cups water
2 tablespoons finely chopped parsley

Preheated oven temperature: 325°F.
1. Remove rind from pork and trim off excess fat.
2. With a sharp carving knife cut 12 deep, 1-inch-wide slits in the fat side of the meat. Spread the slits apart with a knife or the handle of a wooden spoon to make a hole deep enough to hold the stuffing.
3. With the fingers, fill each hole with a good pinch of the salt mixture, rubbing around to coat well. Place a sliver of garlic, a strip of green pepper and a thin slice of onion in each hole. Rub remaining salt mixture over entire outside of the meat.
4. Place meat, fat side up, on a rack in a shallow roasting pan, and bake in preheated oven 30 to 35 minutes per pound, or until a meat thermometer registers 165°F. Remove meat to cooking rack and let rest 15 minutes.
5. *Prepare pan gravy:* Pour off all the pan drippings from the roasting pan and skim off excess fat. Return 4 tablespoons of the drippings

to the roasting pan. Add flour and cook 3 minutes, stirring constantly. Remove from heat. Slowly stir the water into the flour mixture, stirring constantly to blend. Return the mixture to heat and boil a few minutes, stirring constantly with a wooden spoon to loosen the bits that cling to the sides and bottom of the roasting pan. Reduce heat and cook 8 to 10 minutes, or until the gravy has thickened. Add parsley and more salt and pepper if desired. Serve hot over cooked rice.

Serves 10 to 12.

Stuffed Pork Chops

These are double loin chops, trimmed of most of the fat, cut horizontally to the bone and filled with a well-seasoned stuffing. Southern cooks use either a bread-sage or bread-fruit stuffing.

Almost nothing is more popular with my dinner guests than a wintertime treat of pork chops with bread-sage stuffing and sweet potatoes baked in their skins, accompanied by a semi-dry white California wine.

Most butchers will gladly trim and cut pork chops for stuffing. This is not a chore for the home cook unless you have a very sharp small knife with a fine point. Double loin chops should be about 1½ inches thick.

Method:
1. Trim most of the fat off 6 double loin chops.
2. Place the palm of one hand flat on a chop.
3. With a sharp knife in your other hand, cut horizontally to the bone of each chop to form a pocket to hold the stuffing.

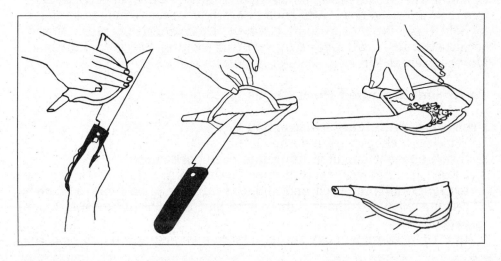

The recipes that follow make enough stuffing to fill 6 double loin chops. Recipes can be doubled or tripled. Do not use packaged dry bread crumbs for either of the following stuffings because the texture is all wrong.

Bread-Sage Stuffing for Pork Chops

2 cups fresh home-style white bread crumbs

¾ teaspoon salt

¼ teaspoon freshly ground black pepper

1½ tablespoons finely chopped parsley

1 teaspoon ground sage

1 tablespoon finely chopped onion

3 tablespoons milk

Combine all ingredients in a medium-sized bowl and stir gently to blend. May be prepared in advance and refrigerated.

Apple-Sage Stuffing for Pork Chops

2 cups home-style white bread cubes

2 tablespoons finely chopped onion

½ cup chopped tart apple, unpeeled

¼ cup melted unsalted butter

1 teaspoon salt

¼ teaspoon freshly ground black pepper

1 teaspoon ground sage, or more to taste

2 to 3 tablespoons chicken broth or water

Combine the bread cubes, onion, apple, butter, salt, pepper and sage in a medium-sized bowl. Add enough broth or water to moisten enough to hold the mixture together. *Caution:* Do not use too much liquid, because the apple will give off juice during cooking. Stir gently to blend. May be prepared in advance and refrigerated.

To Assemble Stuffed Pork Chops

Preheated oven temperature: 350°F.
1. Wipe pork chops with a damp cloth.
2. Spoon about ⅓ cup of stuffing into each pork chop.
3. Close opening with toothpick or poultry pin. *Caution:* Count the toothpicks or pins used and note the number to be removed before serving. Sprinkle chops lightly with salt and freshly ground black pepper.
4. In a 10-to-12-inch heavy skillet heat ⅛ inch peanut oil and heat the

stuffed chops on both sides until brown. Transfer to a baking pan large enough to hold the chops without touching. Add about ¼ inch boiling water to bottom of baking pan. Bake uncovered in preheated oven about 1 hour, or until tender. Serve hot. **Serves 6.**

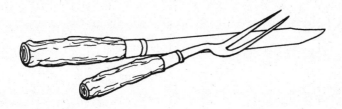

Homemade Pork Sausage

Homemade sausage, redolent of sage and highly spiced with both black and cayenne pepper, is one of the by-product delicacies of the provident pig. Use for stuffing or shape into 2-inch patties and fry until crisp. Served with pancakes and maple syrup, this makes a splendid company breakfast.

Back in the old days of home butchering, all the trimming and grinding necessary for making sausage was an ordeal reserved for the male members in our family. With the modern food processor this chore can be performed in seconds.

Fresh sausage should be refrigerated several hours to blend flavors and should be cooked within 2 days. Freezing sausage is not recommended—it loses too much of its fresh flavor.

For this recipe you will need lean pork, but not too lean. A little fat running through the sausage enhances the flavor and keeps it from drying out during cooking.

1 pound coarsely ground pork (about 2 cups)
1 teaspoon ground sage
1 teaspoon salt

½ teaspoon freshly ground black pepper
¼ teaspoon cayenne pepper

1. In a large mixing bowl combine all ingredients and stir gently to blend. Refrigerate several hours to blend flavors.
2. Form mixture into a 2-inch roll before refrigerating. Cut into 1-inch-thick slices and fry over medium heat until browned and crisp. Drain on paper towels and serve hot.

Serves 4 to 6.

Medallions of Pork Tenderloin with Cream Sauce
(Smothered Pork Tenderloin)

I revived this regional dish of my childhood after I became aware that a local butcher saves the tenderloin for preferred customers.

The tenderloin—and every porker has two—is the tender strip of meat next to the backbone. It is considered the most delicious part of a pig and should be cooked in a very simple manner. Each tenderloin weighs about 1 pound.

Two 1-pound tenderloins will serve 6 people. Allow 2 medallions per serving.

2 pounds of pork tenderloin
Flour for coating
Salt and freshly ground black pepper to taste
Ground sage to taste

3 to 4 tablespoons rendered bacon fat; or use 1 tablespoon peanut oil and 2 to 3 tablespoons unsalted butter
¾ cup heavy cream
Parsley for garnish

1. Wipe tenderloins with a damp cloth. Cut each tenderloin crosswise into 2-inch slices. You should have 6 slices from each tenderloin.
2. Place each piece of meat, cut side down, between two pieces of clear wrap; pound to ¼-inch thickness to make 12 ovals.
3. Coat the pieces of meat lightly with flour. Sprinkle with salt and pepper to taste. Sprinkle sage to taste on one side only. *Caution:* The sage should enhance the flavor of the pork and not overwhelm the taste of the finished dish.
4. In a 10-to-12-inch, heavy skillet heat the bacon fat or oil and butter until hot but not smoking. Place the medallions in the hot fat and immediately turn the heat to medium. Fry gently on one side and then turn. Reduce heat to medium-low and continue cooking about 25 minutes, until the meat is nicely browned and tender. Cover for the last 10 minutes of cooking time to keep the meat from drying out.
5. Remove the meat from the fat and drain on paper towels. Pour off all the fat in the skillet and add the cream. Stir constantly and boil a few minutes, until thickened. Add a little more salt and pepper if necessary. Arrange the medallions artistically on a platter. Coat lightly with the cream sauce. Garnish with parsley and serve hot.

Serves 6.

Oven-Barbecued Spareribs

Spareribs, both oven-braised and glazed, are delicious if cooked properly. Good old-fashioned cooks prefer to oven-braise the ribs and then glaze them with a spicy barbecue sauce at a high temperature during the final minutes of cooking time.

Because of the large amount of bone involved, allow at least 1 pound of meaty spareribs per serving.

6 pounds or more of spareribs, cut into serving portions
Freshly ground black pepper
1 large onion, sliced thin

½ cup boiling water
1 teaspoon salt
1 recipe All-Purpose Southern Barbecue Sauce (page 173)

Preheated oven temperature: 350°F.

1. Wipe the spareribs with a damp cloth and place in a large roasting pan with a tight-fitting lid. Sprinkle lightly with pepper and strew with the sliced onion. Pour the boiling water into the bottom of the roasting pan and add the salt to the water. Cover and bake 30 minutes per pound, or until almost tender, basting frequently with pan juices.
2. Fifteen minutes before the spareribs are done, remove them from the roasting pan and pour off the pan drippings.
3. Turn the oven temperature up to 375°F. Return the spareribs to the roasting pan and brush well with Barbecue Sauce. Continue cooking, brushing a few times with additional sauce, until the ribs are nicely glazed and tender.

Serves 6.

Ham

A fine American country-style ham has always been held in high esteem by regional cooks, be it a Smithfield, North Carolina, Kentucky, Tennessee, Virginia, Georgia, Maryland or even a Harrington brand Vermont cured and smoked ham.

Ham comes from the two hind legs of a hog—from the hipbone through the meaty part of the shank bone. When my grandmothers sugar-cured hams with a mixture of salt, brown sugar, black and cayenne pepper, they always reserved the left leg, or ham, for a special occasion because they held to the rural theory that the pig scratched with his right leg; therefore, the left ham was likely to be tenderer.

A good country-style ham is expensive but worth the price when one considers that many fine dishes are made with boiled or baked ham. These hams are available locally or by mail order.

Allow about ¾ pound of ham with bone in per serving. With boneless ham, ⅓ pound of meat usually is adequate, depending upon the rest of the menu.

How to Test a Ham with Bone in for Doneness

This is a foolproof technique used by cooks long before the invention of the meat thermometer. The method applies whether the ham is cured or fresh, baked or boiled.

At the shank end of the ham there is a small bone about 4 to 5 inches long called a "spoon bone," so named because the end toward the center of the ham is shaped like a small spoon. When the bone can be removed easily, using two pieces of foil to protect the fingers, the ham is cooked to the correct internal temperature. Any further cooking will only dry out the meat and make it tasteless.

NOTE: The bone in a ham acts as a natural heat conductor and requires less cooking time per pound than boneless ham.

How to Test a Boneless Cook-Before-Eating Ham for Doneness

Follow wrapper instructions or use a meat thermometer and cook to an internal temperature of 160°F. to 165°F.

How to Boil an Aged
American Country-Style Cured Ham

Boil is a misnomer in this case. Actually, the ham is cooked at a very low simmer until tender.
NOTE: Well-aged hams do not need a long cooking time.
Preheated oven temperature: 400°F.
1. Unless the wrapper instructions advise otherwise, soak the ham overnight or longer (at least 12 to 18 hours) in enough cold water to cover.
2. Drain and scrub the surface of the ham thoroughly with a stiff brush.
3. Place the ham in a roasting pan with a tight-fitting lid. Cover again with fresh cold water and bring to the simmering point only. Do *not* boil. Simmer the ham 20 to 25 minutes per pound, or until the "spoon bone" can be removed easily. Remove from heat and allow the ham to cool to room temperature in the broth.
NOTE: If the broth is not too salty, skim off the fat and reserve for making bean soup.
4. Remove rind and excess fat. With a sharp knife cut fat ½ inch deep in a diamond-shaped pattern and spread with one of the traditional glazes below. Bake in preheated oven 25 minutes, or until surface is nicely glazed. Serve hot or cold, cut into paper-thin slices.

Glazes

Bourbon Glaze

Mix 1 cup light brown sugar with 1 teaspoon dry mustard or 1 tablespoon Dijon-style mustard and ½ teaspoon ground cloves. Add just enough bourbon to moisten and make a stiff paste. Pat this mixture over the fat.

Bread-Crumb Glaze

Mix ¾ cup dry white bread crumbs without crust and ¾ cup light brown sugar. Pat the mixture over the fat. Dot the center of each diamond with a whole clove.

Honey Glaze

Spoon a light coating of strained honey over the fat.

Cranberry Glaze

Cook 2 cups fresh cranberries with 1 cup of maple syrup until skins pop open. Process mixture in blender or food processor until smooth. Spread over ham.

How to Bake Modern Hams

These are the lightly cured bone-in hams available at any market. Often they are specially priced, making them a very good buy.

Preheated oven temperature: 325°F.

1. Place ham, at room temperature, on rack in a roasting pan, skin side up. Cover with foil if the pan does not have a lid. Bake approximately 20 to 22 minutes per pound, or until the "spoon bone" can be removed easily.

NOTE: If using a meat thermometer, insert it in the fleshiest part of the ham and bake until the thermometer reads 165°F. Remove from oven and cool slightly.

2. Remove rind and excess fat from ham. With a sharp knife, cut fat ½ inch deep in a diamond-shaped pattern. Spread with any of the glazes suitable for boiled ham (page 197).
3. Turn oven temperature up to 400°F. Bake ham another 15 minutes to set the glaze. Slice and serve hot or cold.

Bourbon-Baked Ham

Southern cooks claim that bourbon does something for ham that nothing else does. This recipe is the contribution of friends from Bardstown, Kentucky.

1 10-to-12-pound mildly cured ham with bone in	6 thick slices unpeeled orange or canned pineapple slices ¾ cup bourbon

Preheated oven temperature: 350°F.

1. Line a roasting pan with heavy-duty foil, using enough to wrap ham completely.
2. Place ham in pan, fat side down, and cover with thick slices of unpeeled orange or canned pineapple slices. Pour ¾ cup bourbon over top of ham.

3. Seal the foil tightly around the ham.
4. Pour boiling water into the bottom of the pan to measure halfway up on the outside of the ham. Place lid on roaster. Bake in preheated oven 18 minutes per pound.
5. Remove ham from foil and turn fat side up. Discard fruit. Remove rind and excess fat from ham. With a sharp knife, cut fat ½ inch deep in a diamond-shaped pattern and spread with Bourbon Glaze (page 197).
6. Return ham to oven and bake about 25 minutes, or until the surface is nicely glazed. Serve cold, sliced thin.

Serves 12 to 14.

Maryland Stuffed Ham

Stuffing ham is a time-honored Southern culinary tradition. Perhaps the most classic stuffed ham of all is this one from Southern Maryland.

Originally, ham stuffed with spring greens and wild onions was a traditional Easter dish. Some Southern Marylanders served it with plenty of hot biscuits for Easter breakfast; others reserved the treat for Easter dinner. When the ham is sliced, the effect is of green veining through the pink meat. The ham may be served hot or cold, accompanied with a little cider vinegar, if desired.

One should use a mildly cured 12-pound ham. A ham that has been aged for a longer time should not be used because the meat will be too hard to pull apart and stuff with vegetables.

Cook the Ham: Prepare ham according to directions for How to Boil an Aged American Country-Style Cured Ham (page 197) through Step 2. In Step 3, after 2 hours cooking time immediately remove the ham from the broth to prevent overcooking; additional cooking time is to follow. Reserve broth and cool ham on rack. Remove rind and excess fat.

Stuffing for Ham

3 pounds kale, chopped fine
1 pound watercress, chopped fine
2 pounds green cabbage, cored and chopped fine
2 cups finely chopped celery
1 cup chopped green onion with tops
½ teaspoon cayenne pepper

½ teaspoon freshly ground black pepper
1¼ teaspoons dry mustard
¼ to ½ teaspoon Tabasco sauce, or more to taste
1½ teaspoons salt, or to taste
Cold water

1. Place the kale, watercress, cabbage, celery, green onion, cayenne pepper, black pepper, mustard, Tabasco sauce and salt in a large kettle. Cover with cold water and, stirring occasionally, bring to a rapid boil. Boil only until the vegetables are limp. Remove from heat.
2. Drain vegetables well in a sieve over large bowl, reserving the broth.
3. Turn the vegetables into another large bowl. Add more Tabasco sauce and salt, if desired.

To Stuff the Ham

1. With a sharp carving knife, make X-shaped cuts 3 inches deep and 1 inch apart all over the surface of the ham.
2. Spread the cuts apart with a knife or the handle of a wooden spoon to make pockets to hold the stuffing. Starting on the underside of the ham, using the fingers, fill the pockets with as much vegetable mixture as possible, pushing down filling with the handle of the wooden spoon.
3. Place stuffed ham in the center of a large piece of double-thickness cotton cheesecloth. *Caution:* Do not use cheesecloth made of synthetic material. As an alternative to cotton cheesecloth, use a clean piece of muslin.
4. Arrange any remaining stuffing evenly over the top of the ham. Tie the cheesecloth or sew the muslin around the ham to hold the stuffing in place.

5. Return the stuffed ham to the roasting pan containing the ham broth. Add the reserved vegetable broth and enough water to cover the ham completely. Cover and return the liquid to a rapid boil. Reduce heat and simmer an additional 15 minutes per pound, adding water as needed to keep ham and stuffing covered.
6. Remove the stuffed ham from the heat and allow to cool in the broth 1 hour.
7. Transfer the ham to a cooling rack. Unwrap the cheesecloth or muslin and discard. Place stuffing on top of the ham in a vegetable dish and serve on the side. Slice ham and serve.

Serves 16.

Schnitz Un Knepp

Referred to as "apples and buttons" by the older generations, this dish of dried apple snits, or slices, a glorious slab of country-cured ham and mammoth dumpling balls is a traditional Pennsylvania Dutch meal.

Rarely found on restaurant menus, this recipe was penned for posterity by a kindly lady of the region. This back-to-basics recipe proved to be one of the stars of the test kitchen. Arrange the ham on a large, round platter and encircle with apples and dumplings. Serve piping-hot.

A large stockpot is ideal for preparing this dish.

Apples and Ham

2 cups (2 4-ounce packages) dried
  sliced apples
Water to cover apples
3-to-4 pound center-cut country-cured
  ham

Water to cover ham
2 tablespoons brown sugar

1. Cover the dried apples with water and soak 8 hours or overnight but do not drain.
2. Place the ham in a large, deep kettle with a tight-fitting lid. Cover the ham almost completely with water. Cover and simmer 2 hours.
3. Add the apples, the water in which they were soaked and the brown sugar; cover and simmer an additional 1 hour.

Dumplings

2 cups all-purpose flour
4 teaspoons baking powder
1 teaspoon salt
½ teaspoon freshly ground black pepper

1 large egg, well beaten
½ cup milk
3 tablespoons melted unsalted butter

4. While the apples and ham are cooking, sift together the flour, baking powder, salt and pepper into a medium-sized bowl.
5. With a fork, stir in the egg, milk and melted butter. Continue stirring to make a stiff dough.
NOTE: Originally these dumplings were made with bread dough.
6. Twenty minutes before the apples and ham have finished cooking, pinch off golf-ball-size pieces of dough and place them well apart over simmering apples and ham. (The dough will almost double in size during the cooking.) Cover tightly and cook 20 minutes. *Caution:* Do not lift lid before cooking time is over. Arrange ham, apples and dumplings on a platter. Slice ham on the cross-grain and serve hot with apples and dumplings.
Serves 6 to 8.

Spiced Ham Loaf
(Basic Recipe)

A traditional ham loaf should be a solid, pâté-like, lightly spiced mixture. Serve hot with tart mustard sauce or cold in sandwiches spread with mustard mayonnaise.

1 cup fresh finely ground home-style bread crumbs
½ cup milk
2 cups mildly cured cooked ham, ground fine

½ cup finely ground lean fresh pork
1 tablespoon brown sugar
¼ teaspoon ground cloves
⅛ teaspoon cayenne pepper
1 large egg, lightly beaten

Preheated oven temperature: 350°F.
1. Combine the bread crumbs and milk in a small bowl. Set aside.
2. In a large bowl combine the ham, pork, brown sugar, cloves and cayenne pepper. Stir gently to blend. Add the bread crumb mixture and egg. Stir with a fork only until egg is barely incorporated.
3. Pack the mixture into a 5-cup loaf pan. Bake in preheated oven 50 minutes. Let rest 10 minutes before unmolding. Slice into serving portions.
Serves 6.

Variation: Caramel Ham Loaf

Butter or oil the bottom of the loaf pan. Combine ½ cup firmly packed brown sugar and ¼ teaspoon ground cloves. Spread evenly in the bottom of the loaf pan. If desired, arrange slices of canned pineapple over the brown sugar mixture. Pack the meat mixture firmly over the bottom layer. Bake as above.

Classic Regional Ham Sauces

Tart Mustard Sauce

1 chicken bouillon cube
½ cup cider vinegar
⅓ cup sugar

1½ tablespoons dry mustard
1 large egg, well beaten

1. In a small, heavy saucepan heat the bouillon cube, vinegar, sugar, and mustard until the sugar is dissolved.
2. Slowly whisk the hot mixture into the beaten egg.
3. Return the mixture to the saucepan and cook over low heat stirring constantly until thickened.

NOTE: This is a thin sauce; for thicker sauce use 2 large eggs. Serve hot or cold.
Yield: About ¾ cup.

Cold Mustard Sauce

This is a creamy, cold sauce to serve with sliced cold baked ham or ham mousse.

½ cup heavy cream
2 teaspoons sugar

3 tablespoons Dijon-style mustard

Whip the cream very stiff. Fold in sugar and mustard.
Yield: About 1 cup.

Raisin Sauce

½ cup light brown sugar
1 teaspoon dry mustard
2 tablespoons cornstarch
2 tablespoons cider vinegar

2 tablespoons lemon juice
1½ cups water
½ cup raisins

1. In a 1-quart, heavy saucepan mix the sugar, mustard and cornstarch. Slowly add the vinegar and stir until smooth. Add lemon juice, water, and raisins.
2. Cook over low heat about 5 minutes, stirring constantly, until the mixture has thickened. Serve hot.

Yield: 1½ cups.

Ham Pudding

This is one of the many ingenious Southern ways of using the last morsel of a good country-cured ham. Serve with mushroom or cheese sauce.

3 tablespoons unsalted butter	1½ cups finely ground cooked ham
½ cup finely chopped onion	½ teaspoon paprika
½ cup finely chopped celery	¾ teaspoon Dijon-style mustard
3 tablespoons flour	1 teaspoon baking powder
1 cup half-and-half	Salt (optional)
Yolks of 3 large eggs	Whites of 2 large eggs, stiffly beaten

Preheated oven temperature: 350°F.

1. In a heavy, 2-quart saucepan melt the butter and add the onion and celery. Cook until tender but not brown. Blend in flour and cook 3 minutes, stirring constantly.
2. Remove mixture from heat. Slowly add the half-and-half, stirring constantly to blend.
3. Return mixture to heat and cook slowly, stirring constantly, until thickened. Cool slightly.
4. Add a few tablespoons of the sauce to the egg yolks, 1 tablespoon at a time, stirring constantly to blend.
5. Slowly add the egg mixture to the sauce, stirring constantly to keep the egg mixture from separating. Add ham, paprika, mustard and baking powder. Stir well to blend. Add salt if desired. Gently fold in the stiffly beaten egg whites. Pour into 6 well-oiled 1-cup baking dishes. Bake in preheated oven 30 minutes, or until centers are firm. Unmold onto plates.

NOTE: These puddings will shrink to about ¾ cup per serving. Serve with desired sauce.

Serves 6.

Molded Ham Mousse

Ham mousse is a legacy from the bountiful plantation tables of the Colonial South. Use the leftover bits and pieces of a high-grade cooked, cured ham for this dish. This is one case in which leftover Smithfield ham can be used to good advantage. The blandness of the whipped cream will tame the very salty taste of the meat.

2 tablespoons Knox unflavored gelatin
½ cup boiling water
2 cups finely ground cooked ham
2 teaspoons Dijon-style mustard
4 teaspoons mayonnaise
1 tablespoon freshly grated horseradish, or less to taste
⅛ teaspoon Tabasco sauce

2 tablespoons finely chopped parsley
1 cup heavy cream
Leaf lettuce for garnish
Cold Mustard Sauce (optional, page 203)
Crystallized pickles for garnish (optional)

1. Dissolve the gelatin in the boiling water and set aside to cool.
2. Combine the ham, mustard, mayonnaise, horseradish, Tabasco sauce and parsley in a medium-sized bowl. Stir in the gelatin.
3. Whip the cream until very stiff and fold into the ham mixture.
4. Turn mixture into a 1-quart mold that has been rinsed in cold water or use 6 individual molds. Chill a few hours, until firm. Unmold and garnish with leafy lettuce. Use a pastry tube to decorate with optional Cold Mustard Sauce. Arrange optional sliced pickles around the mold.

Serves 6 to 8.

Fried Country Ham with Red-Eye Gravy

As many outlanders can verify, this is not the simplest dish to prepare. Traditionally served with hot biscuits and grits, this recipe is the Smoky Mountain way, handed down from one generation to another. One must have an iron skillet and a piece of country-cured ham about ¼ inch thick.

1. *Fry the Ham:* Place the ham in a medium-hot skillet; do not add fat. Brown the ham lightly on each side, taking care not to have the heat so high that it will dry out the ham. Transfer ham to a heated platter.
2. Pour off all but 1 tablespoon of ham fat from skillet, leaving browned bits in pan. Sprinkle with ¼ teaspoon sugar.
3. Place over high heat and stir constantly until sugar carmelizes. Do not let the sugar burn. Pour ¼ cup cold strong black coffee in the skillet and bring to a rapid boil, stirring constantly. Reduce the liquid until there is a layer of reddish-brown sauce on the bottom of the skillet. Add water to desired consistency. Bring to a boil again and serve on split biscuits or grits.

Serves 2-3.

Beef

Unlike the numerous improvised and inventive fish dishes in American cooking, those that use beef are relatively few. Granted that New Englanders have their boiled beef dinner and Yankee pot roast, Southerners have spiced beef and chicken-fried steak and Texans have barbecued beef, as a rule American cooks follow the basic tastes of the English, and roast, broil, or sauté quality cuts of beef. Only the less-tender cuts are slowly simmered in broth and seasonings.

Until about 1950, beef was reserved for special occasions. While Americans were luxuriating in postwar affluence, beef consumption began to soar. A well-aged steak on the table was a status symbol, reflecting economic success.

The popularity of the backyard barbecue, in which men demonstrated their cooking expertise at charcoal-grilling steaks and hamburgers, was another factor contributing to the rapid rise of beef consumption. Now that heavy meat-eating is on the decline in this country, I am reminded of the old saying, "The more things change, the more they remain the same." Having gone full cycle, we are back to the custom of eating beef only on special occasions.

Unfortunately, well-aged beef has become almost prohibitively expensive. Cattle, like porkers and poultry, are readied for market on a crash diet of fatting supplements, quickly slaughtered and then rushed to the retailers. A good piece of beef should be aged carefully by hanging in a cooling room at least 3 to 4 weeks to develop full flavor and to tenderize the tissues.

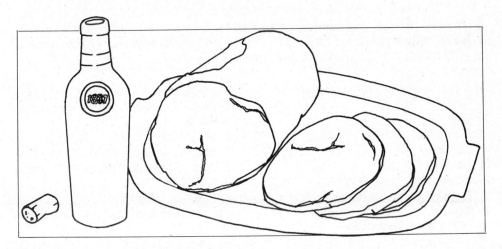

How to Buy Aged Beef

The best source of aged beef is a small individually owned meat market. It is still possible to arrange with a butcher in rural and suburban areas to buy a side of beef or smaller amount. He will hang the beef in his cooling room until aged to your taste. At this point he cuts and freezer-wraps the beef to specifications—that is, so much steak, ground meat, roasts, and so on. This ensures a ready source of good beef, plus the cost averages out per pound to be considerably less than if purchased in individual cuts from a quality market. The steaks and roasts can be prepared English-style; the less-desirable cuts can be utilized in preparing traditional American dishes.

Allow about ½ to ¾ pound of meat per serving, depending upon the amount of bone and gristle and what else is to be served in the menu.

Caution: Thaw meat to room temperature before cooking.

New England Boiled Dinner

A New England boiled dinner is something like a French *pot-au-feu* except that it is made with a large piece of corned beef brisket. Potatoes, carrots, cabbage and rutabagas, beets and sometimes parsnips and onions are arranged around a platter of thin-sliced beef.

The best corned beef is lightly corned, that is, it hasn't been in the brine too long. A reputable butcher is the best source of supply. *Caution:* If prepackaged in liquid, read the wrapper instructions carefully, because the brisket is usually highly spiced and should not be used to prepare this dish. If lightly corned brisket is not available, use kosher corned beef.

The old rules have been changed for cooking the vegetables. Formerly all the vegetables except the beets were tossed into the pot 1 hour before the beef had finished cooking. Modern American cooks prefer to boil or steam the vegetables separately.

1 5-pound lightly corned brisket of beef
Water
1 tablespoon pickling spices
1 bay leaf
1 clove garlic, split
6 whole black peppercorns
1 large whole green cabbage, cut in wedges
6 whole boiled potatoes
6 whole boiled or steamed carrots
6 medium-sized boiled onions (optional)
6 small boiled beets
1 or 2 rutabagas, sliced and boiled
3 large parsnips, halved and boiled (optional)
Parsley for garnish
Prepared mustard and cider vinegar

1. Rinse brisket well under running water to remove brine and place in a large kettle with a tight-fitting lid. Add water to cover, allowing enough room for meat to simmer without boiling over. Stir in the pickling spices, bay leaf, garlic and peppercorns.
2. Heat to boiling, skimming the surface if necessary. Cover and simmer 3 hours, or until meat is tender. Remove from heat and allow meat to cool in broth 1 hour. This can be done in advance.

NOTE: *Preheat in broth before serving.*

3. *Before serving, prepare the vegetables.*
   Steam or boil the cabbage, potatoes, carrots and onions—separately, if possible. Sprinkle lightly with salt and dress with a small amount of melted unsalted butter.
   Cut down tops of beets to ½ inch or less and boil the beets in their skins until tender. Remove skins and serve whole. Canned beets may be substituted.
   Boil the rutabagas and parsnips separately in about 1 inch of water with 1 teaspoon sugar until tender. Sprinkle lightly with salt and dress with a small amount of melted unsalted butter.
4. Remove the beef from the broth to a cutting board. Cut the meat across the grain into thin slices and arrange down the center of a large platter. Arrange the vegetables artistically around the meat. Garnish with parsley. Sprinkle the beets with vinegar and serve mustard from small bowl.

Serves 6 to 8. Use leftover beef and vegetables to make Red Flannel Hash (page 290).

Yankee Pot Roast

This is a no-nonsense one-dish meal with rich gravy. Generations of New England cooks have been taught that during the cooking a pot roast should "catch on" (stick to a cast-iron Dutch oven just enough to brown but not burn), thereby giving the sauce richness and savor.

1 4-to-5-pound boneless round, chuck or rump roast
Salt, freshly ground black pepper and flour for coating
Boiling water
2 thin slices salt pork (⅛ pound)
1 bay leaf
1 sprig parsley
1 teaspoon seedless raisins
2 tablespoons dark rum (optional)
6 whole boiled or steamed carrots
12 small boiled white onions
6 whole boiled potatoes
1 small rutabaga, sliced and boiled

1. Wipe meat with a damp cloth. Sprinkle with salt and pepper to taste. Coat well with flour.
2. Place the salt pork in a large flameproof casserole with a tight-fitting lid and fry until the pork is crisp and brown. Discard the pork.
3. Place the roast in the hot fat over medium-high heat and brown well on all sides. Use two wooden spoons to roll the meat.
4. Add enough boiling water to cover the bottom of the pan—about 1 cup. (Add water as needed to keep bottom of pan covered during cooking.) Add bay leaf, parsley, raisins and optional rum. Cover and simmer gently 3 hours, or until the meat is tender. Discard the bay leaf and parsley.
5. Transfer meat to a heated platter. Arrange cooked vegetables around the meat.
6. Skim as much fat as possible from liquid left in the pan. Return the liquid to high heat. Boil, stirring constantly with a wooden spoon to loosen the bits that cling to the sides and bottom of the pan, until liquid is reduced to gravylike thickness. Add salt and pepper, if desired. Serve with meat and vegetables.

Serves 6. Use leftover beef for sandwiches.

Rolled Roast of Beef

For generations Americans have served generous portions of roast beef and potatoes for family and company dinners. This undoubtedly has helped establish our reputation as a "meat and potatoes nation." Even though the meal may be served less frequently now than in the past, a juicy and tender roast of beef, accompanied by stuffed baked potatoes, is basic American cooking at its very best.

Always buy top quality beef. In selecting a good cut you should have a butcher whom you trust. My butcher recommends eye-round, sirloin-tip and, for very special occasions, the eye of a rib roast. Allow ⅓- to ½-pound of uncooked meat per person. Any butcher will roll and tie the roast, barding (covering) the meat with extra suet fat if necessary. This extra fat protects the roast and will keep it from drying out during cooking.

A reliable meat thermometer is almost a necessity to determine the preferred degree of doneness.

NOTE: A cooked roast should rest 15 minutes before it is to be carved. The internal heat will cook the roast a few degrees beyond the point indicated on the thermometer when the meat was first removed from the oven. Keep this in mind if you plan to serve rare beef.

4-to- 6 pound rolled roast of beef (eye-round, sirloin-tip or rib roast)	Salt and freshly ground black pepper to taste
	Crushed cloves of garlic (optional)

Preheated oven temperature: 500°F.

1. Season the meat by rubbing with salt, pepper and optional garlic.
2. Place the seasoned roast on rack in shallow roasting pan, insert meat thermometer half-way through the middle of the roast and sear at 500°F. for 30 minutes. Reduce heat to 325°F. This method will crisp the surface of the meat. The cooked meat will have a well-done ring around the outside of the slice with a juicy, rare middle. (If you want the beef well-done all the way through, roast at 250°F. the entire cooking time.) Baste the meat with the pan drippings a few times during the roasting period. Roast 15 to 25 minutes per pound or until the thermometer reads from 120°F. to 165°F., depending on how well-done you like your meat.
3. Remove the pan to heated platter. Let rest 15 minutes and remove strings and suet fat. Slice and serve with natural juices or pan gravy.

Serves 8 to 10.

To Serve with Natural Juices:
Remove fat from pan drippings, then reheat the liquid along with juices from the carved meat. Season with salt and freshly ground black pepper. Spoon over meat and serve.

To Serve with Pan-Gravy:
For each cup of gravy, use 2 tablespoons meat drippings, 1½ to 2 tablespoons flour and 1 cup water. Remove roast from pan and pour off all the fat. Measure the amount of drippings needed back into the pan. Blend in the flour with a wooden spoon. The amount of flour will depend on whether you want a thin or slightly thicker gravy. Place pan over low heat and cook, stirring constantly, until mixture bubbles and turns light brown. Remove from heat and gradually add the water, stirring constantly until mixture is smooth. Season with salt and freshly ground black pepper. Return to moderate heat and cook 5 minutes, stirring and scraping the sides of the pan until the gravy has thickened. Serve hot from sauceboat.

Stuffed Flank Steak

Prior to the international influence on American cooking that occurred after the second world war, flank steak usually was stuffed with a savory filling and tenderized by braising in a small amount of water. It was served in appetizing round slices cut across the grain and with pan gravy.

1 2-to-2½-pound flank steak
Add salt and freshly ground black pepper to taste
⅓ cup unsalted butter
2 tablespoons finely chopped green pepper
2 tablespoons finely chopped onion
2 tablespoons tomato paste
½ cup milk

2 cups dry home-style white bread cubes, without crusts
¼ teaspoon ground thyme
¼ teaspoon ground sage
¼ teaspoon ground marjoram
1 cup double-strength beef broth
1½ tablespoons cornstarch

Preheated oven temperature: 500°F.
1. Remove the tough membrane on the outside of the meat with a sharp knife. Pound to even thickness. Score one side of steak in a diamond pattern and rub this side with salt and pepper to taste. Place on a smooth surface, with cut side down.
2. Melt the butter in a medium-sized, heavy skillet. Add the onion and green pepper and cook over low heat, stirring constantly, until tender but not brown. Add 1 tablespoon of tomato paste and cook 5 minutes, stirring constantly. Add milk, bread cubes, thyme, sage and marjoram. Stir gently to blend. Add salt to taste.
3. Place the stuffing lengthwise down the center of the steak but not quite to the ends. Fold the short ends over stuffing and then bring long sides together and overlap to enclose stuffing. Skewer together with poultry pins.

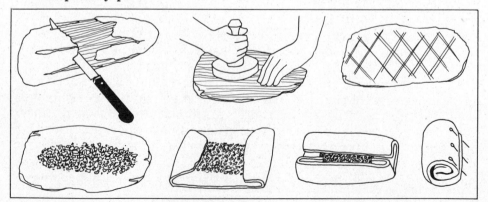

4. Place in a shallow baking pan, seam side down, and roast 15 minutes at 500°F. Reduce heat to 350°F. and continue baking 40 to 50 minutes, or until meat is tender. Remove from oven and transfer to a heated platter.
5. Add the remaining tablespoon of tomato paste to the pan drippings. Cook over low heat 5 minutes, stirring constantly. Blend the broth and cornstarch until smooth and add slowly to the pan mixture, stirring constantly to blend. Boil 1 minute, until the mixture is clear and thickened. Serve with sliced flank steak.

Serves 6.

Variation: Butterflied Flank Steak

After the steak has been trimmed of membranes, split, or "butterfly," it lengthwise, following the grain of the meat. Do not cut all the way through, but leave the steak in 1 piece. (If this seems difficult you can have your butcher do it for you.)

Pot Roast of Beef in the Southern Manner

This meat is cooked in a well-seasoned vegetable sauce that is spooned over whipped potatoes or long-grain white rice.

1 4-to-5-pound boneless round, chuck or rump roast
1 teaspoon salt, or to taste
¼ teaspoon freshly ground black pepper
3 to 4 tablespoons peanut oil or lard
1 cup thinly sliced onion rings
¼ cup finely chopped green pepper
½ cup finely chopped celery
2 tablespoons water
3 cups canned tomatoes with juice
½ cup sliced stuffed green olives
½ teaspoon Tabasco sauce, or less to taste

1. Wipe meat with a damp cloth. Sprinkle with salt and pepper.
2. Pour the peanut oil into a large flameproof casserole with a tight-fitting lid or a Dutch oven (or melt an equivalent amount of lard). Over medium-high heat brown the meat well on all sides; use two wooden spoons to roll the meat. When well browned, remove the meat and set aside.
3. Add the onion rings, green pepper, celery and water to the pan drippings. Cook, stirring constantly, until the vegetables are tender. Add tomatoes, olives and Tabasco sauce. Cook 5 minutes to blend flavors.
4. Return the browned meat to the pan. Cover and simmer gently 3 hours, or until the meat is tender. Transfer meat to a platter and slice.

Serves 8.

Western Swiss Steak
(Basic Recipe)

This recipe, sometimes known as Denver swiss steak, is a Western alteration of New England smothered beef, with many variations. It is generally accepted that the dish should contain tomatoes and onions, but the seasonings can be changed according to regional tastes; that is, with the use of chili powder or herbs, and so on.

1 2-pound boneless round steak, cut 2½ inches thick
½ cup flour
1½ teaspoons salt, or to taste
½ teaspoon freshly ground black pepper, or to taste
2 tablespoons unsalted butter

1 cup thinly sliced onion
½ cup chopped green pepper
1 clove garlic, chopped fine
1 cup peeled, seeded and chopped tomatoes
1 cup boiling water or beef broth
2 tablespoons peanut oil

1. Wipe meat with a damp cloth.
2. Combine the flour, salt and pepper. With a mallet or the edge of a plate, pound all of the flour mixture into both sides of the steak. Refrigerate about 30 minutes.
3. In a small, heavy saucepan melt the butter and add the onion, green pepper and garlic. Cook over low heat, stirring constantly, until vegetables are tender. Add the tomatoes and cook 5 minutes longer. Add the water or broth and more salt and pepper to taste. Set aside.
4. Heat the peanut oil in a flameproof casserole with a tight-fitting lid or in a Dutch oven. Brown the meat well over medium heat on both sides. Pour off any excess fat.
5. Pour the reserved sauce over the meat. Cover and simmer gently about 1¼ hours, or until meat is tender. Add more liquid during the cooking if the sauce begins to stick to the bottom of the pan. Slice meat and serve with sauce.

Serves 6.

My Mother's Country-Fried Steak
(Chicken-Fried Steak)

Pounding and pan-frying round steak is an old-fashioned method of tenderizing a tough cut of meat. Once considered hearty farm fare, steak prepared in this manner currently is featured on the menus of many trendy restaurants in the South. Serve with French fries, country fries or with mashed potatoes and cream gravy.

The steak should be fried to a crisp and crunchy brown in freshly rendered lard or beef suet, or use equal parts peanut oil and unsalted butter. Allow about 6 ounces of meat per serving.

About 2¼ pounds boneless round
  steak, cut ½-inch thick
1 cup flour
1½ teaspoons salt, or to taste
2 teaspoons freshly ground black
  pepper
Freshly rendered lard or suet or peanut oil and unsalted butter for frying

1 tablespoon flour
2 cups milk
Salt and freshly ground black pepper
  to taste
A few sprinklings of cayenne pepper
  (optional)

1. Pound steak with a mallet or the edge of a plate until fibers are broken. *Caution:* Do not cut the surface of the meat. Often the butcher will prepare this for you.
2. Combine the flour, salt and pepper in a plastic bag. (The flavor of freshly ground pepper is important). Shake well to blend and empty out onto a flat baking dish.
3. Cut the meat into individual serving pieces. Coat the pieces all over with the flour mixture and place on a tray; pieces should not touch. Refrigerate at least 30 minutes.
4. Melt lard or suet to a depth of ¼ inch in a 10-to-12-inch cast-iron or electric skillet (or use an equivalent amount of peanut oil and butter). The skillet should be large enough to hold the pieces in one layer without touching. Heat the fat over medium-high heat until hot but not smoking. Carefully place the pieces in the hot fat. Cook, without turning, until golden brown on one side. Turn the pieces and when meat starts to brown, add boiling water to barely cover the bottom of the pan. Partially cover the skillet and reduce heat to medium-low. Continue cooking until meat is tender. Add more water if meat begins to fry. Transfer meat to heated platter.
5. *To make cream gravy:* Pour off all but 2 tablespoons of the fat in the skillet. With a wooden spoon scrape the sides and bottom of the skillet to loosen browned bits. Add 1 tablespoon of flour and cook 3 minutes, stirring constantly. Remove from heat and slowly stir in 2 cups of milk.

   Return to medium heat and boil about 5 minutes, until the gravy has thickened. If a thicker gravy is desired, boil longer. Add more salt and pepper to taste and a few sprinklings of optional cayenne pepper. Spoon over steak and serve very hot.

Serves 6.

Grillades
(Gree-yads)

This is a Creole breakfast dish traditionally served with grits. It is also frequently served by French Quarter restaurants for Sunday brunch and midnight breakfasts on Mardi Gras. Grillades (gree-yads) is a term used in and around New Orleans for pan-sautéed pieces of boneless beef or veal.

1 to 1½ pounds boneless round steak, cut ½ inch thick
Salt and freshly ground black pepper to taste
Cayenne pepper to taste
2 tablespoons peanut oil

1½ tablespoons flour
1 cup chopped onion
½ cup chopped green pepper
1 clove garlic, chopped fine
2 large tomatoes, peeled, seeded and chopped
1 cup hot water

1. Pound steak with a mallet or the edge of a plate until fibers are broken.
2. Cut the meat into grillades about 4 inches square. Season the meat well with salt, black pepper and cayenne pepper.
3. Heat the peanut oil in a 10- to 12-inch, heavy skillet over medium-high heat until hot but not smoking. Brown the meat on both sides. Remove and set aside.
4. Add the flour to the remaining fat in the skillet. Add more oil if necessary. Cook 3 minutes, stirring constantly. Add the onion, green pepper and garlic. Continue cooking until vegetables are tender. Add tomatoes and cook 5 minutes longer. Add hot water and stir to blend; add more hot water if the sauce seems too thick. Add salt and black pepper to taste.
5. Arrange the browned grillades on top of the sauce. Cover and simmer 30 minutes, or until meat is tender. Serve hot with sauce.

Serves 4 to 6.

Stuffed Meat Loaf

Meat loaf is probably the most maligned dish in this country, and one that is almost impossible to find properly prepared in a public eating place. Unlike the French, who relish pâtés, Americans have always preferred to cut their meat with a knife.

The basis for a good meat loaf begins with lean ground round or chuck and quality ingredients.

½ pound fresh mushrooms, chopped fine

2 tablespoons unsalted butter

¾ cup finely chopped onion

½ cup finely chopped celery

½ teaspoon ground thyme

¾ cup heavy cream

1 cup freshly ground home-style bread crumbs

Salt and freshly ground black pepper to taste

2 pounds lean ground round or chuck

2 large eggs, lightly beaten

Preheated oven temperature: 450° F.

1. Cook the mushrooms in a medium-sized, heavy skillet in the butter over medium-low heat until about half the liquid from the mushrooms has evaporated. Add the onion, celery and thyme. Continue cooking until vegetables are tender and all the liquid in the skillet has evaporated. Add ½ cup of the cream and simmer 5 minutes. Gently mix in the bread crumbs and add salt and pepper to taste. Set aside.
2. Very gently mix the ground meat in a large mixing bowl with the remaining ¼ cup heavy cream, the eggs and salt and pepper to taste. *Caution:* Mix only until egg is just incorporated.
3. Line the bottom and sides of an 8-x-4-x-2-inch loaf pan with about three fourths of the meat mixture, leaving enough room for the stuffing. Add the mushroom mixture and pat remaining meat mixture over stuffing, enclosing it completely. Bake in preheated oven 20 minutes; reduce temperature to 350°F. and bake 30 minutes longer. Unmold and slice. Serve hot.

Serves 8.

Creamed Chipped Beef

Dried beef, a standard shelf item prior to World War II, has become an expensive luxury food. Serve over hot biscuits, toast or waffles.

½ pound dried beef

Boiling water

3 tablespoons unsalted butter

3 tablespoons flour

2 cups milk

¼ teaspoon freshly ground black pepper

⅛ teaspoon freshly grated nutmeg (optional)

1. With the fingers, shred the beef into small pieces. Cover with boiling water to freshen. Drain well and set aside.
2. In a heavy, 1½-quart saucepan melt the butter and add the flour. Cook 3 minutes, stirring constantly.
3. Remove from heat and slowly add the milk, stirring constantly to blend. Add the pepper, optional nutmeg and drained beef.

4. Return to heat and cook about 5 minutes, stirring constantly, until mixture has thickened. Serve hot over biscuits, toast or waffles.
Serves 4.

Variation: California-Style Creamed Chipped Beef

In Step 3 add ⅓ cup sliced, pitted ripe olives. In Step 4 add ½ cup cubed avocado just before serving.

Texas Barbecued Beef

Texas barbecue is a legend—famed in story, song and film.

In Texas, real barbecue is cooked very slowly over an enormous open pit with the fire on one end and the meat on the other. It is cooked slowly between 45 and 60 minutes per pound without turning, until very well done. But any backyard chef with a charcoal grill and a few basic cooking skills can do an admirable job.

NOTE: Meat cooked directly over charcoal will require frequent turning and basting. The cooking time should be about 30 minutes per pound.

An authentic Texas barbecue is a festival accompanied with plenty of Lone Star beer, Texas potato salad and lots of fun!

Ground Rules for Barbecuing Texas Style

Brisket is considered the ultimate cut of beef for barbecuing, although no one in Texas knows exactly why. The meat marketing specialist for the Texas Department of Agriculture thinks it may be because briskets formerly were so inexpensive.

Briskets are cut from the breast of the animal and should weigh at least 8 pounds. According to the TDA, those that weigh less come from younger animals and won't have the necessary grain and juiciness. Briskets should be lean but with a moderate amount of fat for flavor; USDA "choice" and "good" grades are considered best. *Caution:* Do not use "prime" grade briskets because they usually have too much fat.

Building a Fire for Barbecuing

Caution: Always start with a clean grill. Besides having a stale taste, old grease can be a fire hazard. Start the fire at least 45 minutes before you plan to begin barbecuing. Texas barbecue is cooked over wood.

Most barbecuers prefer mesquite or oak, and for a little tang, some pecan. "About 2 or 3 pieces the size of your wrist for an 8-hour cooking period," suggests one Texas expert, who says that too much pecan can result in bitterness. For the backyard expert, charcoal and wood chips will suffice. The bed of coals should be several inches longer and wider than the brisket. Coals are ready when white ash forms on the charcoal.

How to Prepare Brisket for Barbecuing

Wipe an 8-to-10-pound brisket with a damp cloth. Rub the meat well with cloves of cut garlic to taste. Season well by rubbing all over with salt and freshly ground black pepper.

How to Barbecue

1. Place the meat over the coals with fat side up. Experts differ on whether to sear the brisket close to the coals for 30 to 40 minutes before raising the grill or to place the meat at least 8 inches from the coals for the entire cooking time at approximately 300°F. Either way is fine. Add additional charcoal and wood chips during the cooking time to smoke-cook the meat.
2. Baste lightly with Basting Sauce (below) every 15 to 20 minutes to keep the meat moist during the long cooking period.

NOTE: Never baste the brisket with barbecue sauce while cooking; this will cause it to burn. A barbecue sauce may be used for basting during the last few minutes of cooking, but usually is served on the side or poured over the meat just before serving.

3. Use tongs to turn meat. For maximum moistness, never stick a fork into the cooking meat. About 1½ hours before brisket is done, wrap in foil to preserve moisture and continue to cook until tender.
    Slice across the grain and serve. Allow about ½ pound meat per serving.

Basting Sauce for Texas Barbecued Beef

1 cup unsalted butter	1 teaspoon salt
½ cup finely chopped onion	1 teaspoon freshly ground black pepper
¼ cup cider vinegar	

1. Melt the butter in a small, heavy saucepan. Add the onion and cook until translucent but not brown. Add vinegar, salt and pepper. Simmer 10 minutes.
2. "Mop" or brush brisket lightly every 15 to 20 minutes with sauce.

Barbecue Sauce for Texas Barbecued Beef

1 14-ounce bottle catsup
1 5-ounce bottle Worcestershire sauce
1 cup cider vinegar
½ cup brown sugar, firmly packed
2 tablespoons dry mustard

2 tablespoons fresh or prepared horseradish
1 tablespoon Louisiana Hot Sauce
1 12-ounce can beer
3 tablespoons unsalted butter
3 tablespoons lemon juice
Salt to taste

Combine all the ingredients in a heavy, 2½-quart saucepan and simmer, stirring often, until sauce is thick. Serve over sliced beef or on the side. **Yield: About 1 quart.**

Texas Barbecued Steak

1 cup red Burgundy wine
1 tablespoon finely chopped parsley
1 bay leaf
½ teaspoon salt
½ cup finely chopped onion

1 clove garlic, crushed
¼ teaspoon ground thyme
2 pounds porterhouse, sirloin, T-bone, club or tenderloin steak, 1½ inches thick

1. Combine the wine, parsley, bay leaf, salt, onion, garlic and thyme in a shallow glass dish large enough to hold the steak in one layer.
2. Place steak in marinade and refrigerate overnight, turning once.
3. Remove steak from marinade. Strain marinade and reserve.
4. Grill the steak over charcoal until desired doneness.
5. Heat the reserved marinade to serve as a meat sauce.
Serves 4.

Texas Barbecued Beef Kabobs

2½ pounds lean beef, cut into 1½-inch cubes
¾ cup peanut oil
¾ cup red wine vinegar
¾ cup finely chopped onion
3 tablespoons Worcestershire sauce
1½ teaspoons dried basil, crushed

1 teaspoon dried rosemary, crushed
¾ teaspoon freshly ground black pepper
½ teaspoon Louisiana Hot Sauce, or more to taste
¾ pound thin bacon slices, blanched and cut into pieces, to wrap steak cubes

Recommended vegetables

Green pepper wedges   Mushroom caps
Cherry tomatoes   Small new potatoes
Onion wedges

1. Trim meat cubes of gristle and excess fat. Place in a large bowl.
2. Combine the peanut oil, vinegar, chopped onion, Worcestershire sauce, basil, rosemary, pepper and hot sauce in a jar and shake well to blend. Pour over the beef cubes, cover and marinate in the refrigerator 4 to 6 hours or overnight.
3. Remove the cubes from the marinade. Strain and reserve the marinade.
4. Wrap steak cubes in bacon slices and thread on skewers, alternating with 3 or 4 of the recommended vegetables.
5. Grill over charcoal until done, approximately 12 to 15 minutes, turning and basting frequently with the strained marinade, until meat is browned and vegetables are tender.

Serves 6.

Hamburgers

A hamburger may be *boeuf haché* in the French language, but when it is placed on a roll and garnished with lettuce, mayonnaise and tomato, it is America's favorite sandwich.

As a teen-ager I worked part-time in a popular sandwich shop on a university campus. The cooks were instructed to make the hamburgers in the manner indicated below, and it has been my favorite cooking method ever since. The secret to making a nice, juicy hamburger is to buy ground chuck with a small amount of fat ground into the beef. Very lean beef makes a dry hamburger.

2 pounds ground beef, preferably   1 tablespoon peanut oil combined
  ground chuck   with 2 tablespoons unsalted butter
2 tablespoons finely chopped onion   6 hamburger rolls
2 teaspoons salt   Mayonnaise, lettuce and tomato slices
Freshly ground black pepper to taste   for garnish
Flour for coating

1. Remove the ground meat from the refrigerator at least 1 hour before using and place on paper toweling. Pat with the toweling to remove excess moisture but do not press hard enough to extract any of the juice in the meat.

2. Mix the onion, salt and pepper into the meat with the fingertips.
   Caution: Do this gently, just enough to distribute the ingredients;
   too much handling will cause the cooked hamburger to be tough and
   hard.
3. Divide the meat into 6 portions. Shape each portion into a patty
   about 1 inch thick in the center and slightly less around the edges.
   With the hands, pat flour coating all over the cakes—not too much,
   just enough to seal in the juices.
4. Heat the oil and butter in a large, heavy, 10-to-12-inch skillet until
   hot but not smoking. Place the patties in the skillet and sauté over
   high heat, turning with a spatula, until both sides are evenly
   browned. Allow a total cooking time of 6 minutes for rare, 10 minutes
   for medium and 15 for very well done. Serve at once on hamburger
   rolls spread with mayonnaise and garnished with lettuce and tomato
   slices.

Serves 6.

Lamb

A lamb is a young sheep under one year of age. Over one year, the slaughtered sheep is referred to as mutton.

In the early 18th century the Fathers in the Spanish missions in the Southwest raised a strain of sheep brought to this country from Spain. However, the English placed strict limitations on the importation of sheep into their American colonies. Consequently, adventurous sea captains profiteered by smuggling the animals into eastern ports, where they were sold in the black market.

After the Revolution, fresh lamb became more plentiful and was a staple of the American table. Albeit probably overcooked, lamb and mutton graced the tables of Martha Washington, Thomas Jefferson, Dolley Madison, Rachel Jackson and other notables of the period. Subsequent generations of American farmers have continued to improve strains of sheep, producing larger, meatier animals than those first scraggly ones smuggled into the colonies.

Lamb Cooking Basics

Good-quality lamb, like beef, should be aged to develop flavor and tenderness.

If cooked properly, lamb will not have an unpleasant flavor. Except as a steak, lamb never should be cooked beyond medium-rare; that is, nice, pink and juicy on the inside and crisp and brown on the outside. To determine the degree of doneness, one should use a reliable meat thermometer. When the thermometer reaches the desired temperature, remove meat immediately to a hot platter to prevent overcooking.

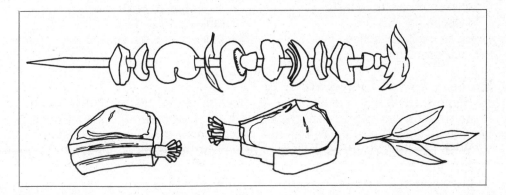

How to Purchase Lamb

The color of lamb varies with the age of the animal. Very young lamb will be very lean and light pink. Spring lamb, young animals slaughtered between March and September, will still be lean but will be a deeper pink. A dark pinkish-red lean meat indicates the lamb is about one year of age. The fat on good-quality lamb should be firm, white, waxy and somewhat brittle.

Three Meals from a 6-to-8-Pound Leg of Lamb*

1. Have the butcher remove the sirloin portion of the lamb leg or do it yourself.
NOTE: If doing it yourself, first remove the parchmentlike tissue called the fell, which covers the outer fat. The sirloin is delicious as a small roast for 4 or sliced into 4 sirloin steaks for broiling or grilling.
2. Trim the remaining lamb of bits and pieces to make stew for 4 servings.
3. About three fourths of the trimmed leg of lamb will be left to roast or grill—bone in, bone out or butterflied. Serves 4.
*(Recommended by the American Lamb Council)

Farm-Style Roast Leg of Lamb

Sometimes known as Swedish roast lamb or Swedish-American farm-style leg of lamb, this is a popular recipe in the Midwest.

1 5-to-6-pound leg of lamb, with bone in	1 cup plus 2 tablespoons heavy cream
1 to 2 cloves of garlic, slivered	¼ cup brandy
1 tablespoon salt, or to taste	2 tablespoons water
1 teaspoon dry mustard	3 tablespoons flour
1 cup strong black coffee	2 tablespoons red currant jelly
2 teaspoons sugar	

Preheated oven temperature: 350°F.
1. Remove the fell and most of the fat from the meat or have the butcher do this for you. With a small, sharp knife make enough 1-inch-deep cuts all over the top of the meat to accommodate the slivers of garlic. With the fingertips, push the garlic well into the meat. Combine the salt and mustard and rub the mixture well over the entire surface of the meat. Place on rack in a shallow roasting pan.

2. In a small bowl combine the coffee, sugar, the 2 tablespoons cream, the brandy and water.
3. Brush coffee mixture over the surface of the prepared roast. Place in preheated oven. Baste the meat frequently with the coffee mixture.
4. After the roast has been in the oven 1 hour, insert a meat thermometer into the thickest part of the meat, being careful not to touch the bone. Allow about 15 minutes roasting time per pound of meat, or until the thermometer registers 130°-135°F. for rare, 140°-145°F. for medium-rare or 160°F. or more for well done. Remove the roast to a hot platter and let rest 10 to 15 minutes before carving.
5. Skim off the fat from the sauce in the roasting pan and add the flour. Cook 3 minutes, stirring constantly.
6. Remove from heat and slowly stir in the 1 cup heavy cream, stirring constantly until smooth.
7. Return mixture to low heat. Stir in jelly and cook 2 minutes, or until thickened. Serve hot over sliced meat or from a sauceboat.

Serves 8.

Boned Leg of Lamb with Chestnut Stuffing

This recipe is a legacy from the days when chestnut trees covered much of the eastern part of this country. Canned chestnut puree can be substituted here for the tedious task of boiling or roasting, peeling and mashing whole chestnuts. Garnish the roast lamb with prunes, pitted and stuffed with a whole roasted chestnut or a teaspoon of mint or red currant jelly.

1 6-to-7-pound leg of lamb, boned and trimmed of excess fat
Juice of 1 lemon
Salt to taste
Freshly ground black pepper to taste
2 tablespoons unsalted butter
2 cups chestnut puree
2 cups coarsely ground dry bread crumbs
1 teaspoon lemon juice
¼ teaspoon freshly ground nutmeg

1 teaspoon salt, or to taste
¼ teaspoon freshly ground black pepper, or more to taste
1 large carrot, diced
1 large onion, coarsely chopped
½ teaspoon dried rosemary
1¼ cups double strength chicken broth
1¼ cups beef broth
1 cup dry white wine

Preheated oven temperature: 400°F.
1. Have the butcher remove the fell and butterfly the lamb—that is, bone and shape it so that it lies as flat as possible. Place the lamb on a flat surface, skin side down, and rub it with lemon juice. Then season it well with salt and pepper.

2. To make the stuffing, melt the butter in a heavy skillet. Stir in the chestnut puree, bread crumbs, lemon juice, nutmeg, salt and pepper. Whip with a wooden spoon until fluffy.
3. Spread the stuffing mixture over the lamb and into the pockets left by the boning.
4. Roll the meat into a cylindrical shape to enclose the stuffing completely. Tie loops of string around the roll to hold its shape and place in a roasting pan. Surround the lamb with the carrot, onion and rosemary and place in preheated oven.
5. Combine the chicken broth, beef broth and wine. Baste the lamb with this mixture after 15 minutes of roasting. Continue basting every 10 to 15 minutes for another 1 hour and 10 minutes, or until the roast is medium-rare (140°-145°F.). Remove roast to a hot platter and let rest 10 minutes before carving.
6. Puree the sauce left in the pan in a blender or food processor. Add more salt and pepper to taste. Reheat the sauce and serve very hot from sauceboat.

Serves 8 to 10.

Chestnut Puree

1 pound unshelled chestnuts   Cold water to cover

1. With a sharp knife cut a gash in the flat side of each chestnut.
2. Cover nuts with water and boil for 15 to 20 minutes or until tender. Remove a few at a time, leaving the remainder in the hot water, and peel off outer and inner skins.
3. Force the chestnuts through a food mill or process in food processor until smooth.

Yield: 2 cups puree.

Barbecued Leg of Lamb

The ground rules for barbecuing a leg of lamb are the same as for Texas Barbecued Beef, page 218.

1 8-pound leg of lamb with bone in   Basting Sauce
4 to 6 cloves garlic   Barbecue Sauce
Salt and freshly ground black pepper
  to taste

1. Remove the fell and trim off the excess fat from an 8-pound leg of lamb with bone in.
2. Rub the meat well with cloves of garlic to taste. Season by rubbing all over with salt and freshly ground black pepper.
3. Follow instructions for barbecuing beef. Baste frequently with Basting Sauce. Cook lamb until the thermometer registers 130°-135°F. for rare, 140°-145°F. for medium-rare or 160°F. or more for well done.

NOTE: The cooking time for lamb is considerably less than for well-done brisket of beef; the timing depends upon the heat and depth of the coals, etc.

During the last 30 minutes of cooking, brush the lamb with Texas Barbecue Sauce. Serve extra sauce on the side.

Serves 8 to 10.

Braised Lamb Shanks

This is a Southern dish with a hearty flavor. Serve with rice or noodles.

6 lamb shanks
1 teaspoon salt, or to taste
Freshly ground black pepper to taste
¼ cup peanut oil
2 tablespoons flour
1 cup chopped onion
2 cloves garlic, chopped fine
½ cup chopped celery

1 large carrot, peeled and chopped
⅔ cup tomato puree
1 cup chicken broth or water
1 bay leaf
½ cup dry red wine
Salt and freshly ground black pepper to taste

Preheated oven temperature: 350°F.
1. Wipe the lamb shanks dry with paper towels and rub well with salt and pepper.
2. Heat the oil in a 10-to-12-inch, heavy skillet until hot but not smoking. When the oil is sizzling, add the lamb shanks and quickly brown on all sides. As shanks brown, remove and place in a large, heavy roasting pan with a tight-fitting lid.
3. After all the shanks have been removed to the roasting pan, add the flour to the skillet and cook 3 minutes, stirring constantly. Add the onion, garlic, celery and carrot. Cover the skillet and cook, stirring occasionally, until the vegetables are tender. Add the tomato puree and cook an additional 5 minutes. Stir in the chicken broth or water, bay leaf and red wine. Season to taste with salt and pepper.
4. Transfer all ingredients to the roasting pan with the meat. Cover and bake in preheated oven 1½ to 2 hours, or until meat is tender. Discard bay leaf. Serve sauce over lamb shanks.

Serves 6.

Veal

Traditional American cooking does not include many veal dishes. Perhaps the reason is that in this country grassland is plentiful and there is little point in slaughtering very young dairy bull calves.

During the Great Depression unscrupulous restaurants often substituted veal for chicken, which was more expensive and preferred by most Americans. In fact, in older cookbooks you often will see veal referred to as "mock chicken."

Veal comes from calves that weigh approximately 90 to 100 pounds at birth. How the calves are fed and cared for determines the quality and type of veal.

Bob veal comes from calves that are slaughtered early, usually less than a week old. The flesh is pale in color and has not matured sufficiently to be satisfactory for eating.

Grain-Fed veal comes from calves that are allowed to grow about 16 weeks. The color of the meat is fairly red and the taste is considered less delicate than milk-fed veal. It is often referred to as "baby beef."

Milk-Fed veal comes from calves raised for about 15 weeks to a weight of 325 to 350 pounds. The animals are pampered by being kept in individual stalls in temperature- and humidity-controlled barns and fed a special milk formula fortified with vitamins and minerals. This is the finest quality veal available. It can be distinguished by its creamy pink color, firm texture and even marbling throughout. Milk-fed veal is being distributed all across the United States. If necessary, ask your local butcher to special-order for you.

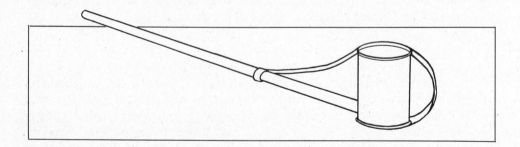

Veal Cooking Basics

The important thing to remember about veal is that it shouldn't be overcooked.

Grain-fed veal is the quality most often available in this country. Roasting and braising are the two most preferred cooking methods. Braising requires the veal to be cooked in a small amount of liquid or veal stock. Veal stock can be made in quantity and frozen in 2-cup portions. Otherwise substitute double-strength chicken broth (page 26).

Marinated Roast of Veal

This is a Southern-style method of roasting veal. Serve with buttered noodles or new potatoes and a green salad.

1 5-to-6 pound boneless shoulder or rump of veal, rolled and tied
2 thin slices lean bacon, blanched and diced
1 teaspoon dried marjoram
1 teaspoon ground thyme
¼ cup freshly chopped parsley

1 cup finely chopped onion
1 clove garlic, chopped fine
½ cup light olive or vegetable oil
½ cup lemon juice
Salt and freshly ground black pepper to taste
About 1 cup chicken broth

Preheated Oven Temperature: 325°F.
1. Place the veal in a large, shallow roasting pan.
2. Combine the bacon, marjoram, thyme, parsley, onion, garlic, oil and lemon juice in a small saucepan. Simmer over low heat 5 minutes to blend flavors. Pat mixture over meat. Cover and marinate in the refrigerator at least 12 hours.
3. Remove the meat from the marinade and reserve marinade. Wipe the meat dry with paper towels and rub with salt and pepper to taste.
4. Return the meat to the roasting pan and insert a meat thermometer. Place in preheated oven and baste about every 20 minutes with reserved marinade. When the meat has reached an internal temperature of 160°–165°F., about 2½ hours, remove to a warm platter. Let rest 10 to 15 minutes before carving.
5. Strain the pan juices and return to roasting pan. If necessary add chicken broth to thin out the sauce. Reheat and serve hot from a sauceboat.
Serves 10 to 12.

Veal Daube
(Pot Roast)

This highly seasoned pot roast is a superb example of Creole cooking. Use a less-expensive, grain-fed veal roast in preparing this recipe. Serve with rice and a green salad.

1   4-to-5 pound boneless shoulder or rump of veal, rolled and tied
2   tablespoons bacon drippings
1   clove garlic, chopped fine
1   teaspoon salt
¼   teaspoon cayenne pepper, or less to taste
¼   teaspoon freshly ground black pepper
⅛   teaspoon ground mace
⅛   teaspoon ground cloves
¼   teaspoon ground allspice
2   bay leaves, crushed

½   teaspoon ground thyme
½   teaspoon ground sage
¼   cup flour
¼   cup unsalted butter, combined with ¼ cup peanut oil
1   cup chopped onion
4   carrots, sliced thin
1   white turnip, quartered
½   cup chopped celery
½   cup chopped red or green pepper
1   cup boiling veal stock or chicken broth

1. Wipe the meat dry with paper towels and rub well with the bacon drippings.
2. Combine the garlic, salt, cayenne, black pepper, mace, cloves, allspice, bay leaves, thyme, sage and flour in a blender or food processor. Process until well mixed. Rub this mixture well all over the meat and set aside.
3. In a Dutch oven or flameproof casserole with a tight-fitting lid heat the butter and peanut oil until hot but not smoking. Brown the meat on all sides. Remove and set aside. Add the onion, carrots, turnip, celery and red or green pepper to the fat remaining in the pan and cook until all the vegetables are lightly browned. Add more butter and oil if necessary.
4. Return the meat to the pan and add the veal stock or chicken broth. Cover and simmer 2 to 2½ hours, or until the meat is tender. Remove the meat to a heated platter and let rest 10 to 15 minutes before serving.
5. Skim off fat and puree the pan juices in blender or food processor; return to pan. If necessary, add more veal stock or chicken broth to thin out the sauce. Reheat and serve hot from sauceboat.

Serves 8.

Veal Birds

Veal birds are thin slices of meat filled with bread stuffing, rolled, tied and slowly braised until tender.

6 slices of veal cut from the leg, about 5 inches square, pounded ¼-inch thick

Lemon juice
Salt and freshly ground black pepper to taste

Stuffing

3 tablespoons unsalted butter
2 tablespoons chopped onion
½ cup chopped celery
¼ teaspoon salt

¼ teaspoon freshly ground black pepper
¼ teaspoon ground sage
1¼ cups fresh bread crumbs

Sauce

3 tablespoons unsalted butter
2 tablespoons peanut oil
2 cups thinly sliced mushrooms (optional)
1¼ cups veal stock or chicken broth

1 tablespoon cornstarch, combined with 1 tablespoon water
½ cup heavy cream or sour cream
Lemon slices and parsley for garnish

1. Rub the veal with lemon juice and sprinkle with salt and pepper to taste. Set aside.

Stuffing
2. Melt the butter in a heavy skillet and add the onion and celery. Cook until vegetables are tender but not brown. Add the salt, pepper, sage and bread crumbs and stir well to blend.
3. Divide the stuffing mixture into sixths and place a dollop on the end of each square of veal. Roll up each square and then tie both ends with thin string.

Sauce

4. Heat the butter and peanut oil in a 10-to-12-inch, heavy skillet until hot but not smoking. Sauté rolls on all sides until nicely browned. Add the optional mushrooms and continue cooking 1 minute. Add the veal stock or chicken broth and bring to a boil. Cover and simmer over very low heat 35 to 40 minutes, until tender. Remove veal rolls to a heated platter and keep warm.

5. Add the cornstarch mixture to the sauce in the pan and stir well to blend. Add the heavy cream or sour cream and reheat to serving temperature. *Caution:* To prevent the sauce from curdling, do not boil the mixture after the cream is added. Remove string, pour the sauce over the veal rolls and garnish the platter with thin lemon slices and fresh parsley.

Serves 4 to 6.

Variety Meats

Heart, tongue and liver from pork, young calves and beef cattle are the three most often used variety meats in American kitchens.

Sometimes partially prepared meats, including scrapple, head-cheese and sausages made from combinations of ground meat also are classed as variety meats.

Stuffed Tongue Acadienne

Cajun cooks, with their French ancestry, have used veal and beef tongues to create distinctive American regional recipes. This one is a fine example. Slice in rounds and serve with white rice and pan gravy.

1 fresh veal or beef tongue, cleaned (about 2 pounds)
1 tablespoon salt
Water to cover tongue
4 cloves garlic, slivered
Salt to taste
Freshly ground black pepper to taste

1 whole carrot, peeled
½ cup chopped green pepper
¼ cup peanut oil or bacon drippings
1 cup chopped onion
About 1 cup water
¼ cup red wine (optional)

1. Boil tongue in water to cover with the 1 tablespoon salt in a large kettle for 15 minutes. Remove the water and cool enough to handle. Discard water.
2. Cut off bone and gristle at thick end of tongue. With a sharp knife cut a pocket in the side of the tongue large enough to hold the whole carrot and green pepper.

3. With a sharp, pointed knife cut small slits, evenly spaced, all over the surface of the tongue and insert the garlic slivers.
4. Rub salt and pepper all over the inside and outside of the tongue. Place the carrot and green pepper in the pocket. Sew or skewer opening together.
5. In a Dutch oven or flameproof casserole with a tight-fitting lid, brown the tongue all over in the peanut oil or bacon fat and set aside.
6. Cook the onion lightly in the remaining fat, adding more oil if necessary to keep the onions from burning.
7. Return the meat to the pan with the onion. Add about 1 cup of water and the optional wine to the pan. Cover and simmer about 2 hours, or until the tongue is tender, adding more water as needed.
8. Remove to a platter and slice in ¼-inch rounds. Slice the narrow part of tongue on a diagonal, gradually turning knife, until the thickest part is cut into crosswise slices. Serve with pan gravy.

Serves 6.

Braised Veal Hearts

Veal hearts have always been held in high regard in my family. This recipe has had much use. You will need a large, heavy skillet with a tight-fitting lid. Serve with buttered noodles and a green salad.

4 veal hearts	½ canned pimiento, chopped
Flour for coating	1 teaspoon salt, or to taste
4 slices lean bacon	Freshly ground black pepper to taste
1 large onion, sliced thin	1 small bay leaf
1 cup veal stock or chicken broth	

1. Clean hearts and remove membrane and large veins with a sharp knife. Cut into ½-inch slices and coat with flour. Refrigerate until needed.
2. Fry the bacon until crisp; crumble and reserve.
3. Place the coated slices in the hot fat and fry until crisp and brown on both sides. Remove and set aside.
4. Add the onion to the fat remaining in the skillet and cook, stirring constantly, until tender but not brown.
5. Return the browned slices of meat to the skillet. Add the veal stock or chicken broth, pimiento, salt, pepper and bay leaf. Cover and simmer 1½ hours, or until tender. Add the crumbled bacon 5 minutes before serving.

Serves 6 to 8.

Old-Fashioned Pan-Fried Liver and Bacon

If using beef liver, soak in milk to cover for several hours and then wipe dry with paper towels before coating with seasoned flour.

8 slices calves' or beef liver, ¼ inch thick
1 teaspoon salt
¼ teaspoon freshly ground black pepper
¼ teaspoon dried marjoram

¼ cup flour
8 strips lean bacon
2 tablespoons unsalted butter
3 tablespoons lemon juice
Chopped parsley for garnish

1. Remove the skin and tough membrane from liver with a sharp knife.
2. Combine the salt, pepper, marjoram and flour in a plastic bag. Shake well to blend and empty out onto a flat baking dish.
3. Coat the slices of liver well all over with the flour mixture and place on a tray; pieces should not touch. Refrigerate until ready to use.
4. In a large, heavy skillet fry the bacon until crisp. Reserve the bacon and pour off all but ¼ cup of the drippings in the pan. Add the butter to the pan and heat until hot but not smoking. Place the coated liver slices in the pan and cook until brown and crisp on both sides. To test for doneness, pierce with fork; rare liver will be nice and juicy, well done will have no juice rising to the surface. Remove to a hot platter. Stir lemon juice into pan juices; spoon over liver. Garnish with parsley and serve with fried bacon.

Serves 4.

Philadelphia Scrapple

Scrapple, the herb-flavored blend of cornmeal with headcheese, is a traditional Philadelphia breakfast. The tradition has survived to the extent that it is listed on the breakfast menu of a prestigious New York hotel, along with the equally famous Philadelphia Sticky Buns.

Scrapple is the diminutive of scrap. In this case it means the scraps from a freshly killed young porker, including the heart, liver and any leftover pork bits. Since it is improbable that a modern cook would have access to these ingredients, the following recipe is modified to use the less-expensive blade end of a pork roast.

Scrapple should be sliced and fried plain on both sides in a small amount of bacon drippings or other fat. Southern style, the scrapple is sometimes dipped in a light batter and then fried to a crisp turn. It is the Pennsylvania Dutch custom to serve eggs or fried apple rings with scrapple. The meal is suitable for breakfast or a light supper.

1 2½-pound pork roast, blade end
1 quart water
2 teaspoons salt
1 cup yellow or white cornmeal
1 cup cold water
¼ to ½ cup finely chopped onion,
    according to taste

1 teaspoon ground sage
¼ teaspoon ground thyme
1 teaspoon ground marjoram
¼ teaspoon freshly ground black
    pepper, or more to taste
Flour for coating
Bacon drippings or other fat

1. Combine the pork roast, 1 quart of water and the salt in a large, heavy saucepan. Cover and cook over medium heat about 1 hour, or until pork is well done and comes away from the bone. Drain broth, skim fat from surface and reserve 2 cups.
2. Remove meat from bone of roast. Chop the meat very fine with a chef's knife or use a food processor. Set aside.
3. In a medium-sized, heavy saucepan combine the cornmeal, 1 cup of cold water and the reserved 2 cups of broth. Stir until no longer lumpy.
4. Slowly simmer the mixture until thick, stirring occasionally. Add chopped meat, onion, sage, thyme, marjoram and pepper. If desired, add more salt.
5. Cover and simmer about 1 hour, stirring often, until mixture is thick and comes off the sides of the saucepan.
6. Rinse an 8-x-4-x-2-inch loaf pan with cold water. Pour in the hot scrapple. Cool and refrigerate until firm. Cut scrapple into thin slices, coat with flour and fry in bacon drippings or other fat until crisp and golden brown on both sides.

Serves 8 to 10.

SAUCE
MAKING

I learned the basics of sauce-making at a very tender age, and I've always regarded the preparation of a flavorful sauce as one of the pleasures of the kitchen.

Sauce and gravy are interchangeable terms in American cuisine. Basically, a sauce is any liquid seasoning. Gravy is a sauce made by thickening the liquid seasoning with a starch such as flour.

One of the most deplorable American kitchen practices I can think of is thickening gravy with a paste mixture of flour and water. New England and Southern cooks are particularly guilty of this bad habit. They use a flour and water base to thicken sauces—something they must have learned at their mother's elbow, and she probably learned from her mother, and so on back to the beginning of American cooking.

Properly cooked sauces and gravies are light and smooth, never heavy, gummy or floury. A properly cooked sauce or gravy should have just enough body to coat the food. The French term is "à la nappe," the ability to coat the food without running off.

Sauce-making Basics

First, you make a *roux*. This is basic to any sauce that uses flour as a thickening agent. A *roux*—the French, Creole and Cajun term for a mixture of flour and fat cooked together to thicken chowders, soups, stews and sauces—can be one of three types: brown, blond and white. For best results, use equal portions of flour and fat.

Brown *roux* is used mainly in gumbos, stews and meat dishes. It involves cooking the fat and the flour over low heat until the mixture is lightly browned (the color of peanut butter) but not burned, or the sauce will not thicken evenly.

Blond *roux* is a *roux* made with flour and fat that is used in cream gravies and sauces. It is cooked to a pale gold color in less time than a brown roux.

White *roux* is always made with butter and is used for refined white sauces. It is cooked for a shorter time than the blond, but not less than 3 minutes over low heat.

Caution: Always cook any *roux* at least 3 minutes to avoid the pasty flavor of raw flour. See individual recipes for cooking instructions. Never cook a *roux* over high heat (low to moderate heat should be used), or the resulting thickened liquid will have a poor texture.

Sauce also can be thickened by reduction, that is, boiling the pan liquids until the sauce is the desired consistency.

Egg yolks and heavy cream are often used in American cooking to thicken sauces. *Caution:* When you add the egg yolk mixture to the sauce, it must be stirred constantly; the moment it reaches the boiling point it must be removed from the heat and stirred quickly for a minute or two until the mixture cools down slightly.

All sauces should be made in a heavy saucepan and stirred with either a whisk or a wooden spoon. It is important to use a heavy saucepan so that the heat will spread evenly over the bottom of the pan. Never use a thin metal pan because even with constant stirring, the *roux* will scorch easily.

Use a 1-to-1½-quart saucepan for making 1 to 2 cups of sauce. A smaller saucepan is not practical because the sauce must be stirred constantly while being cooked. Use a 2-to-2½ quart saucepan for making more than 2 cups of sauce.

Ingredients

Use only the freshest ingredients to make a good sauce.

Butter. To make a *roux* for basic white sauce, nothing compares with unsalted butter. Salted butter is not recommended because salt is added to prolong the shelf life and sometimes gives an off-flavor to the finished sauce.

Fat. Usually bacon or salt pork dripping. Blanch to remove excessive salt before frying.

Oil. Use peanut oil or vegetable oil of high quality.

Flour. Use unsifted, all-purpose white.

Liquid. This can be broth, juice, milk, half-and-half or cream. To add the liquid to the cooked *roux* heated or unheated is a matter of personal preference. In professional kitchens the liquid is scalded, to obtain a more thorough joining of fat and flour with the liquid. This gives a smoother, silkier texture to the finished sauce. In the home kitchen if the *roux* is removed from the heat before the liquid is added, it is not absolutely necessary to preheat the liquid. However, in my opinion, any liquid should be no cooler than room temperature.

Storing Sauces

You can make any sauce ahead of time if you reheat it very slowly over low heat, stirring constantly to keep the mixture from separating.

Sauces containing milk, cream or eggs should not be refrigerated more than 1 or 2 days. *Caution:* Never freeze these sauces.

Sauces made with broth or juice can be refrigerated about 1 week in airtight containers. In most cases they also can be frozen from 1 to 2 months. However, they will lose some flavor and more seasoning probably will be needed when they are reheated.

Basic roux—the cooked flour and fat mixture—can be made in quantity and refrigerated in an airtight container to be used as needed.

White Sauce
(Basic Recipe)

Every good cook should have a thorough knowledge of white sauces, so important in American cooking. On the principle that all of us need an occasional refresher course, here are basic instructions for making thin, medium and thick white sauce in 2-cup portions. Quantities may be doubled to make 1-quart portions.

Thin White Sauce

2 tablespoons unsalted butter, fat or oil

2 tablespoons all-purpose white flour, unsifted

2 cups milk or half-and-half

½ teaspoon salt, or to taste

¼ teaspoon freshly ground black or white pepper

Medium White Sauce

¼ cup unsalted butter, fat or oil

¼ cup all-purpose white flour, unsifted

2 cups milk or half-and-half

½ teaspoon salt, or to taste

¼ teaspoon freshly ground black or white pepper

Thick White Sauce

½ cup unsalted butter, fat or oil
½ cup all-purpose white flour, unsifted
2 cups milk or half-and-half

½ teaspoon salt, or to taste
½ teaspoon freshly ground black or
  white pepper

1. Melt the butter or fat in a heavy saucepan over low heat. (If using oil, mix the oil with the flour before placing over low heat.) Gradually add the flour to the melted butter or fat. Cook the mixture over low to medium heat 3 minutes, stirring constantly, until the mixture is foaming. Remove from heat.
2. Gradually add the milk or half-and-half to the mixture, stirring constantly with a whisk or wooden spoon until smooth. *Caution:* Be sure that all the butter-flour mixture is blended into the liquid. Any particles that are not mixed in will make the sauce lumpy.
3. Return the mixture to medium heat and cook, stirring constantly. Add the salt and pepper and cook 5 minutes until sauce has thickened.

Variations

Use 2 cups (1 recipe) *medium* white sauce as the basis for each sauce.
Basic Cheese Sauce Add 1 to 1½ cups shredded or grated mild, sharp or extra-sharp aged Cheddar cheese to the thickened white sauce. Stir over low heat until cheese is melted. Add ¼ teaspoon dry mustard and ¼ teaspoon paprika. Cook over low heat a few minutes, stirring constantly, to blend flavors.
Basic Mushroom Cream Sauce Cook 1 cup of finely chopped mushrooms in 2 tablespoons unsalted butter until the liquid has evaporated. Add the mixture to the *roux* before the sauce has thickened.
Basic Tomato-Cream Sauce In a 2-quart saucepan combine 2 cups peeled, seeded and chopped fresh tomatoes, or 2 cups canned crushed tomatoes; 1 rib celery with leaves, chopped; 2 tablespoons finely chopped onion; ½ teaspoon salt, and a few sprinklings of cayenne pepper. Cook uncovered over medium-high heat 20 minutes. Process the mixture in a blender or food processor until smooth. Add mixture gradually, stirring constantly, to thickened white sauce. Continue to cook over low heat a few minutes to blend flavors.

Basic Creole Sauce

This is an excellent recipe for a basic sauce from the private collection of a New Orleans cook. Use with fish, meat, poultry, seafood and vegetables.

½ cup chopped onion
¼ cup chopped green pepper
2 ribs celery, chopped
1 clove garlic, chopped fine
2 tablespoons unsalted butter
1 teaspoon chili powder, or to taste

2 cups canned tomatoes with juice
½ teaspoon sugar
1 bay leaf
¼ teaspoon ground thyme
Salt and freshly ground black pepper
   to taste

1. In a 10-to-12-inch, heavy skillet cook the onion, green pepper, celery and garlic in the butter until tender.
2. Add chili powder and cook 5 minutes, stirring constantly. Add tomatoes, sugar, bay leaf, thyme, salt and pepper. Cook uncovered over very low heat 40 minutes. Add a little more tomato juice if the mixture seems too thick. Remove from heat, discard bay leaf and let stand at room temperature several hours to blend flavors. Reheat and serve.

Yield: 2½ cups.

Old-Fashioned Horseradish Sauce

Recommended for meat dishes. This recipe takes a little more effort than merely whipping heavy or sour cream and adding salt, paprika, horseradish and lemon juice—the standard recipe for horseradish sauce.

1 cup Thin White Sauce (see Basic
   Recipe, page 240)
¼ cup freshly grated horseradish
¼ cup freshly ground white bread
   crumbs

½ teaspoon salt, or to taste
¼ teaspoon paprika
2 tablespoons lemon juice
1 tablespoon white wine vinegar

Prepare the white sauce in a heavy, 1-quart saucepan. Add the horseradish, bread crumbs, salt and paprika. Stir well and simmer a few minutes to blend flavors. Add lemon juice and vinegar. Serve hot from a sauceboat.

Yield: About 1⅓ cups. Recipe may be doubled.

Cherried Cranberries
(*All-Purpose Cranberry Sauce*)

This a very nice recipe to use for gift-giving. The sauce is not overly sweet and the berries retain their shape and bright red color.

4 cups whole fresh cranberries
2 cups sugar
¾ cup water

½ teaspoon salt
¼ teaspoon baking soda

1. Combine all ingredients in a heavy, 2½-quart saucepan with a tight-fitting lid. Stir well to blend ingredients.
2. Bring to a low boil over medium heat. Cover with a tight-fitting lid and cook gently for exactly 15 minutes. Remove the covered pan to a cool spot and allow to cool to room temperature. Do not remove the lid until the sauce has cooled to room temperature. Can be refrigerated until needed. Serve from sauceboat.

Yield: 2 pints.

Dessert Sauces

Dessert sauces are used extensively in American cooking as toppings for ice cream, pudding and unfrosted cakes. They should be of a contrasting and agreeable flavor. That is, if the dessert is bland, then the flavor should be lifted with a tart or rich sauce. If the reverse, then use a bland sauce to reduce the tart or rich flavor.

Vanilla Sauce
(Basic Recipe)

2 cups half-and-half or light cream
Yolks of 5 large eggs
½ cup sugar
1 teaspoon cornstarch or 2 teaspoons flour

⅛ teaspoon salt
1 teaspoon vanilla
½ cup heavy cream (optional)

1. Scald the half-and-half or cream in a heavy, 1½-quart saucepan. Set aside.
2. Combine the egg yolks, sugar, cornstarch or flour and salt in blender or food processor. Process 20 seconds until mixed. With the motor running, slowly add the half-and-half or light cream. Process until smooth.
3. Return mixture to saucepan and place over medium-low heat. Stir vigorously with a wooden spoon until the mixture coats the back of the spoon. Stir in vanilla and cool to room temperature.
4. Whip the optional heavy cream in a small bowl. With a rubber spatula fold the cream into the cooled sauce.

Yield: About 2½ cups.

Variations: Chocolate Sauce

In Step 1 add 1 to 2 squares (1 to 2 ounces) unsweetened chocolate, chopped.

Raisin-Nut Sauce

Add ½ cup chopped raisins, ½ cup chopped walnuts or pecans and 1 tablespoon grated orange rind to cooked sauce.

Chocolate Sauce
(Basic Recipe)

2 squares (2 ounces) unsweetened chocolate, chopped
1 tablespoon unsalted butter
⅓ cup boiling water

1 cup granulated sugar, sifted
2 tablespoons light corn syrup
½ cup walnuts or pecans, chopped (optional)

1. Melt chocolate in the top of a double boiler over simmering water. Add butter and stir until melted; add water and stir until well blended. Add sugar and corn syrup. Stir well to blend.
2. Place top of double boiler over direct heat and boil over medium-high heat for 8 minutes. Keep the heat low enough to prevent the mixture from burning on the bottom of the pan but *do not* stir. Cool to room temperature without stirring. Just before serving, add the optional nuts. The mixture will be very thick. Serve cold or reheat over simmering water.

Yield: About 1½ cups.

Variation: Chocolate Bourbon Sauce

Add 3 tablespoons bourbon to the cooled mixture and reheat.

Southern Lemon Sauce

½ cup unsalted butter
1 cup sugar
¼ cup water

1 large egg, well beaten
3 tablespoons lemon juice
Grated rind of 1 lemon

Combine all ingredients in a heavy, 1-quart saucepan. Cook over medium heat, stirring constantly, until mixture comes to a boil and the sauce is clear and thickened. Remove from heat immediately. Cool.

Yield: About 1½ cups.

Quick and Easy Butterscotch Sauce

1 cup light brown sugar, firmly packed
⅔ cup undiluted evaporated milk, or use heavy cream

⅓ cup unsalted butter

Simmer the sugar, evaporated milk or heavy cream and butter in a heavy, 1-quart saucepan over low heat 5 minutes, stirring constantly, until slightly thickened. Serve hot.
Yield: About 1 cup.

Hot Cinnamon Sauce

½ cup sugar
1 tablespoon cornstarch
1 cup water

1 tablespoon unsalted butter
1 teaspoon ground cinnamon
1 teaspoon vanilla

1. Combine the sugar and cornstarch in a heavy, 1-quart saucepan. Stir in the water and blend until smooth.
2. Cook over medium heat, stirring constantly, until thickened. Add the butter, cinnamon and vanilla; cook 2 additional minutes. Serve hot.

Yield: About 1 cup.

Fruit Sauce

Almost any crushed fruit or berry may be used to make this sauce. If using berries with seeds, strain out the seeds.

2 cups crushed fruit with juice: raspberries, strawberries, peaches, canned pineapple, etc.
¼ cup sugar or more, depending upon the sweetness of the fruit

2 teaspoons cornstarch
1 tablespoon unsalted butter
¼ teaspoon salt

1. Combine the fruit, juice, sugar and cornstarch in a heavy, 1½ quart saucepan. Stir to blend.
2. Cook over medium heat, stirring constantly, until thickened. Add the butter and salt and cook 1 minute longer. Serve hot or cold.

Yield: About 2 cups.

Kentucky Bourbon Sauce

1 tablespoon unsalted butter
2 cups light brown sugar, firmly packed
2 teaspoons cornstarch

1 cup cold water
¼ cup bourbon, or more to taste

1. In a medium-sized bowl cream the butter, sugar and cornstarch to a smooth paste. Gradually add the water. Transfer the mixture to a heavy, 1½-quart saucepan.
2. Cook the mixture over medium heat, stirring constantly, until thickened. Cool to lukewarm and add bourbon. Stir well to blend.

Yield: About 2 cups.

Bourbon Hard Sauce

1 cup unsalted butter
1½ cups sugar
⅛ teaspoon salt
1 large egg

1 cup heavy cream
2 tablespoons bourbon, or less to taste

1. In a bowl cream the butter, sugar and salt. Add the egg and beat well. Beat in the cream. Transfer mixture to a heavy, 1½-quart saucepan.

NOTE: Mixture also may be cooked in the top of double boiler over simmering water.

2. Cook over low heat, stirring constantly, until thickened. Do not let the mixture boil, or the egg will curdle. Cool to lukewarm and add bourbon. Stir well to blend.

Yield: About 2 cups.

EGGS, CHEESE, CORNMEAL, RICE, NOODLES

Eggs

In this country when we cook with eggs, we mean hen's eggs. Occasionally duck or goose eggs are fried or poached, but they are never used for baking purposes for two reasons: One, the unpleasantly strong flavor of the yolk; and two, the whites will not whip.

HOW TO BUY STRICTLY FRESH EGGS   An egg is called "strictly fresh" if it is no more than 12 hours from the laying hen and is bought directly from a poultry farm. Strictly fresh eggs are used *only* for frying and poaching. *Caution:* Eggs must be at least 3 days old before they can be hard-cooked or before the whites can be whipped to proper volume for baking purposes. It will be difficult to peel a strictly fresh hard-cooked egg. Whites of strictly fresh eggs can never be whipped until stiff peaks form.

HOW TO JUDGE A FRESH EGG   The position of the yolk, the condition of the white surrounding the yolk and the size of the air space at the large end of the egg determine the freshness. When broken out onto a flat plate a high-quality egg will have a high, curved yolk that is well centered and surrounded by a thick white.

As the egg loses freshness the air space becomes larger because of moisture loss within the egg. The yolk flattens and moves to the side of the egg and the white becomes watery and thin.

Biological irregularities sometimes appear in eggs as blood spots or dark specks. They may be lifted out of the egg before cooking but they do not alter the nutritive value and may be left in.

WHITE EGGS VS. BROWN EGGS   Shell color does not affect flavor, the nutritive value or the cooking performance. White-feathered hens lay white eggs, those with darker feathers lay brown eggs. The color of the yolk is determined by the breed of chicken and the diet, which do not affect the flavor or nutritive value.

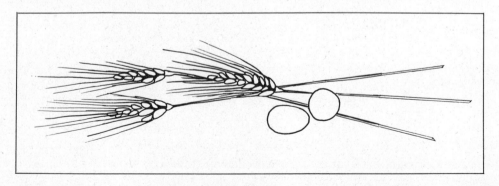

SIZES OF EGGS   Eggs are grouped according to weight. The standard sizes are:

Jumbo .... averaging 2½ ounces per egg
Extra Large .... averaging 2¼ ounces per egg
Large .... averaging 2 ounces per egg
Medium .... averaging 1¾ ounces per egg
Small (pullet) .... averaging 1½ ounces per egg

NOTE: Most recipes in American cooking specify large eggs.
    STORING   The American Egg Board suggests that eggs be stored in their original cartons in the refrigerator—not in the refrigerator egg tray. The carton acts as a barrier to keep air and odors from penetrating through the pores of the shell. Fresh eggs will keep in the refrigerator at least 4 to 5 weeks. Hard-cooked eggs should be refrigerated as soon as they have cooled; use within 1 week.
NOTE: Make a pencil mark on hard-cooked eggs to keep them from getting mixed up with the uncooked.
    Store leftover whites in an airtight container in the refrigerator; use within 10 days. Store leftover yolks, covered with water, in an airtight container; use within 3 days.
    FREEZING   Separate the whites from the yolks. Store in airtight containers. Use within one year.

Egg Cooking Basics

1. Take from refrigerator only the number of eggs needed.
2. Remove eggs from refrigerator about 45 minutes before using, unless they are to be separated. Separating yolks from whites is easier if eggs are cold.
3. Both egg yolks and whites beat up faster to more volume when they are at room temperature.
4. Cook eggs at low to moderate temperature to ensure uniform tenderness. *Caution:* High temperature and overcooking toughen eggs.
5. In combining hot mixtures and eggs, as in sauces, custard and cream fillings, spoon a small amount of the hot mixture slowly into the beaten egg, stirring or beating constantly, before incorporating the egg into the hot mixture. If the beaten egg is added directly to the entire hot mixture, the high temperature will cause curdling or watering.
    FRIED, METHOD #1   Heat 1 to 2 tablespoons unsalted butter in a skillet just hot enough to sizzle a drop of water.

NOTE: Unsalted butter is preferable to bacon or ham drippings for frying eggs; most cured meat contains sugar, and this will cause eggs to stick to the pan.
Caution: Do not salt eggs until they are cooked; salt will toughen the white during cooking. Break and slip eggs into skillet—from a sauce dish if preferred. Reduce heat immediately. Cook over low heat 3 to 4 minutes, to desired doneness.

Baste with butter during cooking. As an alternative, skillet may be covered or eggs may be turned over.

FRIED, METHOD #2   Use just enough butter to keep eggs from sticking and heat as above. Cook over low heat until edges turn white, about 1 minute. Add ½ teaspoon water for one egg, decreasing proportion slightly for each additional egg. Cover skillet tightly to hold in steam, which bastes the egg. Cook to desired doneness.

POACHED   Use a heavy, shallow pan. For each 2 eggs use 1 quart of water and 2 tablespoons white or cider vinegar. Before adding the eggs, bring the water and vinegar to a boil.

Break eggs into a saucer and carefully slip into gently boiling water. Reduce to a simmer, remove from heat and cover. Let stand about 3 to 5 minutes, or until eggs are as firm as you want them. Remove eggs carefully with a slotted spoon and serve on toast. Add salt and pepper to taste.

HARD-COOKED   These eggs should be simmered, not boiled. Fill a heavy saucepan (not aluminum) with enough cold water to cover eggs completely.
NOTE: An optional handful of salt may be added to the water; this keeps the shell from sticking when the eggs are peeled.

Place eggs in pan. Bring to a boil over medium-high heat and then reduce heat so that water is barely bubbling. Cook 3 to 4 minutes for soft-cooked eggs, 12 minutes for hard-cooked eggs. Rinse under cold water until cool. To peel, tap the shell all over on the rounded edge of the sink or rub egg between hands; start peeling at broad end. Rinse off any remaining bits of shell. Pat dry and use as in recipe instructions.

SCRAMBLED   For each 2 eggs use 1 tablespoon milk or water and 1 tablespoon unsalted butter. Crack eggs into a bowl. Add the milk or water and beat with a fork only enough to break the yolks and slightly incorporate them into the whites. Heat butter in a skillet until just hot enough to sizzle a drop of water. Pour in egg mixture and cook over low heat until soft and creamy but not dry, stirring and scraping mixture from bottom and sides of pan occasionally. *Caution:* Do not stir too much or eggs will dry out. Add salt and pepper to taste. Serve at once on a warm plate.

Scalloped Eggs and Cheese

This is a very old and traditional Easter dish.

1½ tablespoons unsalted butter
1½ tablespoons flour
1 cup half-and-half
¼ teaspoon salt, or to taste
⅛ teaspoon freshly ground black pepper, or to taste
⅛ teaspoon paprika
1 teaspoon Worcestershire sauce

½ cup dry white bread crumbs, without crusts
6 hard-cooked eggs, sliced
½ cup grated sharp Cheddar cheese
½ cup dry white bread crumbs, combined with 3 tablespoons melted unsalted butter
Toast triangles and additional sliced eggs for garnish (optional)

Preheated oven temperature: 350°F.
1. Melt the butter in a heavy, 1-quart saucepan over low heat; add flour. Cook over low to medium heat 3 minutes, stirring constantly. Remove from heat.
2. Gradually add the half-and-half, stirring constantly, until smooth.
3. Return the mixture to medium heat and add the salt, pepper, paprika and Worcestershire sauce. Cook 5 minutes, stirring constantly, until the mixture has thickened.
4. Place the unbuttered bread crumbs in a well-buttered 1-quart shallow casserole. Evenly space the egg slices over the bread crumbs and then sprinkle eggs with cheese. Cover evenly with hot sauce. Top with buttered bread crumbs and bake in preheated oven 15 minutes, or until the mixture is bubbly and the bread crumbs golden brown. Before serving, arrange toast triangles around the edge of the dish and place the egg slices flat in the center to form a design. Serve very hot.

Serves 4.

Creole Eggs

You will need to make a white sauce and tomato sauce for this layered dish. Serve over white rice.

2 cups thick white sauce (use Basic Recipe, page 240)
¼ cup unsalted butter
¼ cup chopped onion
¼ cup chopped green pepper
1 clove garlic, chopped fine
1 tablespoon chili powder, or to taste
2 cups canned crushed tomatoes

Salt and freshly ground black pepper to taste
8 hard-cooked eggs, sliced
1 cup grated or shredded mild Cheddar cheese
1 cup finely ground cracker crumbs, combined with 1½ tablespoons unsalted melted butter

Preheated oven temperature: 350°F.
1. Prepare white sauce and set aside.
2. To make the tomato sauce, melt the butter in a heavy, 2-quart saucepan. Add the onion, green pepper, garlic and chili powder. Cook over low heat, stirring constantly, until the vegetables are tender. Add the tomatoes and cook uncovered over medium-low heat about 15 minutes, or until the mixture is very thick. Add this mixture to the white sauce and stir well to blend. Add salt and pepper to taste.
3. Place alternate layers of sauce and eggs in a 1½-quart buttered casserole, beginning and ending with the sauce. Cover evenly with cheese and sprinkle top with the cracker and butter mixture. Bake in a preheated oven about 15 minutes, or until hot and bubbly and the crumbs are golden brown.

Serves 6.

Huevos Rancheros
(Rancher's Eggs)

There are many versions of this recipe. Here the eggs are poached in chili sauce, but they also can be scrambled in the sauce and served over fried corn tortillas.

6 dried chili peppers	½ cup chopped tomatoes
1 cup water	Salt to taste
1 teaspoon bacon drippings	4 to 6 large eggs
½ cup chopped onion	Fried bacon

1. Boil the chili peppers in the water until tender but do not drain. Puree the mixture in a blender or food processor. Set aside.
2. In a large, heavy skillet heat the bacon drippings and add the onion. Cook, stirring constantly, until the onion is translucent but not brown. Add the chili mixture, tomatoes and salt; simmer about 5 minutes. Remove from heat.
3. Break the eggs over the sauce in the skillet. Cover and cook over low heat until eggs are cooked to desired doneness. Spoon sauce over eggs and serve with bacon.

Serves 4 to 6.

American Omelets

American cooks, like the French, have adapted the omelet to accommodate the ingredients at hand. Probably the most popular is the Western omelet, which is made with sautéed chopped onion, green peppers and diced ham. An American Spanish omelet, which differs from an authentic egg and potato omelet as made in Spain, is made with a tomato based sauce. A California omelet combines fresh tomatoes and avocado slices.

Spanish Omelet

1 tablespoon light olive oil
1 cup finely chopped onion
½ cup chopped green pepper
¼ cup finely chopped celery
1 clove garlic, chopped fine
3 medium-sized fresh tomatoes, peeled, seeded and chopped
1 cup *petit pois* (early green peas), canned or frozen, drained

½ cup thinly sliced mushrooms, sautéed
Salt and freshly ground black pepper to taste
6 large eggs
½ teaspoon salt, or to taste
2 tablespoons water
2 tablespoons unsalted butter
2 tablespoons chopped parsley for garnish

1. Heat oil in a 2-quart, heavy saucepan. Add onion, green pepper, celery and garlic. Cook until the vegetables are tender. Add tomatoes and simmer uncovered 10 minutes. Add peas and mushrooms and season to taste with salt and pepper.
NOTE: If using frozen peas, cook following package instructions. Keep warm over low heat.
2. In a medium-sized bowl beat eggs with the ½ teaspoon salt and the water.
3. Melt the butter in a large, heavy skillet, add eggs and cook over low heat, lifting edges and allowing liquid to run beneath, until eggs are almost set. Spoon tomato mixture over surface and garnish with chopped parsley. Cut into serving portions and serve immediately on warm plates.
Serves 4 to 6.

Variation: California Omelet

Omit chopped celery, peas and parsley garnish. Add 1 teaspoon dried crushed basil to cooking tomato mixture. Garnish omelet with 1 ripe avocado, cut into wedges or slices.

Old-Fashioned Deviled Eggs

If possible, use small eggs—the filled egg will be a more appetizing size for serving.

8 hard-cooked small eggs
¼ cup mayonnaise or boiled salad dressing
2 teaspoons heavy cream
2 teaspoons cider vinegar
2 teaspoons Dijon-style mustard

½ teaspoon sugar
½ teaspoon salt
⅛ teaspoon freshly ground black pepper
Paprika for garnish

1. Cut eggs in half lengthwise; remove yolks. Rinse the whites under cold, running water and turn upside down on paper towels to drain.
2. Press yolks through a fine sieve or process until smooth in blender or food processor. Add the mayonnaise or boiled salad dressing, the heavy cream, vinegar, mustard, sugar, salt and pepper. Blend until smooth and fluffy. Spoon the mixture into the egg whites or spoon into a cake-decorating bag with a large star tip and fill the eggs. Sprinkle paprika lightly over the yolks. Refrigerate and serve cold.

Yield: 16 halves.

Pickled Red Eggs

These often appeared in my grandmother's kitchen at Eastertime, when there was likely to be an abundance of hard-cooked eggs left over from the children's egg hunt.

2 cups canned beet juice
1 cup cider vinegar
¼ teaspoon ground cloves

Salt and freshly ground black pepper to taste
10 hard-cooked large eggs, peeled

1. Drain the juice from canned beets to measure 2 cups. Reserve beets for another use. In a 1-quart pan simmer the beet juice, vinegar, cloves, salt and pepper 5 minutes to blend flavors.
2. Place eggs in bowl and cover with juice mixture. Cover and refrigerate 1 to 2 days, turning occasionally, so eggs will be evenly coated. Serve cold in a bowl with juice, or drain and arrange on platter.

Yield: 10 eggs.

Cheese

America's lush pastures produce some of the world's best-fed cows. They in turn gratefully turn out the raw material for cheese equal to the European originals. The most frequently used cheeses in American cooking are:

Hard: Freshly grated Parmesan
Semihard: Cheddar, mild, sharp and extra-sharp
Colby
Longhorn
Semisoft: Monterey Jack
Uncooked soft: Cottage
Cream

Baked Cheese

This is a delicious brunch dish to serve with homemade sausage patties and broiled tomato halves.

1½ cups hot milk
1⅓ cups dry bread crumbs, without crusts
1 tablespoon unsalted butter
Yolks of 4 large eggs

1 cup mild, sharp or extra sharp Cheddar cheese, cubed
½ teaspoon salt
⅛ teaspoon Tabasco sauce
Whites of 4 large eggs, stiffly beaten

Preheated oven temperature: 350°F.
1. Combine the milk, bread crumbs and butter in a blender or food processor. Process until smooth. Add the yolk eggs one at a time and continue processing until smooth. Stop the blender or food processor, add cheese, salt and Tabasco sauce. Process until the cheese is coarsely grated. Pour mixture into a large mixing bowl.

2. Blend one fourth of the egg whites into the cheese mixture and stir well to mix. With a rubber spatula gently fold in the remaining egg whites. *Caution:* Do not overblend, or the mixture will not puff up during baking.
3. Spoon the mixture gently into a well-buttered, shallow, 2-quart baking dish. Bake in preheated oven 30 minutes, or until the center is firm. Serve immediately.

Serves 4 to 6.

American Welsh Rarebit

This recipe is the traditional New England adaptation of the original English dish brought over by the early colonists. Can be prepared easily and quickly in a blender or food processor. Serve over toast.

½ cup unsalted butter, melted
2 teaspoons Worcestershire sauce
1 teaspoon salt, or to taste
1 teaspoon paprika
¼ teaspoon dry mustard

1 pound sharp Cheddar cheese, cubed
1 cup milk or beer, lukewarm
2 large eggs

1. Place all ingredients in a blender or food processor and blend until smooth.
2. Pour into a 1½-quart, heavy saucepan. Cook over medium heat, stirring constantly, until mixture starts to bubble. Immediately turn the heat to medium-low and continue cooking 5 minutes, stirring constantly, or until mixture has thickened. Serve hot.

Serves 4.

Baked Macaroni and Cheese

This is a classic potluck or church-supper dish. Serve with a platter of fresh tomato slices or broiled tomato halves.

2 cups elbow macaroni
2 tablespoons unsalted butter
2 tablespoons finely chopped onion
2 tablespoons flour
2 cups half-and-half
1 cup grated or shredded sharp or exta-sharp Cheddar cheese
½ cup freshly grated Parmesan cheese

¼ cup finely chopped canned pimiento (optional)
1 tablespoon chopped parsley (optional)
Salt and freshly ground black pepper to taste
¾ cup dry bread crumbs, without crusts, combined with 1 tablespoon melted unsalted butter

Preheated oven temperature: 350°F.
1. Cook the macaroni following instructions on package. Drain, rinse under cold water and transfer to a well-buttered 2-quart baking dish.
2. In a 2-quart, heavy saucepan melt the butter and add the onion. Cook until onion is tender but not brown. Add flour and cook 3 minutes, stirring constantly.
3. Remove from heat and slowly blend in half-and-half, stirring constantly until mixture is smooth.
4. Return to heat and cook at least 5 minutes, stirring constantly, until the mixture has thickened.
5. Remove from heat and blend in the cheese, optional pimiento and parsley, salt and pepper. Stir until cheese is melted. Pour mixture over macaroni and sprinkle top with buttered bread crumbs. Bake in preheated oven 25 to 30 minutes, or until the crumbs are golden brown.

Serves 4 to 6.

Variation: Baked Macaroni, Cheese and Tomato

Substitute 2 cups thick tomato juice for the half-and-half.

Cornmeal

Grits in American cooking refers to ground corn, which is known in Southern cooking as hominy grits. Cooked grits can be eaten as a cereal with milk, with butter or pan gravy as a sauce and served in place of potatoes or rice.

Boiled Grits
(Basic Recipe)

4 cups water
1 teaspoon salt
1 cup grits

Unsalted butter
Freshly ground black pepper

Bring water and salt to a boil in heavy, 2-quart saucepan. Slowly pour the grits into the boiling water, stirring constantly to keep mixture from becoming lumpy, until the water returns to a rolling boil. Reduce heat to a very low simmer. Cover and continue cooking, stirring frequently, until the mixture is translucent and the grits are tender. *NOTE: Cooking time will vary according to the brand; follow package cooking instructions for correct timing. Serve very hot.*
    Spoon onto serving plates and dot with butter and sprinkle with pepper.
Serves 4.

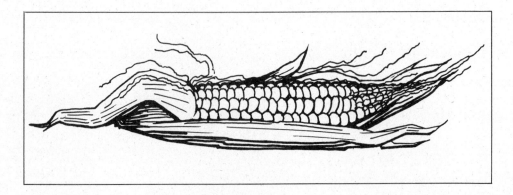

Baked Cheese Grits

This zesty combination of cheese, grits and seasonings is typically southern Louisiana cooking.

6 cups water

1½ teaspoons salt, or to taste

1½ cups grits

4 cups grated or shredded sharp Cheddar cheese

2 large eggs, well beaten

1 teaspoon Worcestershire sauce

1 clove garlic, or more to taste, chopped fine

½ cup unsalted butter

¼ teaspoon Tabasco sauce, or to taste

Preheated oven temperature: 350°F.

1. Bring water and salt to boil in heavy, 2½-quart saucepan. Slowly pour the grits into the boiling water. Continue cooking as for making Boiled Grits (Basic Recipe, page 260). Cool slightly. Add the cheese, eggs and Worcestershire sauce, stirring well to blend. Keep warm.
2. In a small skillet cook the garlic in the butter until limp but do not burn. Stir in the Tabasco sauce and combine with the grits and cheese mixture. Pour into a well-buttered 1½-quart baking dish and bake in preheated oven about 45 minutes, or until the center is firm. Serve very hot.

Serves 6.

Cornmeal Mush

Cornmeal mush is another name for hasty pudding, a favorite supper dish of early New Englanders. Any leftover pudding was poured into a loaf pan, sliced and fried for breakfast. Back-to-basics cooks are returning this wholesome natural food to the breakfast table. Serve hot in cereal bowls with molasses or rich milk, with brown sugar, butter and a sprinkling of nutmeg. Serve fried with molasses and homemade pork sausage patties.

5 cups water

1 teaspoon salt

1 cup yellow or white cornmeal, preferably stone-ground

Bring water and salt to a boil in heavy, 2-quart saucepan. Slowly pour the cornmeal into the boiling water, stirring constantly to keep mixture from becoming lumpy, until the water returns to a rolling boil. Cover and reduce heat low enough to steam-cook mixture. Cook 30 minutes, stirring occasionally. Serve very hot in bowls.

Serves 4.

Variation: Fried Cornmeal Mush

Cool cooked mush. Rinse a 5-cup loaf pan with cool water and fill with the cooked mush. Refrigerate overnight, until firm. Slice the mush about ¼ inch thick and coat lightly with flour. Fry in a small amount of unsalted butter or bacon drippings until crisp and golden brown on both sides. Serve very hot with molasses or maple syrup.

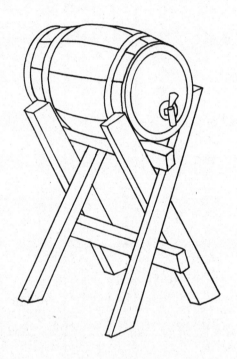

Rice

Most Americans do not realize that the high-quality rice they enjoy is grown in Arkansas, California, Louisiana, Mississippi, Missouri and Texas. In recent years this country has been the world's leading exporter of rice. It is in demand worldwide because of its superior quality, uniform grain size and dependable cooking characteristics.

Rice has been a staple in kitchens in the South since it first appeared in South Carolina cooking and the Spanish-tinged Creole cookery of New Orleans. Rice was undoubtedly combined with Mexican food by the conquering Spanish to cool their chili-seared palates. As time went on, Mexican culture markedly influenced much of Texas cooking, resulting in the term "Tex-Mex."

Types of Rice

Regular-milled long-grain white rice is the most widely used rice in American cooking. Forms separate, fluffy grains when cooked.

Medium- and short-grain white rice is used in desserts, molds and other dishes in which a stickier rice is desired.

Parboiled rice is rice that has undergone a special steam-pressure process that aids in the retention of the natural vitamin and mineral content. Uncooked, the grain has a slightly golden color.

Precooked rice is rice that has been fully cooked and then dehydrated. It requires a minimum of cooking.

Brown rice is the same as white rice except that white rice has been "polished" to remove the bran layers. Brown rice is higher in nutrients, but it is also higher in calories.

Special aromatic rices are varieties that are mutations of natural long-grain rice. Some have a subtle pecanlike flavor, one has an aroma similiar to that of hot buttered popcorn! These rices are extra fluffy when cooked and are especially good with poultry and game dishes.

Wild rice actually is not rice but a tall aquatic grass of North America that bears an edible grain. There are two types of this rice being sold on the market today: Indian wild rice and paddy rice. Run cold water over both varieties until the water runs clear before using. Cook uncovered.

Indian wild rice grows wild, is harvested by canoe and is a source of income for reservation Indians. Those interested in details of the differences between Indian wild rice and cultivated paddy rice may write to: Bob E. Shetterly, Albany Free Traders, New Osnaburgh, Ontario, Canada POV 2H0; or to Cheryl Shetterly, Pitt Store Wild Rice Co., Pitt, Minnesota 56665.

Paddy rice is cultivated rice and shares only a genetic background with Indian wild rice. Unfortunately this farm-grown rice is being sold as Indian wild rice. Paddy rice is fertilized with potassium and phosphorus when planted, top-dressed with nitrogen in June. Other insecticides are applied for control of insects, weeds, rust control and to keep the birds away. Paddy rice does not compare favorably with the true taste of Indian wild rice.

Rice Cooking Basics

Cooking rice is simple. The secret to successful rice cookery is combining the proper ratio of liquid and rice, plus accurate timing. Following package directions is always recommended, because various forms of rice require different amounts of liquid and cooking times.

UTENSILS   Use the correct size of a heavy saucepan with a tight-fitting lid.

1 cup rice—use 2-quart saucepan
2 cups rice—use 4-quart saucepan
3 cups rice—use 6-quart saucepan

YIELD

1 cup regular-milled long-grain white rice = about 3 cups cooked
1 cup medium- and short-grain white rice = about 3 cups cooked
1 cup parboiled = about 4 cups cooked
1 cup brown rice = about 4 cups cooked
1 cup special aromatic rice = about 4 cups cooked
1 cup Indian wild rice = about 4 cups cooked
1 cup paddy rice = about 4 cups cooked

PREPARATION   Do not prewash rice commercially grown in the United States. Rinsing will only wash away precious nutrients of enriched rice. Rice grown in this country is never touched by human hands during cultivation and harvesting and is packaged under sanitary conditions.

LIQUID   Make good use of chicken or beef broth by substituting them for water as the cooking liquid for rice. Vegetable and fruit juices may be used, but dilute them half and half with water.

COOKING RICE   Timing is a matter of personal taste. The following guidelines are suggested by the Rice Council of America: If package directions are not available, follow the *1-2-1 method*. Combine 1 cup uncooked rice, 2 cups boiling liquid for regular-milled long-grain, medium- and short-grain rice, 2½ cups boiling liquid for parboiled, brown and special aromatic rices, 1 tablespoon butter or margarine and 1 teaspoon salt in a 2-to-3-quart saucepan. Reheat to boiling. Stir once or twice. Reduce to simmer; cover and start timing. *For drier rice* use 2 tablespoons less liquid when cooking long-grain, medium- and short-grain rice; use ¼ cup less liquid for parboiled, brown and special aromatic rice.

TIMING

Regular milled long-, medium- and short-grain rice—15 minutes (I
    prefer 17 to 20)
Parboiled—20 to 25 minutes
Precooked—follow package instructions
Brown and special aromatic rices—45 minutes
Indian wild rice—1 hour, using 1 cup well-washed rice to 2½ cups liquid
Paddy rice—follow package instructions

OVEN METHOD FOR COOKING RICE   Rice cooks well in a tightly covered baking dish in the oven. This is an energy-saving method to use when there are other foods baking at the same time. Use the same quantity of ingredients listed on the package or see the 1-2-1 chart above. However, first bring the liquid to a boil; then stir the rice, salt and butter into boiling water and pour into a well-oiled or buttered baking dish. Cover tightly; bake in a pre-heated oven at 350°F. 25 minutes. Bake parboiled rice 35 to 40 minutes; brown and special aromatic rices about 1 hour, or until rice is tender and liquid is absorbed.

MICROWAVE METHOD   Cooking rice in a microwave oven does not save time, but there are savings in energy and cleanup time. In a covered deep, 2-quart container combine 1 cup uncooked rice, 2 cups liquid for regular-milled, parboiled, brown and special aromatic rices, 1 tablespoon butter or margarine and 1 teaspoon salt. (If plastic wrap is used, vent slightly.) For regular-milled and parboiled rice, cook on high (maximum power) 5 minutes. Reduce setting to 50% power and cook 15 minutes longer. For brown rice and special aromatic rices, cook on high 5 minutes. Reduce setting to 30% power and continue cooking 45 minutes. In the absence of variable power settings, follow manufacturer's directions.

TO TEST FOR DONENESS Spoon out a few grains of cooking rice and bite them. If grains are tender throughout but still firm, the rice is done.

TO SERVE As soon as the rice is done it should be fluffed with a fork immediately. This will allow steam to escape and will keep the rice from packing. Serve immediately.

TROUBLE-SHOOTING FOR RICE COOKING PROBLEMS
—courtesy Rice Council of America

Problem	Cause	Cure
Stickiness	too much liquid	use less liquid
	stirring during cooking	don't stir while cooking
	leaving cooked rice in pan too long	fluff with fork and transfer to serving dish
Grains too firm	not enough liquid	add a little more liquid and cook longer
	pan too large, resulting in over evaporation	use smaller pan
	loose-fitting lid	use a tight-fitting lid and do not remove it—keep steam in
Liquid not absorbed	incorrect proportions of rice and liquid	measure accurately
	heat too low	increase heat, replace lid and cook 2 to 4 minutes longer
	excess liquid	
Becomes hard when refrigerated	typical of long-grain rice	when reheating add 2 tablespoons water for each cup rice

Molded Rice Ring

A perforated rice ring mold with a clamp-on lid is available at cookware stores. To improvise, use a well-oiled standard 1½-quart ring mold. Cook 2 cups rice following basic instructions, above. After the rice is cooked and the liquid absorbed, add ½ cup finely chopped parsley and fluff mixture lightly with a fork to mix. Pack into the ring mold. Carefully unmold on a hot platter. Fill the center with any creamed mixture. Serve immediately.

Tex-Mex Rice

This recipe is made as many different ways as there are Texas households.

1 cup finely chopped onion
1 teaspoon finely chopped garlic
1 cup chopped green pepper
½ cup chopped celery

3 tablespoons corn oil or unsalted butter
2 teaspoons chili powder, or to taste
1½ teaspoons salt, or to taste
3 cups cooked long-grain white rice

In a 10-to-12-inch, heavy skillet cook onion, garlic, green pepper and celery in oil or butter until tender but not brown. Add chili powder and salt; cook 5 minutes to develop flavor and color. Stir in rice. Cook over low about 5 minutes, stirring occasionally, until flavors are blended. **Serves 4 to 6.**

Texas Jack

Sometimes known as Texas hash, this is a rice-topped dish concocted during frontier days by chuck-wagon cooks on long cattle drives. This dish is low in cost, high in nutrition and hearty in taste.

4 slices bacon
1 medium-sized onion, sliced thin
1 cup chopped green pepper
2 tablespoons chili powder, or to taste
3 large tomatoes, peeled, seeded and chopped

2 1-pound cans red kidney beans
1 teaspoon salt, or to taste
¼ teaspoon freshly ground black pepper
½ pound sharp Cheddar cheese, shredded or grated
4 cups cooked long-grain white rice

1. In a 10-to-12-inch, heavy skillet fry bacon until crisp. Remove and drain on paper towels. Pour off all the fat and return 2 tablespoons to skillet. Add onion, green pepper and chili powder; cook until

vegetables are soft and the mixture takes on color. *Caution:* Take care that the mixture does not burn. Add the tomatoes and cook 10 minutes, stirring occasionally. Add the beans, salt, pepper and cheese. Heat, stirring constantly, until cheese melts.

2. Crumble the bacon and add to the hot bean mixture. Serve very hot in wide soup plates topped with scoops of rice.

Serves 8.

Charleston Red Rice

This is a one-dish meal that also can be made with pork sausage or diced ham instead of bacon.

6 thin slices smoked cured bacon
1 cup chopped onion
½ cup chopped green pepper
1 6-ounce can tomato paste
2 cups canned crushed tomatoes
¼ teaspoon ground sage
¼ teaspoon ground thyme

½ teaspoon salt, or to taste
Freshly ground black pepper to taste
A few drops of Tabasco sauce (optional)
1 cup uncooked long-grain white rice
2 cups water

1. In a heavy, 4-quart saucepan or heavy, 10-to-12-inch skillet with a tight-fitting lid fry the bacon until crisp. Remove and drain on paper towels. Pour off all the fat and return 2 tablespoons to skillet. Add onion, green pepper and tomato paste; cook at least 5 minutes, stirring constantly, until the vegetables are soft. Add tomatoes, sage, thyme, salt, pepper and optional Tabasco sauce. Simmer uncovered 10 minutes to blend flavors and reduce the liquid in the tomatoes.

2. Crumble the bacon and add to the sauce. Stir in the rice and water. Bring mixture to a boil. Stir once or twice, cover tightly and simmer about 20 minutes. Taste for tenderness after 17 minutes.

NOTE: The rice should be tender and the liquid absorbed. Fluff with a fork and serve hot.

Serves 4.

Indian Wild Rice Supreme

The Sioux were plains Indians and the Algonquins were river Indians. Their life-styles were markedly different. But so much did they prize the wild-rice territory of Minnesota and Wisconsin that they fought repeated battles over the *mahnomen*, which literally translated means "good berry."

Wild rice is delicious served simply with butter, salt and pepper for seasoning; or it can be served with a sauce and combined with meat as a main-course dish. This recipe is an adaptation of one given to me by the Shetterly family, who sell top-quality Indian wild rice by mail order through the Pitt Store Wild Rice Co., Pitt, MN 56665. Price list available on request.

1 cup uncooked Indian wild rice
3 cups boiling water
½ teaspoon salt
2 cups Mushroom Cream Sauce (use Basic Recipe, page 241)
1½ teaspoons Worcestershire sauce

1 pound well-seasoned pork sausage
Additional salt to taste
Freshly ground black pepper to taste
½ cup dry bread crumbs, without crusts, combined with 1 tablespoon melted unsalted butter

Preheated oven temperature: 350°F.
1. Run cold water over the rice until the water is clear. Drain.
2. Put rice in a heavy, 2-quart saucepan, add the water and ½ teaspoon salt. Bring to a rapid boil and stir once or twice; reduce heat to simmer and cook uncovered about 1 hour, or until the grains of rice are puffed open. Drain well.
3. While the rice is cooking, prepare the Mushroom Cream Sauce. Add Worcestershire sauce and set aside.
4. Fry the sausage until crisp and brown. Drain off as much fat as possible.
5. Combine the cream sauce, rice and sausage. Season to taste with salt and pepper and pour into a well-buttered 2-quart baking dish. Sprinkle top with buttered crumbs. Bake in preheated oven about 25 minutes, until the mixture is bubbling-hot and the crumbs are golden brown. Serve hot.

Serves 8.

Noodles

Homemade Egg Noodles

These are the old-fashioned, farm-style noodles, made by hand. Not the least bit fancy looking, but so good when cooked in rich chicken broth or topped with butter. The noodles may be rolled out in a pasta machine, but they will absorb more flavoring if rolled by hand.

1 large egg, lightly beaten
2 tablespoons milk
½ teaspon salt
About 1 cup all-purpose flour, unsifted

4 to 5 quarts rapidly boiling water
  or broth
Salt (optional)

1. In a medium-sized bowl combine egg, milk and salt. Stir in enough flour to make a stiff dough. Cover bowl and let dough rest 10 minutes.
2. Knead mixture a few minutes, until smooth and elastic, and then roll out on a floured surface into a very thin 18-x-12-inch rectangle. Let dry 20 minutes.
NOTE: On a damp day the dough will need to dry longer.
3. Roll dough loosely, jelly-roll fashion, and slice into ¼-inch-thick rounds. Immediately unroll strips and spread them out on a clean cloth to dry 2 hours. At this point they can be sealed in plastic bags and frozen for future use or they may be cooked following recipe instructions.
4. To cook, add strips slowly to boiling salted liquid and boil about 10 minutes, or until noodles are tender. Drain and use as in recipe instructions.

Yield: About 3 cups cooked noodles.

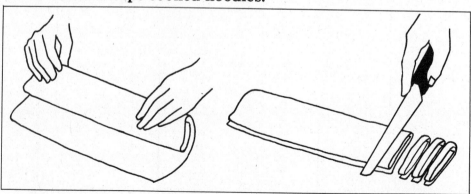

Pennsylvania Dutch Egg Noodles
(Potpie Dough Squares)

These noodles can be cooked with any poultry stew until they are tender. The dish then becomes a Pennsylvania Dutch potpie.

2 large eggs
½ teaspoon salt
⅔ cup milk

About 3 cups all-purpose flour, un-sifted

1. In a medium-sized bowl beat the eggs and add the salt and milk. Gradually beat in enough flour to make a soft but not sticky dough.
2. Remove the dough from the bowl and knead 5 minutes. Cover with a cloth and let rest 30 minutes.
3. Divide the dough into thirds. Roll out one portion at a time on a floured surface into a very thin rectangle. Cut into 2-inch squares.
4. Drop noodle squares into a simmering broth a few at a time, pushing them down gently. Cover with a tight-fitting lid and simmer 20 minutes.

Yield: 8 generous servings.

VEGETABLES AND VEGETABLE DISHES

Vegetables

The climate and rich soil of this country have provided American cooks with an abundance of fresh vegetables. As a result, many distinctive dishes have been created from the produce of kitchen gardens. Most of them are variations of the basic recipes in this chapter.

Vegetable Cooking Basics

In this country the habit of eating overcooked vegetables has all but disappeared in the past decade. How long to cook vegetables is a matter of choice. Except for a few traditional Southern dishes, Americans of this generation generally prefer to undercook vegetables slightly so that they will retain their nutrients, bright color and crisp tenderness. My personal preference is to cook them just to the point where they can be pierced with the sharp point of a paring knife, at the same time remaining slightly firm. This is a cooking technique of professional chefs.

HOW TO PURCHASE VEGETABLES   Modern transportation has greatly extended the range of out-of-season fresh vegetables, making them available in markets the year round. Usually, after they have been hauled from faraway places, they lack flavor and freshness. Try to buy fresh vegetables in season; otherwise use frozen or dried vegetables.

HOW TO SELECT FRESH VEGETABLES   Vegetables should be fresh, firm (not hard) and ripe. Do not buy vegetables that lack these characteristics. Leafy vegetables should be of good color with few waste leaves. Cauliflower and eggplant should be firm with no blemishes. Peas and beans should have crisp pods. Buy vegetables of even size and regular shape.

AMOUNTS OF FRESH VEGETABLES TO BUY   In general, buy only the amount of fresh vegetables you can use immediately, because they deteriorate in quality and lose their nutrients and vita-

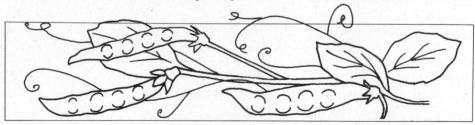

mins very quickly. Winter vegetables and root vegetables may be bought in larger amounts if there is a suitable dry, cool place for storage—not the refrigerator!

TO PREPARE VEGETABLES FOR COOKING   Wash all vegetables before cooking. Even though they look clean, they may have come in contact with insecticides or other impurities. Leafy vegetables need to be washed several times. The leaves should be lifted out of the water rather than pouring the water off. This permits any sand to sink to the bottom of the pan. Drain well before using.

HOW TO COOK VEGETABLES

Blanching. Use this method to cook fresh vegetables (frozen vegetables are blanched before freezing). Cook vegetables briefly, uncovered, in boiling salted water. Immediately rinse under cold running water and drain. Used in baked vegetable dishes.

Boiling. This is the plainest method of cooking vegetables. Immerse vegetables in boiling salted water and cook, covered, until desired tenderness; drain before seasonings are added.

Baking. Dry baking applies to vegetables cooked in their skins.

Baked Stuffed Vegetables. There are many well-seasoned stuffed vegetable dishes in American cooking. These are made of bread crumbs or cooked rice and seasonings with whatever fresh vegetables are at hand.

Au Gratin and Scalloping. In au gratin dishes, blanched vegetables are baked in a sauce with a covering of bread crumbs and cheese. In scalloped or escalloped dishes the vegetables are layered in a baking dish with a sauce or liquid and seasonings, sometimes with a cheese or bread crumb topping.

Frying. The sliced, shredded, grated or chopped vegetable is added to hot fat in a skillet and cooked until desired tenderness.

Deep-Frying. The vegetable is sliced or cut into convenient-sized pieces and submerged in enough hot fat to cover. This is a very quick type of cooking. With the exception of potatoes, most vegetables are dipped in batter for deep-frying.

Steaming. This is one of the best ways to cook vegetables to ensure that all the flavor is retained during cooking. There are several types of vegetable steamers that resemble double boilers with holes in the bottom of the top half. There are also steamer inserts for saucepans. All steamers must have tight-fitting lids, and the constantly boiling water must be kept well below the level of the vegetables during the entire cooking time. Steam vegetables until just tender and then rinse immediately under cold running water. Drain well. Reheat with butter or sauce and seasonings.

Creamed Vegetables
(Basic Recipe)

Cream-style vegetables are currently out of fashion in chic food circles. Perhaps the reason for the decline in popularity of vegetables prepared in this manner is that cooks today tend to serve meat, poultry, fish and seafood dishes with sauces. And in the interest of texture and taste, a menu should include no more than one sauce.

Creative modern cooks have a large range of fresh vegetables at their disposal to combine with a silky, well-seasoned basic cream sauce. Cheese and chopped walnuts combine well with lima beans, pecans with eggplant, almonds with celery, curry with cauliflower, chives with potatoes, parsley with carrots. A pinch of nutmeg lifts the flavor of spinach—the combinations are endless.

Basic Preparation

For 4 servings, add 1 cup hot medium Basic White Sauce (page 240) or 1 cup heavy cream to 2 cups well-drained hot cooked vegetables. *NOTE: Use only a few tablespoons of sauce or cream for spinach or kale. Vegetables should be coated with, but not swimming in, sauce. If using Basic White Sauce, reheat briefly; if using heavy cream, boil 2 minutes. Serve immediately.*

Recommended Vegetables

Asparagus	Celery	Parsnips
Lima beans	Corn	Peas
Cabbage	Chopped kale	Potatoes
Carrots	Mushrooms and wild morels	Chopped spinach
Cauliflower	Small white onions	Turnips

Deep-Fried Batter-Coated Vegetables
(Basic Recipe)

Deep-fried batter-coated vegetables often were used as a meat substitute by early American cooks.

For deep-frying, vegetables need a special coating—one that crisps the instant it touches the hot oil, allowing no oil to seep inside and cause the coating to be greasy or soggy. Batter proportions must be perfect: A very rich batter will absorb oil, one with too much sugar or shortening will not adhere to the vegetables. All-Purpose Dipping Batter (page 145) is a good one.

Use only hydrogenated fats such as shortening, corn or peanut oil for deep-frying. All are stable at the high temperatures necessary for this kind of cooking.

Sweet potato, cucumber and squash rounds

Whole green beans

¼-inch-thick large onion rings

⅓-inch-thick slices of unpeeled egg-plant

Small halves of green pepper

Okra

Mushrooms, including wild morels

Cauliflower and broccoli florets

Asparagus tips

Artichoke bottoms

Pumpkin and squash blossoms

1. It is important to wash and dry all vegetables. Otherwise the batter will not adhere.
2. To heat the fat, use a deep, heavy pan with steep sides and never fill more than half full (just enough fat to cover food is ideal). Heat fat slowly; 350°F. is the right temperature for batter-coated vegetables. To test without a thermometer, drop a cube of day-old bread into the hot fat; if browning takes *exactly* 1 minute, the fat is 350°F.
3. Dip vegetable pieces in the batter one at a time and gently shake off the excess before lowering slowly into hot fat. Fry until golden brown and remove with a slotted spoon. Drain on paper towels and serve hot.

Acorn Squash Stuffed with Ham and Apple

This recipe demonstrates the ingenuity of American cooks in adapting the foods at hand to create an interesting dish.

3 medium-sized acorn squash, about 2¾ pounds

½ teaspoon salt, or to taste

Boiling water

1 cup peeled and diced tart cooking apple

2 cups chopped cooked ham

1 teaspoon dry mustard

¼ teaspoon freshly ground black pepper

¼ cup melted unsalted butter

Preheated oven temperature: 425°F.

1. Wash and cut squashes in half lengthwise. Remove seeds. Sprinkle inside with salt. Place in a baking pan with cut side down. Pour boiling water to cover bottom of pan to a depth of about ¼ inch. Bake in preheated oven about 30 minutes, or until barely tender.

Remove from oven and cool enough to handle. Reduce oven temperature to 375°F.
2. Turn squash halves cut side up. Cut each half into two wedges; you will have a total of 12 wedges.
3. In a medium-sized bowl combine the apple, ham, mustard and pepper. Divide the mixture evenly to fill the squash cavities and brush lightly with melted butter. Place on a large baking pan, return to preheated 375°F. oven and bake an additional 20 minutes, or until the apples and squash are tender. Serve hot.

Serves 6.

Asparagus-Stuffed Eggplant
(Basic Recipe)

This is a typically American recipe for stuffed eggplant. The flavor depends upon whether the stuffing is made with ham or shellfish.

2 cups fresh or frozen asparagus pieces

2 small eggplants, halved lengthwise

½ cup finely chopped onion

1 clove garlic, chopped fine

1 cup finely chopped celery

2 tablespoons unsalted butter

1 cup chopped cooked ham, shrimp or crabmeat

1 cup dry bread cubes

⅓ cup grated or shredded mild Cheddar cheese

Salt and freshly ground black pepper to taste

Preheated oven temperature: 350°F.
1. Blanch fresh asparagus in highly salted water; make sure the pieces are undercooked so that they will retain their color. (It is not necessary to blanch frozen asparagus.) Immediately rinse under cold water and place on paper towels to drain.
2. Scoop pulp from eggplant, leaving ½-inch shell. Chop the pulp.
3. In a large, heavy skillet cook the onion, garlic and celery in the butter until tender. Add the chopped eggplant and cook uncovered until the eggplant is tender. If using fresh shrimp, add them to the mixture and cook 2 minutes.
4. Remove from heat and add the ham or crabmeat, bread cubes, cheese, salt and pepper. Gently blend the mixture with a fork. Pile lightly into eggplant shells. Place on a lightly-oiled baking pan and bake in preheated oven about 30 minutes, or until the filling is hot and lightly browned.

Serves 4.

Glazed Carrots

This recipe is referred to as "company carrots" in some cookbooks.

1 tablespoon vegetable oil, combined with 1 teaspoon unsalted butter

12 medium-sized carrots, cut on the diagonal into ½-inch slices

⅓ cup boiling water or beef broth

½ teaspoon salt, or to taste

2 tablespoons light brown sugar, firmly packed

1 teaspoon grated lemon rind

1 tablespoon lemon juice

2 tablespoons unsalted butter

2 tablespoons chopped parsley

1. Heat the oil and butter in a large, heavy skillet until hot. Add the carrots and sauté 2 minutes, stirring constantly, until the carrots are shiny. Add water or broth and the salt; cover and simmer until the carrots are barely tender.
2. Sprinkle the brown sugar, lemon rind and juice over the carrots. Add the 2 tablespoons butter and stir well to mix. Simmer uncovered until sugar is melted, the liquid has evaporated and the carrots are nicely glazed. Sprinkle with parsley and serve hot.

Serves 6 to 8.

Celery Soufflé

This is a traditional Kentucky dish with a puddinglike consistency and a delicate pale-green color. The term "soufflé" probably developed because aristocratic Southerners considered it very fashionable to give their regional dishes French titles after France came to the aid of the beleaguered revolutionists in 1778. This dish usually is served with Kentucky baked ham, and can be substituted for potatoes, rice or noodles. It also can be baked separately and served as a poultry stuffing.

½ cup chopped onion

¼ cup unsalted butter, bacon drippings or rendered chicken fat

1 cup dry bread crumbs, without crusts

1 cup chicken broth

¼ cup light cream or half-and-half

1½ cups finely chopped celery leaves (do not use white part of celery)

Salt and freshly ground black pepper to taste

4 large eggs, separated

Preheated oven temperature: 375°F.
1. In a small skillet cook onion in the butter, bacon drippings or chicken fat until translucent but not brown. Transfer to a medium-sized mixing bowl and stir in bread crumbs, chicken broth, cream or half-and-half and celery leaves. Season to taste with salt and pepper.
2. Beat the egg yolks well and blend into the bread mixture. Stir in

about one fourth of the egg whites. Beat the remaining egg whites until stiff peaks form and gently fold in with a rubber spatula. *Caution:* Do not overblend—some of the egg white should be visible.

3. Pour mixture into a well-buttered 1-quart baking dish and place inside a larger pan. Pour boiling water to measure a quarter of the way up the side of baking dish. Place in preheated oven and bake about 45 minutes, or until soufflé is firm to the touch.

NOTE: The texture will remain firm, the soufflé can be reheated. Serve hot.

Serves 4 to 6.

Corn Pudding

There are many regional versions of baked corn, scalloped corn and corn pudding, but they all are basically the same dish.

This is a favorite Indiana recipe that uses cracker crumbs and eggs to bind the ingredients together. When fresh corn is in abundance, several puddings can be made and frozen. They will retain much of their original flavor when reheated.

4½ cups fresh, frozen or canned corn (10 to 12 ears fresh corn)

2 tablespoons sugar

½ cup finely ground cracker crumbs

1 teaspoon salt, or to taste

¼ teaspoon freshly ground black pepper

2 large eggs, well beaten

2 tablespoons melted unsalted butter

1½ cups half-and-half

Preheated oven temperature: 375°F.

1. In a large mixing bowl combine the corn, sugar, cracker crumbs, salt and pepper. Stir well to blend. Blend in the eggs and butter. Stir in the half-and-half and mix well.

2. Butter a 6-cup baking dish about 2½ inches deep. *Caution:* The size of the baking dish is important; if using a shallow baking dish, the baking time will have to be adjusted or the pudding will be over-cooked. Pour the mixture into the baking dish and cook in preheated oven about 1 hour, or until light brown on top and the center is firm to the touch.

Serves 8 to 10.

Variation: Creole Corn Pudding

Sauté 2 tablespoons chopped onion and 2 tablespoons chopped green pepper in the batter until onion is translucent and not brown. Add to the corn mixture in Step 1.

Sautéed Corn
(Fried Corn)

People in other nations have the impression that Americans eat cooked corn straight off the cob, regardless of the occasion. That's fine for informal dining, but often the kernels are cut off the cob and then sometimes creamed (see Basic Recipe, page 276) or lightly cooked in butter and seasoned with salt and pepper.

4 cups very fresh corn (about 9 to 10 ears)

¼ cup melted butter
Salt and freshly ground black pepper

1. With a very sharp knife cut the kernels off the cobs into a large bowl. Scrape the sides of the cobs to release the milky pulp. *Caution: Do not cut any of the fiber from the cobs into the mixture.*
2. In a 10-to-12-inch, heavy skillet melt the butter and add the corn. Cook over medium-high heat 3 minutes, turning the mixture with a spatula. Taste for tenderness.

NOTE: If the corn is not strictly fresh, it probably will need about 5 minutes cooking time.

Season to taste with salt and pepper. Serve immediately.
Serves 6 to 8.

Variation: Calico Corn

Sauté ¼ cup each chopped green and red pepper in the butter until tender before adding the corn.

Corn Fritters
(Basic Recipe)

This recipe for fried corn cakes is also known as fresh corn griddle cakes and corn "oysters." New England Maryland cooks often serve them as an accompaniment to seafood dishes.

1 large egg, well beaten
½ cup half-and-half
2 cups fresh, frozen or canned corn
1½ cups sifted all-purpose flour
2 teaspoons baking powder
1 teaspoon salt, or to taste
Freshly ground black pepper to taste

A few sprinklings of cayenne pepper (optional)
1 tablespoon bacon drippings or melted unsalted butter
Peanut oil combined with unsalted butter for frying

1. Combine the egg, half-and-half and corn in a medium-sized bowl.

2. Sift the flour before measuring and combine with baking powder, salt, black pepper and optional cayenne pepper. Sift the mixture over the corn. Stir well to blend; then add the bacon drippings or melted butter and mix well.
3. Add peanut oil and an equal amount of melted butter to a depth of ½ inch in a large, heavy skillet; heat until hot but not smoking (375°F.). Drop the corn mixture by tablespoonfuls into the hot fat and fry until fritters are golden on both sides. Drain on paper towels and serve very hot.

Serves 4.

Baked Eggplant with Pecans

This is a deliciously rich, old-fashioned Southern dish for lovers of eggplant. Serve with broiled lamb chops.

In this recipe it is important to drain the cut eggplant wedges well before coating them with the pecan mixture.

1 large or 2 medium-sized eggplants	¼ teaspoon ground allspice
Lemon juice	Salt and freshly ground black pepper to taste
Salt	
½ cup finely ground pecans	¼ cup unsalted butter, melted
½ cup finely ground dry bread crumbs, without crusts	1 cup heavy cream
1 tablespoon flour	Chopped parsley for garnish

Preheated oven temperature: 350°F.
1. Cut unpeeled eggplant lengthwise into ½-inch wedges. Dip in lemon juice and sprinkle lightly with salt; place on a rack to drain for about 1 hour. Wipe dry with paper towels.
2. Combine the pecans, bread crumbs, flour and allspice in a plastic bag and pour onto a flat baking dish.
3. Sprinkle the drained eggplant wedges with salt and pepper to taste; then coat them with the pecan mixture. Arrange coated wedges in a shallow baking dish, skin side down. Brush lightly with melted butter.
4. Bake in preheated oven about 10 minutes, or until the pecans begin to brown. Cover evenly with cream and cook an additional 20 minutes, or until the eggplant is tender and the cream absorbed. Serve hot, garnished with a sprinkling of parsley.

Serves 6 to 8.

Escalloped Cabbage

This colorful dish is probably of Pennsylvania Dutch origin.

1 head cabbage, about 2½ pounds
1 cup water
1 teaspoon salt
3 tablespoons unsalted butter
2 tablespoons flour
1 cup milk

1 tablespoon sugar, or less to taste
Salt and freshly ground black pepper to taste
1 cup grated or shredded mild or sharp Cheddar cheese
Paprika for garnish

Preheated oven temperature: 350°F.
1. Discard outer leaves from cabbage and cut into 12 wedges. Place in a 10-to-12-inch, heavy skillet with a tight-fitting lid. Add the water and 1 teaspoon salt. Cover and bring to a boil; cook 5 minutes over high heat. Drain on paper towels.
2. While the cabbage is draining, prepare the sauce. Melt the butter in a heavy, 1-quart saucepan. Add the flour and cook 3 minutes, stirring constantly.
3. Remove mixture from heat and slowly stir in the milk, stirring constantly until mixture is smooth. Blend in sugar, salt and pepper to taste.
4. Return mixture to medium heat and cook 5 minutes, stirring constantly, until the mixture has thickened. Cool slightly.
5. Place the cabbage wedges in a well-buttered shallow, 1½-quart baking pan. Pour sauce evenly over cabbage and sprinkle with cheese. Garnish surface with a sprinkle of paprika. Bake in preheated oven 25 minutes, or until the cheese is lightly browned.

Serves 6.

Harvard Beets

Where the name Harvard Beets originated, no one knows. New England cooks have prepared them this way for over 150 years.

2 teaspoons cornstarch
2 tablespoons strained honey
Salt to taste
½ cup cider vinegar

¼ cup beet juice
2 cups cooked cubed beets
2 tablespoons butter

1. Combine the cornstarch, honey and salt in 1-quart saucepan. Slowly add the vinegar and beet juice and stir until smooth.
2. Place over medium-high heat and cook until thickened. Add beets and butter. Serve hot.

Serves 4.

Variation: Yale Beets

Omit vinegar and substitute ½ cup orange juice and 1 tablespoon grated orange rind.

Baked Lima Beans

This is a country dish often served with baked ham.

¾ cup thinly sliced onion
½ cup chopped celery
¼ cup unsalted butter
2 cups canned crushed tomatoes
¼ teaspoon dried basil
1 teaspoon salt, or to taste

Freshly ground black pepper to taste
¼ cup finely chopped parsley
3 cups fresh shelled lima beans; or 2 10-ounce packages frozen lima beans, thawed

Preheated oven temperature: 350°F.
1. In a heavy, 1½-quart saucepan cook the onion and celery in the butter until tender but not brown. Add the tomatoes, basil, salt, pepper and parsley. Simmer 5 minutes to blend flavors.
2. Combine the lima beans with the sauce and pour into a well-buttered 1½-quart baking dish. Bake in preheated oven 1 hour, or until the beans are tender. Serve hot.
Serves 6 to 8.

Stuffed Baked Mushrooms

This versatile and delicious recipe comes from my friend Claudette Price. It became a regional favorite after it appeared in the food column of a local newspaper. Serve as a hot appetizer or as a light entrée. These mushrooms can be filled and frozen unbaked; bake frozen about 22 minutes, or until done.
NOTE: It is important to use fresh cracker crumbs, not packaged, and Monterey Jack cheese.

12 large fresh mushrooms
1 tablespoon freshly ground cracker crumbs
1 tablespoon finely chopped onion
1 cup (½ pound) very lean ground beef
½ cup coarsely grated Monterey Jack cheese

1 tablespoon softened unsalted butter
1 teaspoon ground dried thyme
½ teaspoon salt, or to taste
2 tablespoons freshly ground cracker crumbs, combined with 1 teaspoon melted unsalted butter

Preheated oven temperature: 350°F.
1. Clean and stem mushrooms. (Save stems for another purpose.) If necessary, cut a sliver from the rounded bottom of the mushrooms so that they will stay upright in the baking pan. Place mushrooms in lightly oiled shallow baking pan.
2. In a bowl combine the 1 tablespoon cracker crumbs, the onion, beef, cheese, 1 tablespoon butter, the thyme and salt. Stir gently with a fork to combine. Fill mushrooms and sprinkle the cracker crumbs and butter mixture evenly on top of filling. Bake in preheated oven 15 minutes, or until meat is cooked and the topping browned. Serve hot.

Yield: About 12 stuffed mushrooms.

Stuffed Baked Green Peppers
(*Basic Recipe*)

Green peppers can be filled with almost any precooked food. This is a dish favored by Southern, Creole and Cajun cooks.

6 large green peppers	1 cup fresh bread crumbs or cooked rice
½ cup chopped onion	
1 clove garlic, chopped fine	1 large egg, well beaten
1 tablespoon unsalted butter	1 tablespoon chopped parsley
4 cups chopped cooked lamb, pork, ham, veal or shrimp	1 teaspoon salt, or to taste
	Freshly ground black pepper to taste
	Melted unsalted butter

Preheated oven temperature: 350°F.
1. Slice tops from green peppers; remove seeds and membrane. Blanch in boiling water 5 to 6 minutes. Immediately rinse under cold running water and place on paper towels to drain.
2. In a large, heavy skillet cook the onion and garlic in the 1 tablespoon butter until translucent but not brown. If using fresh shrimp, add them to the mixture and cook a few minutes, or until translucent. *Caution:* Do not overcook, or they will be tough.
3. Remove from the heat and add the chopped meat, bread crumbs or rice, egg, parsley, salt and pepper. Gently blend the mixture with a fork. Fill peppers and brush tops with melted butter. Place in a lightly oiled baking pan and bake in preheated oven 15 to 20 minutes, depending upon the size of the peppers, until the tops are brown. Brush peppers with more melted butter halfway through the baking.

Serves 6.

Variation: Green Peppers Stuffed with Corn

Omit meat or shrimp. Substitute 4 cups cooked corn.

Molded Spinach Ring
(Basic Recipe)

According to old Southern cookbooks, this useful recipe has been around a long time. The ring can be filled with creamed vegetables, ham, poultry, fish or seafood. One suggestion is to fill the center with creamed cauliflower and border the ring with sliced buttered carrots.

3 pounds fresh spinach or 3 10-ounce packages frozen chopped spinach
2 tablespoons unsalted butter
2 tablespoons finely chopped onion

½ cup freshly ground white bread crumbs
⅛ teaspoon freshly grated nutmeg
Salt and freshly ground white pepper to taste
3 large eggs, well beaten

Preheated oven temperature: 325°F.
1. If using fresh spinach, wash thoroughly in at least 3 changes of water to remove sand; place in a large heavy saucepan. Cover the pan and cook over medium heat until wilted. (If using frozen chopped spinach, there is no need to precook.) Chop cooked fresh spinach.
2. Place spinach in a sieve (or use a potato ricer) and press down with rubber spatula until all liquid has been extracted. The drained spinach should be dry and crumbly. Discard liquid—it has a bitter taste.
3. In a large, heavy skillet melt the butter and cook the onion until translucent but not brown. Add the bread crumbs and stir well to mix. Add the spinach, nutmeg, salt and pepper. Blend well and then gently stir in the eggs.
4. Pack mixture into a well-buttered 4-cup ring mold. Place mold in a larger pan and pour boiling water 1 inch up the side of the ring mold. Bake in preheated oven 25 minutes, or until the mixture is firm to the touch.
5. To unmold, place a flat plate on top of the mold and turn upside down. Let rest about 5 minutes, lift off the mold and fill ring with any desired mixture. Serve hot.

Serves 6.

Potatoes

Since World War II, traditional American potato dishes have been available in dehydrated ready-mix or frozen packages. In my opinion, no matter how well prepared these convenience foods may be, it is impossible to recapture the flavor of dishes carefully made from scratch with fresh ingredients. The recipes that follow are those prepared by generations of American home cooks.

Creamed Mashed Potatoes
(Basic Recipe)

In this recipe allow 1 medium-sized potato for each serving. Recipe may be doubled or tripled.

4 medium-sized all-purpose potatoes, peeled and quartered
Salt to taste
2 tablespoons unsalted butter

½ to ¾ cup heavy cream
Salt and freshly ground black or white
  pepper to taste

1. Put the potatoes in a heavy saucepan with water to cover and add salt to taste. Cover, bring to a boil and cook about 20 minutes, or until the potatoes are tender but not mushy. Remove from heat and drain well. If desired, reserve liquid for making gravy or sauce.
2. Set the pan of potatoes back on very low heat and shake the pan gently to remove any moisture from the potatoes. Leave over heat

and add the butter. With an electric hand mixer whip the potatoes with sweeping strokes until smooth and creamy. (If electric hand mixer is not available, rice the potatoes and return to the pan. Beat until smooth and creamy with a large whisk.) Slowly beat in enough cream to make a mixture almost as light as meringue. Season to taste with salt and pepper. To keep warm, cover and place pan over boiling water no longer than 10 to 15 minutes. Serve very hot. **Serves 4.**

Variations: Potato Cakes

Cook 2 tablespoons finely chopped onion in 1 tablespoon unsalted butter until tender but not brown. Combine with 2 cups cold leftover creamed mashed potatoes and 2 tablespoons flour. Form into 6 flat cakes and fry in 2 tablespoons bacon drippings until nicely browned on both sides. Traditionally served with bacon and eggs.

Potato Fritters

Beat 1 large egg and combine with 2 cups leftover Creamed Mashed Potatoes, 2 tablespoons flour, 1 teaspoon baking powder and salt and pepper to taste. Beat well to blend ingredients and gradually beat in ¼ cup milk, or enough to make a thick pancakelike batter. Spoon onto a well-oiled hot griddle and fry until nicely browned on both sides. **Serves 4** as a breakfast side dish.

Creamed Potatoes and Peas

For those of us who have grown up close to the soil, nothing is as special as the fresh taste of just-shelled early June peas combined with tiny, marble-size red potatoes in a lightly seasoned cream sauce.

About 1¼ pounds small red-skinned "new" potatoes

1 cup half-and-half

½ cup heavy cream

Salt and freshly ground black or white pepper to taste

2 cups fresh or frozen peas

1. Put the potatoes in a saucepan with water to cover and salt to taste. Bring to a boil and simmer 20 minutes, or until the potatoes are tender without being mushy. Remove from heat and drain.
2. When the potatoes are cool enough to handle, remove skins and leave them whole if they are small, or cut them into slices about ¼ inch thick.

3. Return potatoes to the saucepan and add the half-and-half and cream. Add salt and pepper to taste.
4. Return to heat and simmer uncovered 5 minutes.
5. Cook peas in boiling salted water until barely tender. Drain well and add to the potatoes. Cook uncovered 1 minute. Serve hot.

Serves 4 to 6.

Potatoes Au Gratin

Before American cooks decided to "Frenchify" this dish, it was called potato and cheese scallop.

4 cups sliced all-purpose potatoes
2 tablespoons unsalted butter
2 tablespoons flour
2 cups milk
1 cup grated or shredded sharp Cheddar cheese

Salt and freshly ground black pepper to taste
¾ cup fresh bread crumbs, without crusts, combined with 3 tablespoons melted unsalted butter

Preheated oven temperature: 350° F.
1. Parboil the potatoes in salted water to cover about 5 minutes, or until barely tender. Drain well and set aside.
2. In a heavy, 2-quart saucepan melt the butter and add the flour. Cook 3 minutes, stirring constantly. Remove from heat.
3. Gradually add the milk to the mixture, stirring constantly until smooth.
4. Return to medium heat and cook 5 minutes, stirring constantly, until the mixture has thickened. Lower heat, add cheese and stir well to blend. Season to taste with salt and pepper. Remove from heat.
5. Place half the potatoes in a well-buttered, shallow, 1½-quart baking dish. Pour half the cheese sauce over potatoes, lifting potatoes with a fork so that all slices are covered with the sauce. Repeat with the remaining potatoes and sauce. Sprinkle top evenly with bread crumb mixture. Bake in preheated oven 30 minutes, or until potatoes are tender and the crumbs golden brown.

Serves 6.

Hash-Brown Potatoes
(Basic Recipe)

3 cups chopped cold boiled or baked potatoes
3 tablespoons flour
1 tablespoon finely chopped onion (optional)
¼ cup half-and-half

1 teaspoon salt, or to taste
¼ teaspoon freshly ground black pepper, or to taste
2 tablespoons bacon drippings; or 1 tablespoon peanut oil and 1 tablespoon unsalted butter

1. Combine the potatoes, flour, optional onion and half-and-half in a medium-sized mixing bowl. Season with salt and pepper and stir well to blend.
2. Heat the bacon drippings or peanut oil and butter in a 9-inch skillet until hot but not smoking. Pack the potato mixture into the skillet to form a round cake; flatten with a spatula. Cook over medium heat until the underside is crusty and golden brown.
3. *Method #1:* Turn half the potato cake over onto the other half. Place on a heated platter and serve very hot.
   Method #2: Turn the potato cake out onto a flat plate. Wipe the skillet clean with paper towels. Add an additional 1 tablespoon of fat to the skillet. Slip the potato cake back into the skillet, brown side up, and cook until bottom is brown. Shake skillet gently to keep cake from sticking. Turn out onto a hot platter, cut into wedges and serve very hot.

Serves 4.

Variations: Corned Beef Hash

In Step 1 add 3 cups chopped cooked corned beef.

Red-Flannel Hash

In Step 1 add 1 cup chopped cooked corned beef and 1 cup chopped cooked beets. Traditionally made from the leftovers of a New England Boiled Dinner (page 208).

Baked Stuffed Idaho Potatoes

An Idaho potato with its fluffy, mealy texture is one of America's culinary treasures. Avoid using a covering of foil when baking potatoes. The foil holds in moisture and steams the potato, rather than baking the skin. If foil-wrapped after baking, it also closes in the steam and softens the skin. Always pierce the skin before baking with a fork to prevent possible bursting in the oven. This helps the steam escape and the mealy texture to develop.

4 to 5 large Idaho baking potatoes	Salt and freshly ground black pepper to taste
8 to 10 tablespoons unsalted butter	
8 to 10 tablespoons sour cream	Melted unsalted butter for topping
	Crumbled bacon
	Fresh dill for garnish, optional

Preheated oven temperature: 425°F.
1. Wash and scrub the potatoes and place on baking sheet in single layer and do not crowd. Bake in preheated oven 55 to 65 minutes, or until cooked through.
2. When the potatoes are cooked, cut them into halves lengthwise and quickly scoop out the insides. Mash potatoes well and for each half add 1 tablespoon of butter and 1 tablespoon of sour cream. Season to taste with salt and pepper and whip until fluffy.
3. Return mixture to shells and brush tops with melted butter. Sprinkle with crumbled bacon and return to preheated oven to heat through. Garnish with optional sprigs of dill. Serve very hot.

Serves 8 to 10.

My Mother's Country-Fried Potatoes

In this recipe the potatoes should be fried in an iron skillet so that they will brown slowly and evenly. Use a mature all-purpose potato for best results.

4 cups thinly sliced potatoes	Salt and freshly ground black pepper to taste
¼ cup bacon drippings	
1 cup thinly sliced onion (optional)	

1. Submerge the sliced potatoes in ice-cold water 30 minutes to remove excess starch.
2. Drain the potatoes well and turn out onto a clean, absorbent cloth towel. Turn the slices in the towel and dry thoroughly on both sides.
3. Heat the bacon drippings in a 9-to-10-inch, heavy skillet over medium-low heat. Place the potatoes and optional onion in skillet and turn to coat well with the drippings. Season to taste with salt and pepper. Cover and cook slowly until bottom is crusty and nicely browned. Remove cover for remainder of cooking time. Turn mixture

with a wide spatula a few times to brown the potatoes evenly. *Caution:* Do this no more than necessary, or the potatoes will break up and be mushy. Serve immediately.
Serves 4.

Scalloped Potatoes and Ham

This is a traditional wintertime country dish.

2 cups Medium White Sauce or Mushroom Cream Sauce (use Basic Recipe, page 241)
5 cups thinly sliced potatoes

1 cup or more thinly sliced or cubed ham
½ cup grated or shredded Cheddar cheese (optional)

Preheated oven temperature: 350°F.
1. Soak the peeled potatoes in cold water and drain thoroughly on paper towels.
2. Place the ham and potatoes in three layers in a well-buttered deep-sided 2-quart baking dish; add a portion of the sauce to each layer and end with a covering of sauce. Sprinkle top with optional cheese. Bake in preheated oven 1 hour, or until the potatoes are fork-tender. If the top seems to be browning too rapidly, cover loosely with foil. Serve hot.
Serves 6 to 8.

Potato Filling

This is an old Pennsylvania Dutch stuffing for poultry. Modern cooks of the area serve it as an accompaniment to meat. The secret of this dish is to add the hot milk gradually during the mixing of the ingredients—this keeps the filling light and fluffy.

6 medium-sized all-purpose potatoes, peeled and cubed
3 cups hot milk
½ cup chopped onion
½ cup chopped celery
2 tablespoons unsalted butter
1 cup dry bread cubes

2 large eggs, well beaten
1 tablespoon finely chopped parsley
½ teaspoon poultry seasoning (optional)
1 teaspoon salt, or to taste
¼ teaspoon freshly ground black pepper, or to taste

Preheated oven temperature: 400°F.
1. Boil the potatoes in salted water to cover until tender but not mushy. Drain well and beat with an electric mixer or run through a ricer. Beat in about 1 cup of the hot milk.

2. In a medium-sized skillet cook the onion and celery in the butter until tender but not brown. Add the bread cubes and stir well to coat.
3. Add the bread cube mixture to the mashed potatoes and beat in a second cup of hot milk. Add the eggs, parsley, optional poultry seasoning, salt and pepper. Beat well to mix and add the third cup of milk. Continue beating until well blended. The mixture will be thin, but it will thicken during the baking. Pour into a well-buttered, shallow, 2-quart baking dish and bake in preheated oven 30 minutes, or until the top is nicely browned. Serve hot.

Serves 6 to 8.

Potato Chips

Potato chips were first contrived in the 19th century by a chef at a resort hotel in Saratoga, New York. For several generations they were known as Saratoga chips.

Use only mature baking potatoes and slice them evenly and paper-thin. *Caution:* Freshly dug potatoes will not brown properly. To slice, use a manual or electric vegetable slicer. Scrub skins thoroughly with a vegetable brush. To peel or not is a matter of choice; I prefer to leave the skins on. If the potatoes are peeled, the skin can be removed with a sharp knife or vegetable peeler in long spirals and fried separately to serve as predinner hors d'oeuvre nibbles or as accompaniments to steak and hamburgers.

Freezing: Potato chips can be deep-fried in quantity and frozen. Drain unsalted chips on paper towels and cool to room temperature. Pack loosely in plastic bags, leaving ½ inch head space; seal the bag airtight. To reheat, spread chips on a baking sheet and crisp in a 350°F. oven a few minutes. Sprinkle with salt and serve.

3 pounds of baking potatoes   Coarse salt
Peanut oil for deep-frying

1. Slice potatoes crosswise into very thin, even rounds. Immediately submerge the slices in ice-cold water. After all the potatoes are sliced, change the water 2 or 3 times. Refrigerate at least 1 hour.
2. Drain the potatoes well and turn out onto a clean, absorbent cloth towel. Turn the slices in the towel and dry thoroughly on both sides.
3. Fill a deep, 2-quart kettle or a deep-fat fryer with oil to a depth of about 3 inches. Heat to 375°F.

4. Fry a few potato slices at a time until golden brown. Depending upon the variety of potato, this should take about 4 to 5 minutes per batch.
5. Drain on paper towels and continue frying remaining slices. *Caution:* Keep fat at constant 375°F. Sprinkle with salt and serve warm.
Serves 4 to 6.

Variation: American-Style French Fries

In Step 1 cut each potato lengthwise into ⅜-inch slices and then cut each slice into ⅜-inch strips.

Sweet Potato Pone

The word "pone" means baked. Sweet potato pone was originally an American Indian dish made with grated raw sweet potatoes, nut meal and honey. From this rough beginning evolved many fanciful sweet potato recipes. The two that follow are traditional Southern favorites.

Famous Sweet Potato Pudding of 1828

This is a light-textured pudding served with Thanksgiving and Christmas dinners in the South. This recipe is quite large and can be halved and baked in a 1-quart dish. In that case, the baking time is reduced to 45 minutes.

1 pound boiled, peeled sweet potatoes (about 3 to 4 medium-sized)
1 cup sugar, or less to taste
½ cup melted unsalted butter
Yolks of 6 large eggs
Grated rind of 1 lemon

½ teaspoon ground mace or ¼ teaspoon freshly ground nutmeg
1 cup orange juice
White of 6 eggs, stiffly beaten
Sugar and slivers of citron for topping

Preheated oven temperature: 350°F.
1. Press the cooked sweet potatoes through a sieve or a potato ricer into a large bowl. Add sugar and melted butter and beat well to mix.
2. Add egg yolks one at a time, beating well after each addition. Add lemon rind, mace or nutmeg and orange juice. Beat until light and fluffy. Stir in one fourth of the beaten egg whites. Fold in the remainder gently with a rubber spatula. *Caution:* Do not overblend; traces of egg white should be visible.

3. Gently pour the mixture into a well-buttered 2-quart soufflé dish. Sprinkle the top with sugar and decorate with slivers of citron. Bake in preheated oven 1 hour and 15 minutes, or until the top springs back when gently pressed with the finger. Serve hot.
Serves 10 to 12.

Candied Sweet Potatoes

These are delicious served with baked ham, pork roast or duck.

6 large sweet potatoes
Salt to taste
¾ cup brown sugar, firmly packed, or less to taste

½ teaspoon grated lemon rind
1½ tablespoons lemon juice
2 tablespoons unsalted butter
2 tablespoons bourbon (optional)

Preheated oven temperature: 375°F.
1. Boil unpeeled sweet potatoes in water until they are almost tender. Peel and cut lengthwise into ½-inch slices.
2. Layer the slices in a well-buttered, shallow, 1½-quart baking dish. Sprinkle each layer with salt, brown sugar, lemon rind and juice. Dot top with butter.
3. Place in preheated oven and bake 20 minutes, basting occasionally with the melting mixture, until the potatoes are nicely glazed. If using the optional bourbon, pour evenly over the potatoes during the last 10 minutes of baking time. Serve hot.
Serves 6.

Variations:
Candied Sweet Potatoes with Marshmallows

Space large marshmallows evenly over top of baked sweet potatoes. Place in broiler 3 inches from heat source for about 30 seconds, or until marshmallows are golden.

Sweet Potato and Apple Scallop

Use 3 large sweet potatoes, 3 cups peeled tart apple slices and ½ cup chopped walnuts (optional). In Step 2 layer the sweet potatoes, apples and nuts. Sprinkle each layer with salt, brown sugar, lemon rind and juice.

Baked Yellow Summer Squash

This is a Tarheel dish and a favorite of all Southerners.

6 cups sliced yellow summer squash
1 cup chopped onion
1 cup chopped green pepper
6 tablespoons melted unsalted butter
¾ cup crushed cracker crumbs

3 large eggs, lightly beaten
Salt and freshly ground black pepper to taste
½ cup grated or shredded Cheddar cheese, or more to taste

Preheated oven temperature: 375°F.
1. Steam the squash, onion and green pepper, covered, until barely tender.
2. Transfer vegetables to a medium-sized bowl and stir in butter, cracker crumbs, eggs, salt and pepper. Pour mixture into a well-buttered 1½-quart baking dish. Sprinkle top with cheese and bake in preheated oven 45 minutes.

Serves 6.

Tomato Pudding

This is a dressed-up version of scalloped tomatoes. The original recipe called for 1 cup of sugar, and the pudding was served both as a vegetable and for dessert. It has been modernized in this recipe to serve as an accompaniment to meat.

1 cup chopped onion
2 tablespoons unsalted butter
3 cups peeled, seeded and chopped fresh tomatoes, or use 3 cups canned crushed tomatoes
½ cup boiling water

¼ cup brown sugar, firmly packed, or less to taste
2 tablespoons chopped parsley
½ teaspoon salt, or to taste
Freshly ground black pepper to taste
2 cups dry white bread cubes
¼ cup melted unsalted butter

Preheated oven temperature: 375°F.
1. In a heavy, 2-quart saucepan cook the onion in the 2 tablespoons of butter until translucent but not brown.
2. Puree the tomatoes in a blender or food processor.
3. Add the tomatoes, boiling water, brown sugar, parsley, salt and pepper to the onion. Cook over medium heat 10 minutes, stirring occasionally.

4. Coat the bread cubes well with the ¼ cup melted butter. Spread mixture evenly in the bottom of a lightly buttered 1-quart baking dish. Spoon tomato mixture over the bread cubes. Cover with a lid or foil and bake in preheated oven 40 minutes, or until the mixture is firm. Serve hot.

Serves 6.

Okra and Tomatoes

This is a time-honored Creole and Southern vegetable dish to serve with white rice. It can be made in large quantities and frozen, to be used as a base for gumbos (see Gumbo-making Basics, page 59). *Caution:* Do not prepare in an iron or aluminum pan.

2 tablespoons bacon drippings
1 cup chopped onion
1 teaspoon finely chopped garlic, or to taste
1 pound fresh or frozen okra, sliced
1 cup diced fried ham
Water

1½ cups peeled, seeded and chopped tomatoes
¼ teaspoon sugar
1 teaspoon salt, or to taste
¼ teaspoon freshly ground black pepper
A few sprinklings cayenne pepper (optional)

1. In a large, heavy, 10-to-12-inch skillet, preferably electric, heat the bacon drippings and add the onion, garlic, okra and ham. Cook, turning occasionally with a spatula, until okra ceases to be gummy and the slices separate. Add water 1 tablespoon at a time to keep mixture from sticking to the bottom of the skillet.
2. Add tomatoes, sugar, salt, black pepper and optional cayenne pepper. Cover and simmer 15 minutes. Serve hot.

Serves 4.

Fried Green Tomatoes

This simple dish has many possibilities. Serve as an accompaniment to broiled steaks and chops or on toast as an open-faced sandwich.

3 or 4 firm green tomatoes
½ cup flour; or use ¼ cup flour and ¼ cup cornmeal
Salt and freshly ground black pepper to taste

Peanut oil combined with unsalted butter for frying; or use bacon drippings

1. Slice the tomatoes into ¼-inch rounds.
2. Combine the flour, or flour and cornmeal, salt and pepper in a plastic bag. Pour out into a flat baking dish and coat each slice of tomato well with the mixture. Place on a tray lined with wax paper.
3. Add peanut oil and an equalamount of melted butter to a depth of ¼ inch in a large, heavy skillet, or use bacon drippings. Heat until hot but not smoking (365°F.). Gently place the coated tomato slices in the hot fat, making sure they do not touch. Fry on both sides until golden and crisp, using a spatula to turn the slices. Drain quickly on paper towels and serve immediately.

Serves 4.

Baked Stuffed Tomatoes

6 firm ripe tomatoes
6 slices lean bacon
¼ cup finely chopped onion
¼ cup finely chopped celery
2 tablespoons chopped parsley
1 cup fresh white bread crumbs

Salt and freshly ground black pepper to taste
6 tablespoons grated or shredded Cheddar cheese; or use half Cheddar and half Parmesan
3 teaspoons unsalted butter

Preheated oven temperature: 350°F.
1. Slice stem tops from tomatoes. With a spoon scoop out the centers and reserve the pulp. Place tomatoes upside down to drain.
2. Fry the bacon in a skillet until crisp. Crumble and place on paper towels to drain. Pour off all but about 2 teaspoons of the drippings. Add the onion and celery and cook until tender. Add crumbled bacon, parsley, bread crumbs, salt and pepper. Stir lightly until well blended.
3. Fill the tomatoes with the bread mixture, top each with 1 tablespoon cheese and dot with ½ teaspoon butter. Place in lightly oiled 1-cup baking dishes or large muffin tins. Bake in preheated oven 30 minutes, until the cheese is nicely browned. Serve hot.

Serves 6.

Creamed Mashed Turnips

Use basic recipe for Creamed Mashed Potatoes, page 287, substituting 1 pound of white or yellow turnips for the potatoes. Add ⅛ teaspoon freshly grated nutmeg. *Caution:* Turnips are too fibrous to run through a ricer; beat by hand or with an electric mixer until smooth and creamy.

Serves 4.

Turnip Soufflé

This is an honest American pudding that will puff only slightly during baking. Can be kept warm in the oven until serving time. Excellent with roast lamb, duck or wild game dishes.

1 pound white turnips
1 pound all-purpose potatoes
1 teaspoon sugar
2 tablespoons unsalted butter
2 tablespoons heavy cream

1 large egg, well beaten
Salt and freshly ground black pepper
  to taste
⅛ teaspoon freshly grated nutmeg
  (optional)

Preheated oven temperature: 400°F.
1. Peel and cube the turnips and potatoes. You will need an amount to measure 4 cups when beaten. Cover and cook with the sugar in 1 inch of water until tender, about 12 to 15 minutes. Drain well. Place over low heat for a few minutes to dry out excess moisture.
2. With an electric mixer beat the butter into the turnip and potato mixture; continue beating until mixture is free of lumps. Beat in the cream and then the egg, beating well after each addition. The mixture should be light and fluffy. Add salt, pepper and optional nutmeg.
3. Spoon mixture into a well-buttered 5-cup soufflé dish. Bake in preheated oven 20 minutes, or until golden brown and slightly puffed.
Serves 6.

Vegetable Ribbon Loaf

This is an old regional recipe brought up to date. Serve cold as a first course or hot as an accompaniment to meat.

Vegetables

1 cup fresh or frozen green peas
½ pound fresh uncut green beans

½ pound fresh baby carrots
8 stalks fresh asparagus

Filling

1 cup cooked fresh or frozen green
  peas, puréed
2 cups heavy cream
1½ cups fresh white bread crumbs

1 large egg plus 1 egg white
1 teaspoon salt
½ teaspoon freshly ground white
  pepper

Preheated oven temperature: 375°F.

1. Blanch the 1 cup of uncooked green peas, the green beans, carrots and asparagus separately in highly salted water, keeping them undercooked so that they retain their color. Immediately rinse under cold water and place on paper towels to drain.

NOTE: Most of the salt will rinse off, leaving just enough to lift the flavor of the vegetables.

2. *To prepare the filling:* Combine the second cup of (cooked) green peas, the cream, bread crumbs, egg and white and salt and pepper. Beat mixture until smooth. This can be done with an electric mixer or all the ingredients can be placed in a blender or food processor and processed until smooth.

3. *To assemble:* Butter a 5-cup loaf pan thoroughly, using plenty of butter. Layer the peas evenly on the bottom. Spoon a ½-inch layer of the filling over the peas. Place a single layer of beans over the filling, pressing down slightly to keep the beans in position. Place another ½-inch layer of filling over the beans. Place a single layer of carrots over the filling, again pressing down. Place another ½-inch layer of filling over the carrots. Place the asparagus spears over the last layer of filling and press down. This will be the bottom of the loaf when it is unmolded. You will have 4 layers of vegetables and 3 layers of filling.

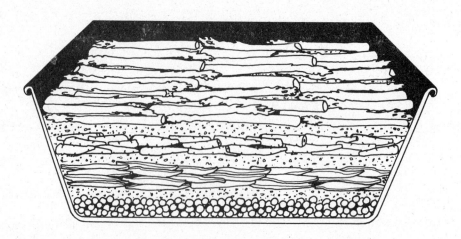

4. Cover the pan securely with foil. Set inside a larger pan and pour boiling water to measure 1 inch up the side of the loaf pan. Bake in preheated oven 45 minutes, or until firm.

5. *To serve cold:* Cool and refrigerate overnight. Turn out onto a platter and slice with a serrated knife, being careful to use long, even strokes so that the layers are neatly sliced and do not run together. Serve with boiled salad dressing or a mustard-flavored mayonnaise thinned out with cream.

Serves 10 to 12 as a first course.

6. To serve hot: Remove from water bath and let rest 15 minutes. Turn out onto a serving platter and slice with a serrated knife in serving portions about 1 inch thick. Transfer to serving plates with a wide spatula. Serve plain or with a mushroom cream sauce.

Serves 8 to 10.

The three regional dishes that follow are dear to the heart of any true Southerner.

Southern-Fried Green Beans

2 pounds fresh green beans
6 slices smoke-cured bacon
1 cup thinly sliced onion

1 teaspoon sugar
Salt and freshly ground black pepper
 to taste

1. Snip the ends off the beans and snap them in 1½-inch pieces. Place in salted water in a large kettle, cover and cook until tender. Drain well.
2. In a large, heavy, iron skillet fry the bacon until crisp. Add the cooked beans and the onion. Cook uncovered 15 minutes. Add the sugar, cover and cook over medium-low heat 1 hour or more. Add salt and pepper to taste.

Serves 6 to 8.

Turnip Greens with Hog Jowl

The liquid left in the bottom of the cooking pan is called "pot likker" and it is served on the side in cups. Serve this traditional dish with corn bread.

1 pound mustard greens
½ pound salt pork, fresh hog jowl or
 smoked ham hocks
1 pound or more tender turnip greens

Salt and freshly ground black pepper
 to taste
About 6 small green onions, chopped

1. Place the mustard greens in a large kettle with the meat and add enough water to barely cover. Cover and cook until meat is tender.
2. Cook the turnip greens in a small amount of salted water in a separate covered pan until tender. Add greens and liquid and simmer a few minutes to blend flavors.

NOTE: Use salt with caution. Salt pork and smoked ham hocks can be very salty.

Drain off the "pot likker" and reserve. Place the greens in a deep dish or platter and arrange the meat over the greens. Cover with chopped green onions.

Serves 6.

Hoppin' John

This is a traditional New Year's Day dish in every Southern household. Serve with corn bread.

2 cups dried black-eyed peas or cowpeas	2 cups white rice
3 quarts water	1 tablespoon salt, or to taste
½ pound salt pork streaked with lean, sliced or cubed	¼ teaspoon freshly ground black pepper
1 cup chopped onion	1 small dried red pepper

1. Bring peas and water to a boil in a large kettle; boil 2 minutes. Cover kettle and let stand 1 hour.
2. In a small skillet sauté the salt pork until crisp and brown. Add the onion and cook until tender and golden brown. Transfer this mixture to the kettle containing the peas.
3. Cover kettle and simmer until peas are tender, about 1 hour. Stir in rice, salt, black pepper and red pepper. Cover and cook 17 to 20 minutes without stirring until rice is tender. Remove red pepper and serve hot.

Serves 8 to 10.

Dried Beans

The common varieties of dried beans used in American bean dishes are native to the New World, dating back to the Indian culture of North and South America.

Dried Bean Basics

PRESOAKING   All varieties of dried beans except split peas and lentils require presoaking for good cooking results.

Quick Method: Add cold water to measure 2 inches over the beans. Bring to a boil. Cover pot and cook 2 minutes; remove from heat. Let stand 1 hour. Drain if desired. Proceed with recipe.

Overnight Method: Add cold water to measure 2 inches over the beans and let stand overnight. Drain if desired. Proceed with recipe.

COOKING BEANS   Beans require long, slow cooking to break down hard-to-digest starches. A little oil added to the cooking liquid helps to prevent the water from boiling over.

SOAKING LIQUID   To cook or not to cook the beans in the soaking liquid is the choice of the cook. The modern cooking theory is to use the soaking liquid because it contains nutrients. I prefer not to use the liquid. It is my opinion that beans cooked in their soaking liquid have a slightly unpleasant off-taste.

New England Baked Beans

The Puritan housewife baked her beans all day Saturday and served them fresh for the Saturday night meal (the beginning of Sabbath); then she warmed them over for Sunday breakfast and served them warm or cold, depending on the heat-holding qualities of her oven, for Sunday's noonday meal, providing she did not consider it necessary for the family to fast from breakfast until sundown on Sunday.

All religious significance was lost years ago, but baked beans (sometimes referred to as Yankee Doodle in a pot) and brown bread are still eaten every Saturday night and Sunday morning by many New Englanders.

The following traditional recipe is from the private collection of a woman from Maine who was born to New England cooking.

1 pound (2 cups) dried pea beans or red kidney beans
¼ pound salt pork or cured bacon, cut into 3 pieces

2 to 3 teaspoons salt
2 tablespoons light brown sugar
3 tablespoons dark molasses
1 tablespoon dry mustard

Preheated oven temperature: 225°F.
1. Presoak the beans, using Quick Method or Overnight Method. Drain, cover with fresh cold water and simmer 30 minutes. Drain and reserve all the cooking liquid.
2. Place 1 piece of the salt pork in the bottom of a 2½-quart bean pot or a heavy, deep-sided, flameproof casserole with a tight-fitting lid; add the beans. Score the remaining 2 pieces of salt pork with ½-inch gashes and press into beans, leaving ¼ inch extending above the beans.
3. Combine the salt, brown sugar, molasses and mustard in a small saucepan. Stir well to blend. Add 1 cup of the reserved bean liquid and bring to a boil. Pour over the beans. Cover and bake in preheated oven 6 to 7 hours, adding more of the reserved cooking liquid every 2 hours.

NOTE: Beans should be covered with liquid during all but the last hour of cooking time. Remove the cover during the last hour of baking to brown the beans and evaporate enough of the liquid so that the beans won't be soupy.
Serves 6 to 8.

Michigan Baked Beans
(Pork and Beans)

There are as many recipes for Michigan baked beans as there are for New England baked beans. This is the recipe used by my aunt, a superb country cook. Serve with homemade wholewheat bread.

1 pound (2 cups) of Michigan navy or great northern beans

¼-pound chunk cured bacon with streaks of lean, cubed

⅓ cup light brown sugar, firmly packed

⅓ cup molasses

½ cup chili sauce

2 cups canned tomatoes, chopped

½ cup finely chopped onion

½ teaspoon dry mustard

1½ teaspoons salt, or to taste

Preheated oven temperature: 325°F.
1. Presoak the beans, using Quick Method or Overnight Method.
2. Place beans in a large, heavy saucepan with cold water to cover.
3. Cover and cook 1 hour, or until the beans are tender. Drain, reserving 1 cup liquid.
4. Add the cubed bacon, brown sugar, molasses, chili sauce, tomatoes, onion, dry mustard and salt to the beans. Stir well to blend.
5. Pour mixture into a well-oiled, shallow, 2-quart baking pan. Cover with foil and bake in preheated oven 1 hour and 15 minutes. Uncover and bake an additional 15 minutes, or until liquid is cooked down but beans are still juicy. Serve hot or cold.

Serves 6.

Frijoles

In Tex-Mex cooking there is only one bean that identifies this dish: the pinto, or painted bean.

1 pound (2 cups) dried pinto beans

½ cup cubed salt pork

1 cup chopped onion

1 large clove of garlic, chopped fine

1 sprig cilantro or ¼ teaspoon dried coriander

1 teaspoon chili powder

1 teaspoon dried cumin

Salt to taste

1. Presoak the beans, using Quick Method or Overnight Method.
2. Place beans in a large, heavy saucepan with cold water to cover.

3. Add the salt pork, onion, garlic, cilantro or coriander, chili powder, cumin and salt. Cover and bring to a boil; reduce heat and simmer slowly about 3 hours, or until beans are tender. Add more water as needed.
Serves 6.

Variation: Frijoles Refritos (Refried Beans)

Begin with a recipe of frijoles that have simmered slowly until almost all the liquid has evaporated. Heat 2 tablespoons of oil or bacon drippings in a heavy skillet and add beans by spoonfuls with a little of the remaining pot liquid; mash to a heavy paste with a large fork or potato masher. Pan-fry 10 to 15 minutes, stirring often to keep from scorching. Stir in some grated Cheddar cheese and heat just enough for cheese to melt. Serve hot with chopped onions and green chili peppers.

SALADS AND DRESSINGS

The innovative Pennsylvania Dutch cook is responsible for many of the traditional American salads we enjoy today. These salads usually are served with the main course.

West Coast salads are in a different category. They can be anything from a simply dressed green salad to a sturdy dish containing meats, poultry, seafood and/or fruits. It is a tradition on the West Coast to serve the salad as a first course.

Now that native wines are coming into their own and are being served with the entrée, many Americans follow the rule of the French and serve the salad after the main course. The reason is obvious—the acidity of most salad dressings interferes with the taste of wine.

Salads in American cooking fall into three categories: Main-dish salads, side-dish salads and fruit salads.

Salad-making Basics

SALAD GREENS   When you shop for greens, select only those that are crisp and fresh-looking, with good color. There is no way to bring wilted greens back to their original freshness.

RECOMMENDED GREENS   Boston, bibb (sometimes called limestone), leaf, salad bowl and romaine lettuce, chicory, escarole, endive, spinach, watercress, dandelion leaves, the green tops of white turnips and beets. Buy iceberg lettuce as a last resort; unless it is garden-fresh at a roadside stand, most iceberg lettuce is hard-ripe and tasteless.

CLEANING GREENS   Separate from the head or main stem as many leaves as you need for the salad. (Refrigerate the remainder—they will stay fresher if not washed.) Wash the leaves well in cold water. Lift the leaves out of the water to avoid pouring the sand back through the leaves. Three changes of water may be necessary if the leaves are excessively sandy.

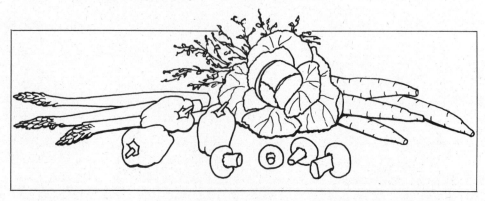

DRYING THE GREENS   Dressing will not cling to wet leaves, so dry the greens thoroughly. Put the leaves in a colander or wire basket and shake off as much water as possible. Then tear the leaves into whatever size is desired, put them in a salad spinner or wrap them in a dry cloth or paper towels and refrigerate until serving time.

Salad Dressings

There are many excellent homemade salad dressings in American cooking. The most classic is "boiled dressing." Making a boiled dressing can be a bit tricky—the egg in the mixture has a tendency to curdle. As a substitute, many years ago cooks began substituting mayonnaise.

VINEGARS   Those used most often in salad dressings are apple cider vinegar, red and white wine vinegar. Distilled white vinegar is used for pickling and is almost never used in salad dressings.

HERBS AND SPICES   American cooks are once again becoming familiar with these treasured seasonings, which were at the fingertips of Colonial cooks. They can be used in any salad dressing, to create tasty variations.

OILS   The usual choices are corn oil and light olive oil. Sometimes they are mixed, half corn oil and half olive oil, because corn oil is too mildly flavored for some people.

Boiled Dressing
(Basic Recipe)

This dressing is referred to in many cookbooks as "cooked mayonnaise." In times past, every home cook had a favorite recipe; it was made in quantity and stored in a glass jar in the refrigerator to use as needed. The thick dressing base was either thinned to desired consistency with unwhipped heavy cream or mixed half and half with whipped cream. Herbs, spices and other condiments were added at the discretion of the cook.

A very heavy saucepan is needed to prepare this dressing. Otherwise, cook the mixture in the top of a double boiler over simmering water.

¼ cup unsalted butter
2 tablespoons flour or 1 tablespoon
  cornstarch
1 tablespoon sugar
½ teaspoon salt

1 cup milk
1 teaspoon dry mustard
2 large eggs
½ cup cider vinegar

1. Melt the butter in a heavy, 1-quart saucepan over low heat. Add the flour or cornstarch, the sugar and salt. Blend mixture until smooth. Slowly add the milk, stirring constantly to blend. Cook over medium-low heat, stirring constantly, until thickened. Remove from heat and cool slightly.
2. Beat the mustard, eggs and vinegar in a small bowl. Slowly pour the mixture into the cooled sauce, stirring constantly until smooth.
3. Return to medium-low heat and cook just under the boiling point until the consistency of soft custard. Cool and refrigerate.
4. Thin to desired consistency with heavy cream.

Yield: 2 cups of salad dressing base.

Blender Mayonnaise
(*Basic Recipe*)

After the blender became a basic kitchen appliance, food editors around the country popularized this recipe. It also can be prepared in a food processor with good results. Follow manufacturer's instructions.

1 large egg
¾ teaspoon salt
½ teaspoon dry mustard
¼ teaspoon paprika

1 tablespoon vinegar and 1 tablespoon lemon juice; or 2 tablespoons vinegar
1 cup corn oil or ½ cup corn oil and ½ cup light olive oil

Put the egg, salt, mustard, paprika, vinegar and lemon juice and ¼ cup of oil into a blender. Cover and process at high speed for a few seconds. Immediately remove feeder cap and, with the motor still running, pour in the remaining oil in a slow steady stream. Use rubber spatula, if necessary, to scrape down sides of blender and keep the ingredients flowing to the processing blades. Keep refrigerated no longer than 7 days.

Yield: About 1¼ cups.

Variation: Mustard Mayonnaise

Substitute 1½ tablespoons Dijon-style mustard for dry mustard. Omit vinegar and substitute 1 additional tablespoon of lemon juice.

Russian Dressing

Add 3½ tablespoons chili sauce and 1 teaspoon prepared horseradish to ingredients in the blender. Fold 2 teaspoons finely chopped green onion into the finished dressing.

Thousand Island Dressing

Add ¼ cup chili sauce and 1 teaspoon Worcestershire sauce to ingredients in blender. Fold 8 finely-chopped stuffed green olives, 1 tablespoon finely chopped onion and 2 tablespoons finely chopped dill pickle into the finished dressing.

Oil and Vinegar Dressing

This is an American adaptation of the classic vinaigrette of French cookery. Use to dress a mixture of salad greens.

2 tablespoons finely chopped onion
1 clove garlic, chopped fine
1 cup of corn oil; or ½ cup corn oil and ½ cup light olive oil
⅓ cup white or red wine vinegar
½ teaspoon salt, or to taste

½ teaspoon dry mustard
½ teaspoon Worcestershire sauce (optional)
½ teaspoon sugar or honey
¼ teaspoon freshly ground black pepper, or to taste

Combine all the ingredients in a 1-pint jar. Shake well to blend. Use sparingly. The greens should be very lightly coated with the dressing. **Yield: About 1½ cups.**

Pennsylvania Dutch Bacon Dressing

This is an old-fashioned hot salad dressing that should be served with raw spinach, dandelion greens, leaf lettuce or cooked green beans. Hard-cooked egg slices may be used for garnish.

2 slices cured bacon
1½ tablespoons flour
¾ cup water, combined with ¼ cup cider vinegar
1 tablespoon sugar, or less to taste
Yolk of 1 large egg, well beaten

⅛ teaspoon dry mustard
Salt and freshly ground black pepper to taste
About 1 pound of salad greens, torn into bite-sized pieces; or 2 pounds cooked green beans

1. Fry the bacon in a medium-sized skillet until crisp. Remove the bacon and drain on paper towels. Add the flour to the bacon drippings in the skillet and cook over medium heat 3 minutes, stirring constantly.
2. Remove from heat and slowly add the water-vinegar mixture, stirring constantly until mixture is smooth.
3. Return to medium heat and cook 5 minutes, stirring constantly, until the mixture has thickened. Remove from heat and quickly

whisk in sugar, beaten egg, mustard, salt and pepper. Return to low heat and cook 2 minutes. Pour at once over salad greens or green beans. Crumble the bacon and add to the salad mixture. Toss well to blend and serve hot.
Serves 6 to 8.

Creamy Dressing for Vegetables

This slightly piquant dressing contrasts well with vegetables in a salad.

1 teaspoon Dijon-style mustard
⅔ cup heavy cream
½ teaspoon salt

½ teaspoon sugar
2 tablespoons white wine vinegar

Combine all the ingredients in a small bowl; beat with a whisk until well blended. Refrigerate a few hours to blend flavors.
Yield: ¾ cup.

Variation: Creamy Blue Cheese Dressing

Decrease salt to ¼ teaspoon. Add 2 to 3 tablespoons crumbled blue cheese.

B&O French Dressing

Before the days of air transportation, many of the railroads were famous for the cuisine served in their dining cars. This was a classic favorite of passengers on the Baltimore & Ohio line.

½ tablespoon sugar
½ teaspoon dry mustard
½ teaspoon salt
⅛ teaspoon white pepper
Dash of paprika
Juice of half an orange

1½ cups olive oil
½ teaspoon Worcestershire sauce
½ cup vinegar
½ tablespoon catsup
½ small onion

1. Mix the sugar, mustard, salt, pepper and paprika in a medium-sized bowl.
2. Combine the orange juice, oil, Worcestershire sauce, vinegar and catsup in a jar. Shake until well mixed.
3. Beat the oil mixture slowly into the dry mixture until well blended. Add the onion but remove it after 15 minutes. Store in a 1-pint jar. Shake well before using.
Yield: 2 cups.

Putch's Famous Spinach Salad

This is a California-style salad that originated in the kitchen of a famous Kansas City, Missouri, restaurant. It's perfect to serve with broiled meats.

1 pound fresh spinach
½ cup finely chopped celery
½ cup finely chopped onion
1 cup cubed Monterey Jack or Cheddar cheese
1 cup mayonnaise, preferably home-made

½ teaspoon salt
½ teaspoon Tabasco sauce
1½ teaspoons cider vinegar
2 hard-cooked large eggs, chopped
¼ cup freshly grated horseradish (optional)

1. Clean spinach following basic instructions, page 308. Trim off stems and chop leaves coarsely with a chef's knife. Place in a large salad bowl. Add celery, onion and cheese.
2. To make the dressing, combine the mayonnaise, salt, Tabasco sauce and vinegar in a small bowl. Stir well to blend.
3. Pour the dressing over the spinach and toss gently to coat well. Serve on individual salad plates. Garnish with chopped eggs. Serve a small portion of optional horseradish on the side of each plate.

Serves 6 to 8.

Vegetable Salad Bowl

The secret of good vegetable salad is to keep the ingredients separated until the final mixing, so that the flavor of each one will stand out.

1 cup green beans, lightly cooked
1 cup asparagus cuts, lightly cooked
½ cup cubed cooked beets
½ cup of your favorite salad dressing
1 cup shredded raw carrots

½ cup chopped celery
4 cups salad greens, torn into bite-size pieces
Salt and freshly ground black pepper to taste

1. Place the beans, asparagus and beets separately in small bowls with 2 tablespoons of salad dressing per bowl; marinate and chill 20 minutes. Reserve the remainder of the dressing.
2. Place the carrots, celery and greens in a large salad bowl. Add the marinated vegetables, the remainder of the salad dressing and the salt and pepper; toss gently to mix well. Serve immediately.

Serves 6.

Orange and Onion Salad

This is a good salad to serve with Tex-Mex food or when a green salad doesn't seem compatible with the rest of the menu.

2 large Spanish onions or any other mild-flavored onion
2 large navel oranges
1 ripe avocado

Lettuce leaves
Any desired tart salad dressing
Dried tarragon leaves (optional)

1. Peel the onions and slice into paper-thin rings. Soak in salted ice water until crisp. Drain on paper towels.
2. Peel oranges, slice into rings and remove seeds. Peel and slice avocado into rings.
3. Arrange lettuce leaves in a shallow salad bowl. Place onion rings alternately with orange and avocado rings. Dress lightly with your favorite tart salad dressing, to which a pinch of optional tarragon leaves may be added.

Serves 4 to 6.

Variation: Grapefruit and Avocado Salad

Omit onion and orange. Substitute peeled grapefruit sliced into rings.

Yellow Wax Beans in Mustard Sauce

Pennsylvania Dutch cooks use yellow wax beans to prepare this vegetable salad dish but green beans taste just as good with the sauce.

2 pounds fresh yellow wax beans or green beans
3 green onions, chopped
2 large eggs
2 tablespoons sugar
2 tablespoons white wine vinegar

½ cup corn oil or light olive oil
1 tablespoon lemon juice
1 teaspoon Dijon-style mustard
½ teaspoon salt
¼ teaspoon freshly ground black pepper

1. Cook the beans in boiling salted water until just tender. Rinse immediately under cold running water. Drain thoroughly.
2. To make the dressing, combine remaining ingredients in a blender or food processor and process 3 minutes. *Caution:* If using a blender, follow manufacturer's instructions; it may be necessary to turn the motor on and off to prevent it from overheating.

3. Pour the dressing into the top of a double boiler and cook over simmering water a few minutes, stirring constantly with a whisk until the mixture thickens. Cool slightly.
4. Spoon sauce over beans and toss to coat well. Serve at room temperature.

Serves 6 to 8.

Hoosier Three-Bean Salad

Indiana farm women undoubtedly created this winter salad from an ample supply of canned produce from the summer garden. Freshly cooked green and yellow wax beans may be substituted.

2 cups cut green beans (1-pound can)
2 cups cut yellow wax beans (1-pound can)
2 cups red kidney beans (1-pound can)
1 cup apple jelly, or to taste
¼ cup vinegar
1 tablespoon cornstarch
1 teaspoon salt, or to taste
2 cups thinly sliced celery
½ cup chopped green onion
Salad greens to line bowl

1. Drain the beans well and place in a large bowl.
2. In a small, heavy saucepan combine the jelly, vinegar, cornstarch and salt. Cook over low heat until the mixture is clear and has thickened. Cool slightly.
3. Pour the warm sauce over the beans. Refrigerate 1 to 2 hours to blend flavors. Stir in the celery and onion. Spoon into a lettuce-lined salad bowl and serve at room temperature.

Serves 12.

Coleslaw

Coleslaw is counted as one of the 7 sweet and 7 sours of Pennsylvania Dutch cooking. There are two types: One is shredded cabbage in a cream dressing; the other is redolent of vinegar and sugar.

Old-Fashioned Creamed "Slaw"

1 small head green cabbage, about 1 pound
¾ cup heavy cream
1 tablespoon white wine vinegar
1 tablespoon sugar, or less to taste

½ teaspoon dry mustard
¾ teaspoon salt
Freshly ground black pepper to taste
A pinch of cayenne pepper (optional)

1. Remove the outer leaves of the cabbage, split head in half and remove the core. Shred or grate the cabbage into a large bowl. You should have about 5 cups.
2. To prepare the dressing, combine the remaining ingredients in a small bowl. Beat with a small wire whisk until the mixture begins to thicken slightly and small bubbles appear.
3. Pour the dressing over the cabbage and toss quickly until well coated. Serve immediately.

Serves 4 to 6.

Pepper "Slaw"

1 medium-size head green cabbage, about 1½-pounds
½ cup chopped green pepper
½ cup cider vinegar
½ cup water

½ teaspoon salt
½ cup sugar or to taste
1 teaspoon celery seed

1. Remove the outer leaves of the cabbage, split in half and remove the core. Shred or grate the cabbage into a large bowl. You should have about 7 cups. Add the green pepper.
2. To make the dressing, combine the vinegar, water, salt, sugar and celery seed in a small saucepan. Place over low heat and stir until sugar is dissolved. Cool.
3. Pour dressing over cabbage mixture and toss until well mixed. Refrigerate, covered, several hours to blend flavors. Serve cold in small side dishes.

Serves 6 to 8.

Cold Potato Salad

This is a standard recipe used by many home cooks.

6 to 7 medium-sized all-purpose potatoes
2 hard-cooked large eggs
⅔ cup finely chopped celery
5 chopped green onions, white part only
⅓ cup chopped sweet pickle or pickle relish

¾ cup Boiled Dressing (use Basic Recipe, page 309); or mayonnaise, preferably homemade
1 teaspoon Dijon-style mustard
1 teaspoon Worcestershire sauce
Salt and freshly ground black pepper to taste

1. Boil the potatoes in their skins until tender; then peel and cube.
2. Separate the yolks from the whites of eggs. Reserve the yolks and chop the whites.
3. Combine the potatoes, chopped egg white, celery, green onion and pickle in a large bowl.
4. To make the dressing, mash the egg yolks in a small bowl with a fork until fluffy; then blend in Boiled Dressing or mayonnaise, the mustard and Worcestershire sauce.
5. Pour dressing over the potato mixture and stir gently to coat the potatoes and blend the ingredients. Add salt and pepper. Serve chilled. *Caution:* If salad is to be kept at room temperature longer than the normal serving time, prepare with Boiled Dressing. A cooked dressing keeps better.

Serves 6.

Variation: Texas Potato Salad

In Step 3, substitute dill pickle for sweet pickle. In Step 4 add ¾ cup crisply fried bacon bits and large firm tomato, seeded and chopped.

German Potato Salad

There are many versions of this salad in American cooking. Some are served hot, others cold, but all are variations of this traditional Pennsylvania Dutch recipe.

6 to 7 medium-sized all-purpose potatoes
8 thin slices cured bacon
⅓ cup water
3 tablespoons cider vinegar
1 tablespoon sugar
2 teaspoons salt, or to taste

Freshly ground black pepper to taste
1 tablespoon Dijon-style mustard
½ cup chopped green onion, white part only
1 cup sour cream
1 tablespoon finely chopped parsley

1. Boil the potatoes in their skins until tender; then peel and slice or cube.
2. Fry bacon in a large skillet until crisp. Drain bacon on paper towels. Crumble and set aside.
3. Pour off all but 2 tablespoons of bacon drippings from the skillet. Add the water, vinegar, sugar, salt, pepper and mustard. Stir over medium heat until mixture boils and the sugar is dissolved.
4. Remove from heat and add potatoes and green onion. Turn carefully with a wooden spoon or spatula until most of the dressing is absorbed. Gently fold in the sour cream, parsley and crumbled bacon. Serve warm.

Serves 6.

Classic Chicken Salad
(Basic Recipe)

In making chicken salad it always is better to use stewed chicken (see Basic Recipe, page 169) because the meat will be tenderer and moister. And of course, the bonus is a delicious broth and enough leftover chicken to use as a base for preparing soup. To use as a sandwich filling, chop the chicken and celery very fine.

4 cups cubed cooked chicken
1 cup chopped celery
⅓ cup cider vinegar
1 cup mayonnaise, made with half corn oil and half light olive oil (page 310)

Salt and freshly ground black pepper to taste
Green lettuce leaves
2 hard-cooked large eggs, shelled and quartered
8 stuffed olives, sliced thin
Paprika for garnish

1. In a large bowl combine the chicken, celery, vinegar, ⅓ cup of the mayonnaise, the salt and pepper. Stir lightly to mix well. Refrigerate several hours or overnight, mixing salad several times to blend flavors.
2. Line a large salad bowl or 6 to 8 individual salad bowls with lettuce. Spoon chicken mixture onto lettuce leaves. Garnish with quartered eggs, olives and a sprinkling of paprika. Top with remaining mayonnaise. Serve immediately.

Serves 6 to 8.

Variation: Turkey Salad

Substitute turkey for chicken. Omit stuffed olives and substitute ½ cup finely chopped sweet pickles or watermelon pickles.

Ham Salad

Ham salad can be served on lettuce leaves or used as a filling for
sandwiches. If using as a sandwich filling, chop the ham and other
ingredients much finer than for a main-course salad.

3 cups cooked cubed ham
1 cup finely chopped celery
½ cup chopped stuffed olives
2 hard-cooked large eggs, chopped
¼ cup finely chopped onion

1 tablespoon lemon juice
1 tablespoon Dijon-style mustard
Freshly ground black pepper to taste
¾ cup mayonnaise, preferably
   homemade

1. In a large bowl combine ham, celery, olives, eggs, onion, lemon juice,
   mustard and pepper. Stir well to blend flavors. Refrigerate several
   hours.
2. Remove from refrigerator and add mayonnaise. Mix well and serve
   on lettuce leaves or use to make sandwiches.

Serves 6, or makes enough filling for 6 large sandwiches.

Crab Louis

No one seems to know who Louis was. According to the food editor of
a San Francisco newspaper, Crab Louis originated in San Francisco
and is popular all along the Pacific Coast. The salad should be made
with fresh Dungeness crab, but any good quality crab—fresh, frozen
or canned—may be substituted.

½ medium-sized head of green lettuce (you may use iceberg if it is
   not too firm and white), shredded
2 cups flaked crabmeat

1 large tomato, cut into wedges
2 hard-cooked large eggs, sliced
8 pitted black olives
8 strips canned pimiento

Louis Dressing

1 cup mayonnaise, preferably
   homemade
½ cup chili sauce
1½ teaspoons finely chopped onion
1 teaspoon freshly grated horseradish, or less to taste

1 teaspoon lemon juice
¼ teaspoon crushed dried tarragon
Salt and freshly ground white pepper
   to taste

1. Arrange shredded lettuce on 4 salad plates.
2. Pick over crabmeat to remove cartilage and shell. Mound the crabmeat in the center of each plate. Garnish with tomato wedges, egg slices, olives and pimiento strips; refrigerate a few hours.
3. To prepare the Louis dressing, combine remaining ingredients. Spoon over chilled salad just before serving.

Serves 4.

Variation: Shrimp Louis

Substitute 2 cups medium-sized cooked shrimp for the crabmeat.

Crabmeat Salad

Maryland and Gulf Coast cooks share this basic recipe for crabmeat salad. It also can be used to fill avocado halves and tomatoes or as a sandwich filling.

½ medium-sized head of green lettuce, shredded
1 pound lump crabmeat, drained
⅔ cup homemade mayonnaise, made with half corn oil and half light olive oil (page 310)
1 teaspoon lemon juice

2 teaspoons capers
Cayenne pepper to taste
Salt to taste
2 tablespoons finely chopped parsley for garnish
Paprika for garnish

1. Arrange shredded lettuce on 6 salad plates.
2. Pick over crabmeat to remove cartilage and shell. *Caution:* Handle the crabmeat gently to keep the pieces as large as possible. Mound the crabmeat in the center of each plate.
3. To prepare the dressing, combine the mayonnaise, lemon juice, capers and cayenne pepper in a small bowl. Taste for seasonings and add salt if desired. Spoon the dressing over the crabmeat. Garnish with parsley and a sprinkling of paprika. Serve chilled but not cold.

Serves 6.

Green Goddess Salad

This is a West Coast main-course salad.

6 cups bite-size pieces of romaine
   lettuce
3 cups torn curly endive
1 cup cooked small shrimp
1 clove garlic, mashed
1 cup mayonnaise, preferably homemade
½ cup sour cream

¼ cup chopped parsley
3 tablespoons finely chopped chives
1-to-2 tablespoons anchovy paste, to
   taste
3 tablespoons tarragon vinegar
1 tablespoon lemon juice
Freshly ground black pepper to taste
Tomato wedges

1. Place romaine, endive and shrimp in large salad bowl.
2. To prepare dressing, rub a small bowl with the mashed garlic. Add mayonnaise, sour cream, parsley, chives, anchovy paste, vinegar, lemon juice and pepper. Mix well and refrigerate 1 hour to blend flavors.
3. Moisten the salad bowl ingredients with ⅓ cup of the dressing; toss gently until all the leaves are coated. Serve on chilled salad plates. Garnish with tomato wedges. Serve remaining dressing from a sauce dish.

Serves 6 to 8.

Maine Lobster Salad

An authentic Maine lobster salad is boiled lobster and dressing served on a bed of shredded lettuce with a sprinkling of paprika for garnish, and nothing more. Maine cooks prefer not to mask the flavor of lobster salad with chopped celery or other distracting ingredients.

3 cups cubed boiled lobster, chilled
   (allow ½ cup per serving)
Boiled Dressing (use Basic Recipe,
   page 309); or homemade mayonnaise

½ medium-sized head of green let-
   tuce, shredded
Lobster claws for garnish
Paprika for garnish

1. Mix the lobster with just enough dressing or mayonnaise to coat the meat, allowing about 1 tablespoon of dressing for each cup of lobster. (Some Maine cooks prefer not to mix the lobster with the dressing but merely add a dollop on top of each portion.) Refrigerate until thoroughly chilled.
2. Arrange shredded lettuce on individual salad plates. Mound the lobster in the center of each plate. Top each serving with a whole lobster claw removed from the shell. Sprinkle with paprika. Serve chilled but not cold.

Serves 6.

Shrimp Salad
(*Basic Recipe*)

This is a standard recipe for shrimp salad. However, any cold seafood sauce (see pages 150–52) can be used to coat the shrimp. Serve on lettuce leaves or use as a stuffing for tomatoes or avocado halves.

2 cups cooked shrimp
½ cup finely chopped celery
2 tablespoons finely chopped sweet pickle
1 teaspoon finely chopped capers
¼ cup mayonnaise, preferably homemade

⅛ teaspoon Tabasco sauce
Salt and freshly ground black pepper to taste
1 hard-cooked large egg, chopped fine
Lettuce leaves

1. If the shrimp are large, cut each one into 2 or 3 pieces; combine in a bowl with the celery.
2. In a separate small bowl combine the pickle, capers, mayonnaise, Tabasco sauce, salt and pepper. Stir well to blend and combine with the shrimp and celery. Gently stir in the chopped egg.
3. Line 4 salad plates with lettuce leaves. Mound shrimp mixture in the middle and serve chilled but not cold.

Serves 4 for salad or will fill 6 avocado halves or 6 medium-sized tomatoes.

Variation: Tuna Fish Salad.

Substitute 2 cups well-drained tuna fish for the shrimp. Substitute ¼ cup sliced stuffed olives for the sweet pickle. Omit capers.

The Original Waldorf Salad

This simple salad has become the victim of too many ingredients, including sugar, whipped cream, grapes, dates, raisins, and so on. Well-flavored ripe apples do not need to be sweetened, and whipped cream makes the salad taste like a dessert.

2 cups cubed unpeeled red apples (use red Delicious, Winesap or any other eating apple)
1 tablespoon lemon juice
1 cup chopped celery

½ cup walnuts
About ½ cup Boiled Dressing (see page 309); or mayonnaise, preferably homemade
Lettuce leaves

1. Combine the apples and lemon juice in a large bowl. Make certain that the apples are well coated with the lemon juice to prevent them from turning dark. Add the celery and walnuts. Stir in enough Boiled Dressing or mayonnaise to bind the ingredients together, no more.
2. Line a large bowl or individual salad plates with lettuce leaves. Arrange salad on lettuce and serve immediately.

Serves 6.

Molded Fresh Cranberry Salad

Fresh cranberry salad is a wonderful palate refresher, and it contrasts well with rich poultry, pork or ham entrées. Past generations have made this recipe with imitation fruit-flavored gelatin dissolved in water. I have substituted unflavored gelatin and bottled cranberry juice in this recipe.

2 tablespoons (2 envelopes) unflavored Knox gelatin
1 cup sugar, or less to taste
1 cup cranberry juice
1 medium-sized orange (2½–3-inch
diameter)

2 cups raw cranberries
1 cup chopped pecans or walnuts
(optional)
Lettuce leaves
Boiled Dressing or mayonnaise, preferably homemade, for garnish

1. Combine the gelatin and sugar in a medium-sized bowl.
2. Heat the cranberry juice in a small saucepan until it just begins to boil. Remove from heat and pour over sugar mixture; stir until gelatin is completely dissolved.
3. Trim 4 thin one-inch squares of peel from orange (no white pith); cut into thin strips. *Caution:* The pith will give the salad a bitter taste. Quarter the orange and remove the seeds.
4. Place the orange peel and quarters in a blender or food processor. Add the cranberry juice mixture and cranberries. Blend at high speed until cranberries and orange peel are chopped fine. Stir in optional nuts.
5. Pour mixture into 6 well-oiled ¾-cup molds. Refrigerate several hours, or until firm. Unmold onto lettuce leaves and top with a dollop of Boiled Dressing or mayonnaise. Serve immediately.

Serves 6.

Variation: Cranberry Ring

Double the recipe and pour into a well-oiled 5-to-6-cup ring mold. Refrigerate several hours, or until firm. Unmold and fill with chicken, turkey or ham salad.

Serves 8 to 10.

Tomato Aspic

This is a Southern recipe for a tangy tomato aspic. It can be served in individual molds or in a large ring filled with poultry or shrimp salad. Cajun cooks frequently serve the aspic with Jambalaya (page 54).

3 cups canned tomatoes
1 clove garlic, chopped
1 teaspoon Worcestershire sauce
1 teaspoon lemon juice
½ teaspoon sugar
A few drops of Tabasco sauce
Salt to taste
2 tablespoons (2 envelopes) unflavored Knox gelatin
½ cup finely chopped celery

¼ cup finely chopped green onion
¼ cup finely chopped stuffed green
  olives
¼ cup finely chopped dill pickle
2 tablespoons finely chopped
  parsley
Lettuce leaves or watercress
Mayonnaise, preferably homemade,
  for garnish
Celery strips for garnish (optional)

1. In a heavy, 1½-quart saucepan (not aluminum)cook the tomatoes, garlic, Worcestershire sauce, lemon juice, sugar, Tabasco sauce and salt over medium-low heat 20 minutes, covered.
2. Transfer to a blender or food processor and process until smooth. Strain back into the saucepan, using a spatula to press down on the pulp; there should be 2 cups of liquid in the pan. Discard the tomato seeds. Reheat the liquid until it just begins to boil.
3. Put the gelatin in a medium-sized bowl; add the boiling tomato mixture and stir until gelatin is dissolved. Chill until slightly thickened.
4. Add the chopped celery, green onion, olives, dill pickle and parsley. Stir well to blend. Pour into well-oiled individual molds. Chill until firm. Unmold onto lettuce leaves or watercress and garnish with a dollop of mayonnaise. Garnish with optional celery strips soaked in ice water until they curl.

Serves 6.

Variation: Tomato Aspic Ring

Double the recipe. Pour into a well-oiled 5-to-6-cup ring mold. Chill until firm. Unmold onto lettuce leaves or watercress and fill with salad. Garnish with optional celery strips.

Serves 10.

Perfection Salad

By all accounts, the popularity of this old-fashioned salad began after unflavored gelatin became available to home cooks. Basically, the salad is molded coleslaw. Perfect to serve with fried fish, shrimp or scallops.

The food processor can be used to make quick work of the chopping necessary to prepare the salad; follow manufacturer's instructions.

3 tablespoons (3 envelopes) unflavored gelatin
3 tablespoons sugar, or less to taste
2 cups boiling water
½ cup tarragon vinegar
2 tablespoons lemon juice
2 cups chopped cabbage

1 cup chopped celery
1 cup chopped red or green pepper
2 canned pimientos, chopped fine
1 teaspoon salt, or more to taste
Lettuce leaves
Boiled Dressing or mayonnaise, preferably homemade, for garnish

1. In a large bowl mix gelatin and sugar; add boiling water and stir until gelatin is completely dissolved. Add vinegar and lemon juice; stir to blend. Chill in the refrigerator until the mixture is the consistency of unbeaten egg whites.
2. Add cabbage, celery, pepper, pimiento and salt. Stir well to blend. Pour the mixture into a well-oiled 9-x-9-inch baking pan or individual molds. Chill several hours, or until firm. Unmold onto lettuce leaves and garnish with a dollop of Boiled Dressing or mayonnaise. Serve chilled.

NOTE: If molded in baking pan, cut into 3-inch-square serving portions.
Serves 8.

BAKING

Breads

Yeast Bread

Up until the period of affluence that followed the First World War, every rural cook set aside one day a week, usually Saturday, to bake enough bread to last the family through the following week. Unfortunately, the nation rapidly developed a taste for overprocessed white bakery bread, and until the sixties very little bread was made in the home kitchen.

For fifteen years I have been teaching the basics of breadmaking in my kitchen workshop and demonstrating the craft before local charity and civic organizations. I have discovered that one basic recipe can be adjusted to make many types of bread. It is the variety of flour—all-white, graham, whole-wheat, rye, oat, cornmeal, or a combination—that determines the type of loaf.

Organization is of key importance when baking bread, in order to keep the chore from being time-consuming. The actual mixing of the ingredients takes very little time, hand kneading takes no more than 10 to 15 minutes and only a few more minutes are needed to shape the loaves and put them in pans. The rising and baking takes more time. Both of these processes take care of themselves, allowing the cook time to perform other unrelated chores around the home.

To many minds, homemade bread is essential to good nutrition. Fortunately, making good bread is within the scope of even the less than moderately skilled cook. The secrets are patience and careful attention to basic instructions.

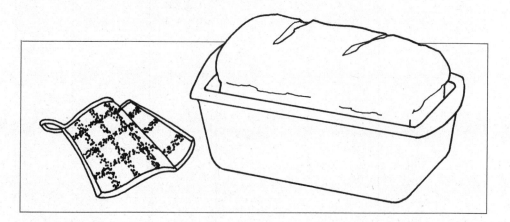

Breadmaking Basics

UTENSILS   You will need a mixing bowl large enough to accommodate a substantial quantity of dough—the larger the better if you plan to make several loaves. You also will need measuring cups, measuring spoons and a large wooden spoon for stirring the dough. A heavy-duty mixer with a dough hook is a laborsaving appliance. However, its bowl will not be large enough to mix dough for more than 3 medium-sized loaves.

KNEADING SURFACE   It is necessary to have a flat surface for kneading dough by hand. Use a large wooden or formica surface, pastry cloth or marble slab.

PANS   Bread pans of any size may be used. Professional bakers prefer dark-colored pans to help absorb heat and give a darker crust, but aluminum, glass or ceramic pans are satisfactory. I prefer to use ovenproof clay or stoneware: their browning qualities are much better in a conventional oven than aluminum, glass or ceramic.

INGREDIENTS

YEAST. There are several types of yeast, and which to use is a matter of personal preference in breadmaking. Yeast is a low form of plant life. When liquid, starch and sugar are provided, like a plant it starts to grow and produces a carbon dioxide gas that leavens the dough, causing it to rise. Carbon dioxide is added to much of the spongy-white, commercially made bread by mechanical means, and this is why the bread is so bland.

Active Dry Yeast. This is dormant dried yeast bought in small, ¼-ounce (7 gram) packages with an expiration date in bold print on each package. *Caution:* Even a few days beyond the expiration date makes a difference in the finished loaf.

Fresh Compressed Yeast. This is live yeast, not dehydrated, which is the reason it needs to be kept refrigerated until used. This yeast is perishable. It should be kept no longer than 10 to 14 days in the refrigerator. It can be frozen indefinitely. One 1-ounce cake of fresh compressed yeast is equivalent to two ¼-ounce packages (2 tablespoons) active dry yeast.

Liquid Starter. This is the earliest form of yeast, which acquired the regional term "sourdough" at the time of the westward gold rush of the 1800s. Liquid yeast usually is made of potato water and flour, which is allowed to ferment long enough to build up enough carbon dioxide to leaven the bread. Two cups liquid starter is equivalent to a ¼-ounce package active dry yeast or ½-ounce fresh compressed yeast.

Gluten. Gluten is a mixture of plant proteins that occurs in cereal grains. The carbon dioxide generated by the growing yeast must have a structure to support it. The framework is provided by the gluten in the flour. The combination of the yeast and gluten in the flour is what makes the bread rise.

FLOUR

All-purpose white is the most commonly used flour in bread-making. It is available bleached and unbleached. Unbleached flour gives the bread more nutrition, texture and flavor.

Rye, Whole-wheat, Graham, Oat and Cornmeal are cereal grains with low gluten content and should be combined with all-purpose white flour. Used alone, they produce a heavy bread.

Stone-Ground. Years ago, when all bread came from the hearth, it was made with stone-ground flour. The grain was ground into flour by huge crushing millstones. This process kept the germ oil in the grain from lumping and becoming rancid. This is the reason many modern breadmakers prefer the freshness of stone-ground flour and meal. Both will stay fresher longer if kept refrigerated or frozen.

Sweeteners. Sweeteners such as honey, molasses and sugar are not necessary ingredients in breadmaking. Any sweetener does add moisture and some flavor to baked bread. Honey is a natural preservative and bread made with it keeps better and stays fresher longer. Sweeteners can be used interchangeably in most bread recipes. Too much sugar will retard the action of the yeast, so it is best to put the major part of the sweetness in the topping, as with sugar-crusted breads and glazed rolls.

Liquids. Milk, water and potato water are the liquids used most frequently in breadmaking. Water gives a crisp crust and a firmer-textured loaf; milk gives spongier texture and a darker crust. Potato water is preferred by many country cooks because it helps the yeast develop.

Eggs. Although not a necessary ingredient, eggs give bread color, texture and flavor. Bread made with eggs will require a considerably longer time to rise.

Fats and oils. These are not necessary ingredients, but they do make the bread tenderer and improve the keeping quality. I prefer to use melted lard or unsalted butter. However, melted margarine, shortening or oil are equally satisfactory.

Salt retards the growth of yeast and should not be added to the ingredients until the yeast mixture has grown strong and lively.

HOW TO KNEAD DOUGH

Turn the ball of risen dough out onto a lightly floured surface and turn to coat with flour. Knead by folding the dough toward you and then pushing down with the heels of your hands. This is called the "heel and push method." Continue kneading, giving the ball of dough quarter turns, until the dough becomes springy to the touch. Sometimes blisters will appear on the dough surface. This is a sure sign that the dough has had sufficient kneading.

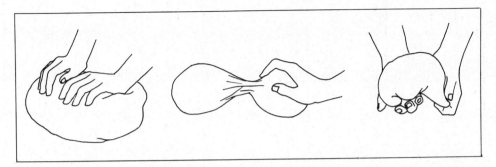

HOW TO SHAPE LOAVES   Pinch dough to divide into equal pieces (do not cut with a knife—this will break the air pockets). Pat each piece of dough into an oval about 1 inch shorter than the length of the baking pan. Fold in half lengthwise, pinching seams lightly to seal. Tuck ends under and place in a well-oiled pan, seam side down.

Preparation. There are important "Do's" and "Don'ts" in the craft of breadmaking.

HOW TO PROOF YEAST   To "proof" literally means to prove that the yeast is active. Those of us experienced in breadmaking prefer to proof by placing the yeast, warm water and sugar or honey in a small bowl for about 10 minutes, or until foamy. In the rapid-mix method the yeast is added directly to the ingredients during the mixing. Then one has to wait until the dough rises enough to be placed in the oven before the yeast has proved to be active.

To Proof Active Dry Yeast: Combine ½ cup warm water (115°F.), 1 teaspoon sugar or honey, a pinch of optional ginger and a ¼-ounce package of yeast in a small bowl. Set in a warm place until foaming nicely, which should take about 10 minutes.

To Proof Fresh Compressed Yeast: Combine ½ cup lukewarm water heated to a temperature of *no more than 95°F.* with 1 teaspoon sugar or honey and a 1-ounce cake of yeast. *Caution:* The temperature of the water is very important. Fresh yeast is as delicate as a flower and can be killed by using water that is too hot. Proceed as with proofing active dry yeast.

To Proof Liquid Starter: See Sourdough Breadmaking Basics, page 346.

TO FREEZE BREAD   Dough should be baked before freezing. (Unbaked dough, unless extra yeast is added, does not rise well after it has been frozen. Cool baked breads or rolls thoroughly. Wrap in airtight paper or place in plastic freezer bags, squeezing out as much air as possible. Storage life is about 6 months. Thaw in wrapper about 30 minutes. Rewrap in foil and place in a preheated 300°F. oven 15 to 20 minutes.

THE "DO" LIST

1. *Do* read through the recipe before you begin to make bread. Make certain that you have the proper ingredients and utensils or suitable substitutes, and that you understand the mixing method.
2. *Do* try the Basic Recipe first if you are just learning to make bread. Watch how the yeast mixture looks when it has been "proofed," how the dough feels and looks when it is being mixed and after it has been kneaded sufficiently. Note how the loaf feels when it is ready for the oven, what happens to it while it is in the oven and when to take it out of the oven. You will discover that breadmaking is truly a pleasure, once you learn the basics.
3. *Do* experiment with herbs, spices, flavorings, combinations of dried fruits and nuts, and the sizes and shapes of the loaves of bread as soon as you have mastered the Basic Recipe. Breadmaking need never be monotonous. Try adding wheat germ or sprouts, for example. Our forebears added any vegetable that contained a sizable amount of starch, such as puree of cooked potatoes, parsnips, turnips, dried peas, lentils or beans.
4. *Do* proof the yeast at the correct temperature—this is very important. Yeast that fails to bubble or foam in the proofing should be discarded. Something is wrong and you should start with another package of yeast and fresh ingredients.

THE "DON'T" LIST

1. *Don't* start to bake bread unless you are reasonably sure you will have time to complete the process.
2. *Don't* fill bread pans more than half full with dough. The dough needs room to rise before it is placed in the oven.
3. *Don't* ruin the baked loaf by trying to cut it with a dull knife. A serrated bread knife should be used.
4. *Don't* wrap the baked bread until it has cooled to room temperature; this will take several hours.

Common Causes of Poor-Quality Bread

Uneven top crust with lumps and bulges is the result of improper mixing and improperly molding dough into loaves.

Top crust cracks are usually the result of too much flour in the dough. *Shell crack* results from uneven oven temperature or from putting the pans of dough so close together that heat cannot circulate evenly. The shell crack comes on the side of the loaf where the temperature is lowest in the oven, and it can be as wide as 3 to 4 inches.

Overhang is when the baked loaf hangs over the edges of the pan. This may come from letting the dough rise too much before it goes into the oven. It also may be caused by putting the loaves into an oven that is not hot enough.

Thick crust may come from dough getting too light, rising too much or from dough that has been under-kneaded.

Thick cell walls develop when there has been too little kneading or too short a fermentation period or a combination of both.

Crumbly and coarse-textured bread usually is caused by using too much flour, which makes the dough too stiff, or from letting the dough rise too much.

Streaks in bread may be caused by adding flour to the dough while molding loaves. Using excess fat on the hands while molding the loaves also may cause streaks.

Compact or heavy texture at the bottom of the baked loaf may result from leaving the pans with the molded loaves on a cold surface while rising before baking. It also may occur if the temperature at the bottom of the oven is too low.

Soggy, heavy bread means that too much liquid and not enough flour was mixed into the dough. It also can be caused by wrapping bread before it has cooled to room temperature.

Tough bread is the result of adding too much flour during the mixing, making the dough heavy. It also can be the result of dough not having risen sufficiently before being placed in the oven.

Air bubbles in the baked bread are a result of insufficient mixing, too long a rising time, or a room that was too warm causing the dough to expand too fast.

White Bread
(Basic Recipe)

Bread made with water has a firmer texture and better slicing qualities than bread made with milk. In the interest of nutrition, I enrich the bread with dried skim milk, which will not affect the desired firm texture.

This recipe makes 2 medium-sized loaves or 6 mini loaves. Recipe ingredients may be doubled for a larger quantity of bread.

Caution: Before you begin breadmaking, be certain you have a bowl large enough to accommodate the dough in the recipe. A 4-quart bowl is the minimum size recommended for successful results. Remember to double the size of the bowl if you double the amount of ingredients.

3 cups warm water (115°F.)
½ teaspoon sugar
1 package (¼-ounce) dry yeast
2½ tablespoons honey, molasses or
  sugar
7 cups all-purpose unbleached white
  flour plus a little more for final
  kneading

¼ cup plus 2 tablespoons dried skim
  milk
2½ teaspoons salt, or to taste
¼ cup melted lard, unsalted butter,
  margarine or vegetable oil

Preheated oven temperature: 375°F.

1. Combine ¼ cup of the warm water, ½ teaspoon sugar and the yeast in a small bowl and let stand in a warm, not hot, place until foaming nicely. This should take no longer than 10 to 15 minutes. The bread will not rise if the mixture does not foam.
2. In a large mixing bowl stir together the 2½ tablespoons of honey, molasses or sugar, 1¼ cups of the warm water, 2 cups of the flour and the dried skim milk. Stir in the foaming yeast mixture, beating well.
3. Cover the bowl with plastic wrap and let stand in a warm place until the mixture, which is called a "sponge," has risen well and is bubbly, about 1 hour.

NOTE: The "sponge" gives the dough a head start and assures good texture. It is particularly effective if whole-grain flours are to be mixed into the dough.

4. Add 1½ cups of the warm water, the salt, melted lard, butter, margarine or oil and beat well. Stir in 3 cups of flour, mixing with a wooden spoon or the dough hook of an electric mixer, until the dough pulls away from the sides of the bowl. *Caution: Do not add additional flour at this point. The dough should be slightly sticky when touched with the fingers.*
5. Spread the remaining 2 cups of flour in a wide circle on a smooth kneading surface. Turn out the dough and knead 10 to 15 minutes (see Breadmaking Basics), using a little additional flour if necessary to make the texture of the dough smooth and satiny.

NOTE: It is almost impossible to overknead bread dough, but the common mistake of the beginner is to knead in too much flour. More flour will be added during the final step while shaping the dough into loaves, and this amount of flour usually is enough.

6. Wash out the mixing bowl and oil the inside lightly. Place the dough in the bowl, turning the dough in a ball so it will be lightly oiled all over. Cover with a damp cloth or plastic wrap. Set in a warm place, free from draft, until double in volume, about 1½ hours. To test, insert 2 fingers about 2 inches into the dough. If indentation remains, turn out onto a lightly floured surface.

7. Knead lightly, using only enough flour to keep dough from sticking. Divide into even portions, shape into loaves (see Breadmaking Basics) and place in oiled 8-x-4-x-3-inch loaf pans. Brush tops of loaves with melted shortening or oil.
8. Cover loaves with a cloth and set in a warm place to rise. Dough should rise slightly over top of pan in a rounded shape. (This rising will take about half the time of the second rising.) *Caution:* If the dough is allowed to rise higher, it will develop large air bubbles during baking. If by accident the dough should rise too much in the pan, remove the dough and knead lightly. Place back in the pan and watch carefully. It will rise rapidly because the yeast is very active.
9. Place loaves well apart on the middle shelf of preheated oven. Bake 45 minutes, or until done. To test, tap the top of the bread with your finger. A hollow sound means the loaf is properly baked. Bake mini loaves about 35 minutes.
10. Remove breads from pans and cool on wire racks. If a shiny top crust is desired, brush the loaves with melted shortening or oil as soon as they are removed from the oven.

Yield: 2 medium-sized loaves or 6 mini loaves.

Variations: Whole-Wheat Bread

In Step 2 substitute 2 cups whole-wheat flour, preferably stone-ground, for the all-purpose unbleached white flour.

Rye Bread

In Step 2 substitute rye flour, preferably stone-ground, for the all-purpose unbleached white flour and add 2 tablespoons caraway seeds or more to taste.

Cornmeal Bread

In Step 2 add 1 cup yellow or white cornmeal.

Raisin Bread

In Step 2 substitute ¼ cup light brown sugar, firmly packed, for the honey, molasses or sugar. In Step 4 add ¾ cup chopped raisins.

Cheese Bread

In Step 4 add 2 cups shredded sharp Cheddar cheese.

Cinnamon Bread

In Step 7 roll each piece of dough into a 14-x-7-inch rectangle. Sprinkle with ¼ cup sugar combined with 1 teaspoon ground cinnamon. Roll as for jelly roll, starting with one 7-inch edge. Press to seal edge and place in pan, seam side down.

Wheat-Germ Bread

In Step 4 add 1½ cups wheat germ.

Rapid-Mix Yeast Bread

For many people time is of the essence in today's busy world and it is not always possible to spend time at home to make bread that requires a triple rising. This recipe for rapid-mix yeast bread is also known as the one-bowl method and batter bread. The baked bread will not have quite as firm a crumb as hand-kneaded dough, but it will fill the house with a welcoming fragrance of delicious bread being baked for dinner.

2 packages dry yeast (¼-ounce)
2¾ cups warm water (115°F.)
6 cups all-purpose unbleached white flour; or 2 cups white flour and 4½ cups whole-wheat flour

3 tablespoons honey, molasses or sugar
1 tablespoon salt
2 tablespoons melted lard, unsalted butter or oil

Preheated oven temperature: 375°F.
1. In the large bowl of an electric mixer sprinkle the yeast into the warm water; let stand 5 minutes and then stir until yeast is dissolved.
2. Add 3¼ cups of the flour, the honey, molasses or sugar, the salt and lard, butter or oil. Mix at low speed; then beat 2 minutes at medium speed. (All of the beating may be done by hand, using 100 strokes.)
3. Beat in remaining flour by hand. Cover the bowl with plastic wrap and let rise in a warm place away from draft until double in volume, about 45 minutes.
4. Stir the batter with a wooden spoon 30 seconds, beating hard.
5. Spread the batter in 2 well-oiled 9-x-5-x-3-inch loaf pans. Cover with a cloth and let rise in a warm place until double in volume, about 20 minutes. Bake in preheated oven 45 to 50 minutes, or until done. Turn out on rack and cool.
Yield: 2 loaves.

Pennsylvania Dutch Egg Twist Bread

Living close to the Pennsylvania Dutch country puts me in touch with some very special recipe sources. This is a large recipe and difficult to divide. Better to enjoy one large loaf of delicious bread warm from the oven and freeze the second until needed.

Saffron is not a necessary ingredient in the recipe, but it is traditional with all cooks of the area. Inexpensive 7-gram amounts may be ordered from Shank's Extracts, Inc., 3130 Columbia Avenue, Lancaster, Pennsylvania 17603.

NOTE: Because of the high egg content of the recipe, double the rising time ordinarily allowed for breadmaking.

½ cup warm water (115°F.)
2 teaspoons sugar
¼ teaspoon ground ginger
2 packages dry yeast (¼-ounce each)
2 cups boiling water
2 tablespoons honey
A pinch of saffron, dissolved in 1 tablespoon hot water (optional)

¼ cup melted unsalted butter or vegetable oil
1 tablespoon salt
3 large eggs plus 1 yolk
About 10 cups unbleached all-purpose flour
White of large egg, beaten with 2 teaspoons cold water

Preheated oven temperature: 400°F.

1. Combine the ½ cup warm water, the sugar, ginger and yeast in a small bowl and let stand in a warm, not hot, place until foaming nicely.
2. In a large mixing bowl combine the boiling water, honey, saffron, butter or oil and salt; cool to a warm temperature (115°F.). Add yeast mixture and eggs, beating well. Add about 8½ cups of flour 1 cup at a time, beating well after each addition, until the dough pulls away from the sides of the bowl.
3. Spread about 1½ cups flour in a wide circle on a smooth kneading surface. Turn out the dough and knead 10 to 15 minutes (see Breadmaking Basics), using additional flour if necessary to keep the dough from being too sticky to handle.
4. Place the dough in a well-oiled bowl, turning the dough in a ball so it will be lightly oiled all over. Cover with a cloth and set in a warm place, away from draft, to rise until double in volume, about 1½ to 2 hours. Punch down, cover, and let rise until double in volume the second time. Turn out onto a lightly floured surface.
5. Knead lightly and divide dough into 6 pieces. Form each piece into a roll about 10 inches long. You will need 3 lengths for each loaf of bread.

6. *To form the twist.* Place 3 rolls together on floured surface. Cross the rolls in the center. *Caution:* Do not pull the rolls too tight; they must have room to double in volume and give the baked bread an attractive appearance. Braid the dough from the middle to each end. Pinch ends together tightly and tuck under the loaf. Repeat to form the second loaf of bread.

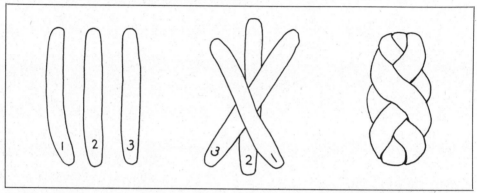

7. Transfer the braided loaves carefully to 2 well-oiled 9-x-5-x-3-inch bread pans.
8. Cover loaves with a cloth and set in a warm place to rise until double in volume. Glaze tops with egg white.
9. Place loaves well apart on the middle shelf of preheated oven. Bake at 400°F. 10 minutes; then reduce heat to 375°F. and bake 35 minutes, or until done.
10. Remove breads from pans and cool on wire racks.
Yield: 2 large loaves.

Anadama Bread

Anna will be remembered forever in American cooking as a lazy New England housewife. According to legend, her irate fisherman husband returned to find nothing on the supper table but hasty pudding (mush). He grabbed the molasses, yeast starter and flour and stirred them into the hasty pudding, immortalizing her with the words, "Anna, damn her," as he placed a loaf of bread dough in the oven. As time passed, thrifty New England housewives added the leftover morning coffee to the ingredients to darken the bread and give it better color.

This recipe will make 2 loaves; one to eat warm from the oven and one to place in the freezer.

2 cups cold water; or 1 cup cold water and 1 cup cold black coffee
½ cup yellow cornmeal, preferably stone-ground
½ cup dark molasses
2 teaspoons salt, or less to taste
½ cup warm water (115°F.)
1 teaspoon sugar
¼ teaspoon ground ginger
2 packages dry yeast (¼- ounce)
About 7½ cups all-purpose unbleached flour
3 tablespoons melted lard or unsalted butter

Preheated oven temperature: 375°F.

1. Combine the cold water or water and coffee and the cornmeal. Bring to a boil in a 1-quart heavy saucepan, stirring constantly and vigorously to keep the mixture from becoming lumpy. Remove from heat and stir in molasses and salt. Cool to a warm temperature (115°F.).
2. Combine the ½ cup warm water, the sugar, ginger, and yeast in a small bowl and let stand in a warm, not hot, place until foaming nicely.
3. In a large mixing bowl combine the cornmeal and the yeast mixture. Stir in 2 cups of the flour, beating well. Add the melted lard or butter and stir in 4 more cups of flour, mixing with a wooden spoon or the dough hook of an electric mixer, until the dough pulls away from the sides of the bowl.
4. Spread the remaining 1½ cups flour in a wide circle on a smooth kneading surface. Turn out the dough and knead 10 to 15 minutes (see Breadmaking Basics) using additional flour if necessary to keep the dough from being too sticky to handle.
5. Place the dough in a well-oiled bowl, turning the dough in a ball so it will be lightly oiled all over. Cover with a cloth and set in a warm place away from draft to rise until double in volume. Turn out onto a lightly floured surface.
6. Knead lightly and divide into 2 even portions, shape into loaves and place in oiled 9-x-5-x-3-inch loaf pans. Brush tops of loaves with melted unsalted butter.
7. Cover loaves with a cloth and set in a warm place to rise until double in volume.
8. Place loaves well apart on the middle shelf of preheated oven. Bake 45 minutes, or until done.
9. Remove breads from oven and brush with melted butter. Turn out of pans and cool on wire racks.

Yield: 2 medium-sized loaves.

Variation: Oatmeal Bread

In Step 1 omit cold water and cornmeal. Pour 2 cups of boiling water over 1 cup rolled oats. Cover and let stand 30 minutes. Stir in molasses and salt.

Sally Lunn Bread

This is a traditional bread of the Tidewater. Originally the bread was made with liquid starter, a mixture of lard and butter and a considerable amount of sugar. This is a modern recipe and makes a bread with a fluffy, spongelike texture. Like most Southern breads, it is at its best when eaten warm from the oven, sliced and spread with pats of fresh butter.

¼ cup warm water (115°F.)
1 teaspoon sugar
⅛ teaspoon ground ginger
1 package dry yeast (¼-ounce)
½ cup warm milk (115°F.)
⅓ cup sugar

½ cup melted unsalted butter
1 teaspoon salt
3 large eggs, lightly beaten
About 4 cups all-purpose bleached flour

Oven temperature: 350°F.

1. In a large mixing bowl combine the warm water, 1 teaspoon sugar, ginger and yeast. Let stand in a warm, not hot, place until foaming nicely. Add the warm milk, ⅓ cup sugar, the butter and salt; stir to mix. Add the eggs and beat well. Add flour 1 cup at a time, beating well after each addition, until the dough pulls away from the sides of the bowl.
2. Transfer dough to a well-oiled bowl, brush top with oil and cover with a cloth. Set in a warm place away from draft, to rise until double in volume.
3. Punch down the dough and transfer to well-buttered 9-inch tube pan. Cover pan with a cloth and set in a warm place until double in volume.
4. Place in the center of the middle shelf of preheated oven. Bake about 45 minutes, or until golden and a cake tester comes out clean.
5. Remove from oven and turn out on rack to cool slightly. Slice and serve.

Serves 8 to 10.

No-Knead Refrigerator Yeast Rolls
(Basic Recipe)

Before bakery rolls were generally available, every home cook made her own. Since mixing a batch of dough every day was a bother, a clever cook devised a formula for what was called "icebox dough."

Yeast dough cannot be refrigerated unless the recipe has been designed to extend the action of the yeast over several days. For this reason it is necessary to use at least ¼ cup sugar in the recipe; the sugar is what feeds the yeast and keeps it alive. This dough will keep 3 days in the refrigerator and can be formed into a variety of roll shapes, as desired.

NOTE: If fluffy-white Southern-type rolls are desired, use all-purpose bleached flour.

¾ cup milk
¼ cup sugar
2 teaspoons salt, or to taste
5 tablespoons melted unsalted butter or margarine
½ cup warm water (115°F.)

1 teaspoon sugar
2 packages dry yeast (¼-ounce each)
1 large egg, well beaten
4½ cups sifted all-purpose bleached or unbleached flour (measure after sifting)

Preheated oven temperature: 400°F.
1. Heat the milk to just under the boiling point in a small saucepan. Stir in the ¼ cup sugar, the salt and butter or margarine. Cool to a warm temperature (115°F.).
2. Combine the ½ cup water, 1 teaspoon sugar and yeast in a large bowl and let stand in a warm, not hot, place until foaming nicely. Stir the lukewarm milk mixture into the yeast mixture.
3. Add the egg and 2 cups of the flour to the yeast mixture, beating until smooth. Add the remainder of the flour and continue beating until smooth.
4. Place dough in a lightly oiled mixing bowl and cover tightly with plastic wrap. Refrigerate at least 2 hours or up to 3 days.
5. To use, remove from the refrigerator, punch down the dough and shape into 1½-inch balls. Place on a lightly oiled baking sheet, cover with cloth and let rise in warm place away from draft until double in volume. Brush tops lightly with melted unsalted butter or margarine and bake in preheated oven 15 minutes, or until done and tops are nicely browned.
Yield: 24 to 30 plain rolls.

Variations: Cloverleaf Rolls

In Step 5 divide the dough in half. Form each half into a 9-inch roll.
Pinch off 9 equal pieces and form into balls. Oil a medium-sized muffin
pan and place 3 balls in each cup. Brush lightly with melted unsalted
butter or margarine. Cover with a cloth and let rise in a warm place
away from draft until double in volume. Bake in preheated 400°F. oven
about 15 minutes, or until done and the tops are nicely browned. Remove from oven and serve hot.
Yield: 18 rolls.

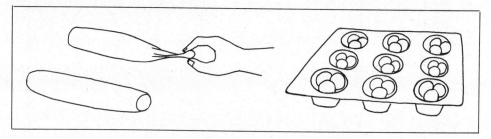

Parker House Rolls (Pocketbook Rolls)

In Step 5 turn dough out onto a lightly floured surface. Divide in half.
Roll out each piece into a 9-inch circle. Cut into 1½-inch rounds. You
should have 12 rounds from each piece. Crease each round slightly off
center with dull edge of knife. Brush lightly with melted unsalted
butter or margarine. Fold larger half over smaller so that edges just
meet. Seal the edges of the dough by pressing with the fingertips. Place
on a lightly oiled baking sheet, cover with a cloth and let rise in a
warm place away from draft until double in volume. Brush tops lightly
with melted unsalted butter or margarine and bake in preheated 400°F.
oven about 15 minutes, or until done and tops are nicely browned. Serve
hot.
Yield: 24 rolls.

Fried Biscuits

In Step 5 roll out the dough into a rectangle ½ inch thick. Pour vegetable
or peanut oil into a kettle or deep-fryer to a depth of about 2 inches.
Heat to 375°F. Cut the dough into 2-inch rounds or squares and drop
into the hot oil a few at a time. When the biscuit is puffed and browned
on both sides, remove with slotted spoon and drain on paper towels.
Serve immediately.
Yield: 24 to 30 biscuits.

Philadelphia Sticky Buns
(Cinnamon Rolls)

As their name implies, these buns are very sweet and sticky and undoubtedly of Pennsylvania Dutch origin. Currently they are in fashion at sophisticated dining places around the country.

Basic Dough

¼ cup warm water (115°F.)

2 teaspoons sugar

¼ teaspoon ground ginger

2 packages dry yeast (¼-ounce each)

1 cup milk

⅓ cup sugar

⅓ cup melted unsalted butter

2 large eggs, well beaten

1 teaspoon salt

About 5 cups sifted all-purpose bleached flour (sift before measuring)

Sticky Bun Mixture

¾ cup unsalted butter

¾ cup dark brown sugar, firmly packed

1 cup coarsely chopped pecans or walnuts

1 cup raisins (optional)

¼ cup melted unsalted butter

¼ cup light brown sugar, firmly packed

2 tablespoons ground cinnamon

Preheated oven temperature: 400°F.

1. Combine the water, 2 teaspoons sugar, the ginger and yeast in a small bowl and let stand in a warm, not hot, place until foaming nicely.
2. Heat the milk to just under the boiling point and pour into a large bowl. Cool to warm temperature (115°F.). Add the ⅓ cup sugar, ⅓ cup melted butter, the eggs, salt and yeast mixture, beating well. Add 4 cups of the flour 1 cup at a time, beating well after each addition, until the dough pulls away from the sides of the bowl.
3. Spread about 1 cup of flour in a wide circle on a smooth kneading surface. Turn out the dough and knead about 5 to 8 minutes, or until smooth, using additional flour if necessary to keep the dough from being too sticky to handle.
4. Place the dough in a well-oiled bowl, turn the dough in a ball so it will be lightly oiled all over. Cover with a cloth and set in a warm place away from draft to rise until double in volume.
5. While the dough is rising, prepare the pans. Cream the ¾ cup butter and dark brown sugar until light and fluffy. Spread the mixture over bottoms and sides of two 9-inch round pans. Sprinkle lightly with one half of nuts and optional raisins.
6. Turn dough out onto a lightly floured surface, knead lightly and divide into 2 pieces. Roll each piece of dough into a 15-x-12-inch

rectangle. Brush the surface of each piece with the ¼ cup melted butter and sprinkle with the light brown sugar, cinnamon and remaining raisins and nuts. Roll as for jelly roll, starting with 12-inch edge. Press to seal edge in place.

7. Slice each roll crosswise into 1½-inch slices. Place in prepared pans, with cut side down. Cover pans with a cloth and set in a warm place to rise until double in volume.

8. Place pans well apart on the middle shelf of preheated oven. Bake 25 minutes, or until done. Unmold on plate and remove pan immediately.

Yield: 24 buns.

Variation: Hot Cross Buns

Prepare Basic Dough as for Philadelphia Sticky Buns except in Step 3 add ⅔ cup currants or raisins and ½ teaspoon ground cinnamon. Omit Step 5 and continue to Step 6. Pat kneaded dough out to ¾-inch thickness; cut with a floured 2-inch round cutter. Shape the rounds into balls and place close together on a lightly oiled baking sheet; brush the tops with 1 lightly beaten egg white. Reserve the remaining egg white. Cover baking sheet with a cloth and set in a warm place until double in volume. Place baking sheet on the middle shelf of a preheated 400°F. oven. Bake about 30 minutes or until golden. Remove to rack. Add enough sifted confectioners' sugar to the reserved egg white to make a thick consistency; fashion a cross with the tip of a teaspoon on the top of each bun.

Yield: 24 buns.

Yeast Doughnuts

These were made in large quantities by my mother and grandmothers. Unfortunately, fried doughnuts do not keep well. They should be consumed within a few hours—which has never been a problem when I have made them for Sunday brunch. Roll them in confectioners' or granulated sugar. For special occasions dip them in honey or bourbon glaze. Use the scraps of dough to form twists.

1¼ cups milk

2 packages dry yeast (¼-ounce each)

1 tablespoon sugar

About 4½ cups all-purpose bleached flour

½ cup sugar

5 tablespoons unsalted butter

¼ teaspoon ground mace or nutmeg

1 large egg, well beaten

¼ teaspoon salt

Peanut oil or corn oil for deep-frying

1. Heat the milk to just under the boiling point. Pour into a medium-sized mixing bowl and cool to warm temperature (115°F.). Add the yeast, 1 tablespoon sugar and 1½ cups of the flour, beating well. Cover the bowl with plastic wrap and let stand in a warm place until mixture has risen well and is bubbly.
2. In a large bowl cream the ½ cup sugar and the butter. Add the yeast mixture, mace or nutmeg, egg and the remainder of the flour 1 cup at a time, until a moderately soft and silky dough has formed.
3. Turn out onto a lightly floured surface and knead briefly, about 4 to 5 minutes.
4. Place the dough in a well-oiled bowl, turning the dough in a ball so it will be lightly oiled all over. Cover with a cloth and set in a warm place away from draft to rise until double in bulk. Turn out onto a lightly floured surface.
5. Punch down the dough. Roll out in a circle to a thickness of about ½ inch. Cut in rounds with a doughnut cutter. (If a doughnut cutter is not available, use any round cutter and a bottle cap or thimble to make a hole in the center.) The fried round centers are time-honored kitchen samples.
6. Place the doughnuts and centers on wax-paper-lined trays. Cover with a cloth and place in a warm place until very light and puffy, about 40 to 45 minutes.
7. Fill a deep, 2-quart kettle or deep-fat fryer with oil to a depth of about 3 inches. Heat to 375°F.
8. Add doughnuts a few at a time and fry about 1 minute on each side or until golden. Drain on paper towels and then roll in sugar or dip in glaze.
Yield: 18 2-inch doughnuts and 18 centers.

Sourdough Bread

Making bread with a natural liquid starter is a fussy business until the yeast and you develop compatible personalities. This depends upon the temperature, humidity, barometric pressure, bacteria count in the air and even the chemicals in your skin. Once you have adjusted to all the little quirks of your particular starter, there is no other type of breadmaking more rewarding.

My starter is known as "Sam" around the kitchen, and he is alive and well after being "started" in 1965. Portions of this original starter have traveled all over the United States and to many countries, including Greenland, to be shared by fellow breadmaking enthusiasts.

In recent years health-oriented periodicals have been circulating the newly developed theory that natural yeast is considerably more nutritious than processed commercial yeast. As a result, many people are interested in working with natural liquid starter.

Sourdough Breadmaking Basics

First you need natural liquid yeast. Always remember that 2 cups of natural liquid yeast is the equivalent of one ¼-ounce package dry yeast. The old frontier adage about obtaining a lively starter is equally good advice today: Beg, borrow or steal a portion from someone who has a particularly strong strain with a high bacteria count. Dehydrated sourdough starters are available. However, people who have tried them tell me that they are not satisfactory unless "seeded" by adding a small amount of active natural starter.

HOW TO BEGIN A STARTER   This is the formula I used. In a medium-sized bowl dissolve a ¼-ounce package dry yeast in 1 cup warm (115°F.) potato water (this is the water in which peeled potatoes have been cooked). Add 1 cup all-purpose unbleached white flour and 1 tablespoon sugar, beating well. Pour the mixture into a large glass or crockery container. Cover it lightly and let it stand in a warm place 48 hours, stirring several times. Never use metal or plastic because of adverse chemical reactions. *Caution:* The starter will begin to grow and must have room to expand. Never cover the jar with a tight lid and always use a container twice the size of the amount of the starter, to allow the starter enough air to breathe. Gases build up inside the container powerful enough to break the jar if they cannot escape. Once the liquid has fermented—and you can tell by the bubbles and "yeasty" odor—it is ready to use at once or to be refrigerated and deactivated for future use.

HOW TO ACTIVATE STARTER   Remove from the refrigerator and pour the starter into a glass or crockery bowl—not metal or plastic. Wash and sterilize the refrigerator container. Add 2½ of flour and 2 cups of warm water to the yeast as soon as it is removed from the refrigerator. Allow 12 hours for fermentation at room temperature before you begin making the bread. This is a two-step process; activating the starter is a preliminary step in working with liquid yeast. Don't let the starter get cold during the 12 hours and do not attempt to shorten the fermenting time. After the fermentation is complete, *always return* 2 cups of fermented starter to the sterilized container. Cover loosely and refrigerate for the next breadmaking session. Otherwise, you will have to make a starter all over again. Follow recipe instructions for making bread.

HOW TO CARE FOR STARTER   If you do not use your starter on a weekly basis, it must be removed about every 10 days and "fed" with 1 cup warm water and 1½ cup flour.

Personal Note: My starter has been refrigerated up to 6 weeks without any special attention. In this length of time it will develop a very dark liquid on the top. Pour this off and discard before you add more water and flour. If you should find yourself with more than half a container of starter, take courage and pour off all but 2 cups—more is not better in this particular instance. *Caution:* Every time you remove the starter from the refrigerator to add water and flour, regardless of whether you plan to bake bread or not, you must leave it at room temperature for 12 hours before returning the starter to the refrigerator.

NOTE: Liquid starter responds to personal attention and lives forever with proper care. Many sad stories are written in frontier history about families who lost their starter to the heat of summer. High temperature kills the bacteria in yeast. Therefore, care must be taken to keep the liquid starter away from too much heat.

NOTE: It is a fatal mistake to place the starter over the oven pilot light without penning a warning to yourself on the front of the oven door. Do not leave starter outside the refrigerator more than 3 days; too much bacteria will build up and sour the starter beyond the point of making good bread.

Basic Sourdough Bread I

There are two methods for making sourdough bread. One is to assist the liquid yeast with commercial dry yeast. This is a faster method than if the bread is made entirely with natural liquid starter and is the method recommended for beginners. The second method requires an extra step called "setting a sponge," and for this method you must have a very strong strain of yeast. After mastering the first method you can easily judge the strength of your individual starter and proceed to the second method, which is the ultimate achievement for breadmakers.

Refrigerated starter

2 cups warm water (115°F.)

2½ cups unbleached white flour, or more

½ cup warm water (115°F.)

1 teaspoon sugar

½ teaspoon ground ginger

1 package dry yeast (¼ ounce)

2 cups warm (115°F.) water

1 cup dried skim milk

¼ cup honey, molasses or sugar

3 cups unbleached white, whole-wheat or rye flour

¼ cup melted lard, unsalted butter or oil

1 tablespoon salt, or less to taste

About 4½ cups unbleached white flour

Preheated oven temperature: 375°F.

1. This is a preliminary step and not to be confused with the actual mixing of the dough. The night before or at least 12 hours before you begin breadmaking, remove the starter from the refrigerator and empty all the starter into a large mixing bowl (do not use metal or plastic). Add 2 cups warm water and 2½ cups white flour, or enough to make a stiff, pancakelike batter. Beat thoroughly. There will be some lumps of flour remaining. These will dissolve during the 12 hours. Cover tightly with plastic wrap and set in a warm place (about 80°–85°F.) to ferment for 12 hours. Now the starter is ready for breadmaking.

2. Stir the starter thoroughly with a wooden spoon. Pour 2 cups into a large mixing bowl. Pour remaining starter back into starter jar (you should have at least 2 cups), cover and return to the refrigerator for your next breadmaking session.

3. Combine ½ cup of the warm water, 1 teaspoon sugar, the ginger and dry yeast in a small bowl and let stand in a warm, not hot, place until foaming nicely.

4. Add 2 cups of warm water, the milk, honey, molasses or sugar and 3 cups of white, whole-wheat or rye flour to the starter in the large mixing bowl. Beat thoroughly and add the foaming yeast mixture as soon as it is ready and continue beating. Beat in the lard, butter or oil and salt. Gradually add 3½ cups of white flour 1 cup at a time, stirring until the dough pulls away from the side of the bowl.

5. Spread the remaining 1 cup of flour in a wide circle on a smooth kneading surface. Turn out the dough and knead 10 to 15 minutes (see Breadmaking Basics, page 329), using a little additional flour if necessary to make the texture of the dough smooth and satiny.

6. Place the dough in a well-oiled bowl, turning the dough in a ball so it will be lightly oiled all over. Cover with plastic wrap. Set in a warm place away from draft until double in volume, about 1½ hours. Turn out onto a lightly floured surface. Divide into 2 even portions, shape into loaves and place in oiled 8-x-4-x-3-inch loaf pans. Brush with melted shortening.

7. Cover loaves with a cloth and set in a warm place to rise. Dough should rise slightly over top of pan in a rounded shape.

8. Place loaves well apart on the middle shelf of pre-heated oven. Bake 45 minutes, or until done.

9. Remove bread from pans and cool on wire rack. If a shiny top crust is desired, brush the loaves with melted shortening or oil as soon as they are removed from the oven.

Yield: 2 medium-sized loaves.

Basic Sourdough Bread II

2 cups starter
2 cups warm water (115°F.)
½ cup sugar
4 cups unbleached white flour; or 2 cups white and 2 of whole-wheat or rye flour
½ teaspoon ground ginger

2 teaspoons honey, molasses or sugar
1½ teaspoons salt
¼ cup melted lard, unsalted butter or oil
About 4 cups unbleached white flour

Preheated oven temperature: 375°F.

1. As in Sourdough Bread I, this is a preliminary step. The night before or at least 12 hours before you begin breadmaking, remove the starter from the refrigerator and continue through Step 1 as in Sourdough Bread I.
2. Stir the starter thoroughly with a wooden spoon and pour 2 cups into a large mixing bowl. Pour remaining starter back into starter jar, as in Step 2 for making Sourdough Bread 1. Add the 2 cups warm water, ½ cup sugar and 4 cups white flour or 2 cups white and 2 cups whole-wheat or rye flour, beating well.
3. Cover the bowl with plastic wrap and let stand in a warm place until the mixture, which is called a sponge, is well risen and bubbly.

NOTE: For extra-tangy sourdough bread, let the mixture stand overnight.

4. Dissolve the ginger in the 2 teaspoons warm water and add to the sponge when it is ready.

NOTE: The ginger is added to help activate the natural liquid starter. Beat in the honey, molasses or sugar, salt and melted lard, butter or oil. Stir in 3 cups of the 4 cups of flour 1 cup at a time, until the dough pulls away from the sides of the bowl.

5. Spread the remaining 1 cup of flour in a wide circle on a smooth kneading surface and proceed as in Steps 5 to 9 for making Sourdough Bread I.

NOTE: After the bread has been kneaded and is ready to be shaped into loaves, pinch off about ½ cup of dough and reserve for the next breadmaking session. Keep this ball of dough in a glass jar in the refrigerator and incorporate it into the first kneading of your next batch of bread. This is an old frontier sourdough breadmaking technique used by my grandmothers to add extra flavor to the bread, and it works beautifully.

Quick Breads

Quick breads are just what their name implies. They are breads or breadlike mixtures that are mixed and baked at once. The leavening agents act quickly and make the mixture light without the prolonged waiting time needed when baking with yeast.

Steamed New England Brown Bread

This regional American bread was created by early cooks to accompany baked beans.

1 cup yellow cornmeal
1½ cups unbleached white flour
½ cup whole-wheat flour
2 teaspoons baking soda
1 teaspoon salt

2 cups buttermilk or sour milk (see note)
¾ cup dark molasses
1 cup chopped raisins

1. Combine the cornmeal, white flour, whole-wheat flour, baking soda and salt in a large bowl. Then combine the buttermilk or sour milk, molasses and raisins in another bowl. Add the buttermilk mixture to the flour mixture, stirring only enough to dampen the flours. Do not overblend.
2. Pour the batter into 2 well-buttered 1-pound coffee cans about three fourths full. Cover the cans with foil well-buttered on the underside. Secure the seal tightly with string.
3. Place the cans on a rack in a large kettle. Pour in enough boiling water to come halfway up the sides of the cans, adding more boiling

water if needed. Cover the kettle tightly and steam 3 hours. Keep the water boiling gently at all times.

4. Lift the cans from the kettle, remove the foil and run a knife around the inside of the cans to loosen the breads. Unmold onto a baking sheet. Place in a preheated 300°F. oven 10 to 15 minutes to firm bread for slicing. To slice without crumbling, wrap a length of strong, fine string around the loaf, cross the ends and pull the string through the bread to make round slices. Serve warm with butter.

Yield: 2 loaves.

NOTE: To sour pasteurized milk, have it at room temperature. For each cup needed, place 1 tablespoon lemon juice or distilled white vinegar in the bottom of the cup. Fill with milk, stir to mix and let stand 5 minutes to clabber.

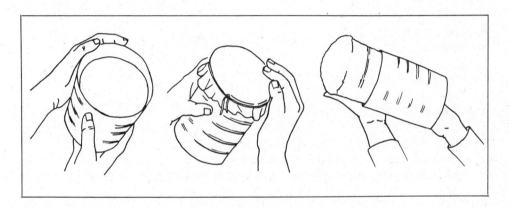

Banana Bread

Banana bread is a universal favorite, especially when it is sliced and spread with peanut butter or cream cheese.

⅓ cup unsalted butter or margarine	2 cups all-purpose flour, unsifted
⅔ cup sugar	2 teaspoons baking powder
2 large eggs, well beaten	½ teaspoon baking soda
2 tablespoons milk	¼ teaspoon salt
1 cup ripe banana pulp, combined with 1 teaspoon lemon juice	1 cup chopped nuts (optional)

Preheated oven temperature: 350°F.

1. Cream the butter or margarine and sugar in a large bowl until light and fluffy. Add the eggs, milk and banana pulp. Stir well to blend.
2. Sift the flour, baking powder, baking soda and salt into the creamed mixture and stir quickly until just blended. Fold in optional nuts.

3. Pour batter into a well-oiled 9-x-5-x-3-inch loaf pan. Bake in pre-heated oven 45 to 50 minutes, or until a cake tester comes out clean. Remove from oven and run a spatula around sides of pan. Turn out on rack and cool. Slice and serve.
Yield: 1 loaf.

California Fresh Date Bread

California fresh dates are easy to prepare. They aren't sticky, so slit them with a sharp knife, slip out their pits and chop coarsely to use as directed.

This is a bread with a good, solid texture, ideal for slicing and to pack in school box lunches.

3 cups sifted all-purpose flour (sift before measuring)
4 teaspoons baking powder
½ teaspoon salt
½ cup sugar
1 cup chopped fresh dates

1 cup chopped walnuts or pecans
1 large egg, well beaten
1½ cups milk
2 tablespoons melted unsalted butter or margarine

Preheated oven temperature: 350°F.
1. Sift the flour with the baking powder, salt and sugar into a large mixing bowl. Stir in the dates and walnuts or pecans.
2. Combine the beaten egg, milk and butter or margarine. Add to the dry ingredients and stir until just blended. *Caution:* Overblending will cause the texture to be dry and tough.
3. Turn into a well-oiled 8-x-4-x-3-inch loaf pan and let rest at room temperature 20 minutes.
4. Bake in preheated oven 55 to 60 minutes, or until firm to the touch. Remove from the oven and let rest in the pan a few minutes to steam slightly; then loosen sides with a spatula and turn out on a rack to cool. Slice and serve.
Yield: 1 loaf

Cranberry-Orange-Nut Bread

This is a beautiful and festive-looking bread for holiday gift-giving.

Juice and rind of 1 medium-sized orange (2½ to 3 inches)
2 tablespoons unsalted butter or margarine
Boiling water
1 cup raw cranberries
1 cup pecans or walnuts

1 large egg, well beaten
2 cups sifted all-purpose flour (sift before measuring)
¾ cup sugar
1½ teaspoons baking powder
½ teaspoon baking soda
½ teaspoon salt

Preheated oven temperature: 350°F.
1. Trim 4 1-inch squares of peel from orange (no white pith). Cut the orange in half and squeeze out juice. Put the peel and juice in a 1-cup measure and pour in enough boiling water to make ¾ cup. Add the butter or margarine.
2. Pour the orange juice mixture into a blender or food processor and process until finely grated. Add the cranberries and nuts; process briefly, until cranberries and nuts are chopped. Pour mixture into a large mixing bowl and stir in the egg.
3. Sift the flour, sugar, baking powder, baking soda and salt into the ingredients in the bowl and stir quickly until just blended.
4. Pour batter into a well-oiled 9-x-5-x-3-inch loaf pan. Bake in pre-heated oven 55 to 60 minutes, or until a cake tester comes out clean. Remove from oven and run a spatula around sides of pan. Turn out on rack and cool. Slice and serve.

Yield: 1 loaf.

Pumpkin Bread

This is a Mormon church recipe for a wholesome bread that keeps marvelously.

1 cup vegetable or corn oil
4 large eggs, well beaten
⅔ cup water
2 cups cooked pumpkin
3⅓ cups sifted unbleached white flour; or 1⅔ cups whole-wheat flour and 1⅔ cups white flour (sift before measuring)

2 cups sugar, or less to taste
2 teaspoons baking soda
1 teaspoon ground cinnamon
1 teaspoon ground nutmeg
1 cup chopped nuts
⅔ cup raisins (optional)

Preheated oven temperature: 350°F.
1. Combine the oil, eggs, water and pumpkin in a large mixing bowl.
2. Sift the flour, sugar, baking soda, cinnamon and nutmeg together. Combine with the ingredients in the mixing bowl. Fold in the nuts and optional raisins.
3. Turn into 2 well-oiled 8-x-4-x-4-inch loaf pans. Bake in preheated oven 45 minutes, or until a cake tester comes out clean. Run a spatula around edges of pan and turn out onto a rack to cool. Slice and serve.

Yield: 2 loaves.

Granny Wagner's Sour Cream Black Walnut Bread

Mrs. Wagner has been making this delicious bread for over fifty years. It is a famous North Carolina recipe, best made with native black walnuts. English walnuts or other nuts may be substituted if black walnuts are not available.

1 large egg
1 cup light brown sugar, firmly packed
1 cup sour cream
2 cups sifted all-purpose flour (sift before measuring)

1 teaspoon baking soda
½ teaspoon baking powder
⅓ teaspoon salt
½ cup chopped black walnuts

Preheated oven temperature: 350°F.
1. Combine the egg, brown sugar and sour cream in a large mixing bowl and beat well.
2. Sift the flour, baking soda, baking powder and salt over the ingredients in the bowl. Stir well to blend and fold in the walnuts.
3. Pour into a well-oiled 9-x-5-x-3-inch loaf pan or 3 small loaf pans. Bake in preheated oven 1 hour for large loaf and about 40 minutes for smaller loaves, or until a cake tester comes out clean. Run a spatula around edges of pan and turn out onto a rack to cool. Slice and serve.
Yield: 1 large loaf or 3 small loaves.

Southern Corn Bread

From Maryland to Texas corn bread is crisp—not sweet—and 100% white cornmeal. To bake this bread crisp, the pan must be shallow for good browning.

2 cups white cornmeal, preferably water-ground
2 teaspoons baking powder
1 teaspoon baking soda
1 teaspoon salt

2 cups buttermilk
2 large eggs
⅓ cup bacon drippings or melted lard

Preheated oven temperature: 425°F.
1. Combine the cornmeal, baking powder, baking soda and salt in a large bowl. Add the buttermilk, eggs and bacon drippings, lard or butter. Stir to blend well but do not beat mixture.
2. Pour mixture into a well-oiled 13-x-9-x-1-inch baking pan and bake in preheated oven 25 minutes, or until done.

NOTE: If the top does not seem to be browning, place under the broiler a few minutes.
Yield: 6 servings.

Variation: Cornsticks

Preheat iron corn-stick pans in the oven and brush wall with oil. Pour batter into pans and bake in preheated 450°F. oven 20 minutes.
Yield: 20 corn sticks.

Northern Corn Bread

North of the National Road, which is the old Cumberland Trail to the West, generations of Americans have been raised on sweet yellow corn bread; except in Rhode Island, where white cornmeal is the rule. Yankee corn bread is a version of New England johnnycake and is made with part flour, part yellow cornmeal and sugar to taste.

1 cup sifted all-purpose unbleached flour (sift before measuring)
2 teaspoons baking powder
1 teaspoon salt
2 to 4 tablespoons sugar, depending on taste

1 cup yellow cornmeal
2 large eggs, well beaten
¾ cup milk
¼ cup melted unsalted butter or margarine

Preheated oven temperature: 400°F.
1. Sift the flour, baking powder, salt and sugar into large bowl. Add cornmeal and mix well.
2. Combine the eggs and milk and add to the flour mixture but do not mix. Add the butter or margarine and mix only enough to dampen flour.
3. Pour into a well-oiled 9-x-9-x-2-inch square pan and bake in preheated oven 25 minutes, or until done.
Yield: 6 servings.

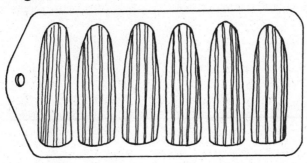

Jalapeño Corn Bread

This is hot and peppery Tex-Mex corn bread, appropriate with South-west cooking.

1 cup yellow cornmeal
2 teaspoons baking powder
1 teaspoon baking soda
1 teaspoon salt
2 large eggs, well beaten
1 cup milk

2 cups cream-style corn
5 small jalapeño peppers, chopped fine
¼ cup bacon drippings
1 cup grated or shredded sharp Cheddar cheese

Preheated oven temperature: 350°F.
1. Combine the cornmeal, baking powder, baking soda and salt in a large bowl.
2. Combine the eggs and milk and stir into the dry ingredients. Add corn, peppers and bacon drippings and stir to blend.
3. Pour half the mixture into a well-oiled 9-x-9-x-2-inch square pan. Sprinkle with the cheese. Cover with remaining batter and bake in preheated oven 1 hour, or until done.
Serves 6.

Southern Spoon Bread

The title bread is apt to mislead the novice not familiar with Southern culinary terms. This really is not a bread but a light-textured baked cornmeal batter, which must be served piping-hot, straight from the oven. It is "spooned" onto the plate, and that is how the dish came by its name. Serve with butter, jelly, jam or gravy. Spoon bread tends to fall easily when it comes out of the oven. The bourbon helps to prevent this from happening and it doesn't alter the taste at all.

1 cup white or yellow cornmeal
2 cups milk
1 cup melted unsalted butter or margarine
½ teaspoon salt

1 tablespoon sugar
5 large eggs, separated
1½ tablespoons bourbon (optional)

Preheated oven temperature: 350°F.
1. In a heavy, 1½-quart saucepan combine the cornmeal and milk. Place over medium-low heat and cook just below the boiling point 5 minutes, stirring constantly and vigorously until the lumps are dissolved and the mixture has thickened. Stir in the butter or margarine, the salt and sugar. Remove from heat and cool slightly.

2. Quickly beat the egg yolks into the mixture and blend thoroughly.
3. Beat the egg whites in a large bowl until soft peaks form and gently fold the egg whites and optional bourbon into the cornmeal mixture with a rubber spatula.
4. Pour the mixture into a well-oiled 1½-quart baking dish and bake in preheated oven 45 minutes, or until nicely browned on top and a cake tester comes out clean. Serve immediately.

Serves 6.

Sour Cream Coffee Cake
(Basic Recipe)

This recipe, with regional variations, has been in circulation since the 1950s. It may be baked in a 13-x-9-x-2-inch pan or a 9-inch tube pan.

½ cup unsalted butter or margarine
¾ to 1 cup sugar
2 large eggs
1 teaspoon vanilla
2 cups all-purpose flour, unsifted
1 teaspoon baking soda
1 teaspoon baking powder

½ teaspoon salt
1 cup sour cream
½ cup chopped nuts, any kind
2 tablespoons unsalted butter or margarine
1 cup light brown sugar, firmly packed
1 teaspoon ground cinnamon

Preheated oven temperature: 350°F.
1. Cream the ½ cup butter or margarine and the sugar in a large mixing bowl until fluffy. Add the eggs and vanilla and beat well.
2. Sift the flour, baking soda, baking powder and salt together and add alternately with sour cream to the ingredients in the mixing bowl, folding with a rubber spatula to blend ingredients. Pour mixture into a well-oiled 13-x-9-x-2-inch pan; if using tube pan, see next step.
3. Combine the nuts, 2 tablespoons unsalted butter, the brown sugar and cinnamon in a small bowl. Crumble with fingertips until lightly mixed. If using a single-layer baking pan, spread the mixture over the top. If using a tube pan, pour half the batter into the pan, spread with half the crumb mixture and continue with the batter; spread the top with the remainder of the crumb mixture.
4. Bake in preheated oven 45 to 55 minutes, or until a cake tester comes out clean. Remove from oven and run a spatula around the edges and center of the tube pan and turn out onto a plate to cool. Slice and serve.

Serves 10 to 12.

Variations: Apple Sour Cream Coffee Cake

In Step 2 fold in 2 cups chopped, peeled apples.

Pear Sour Cream Coffee Cake

In Step 2, fold in 2 cups chopped, peeled pears.

Raisin Sour Cream Coffee Cake

In Step 2 fold in ¾ cup chopped raisins.

Apricot Sour Cream Coffee Cake

In Step 2 fold in 1½ cups chopped dried apricots.

Southern Baking Powder Biscuits

These are so light and flaky that they will float right up in the air if the dough is mixed with a very light touch. This is why the biscuits have become so famous. I grew up with this recipe and I know it well. The dough should be made with very soft all-purpose bleached flour and not unbleached bread flour. Great care should be taken not to blend the shortening and flour to a fine consistency.

2 cups all-purpose bleached flour	1 teaspoon salt
1 tablespoon baking powder	¼ cup cold unsalted butter or lard
	¾ cup milk

Preheated oven temperature: 450°F.

1. Sift the flour, baking powder and salt into a medium-sized bowl. Quickly work or crumble the butter or lard into the flour with the fingertips until flaky. (This means the particles of butter or lard should be about the size of uncooked flakes of regular oatmeal.)
2. Make a well in the center of the mixture and pour in the milk all at once. Stir quickly with a fork and mix only long enough to dampen the flour.
3. Turn out on a lightly floured surface and knead about 6 to 8 seconds, just long enough to form a round ball; then pat out to a thickness of ½ inch. Cut into rounds, place on a lightly oiled baking sheet and bake in preheated oven 12 minutes, or until done.

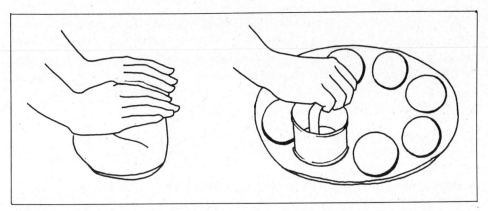

NOTE: For crust on top and bottom only, place on sheet close together; place far apart if crust is desired on sides of biscuits.
Yield: 12 medium-sized biscuits.

Indian Puffs

Up until almost the end of the 19th century, American cooks referred to cornmeal as Indian meal. And this is most likely how these cornmeal popovers came by their name. The batter can be prepared a few hours in advance and refrigerated until needed. The hot bread gives any meal a real American touch.

⅞ cup milk (measure 1 cup and remove 2 tablespoons)
2 large eggs
1 teaspoon melted unsalted butter or margarine

½ cup all-purpose flour, unsifted
¼ cup white or yellow cornmeal
½ teaspoon salt

Preheated oven temperature: 450°F.
1. Combine the milk, eggs, butter or margarine, flour, cornmeal and salt in a blender or food processor. Blend at high speed until smooth.
2. Fill well-oiled muffin pans about two thirds full. Bake in preheated oven 15 minutes; reduce heat to 375°F. and bake another 20 minutes, or until done. Remove from pan immediately and turn on sides to keep the bottoms from steaming.
Yield: 10 medium-sized puffs.

Hush Puppies

These are fried cornmeal balls, which are traditionally served with fried fish in the South. They originated along a Florida river bank—or so the story goes. While the fishermen were frying their just-caught fish they would quiet the howls of their dogs with scraps of fried corn pone and the command to, "Hush, puppy!"

2 cups white or yellow cornmeal
1 tablespoon flour
½ teaspoon baking soda
1 teaspoon salt

1 large egg, well beaten
3 tablespoons finely chopped onion
1 cup buttermilk
Peanut oil or corn oil for deep-frying

1. Combine the cornmeal, flour, baking soda and salt in a large bowl. Add the egg, onion and buttermilk. Mix only enough to blend ingredients.
2. Fill a deep, 2-quart kettle or deep-fat fryer with oil to a depth of about 3 inches. Heat to 365°F.
3. Drop teaspoonfuls into hot oil and fry until golden brown. When they are cooked through, they will float to the top of the hot fat.

Yield: 20 to 25 hush puppies.

Corn Tortillas
(Masa Harina)

Frozen tortillas are available in markets. However, many people prefer to make their own from scratch. To do this, you will need to purchase masa harina, which is dried corn that has been ground fine. This is available in almost all shops that specialize in Mexican and Latin foods. Best known brand is *Quaker Masa Harina* masa mix.

2 cups masa harina mix

1 cup plus 2 tablespoons water

1. Combine the masa harina and water in a bowl, mixing until dough forms a ball. If necessary, add 1 to 2 teaspoons additional water.
2. Shape to form 14 to 16 balls. Cover with a cloth to prevent dough from drying out. Remove balls one at a time for shaping.
3. To roll the tortillas, place each ball between 2 sheets plastic wrap; roll out or press with a tortilla press to form 6-inch circles. Carefully peel off plastic wrap. If using a tortilla press, plastic wrap is not necessary.

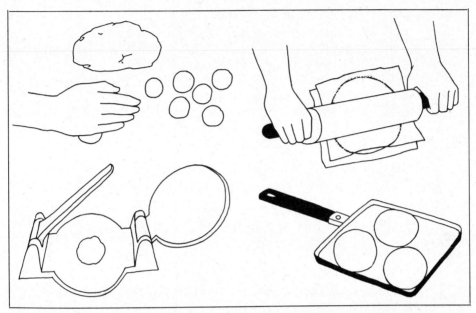

4. Bake on a hot (400°F.) ungreased griddle or in heavy skillet 30 seconds. Turn with your fingers or a spatula; continue baking 15 to 30 seconds. Tortillas should be soft and pliable. Use immediately or layer between sheets of wax paper.

Yield: 14 to 16 tortillas.

Muffins
(Basic Recipe)

Piping-hot, fresh-from-the-oven muffins work wonders with a menu. They are served in this country for breakfast, to fill out a light supper or with a main-course salad for lunch.

Quick stirring is the secret to crisp, tender muffins. Add the liquid and stir only until the flour is dampened. Don't fret if the batter is still lumpy—it's supposed to be that way. Overmixing makes tunnels inside and gives peaked tops to the baked muffins.

3 cups sifted all-purpose flour (sift before measuring)
4 teaspoons baking powder
1 teaspoon salt

3 tablespoons sugar
½ cup unsalted butter or margarine
2 large eggs, well beaten
1¼ cups milk

Preheated oven temperature: 400°F.
1. Sift the flour, baking powder, salt and sugar together into a large bowl. Cut in the butter or margarine with a pastry blender or electric mixer until the consistency of cornmeal.
2. Combine the eggs with the milk and add to the flour mixture; mix only enough to dampen all the flour.
3. Fill well-oiled muffin pans about two thirds full. Bake in preheated oven 20 to 25 minutes, or until done.

Yield: 20 medium-sized muffins.

Variations: Apple Muffins

In Step 2 add 1 cup chopped, peeled apples to the egg-milk mixture. In Step 3 sprinkle tops with a mixture of 2 tablespoons sugar and ¼ teaspoon ground cinnamon before baking.

Raisin-Orange Muffins

In Step 2 add ⅔ cup chopped raisins and 1½ teaspoons grated orange rind to egg-milk mixture.

Raisin-Spice Muffins

In Step 2 add ⅔ cup chopped raisins to the egg-milk mixture. In Step 3 sprinkle tops with a mixture of 2 tablespoons sugar and ¼ teaspoon ground cinnamon before baking.

Date Muffins

In Step 2 add 1 cup finely chopped dates to egg-milk mixture.

Corn Muffins

Corn muffins should not be overly sweet if they are to be served with the main course. This recipe is a Midwestern favorite.

1 cup sifted all-purpose flour (sift before measuring)
4 teaspoons baking powder
½ teaspoon salt
2 tablespoons sugar, or less to taste

1½ cups yellow cornmeal
1 large egg, well beaten
1 cup milk
2 tablespoons melted unsalted butter or margarine

Preheated oven temperature: 400°F.
1. Sift the flour, baking powder, salt and sugar into a large bowl. Add cornmeal and mix well.

2. Combine egg and milk. Add to flour mixture and then add butter or margarine; mix only enough to dampen flour.
3. Fill well-oiled muffin pans about two thirds full. Bake in preheated oven 25 minutes, or until done.

Yield: 12 medium-sized muffins.

Bran Muffins

These are delectable muffins either hot, cold or toasted—and so nutritious!

¼ cup unsalted butter or margarine
½ cup light brown sugar, firmly packed
¼ cup dark molasses
2 large eggs
1 cup milk

1½ cups bran
1 cup all-purpose flour, unsifted
1½ teaspoons baking soda
¾ teaspoon salt
½ cup chopped raisins (optional)

Preheated oven temperature: 400°F.
1. Cream the butter or margarine with the sugar until light and fluffy. Add molasses and eggs and beat well. Stir in milk and then bran.
2. Sift the flour, baking soda and salt into the creamed mixture and stir quickly just until thoroughly blended. Fold in optional raisins. The batter will be very thin—this is normal. The bran will expand and make the mixture firm during baking.
3. Fill well-oiled muffin pans about two thirds full. Bake in preheated oven 15 to 20 minutes, or until done.

Yield: 18 medium-sized muffins.

Maine Blueberry Muffins

These are rich muffins, more like cake than bread, and are traditional with many Maine dishes.

A light touch is needed in mixing the batter; do this by hand. Just in case you have picked fresh blueberries, stem, wash and dry them on paper towels before you begin mixing the ingredients.
NOTE: If the blueberries are not sweet, increase sugar to ½ cup.

2 cups sifted all-purpose flour (sift before measuring)
3 teaspoons baking powder
½ teaspoon salt
⅓ cup sugar

2 large eggs, well beaten
1 cup milk
½ cup melted unsalted butter
1 cup fresh or frozen blueberries

Preheated oven temperature: 425°F.

1. Sift the flour, baking powder, salt and sugar together into a large bowl. Reserve 2 tablespoons of this mixture to coat the blueberries.
2. Combine the eggs, milk and butter. Make a well in the middle of flour mixture with a spoon. Pour in the liquid mixture and mix only enough to dampen all the flour. Coat the blueberries with the reserved 2 tablespoons flour mixture; then fold them lightly into the batter.
3. Fill well-oiled muffin pans about two thirds full. Bake in preheated oven 25 minutes, or until a cake tester comes out clean. Remove from oven and let rest in pan 1 minute. This will keep the muffins from sticking to the pan.

Yield: About 14 medium-sized muffins.

Griddle Cakes

A breakfast of griddle cakes is traditionally American. Serve on warm plates with maple syrup, sorghum or honey and ham, bacon or sausage patties.

Once the griddle is seasoned with oil to receive the first batch of griddle cakes, there is no need to brush it with oil again until the next griddle-making session. Instead, rub with a little bag of salt to smooth the surface before pouring each batch of cakes. For the salt bag, tie ¼ cup salt in doubled cheesecloth.

Heat the griddle over medium heat until a few drops of water sprinkled on the surface dance about.

Buckwheat Cakes

2 cups sifted buckwheat flour (sift before measuring)
2 teaspoons baking powder
1 teaspoon baking soda
1½ teaspoons salt
2 tablespoons sugar
2 large eggs, well beaten
4 cups buttermilk
¼ cup melted unsalted butter or corn oil

1. Sift the flour, baking powder, baking soda, salt and sugar into a large bowl.
2. Combine the eggs and buttermilk and add to flour mixture but do not mix. Add butter or oil. Then mix only enough to dampen flour.
3. Ladle mixture onto hot griddle, allowing about ¼ cup of batter for each cake. Bake on each side until golden, turning with a wide spatula. Serve immediately.

Yield: 24 griddle cakes.

Cornmeal Batter Cakes
(*Indian Griddle Cakes*)

2 cups buttermilk
1 teaspoon salt
1 teaspoon baking soda
1 teaspoon baking powder

1 teaspoon sugar
2 tablespoons flour
2 cups white or yellow cornmeal
1 large egg, well beaten

1. Combine the buttermilk, salt, baking soda, baking powder, sugar and flour in large bowl. Beat well to blend ingredients. Sift the cornmeal over the mixture; add the egg and blend until well mixed.
2. Ladle mixture onto hot griddle, allowing about ¼ cup of batter for each cake. Bake on each side until golden, turning with a wide spatula. Serve immediately.

Yield: 18 cornmeal batter cakes.

Sourdough Pancakes

2 cups liquid yeast starter
2 large eggs, separated
½ teaspoon salt

2 tablespoons sugar
1 teaspoon baking soda, dissolved in 2 teaspoons warm water

1. Prepare the starter the night before as in Step 1 for Basic Sourdough Bread (page 348).
2. In a large bowl beat the egg yolks with the salt until they are thick and light. Stir in the starter.
3. Beat the egg whites in a separate bowl, beating in the sugar, until stiff peaks form; gently fold into the batter with a rubber spatula. Add the baking soda and water mixture and stir gently to blend.
4. Ladle mixture onto hot griddle, allowing about ¼ cup of batter for each cake. Bake on each side until golden, turning with a wide spatula. Serve immediately.

Yield: 18 pancakes.

Cakes

American cakes are unique. In my opinion, they cannot be matched by the most elegant Austrian sacher torte, French *génoise* or Scandinavian cream cake.

The first step in making a successful cake is to put your heart into the project. Cakemaking is an exacting process; the ingredients must be as balanced as a pharmacist's prescription. Perfect cakes are possible for the novice baker who is willing to heed the basics and follow recipe directions with care.

Cakemaking Basics

Read through the recipe to be sure you understand the instructions and have the ingredients and equipment needed.

Use only the best quality flour, shortening and all other ingredients, such as flavorings and dried fruits or nuts.

Always measure all ingredients accurately. Dry ingredients should be measured in cups which come in graduated sizes of ¼, ⅓, ½ and 1 cup. Use these cups also for measuring shortening. To measure liquid ingredients, use a glass cup with a spout. Measure the liquid at eye level. In cake baking do not interchange the cups because there is enough difference between dry and liquid measures to affect the batter.

To measure flour. Sift before measuring. Spoon flour lightly to top of measuring cup; never pack the flour. Then level off the top with a knife. Sift again with rest of dry ingredients.

To measure sugar. Always sift white granulated sugar before measuring. Discard lumps and large crystals. This will make it easier to cream the sugar into the shortening. Pack brown sugar firmly in the cup and level off top with a knife. To measure confectioners' sugar, press through a sieve to remove lumps. Spoon lightly into measuring cup and level off top with knife.

INGREDIENTS   Have all ingredients at room temperature before you begin mixing the batter, unless the recipe specifies otherwise.

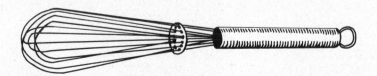

Flour. Most traditional American cakes are made with all-purpose flour, which is a mixture of hard and soft flours, or with cake flour, which is made from "soft" wheat with a low gluten content. Substituting one for the other in a recipe is not recommended. However, in an emergency use ⅞ cup all-purpose flour (1 cup less 2 tablespoons) as a substitute for 1 cup cake flour.

Shortening. Do not substitute liquid oil for solid butter or margarine in a cake recipe. The texture will be poor because air will not be beaten in when adding the fat.

Oil. Use only unflavored corn or vegetable oil.

Eggs. Use large eggs, at least 3 days old, for best results.

Flavorings and Extracts. The modern theory of cakemaking is to add these just after creaming the fat and sugar so that the flavor will be carried throughout the batter during the mixing.

MIXING INGREDIENTS

Complete mixing directions are given with each recipe; however, beginners frequently need additional help in understanding certain cakemaking terms.

To Cream. This applies to working the butter or margarine to a creamy consistency. This can be done by hand with a wooden spoon or with an electric mixer by working the mixture around the bowl until it becomes light and fluffy. The term is not to be confused with mixing or stirring.

Add Sugar Gradually. After the butter or margarine has been creamed, add sugar 2 to 3 tablespoons at a time and continue beating until the mixture becomes smooth and even in texture. If the mixture looks curdled, you have overbeaten the ingredients.

Add Dry Ingredients Alternately with Liquid. This means to add the dry ingredients to the batter, beginning with the flour mixture and alternating with the liquid mixture. The flour mixture should be added in three equal portions and the liquid mixture in two equal portions. This will keep the batter in balance. The entire procedure should be done gently with a rubber spatula in an under-and-over motion and should take no more than 2 minutes. (This step can be done with an electric mixer. Follow manufacturer's instructions for best results.)

Stiffly Beaten Egg Whites. These are egg whites beaten separately until stiff peaks form. The incorporated air helps the batter rise. If the whites become watery during the beating, they have been overbeaten. Begin beating whites after the oven has reached the correct temperature for baking the cake. Fold beaten egg whites into the batter in an under-and-over motion, gradually turning the bowl. If recipe calls for more than two whites, fold in half at a time. Follow recipe instructions for incorporating the whites into the batter.

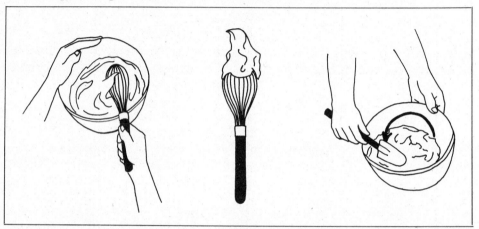

American cooks consider cakemaking a fine art, and everyone has a list of do's and don'ts.

FREEZING CAKES   Almost any cake can be frozen plain. If the cake is to be frosted and frozen, use only a confectioners' sugar frosting made with plenty of butter or margarine. Do not attempt to freeze cakes with cream fillings. *Caution:* Make the cake with pure vanilla extract; imitation vanilla imparts a bitter taste when frozen. Thaw unfrosted cakes unwrapped. Use as soon as possible because thawed cakes dry out rapidly. To thaw frosted cakes, loosen the wrapping but do not uncover while thawing. Thaw in the refrigerator to prevent the frosting from becoming grainy.

THE DO'S

1. Occasionally make certain your oven is the correct temperature. Double-check with a portable oven thermometer or have the oven checked by a serviceman. Even a brand-new oven is likely to be off and will need to be adjusted.
2. Spread the batter evenly in pan before baking, with slightly more batter toward the sides than in the center.
3. To bake properly, the heat must circulate evenly around the cake pan. Place the pan in the center on the middle shelf of the oven.

THE DON'TS

1. Never open the oven door to peek at a cake during the first 15 minutes of baking.
2. Never overbake, or a dry cake will be the result.
3. Never frost a hot cake. Be sure it is completely cool unless the recipe directs otherwise.

One-Two-Three-Four-Cake
(Basic Yellow Cake)

One cup shortening, 2 cups sugar, 3 cups flour and 4 eggs is how many cooks remember the recipe for this old-fashioned cake. This is a versatile basic cake that can be served plain or with a thin lemon glaze, and it also can be dressed up with frosting for any festive occasion.

3 cups sifted all-purpose flour (sift before measuring)
1 tablespoon baking powder
¼ teaspoon salt
1 cup unsalted butter or margarine

2 cups sugar
4 large egg yolks
1 teaspoon vanilla or lemon extract
1 cup milk
4 large egg whites, stiffly beaten

Preheated oven temperature: 350°F.
1. Sift together the flour, baking powder and salt. Set aside.
2. Cream the butter or margarine in a large bowl until light and fluffy. Gradually add the sugar, 2 to 3 tablespoons at a time, and continue beating until the mixture is smooth and even in texture. Add the egg yolks one at a time, beating well after each addition. Stir in the vanilla or lemon extract.
3. With a rubber spatula gently blend in the flour mixture alternately with the milk, beginning and ending with the flour mixture.
4. Fold the egg whites into the batter lightly but quickly, half at a time, with a down-up-and-over motion, gradually turning the bowl.
5. Pour batter into a well-oiled 10-inch tube pan and bake in preheated oven 55 to 60 minutes, or until the cake shrinks slightly from the sides of the pan and cake tester comes out clean.
6. Remove from oven and cool cake in pan on a wire rack 10 minutes; remove from pan. Cool and frost as desired.
Yield: 10 to 12 servings.

Variations: Cocoa Cake

Reduce flour to 2½ cups and add 5 tablespoons cocoa. Sift with dry ingredients.

Spice Cake

Reduce flour to 2¾ cups and add 1 teaspoon ground cinnamon, ½ teaspoon ground cloves and ½ teaspoon ground allspice or nutmeg. Sift with dry ingredients.

Pennsylvania Dutch Golden Saffron Cake

In Step 2 add 8 threads finely crushed Spanish saffron. Flavor with vanilla, not lemon juice. When cool, frost with Lemon Buttercream Frosting (page 389); decorate with poppy seeds, multicolor or yellow crystal sugar.

White Mountain Cake
(Basic White Cake)

This cake probably came by its name because it often was covered with a fluffy white frosting that stood up in high peaks. Substitute 7-Minute Frosting (page 390).

Vegetable food coloring may be added to the cake mixture and frosting if a party cake is desired.

2½ cups sifted cake flour (sift before measuring)
1 tablespoon baking powder
¼ teaspoon salt
½ cup unsalted butter or margarine
1½ cups sugar

1 teaspoon vanilla; or ¾ teaspoon vanilla and ¼ teaspoon almond extract
1 cup milk
4 large egg whites, stiffly beaten

Preheated oven temperature: 350°F.
1. Sift together the flour, baking powder and salt. Set aside.
2. Cream the butter or margarine in a large bowl until light and fluffy. Gradually add the sugar, 2 tablespoons at a time, and continue beating until the mixture is smooth and even in texture. Stir in the vanilla or vanilla and almond extract.
3. With a rubber spatula gently blend in the flour mixture alternately with the milk, beginning and ending with the flour mixture.
4. Fold the egg whites into the batter lightly but quickly, half at a time, with a down-up-and-over motion, gradually turning the bowl.
5. Pour batter into a well-oiled 10-inch tube pan and bake in preheated

oven 50 to 55 minutes, or until the cake shrinks slightly from the sides of the pan and cake tester comes out clean.
6. Remove from oven and cool cake in pan on a wire rack 10 minutes; remove from pan. Cool and frost as desired.
Yield: 10 to 12 servings.

Variation: Orange-Coconut Cake

Substitute 1 tablespoon finely grated orange rind for the vanilla and almond extract. Substitute 1 cup orange juice combined with ½ cup shredded or grated coconut for the milk. Frost with Orange Buttercream Frosting (page 389) and sprinkle with additional coconut.

Preacher's Chocolate Cake
(Basic Chocolate Cake)

Prior to World War I rural communities in southern Indiana were so sparsely populated that the church congregation could not support a full-time minister. As a result, these small churches were attended to by visiting circuit traveling clergymen, commonly referred to as "preachers." It was local custom for the congregation to take turns inviting these traveling men for Sunday dinner, the noonday meal after the church service, and "preacher" expected a bountiful meal—accompanied by a rich chocolate cake. As time went by this old-fashioned rich chocolate cake became known as "Preacher's Cake."

2 cups sifted cake flour (sift before measuring)
1 tablespoon baking powder
¼ teaspoon salt
½ teaspoon baking soda
½ cup unsalted butter or margarine
1 cup sugar
2 large egg yolks, well beaten
3 squares (3 ounces) unsweetened chocolate, melted
1 teaspoon vanilla
1¼ cups milk
2 large egg whites, stiffly beaten

Preheated oven temperature: 350°F.
1. Sift together the flour, baking powder, salt and baking soda. Set aside.
2. Cream the butter or margarine in a large bowl until light and fluffy. Gradually add the sugar, 2 to 3 tablespoons at a time, and continue beating until the mixture is smooth and even in texture. Beat in the egg yolks and add the chocolate and vanilla, stirring well to blend.
3. With a rubber spatula gently blend in the flour mixture alternately with the milk, beginning and ending with the flour mixture.

4. Fold the egg whites into the batter lightly but quickly with a down-up-and-over motion, gradually turning the bowl.
5. Pour batter into a well-oiled 10-inch tube pan and bake in preheated oven about 55 minutes, or until the cake shrinks slightly from the sides of the pan and a cake tester comes out clean.
6. Remove from oven and cool cake in pan on a wire rack 10 minutes; remove from pan. Cool and frost with Chocolate Buttercream Frosting (page 389).

Yield: 10 to 12 servings.

Variations: Chocolate Mocha Cake

Substitute ¾ cup strong black coffee and ½ cup warm water for the milk.

Chocolate Nut Cake

In Step 3 add ¾ cup chopped walnuts, pecans or hickory nuts.

Devil's Food Cake

After angel food cake became an American success, some wit must have had the idea to "give the devil his due" by naming a cake in his honor. Frost with either 7-Minute or Chocolate Buttercream Frosting.

¼ cup cocoa
1 square (1 ounce) unsweetened baking chocolate
½ cup boiling water
1 teaspoon baking soda
½ cup unsalted butter or margarine

2 cups light brown sugar, firmly packed
2 large eggs
2½ cups sifted cake flour (sift before measuring)
1 cup buttermilk

Preheated oven temperature: 350°F.
1. In small, heavy saucepan dissolve the cocoa and chocolate in the ½ cup boiling water over low heat, stirring well to blend. Remove from heat and cool. Add baking soda and stir to mix. Set aside.
2. Cream the butter or margarine in a large bowl until light and fluffy. Gradually add the sugar, about 3 tablespoons at a time, and continue beating until the mixture is smooth and even in texture. Beat in the eggs one at a time, beating well after each addition. Stir in chocolate mixture.
3. With a rubber spatula gently blend in the flour alternately with the buttermilk, beginning and ending with the flour.

4. Pour batter evenly into 2 well-oiled 8-inch square pans. Bake in preheated oven 22 to 25 minutes, or until the cake shrinks slightly from sides of pan and a cake tester comes out clean.
5. Remove from oven and cool cakes in pans on a wire rack 10 minutes. Remove from pans and cool thoroughly before frosting. Use 7-Minute Frosting or Chocolate Buttercream Frosting (page 389).
6. Place one layer on a cake plate and cover top with frosting. Place second layer on top and cover the entire cake with frosting.

Yield: 10 to 12 servings.

Chocolate Bourbon Cake

This recipe originated in Kentucky, where cooks have used their justly famous bourbon as flavoring for at least 200 years. This is a superb party cake, but very rich. The batter can be baked as a sheet cake or in a tube pan. Frost with Chocolate Bourbon Frosting.

2 cups sifted cake flour (sift before measuring)
2 teaspoons baking powder
¼ teaspoon salt
½ cup unsalted butter or margarine
2 cups sugar
4 squares (4 ounces) unsweetened baking chocolate, melted

2 large egg yolks, well beaten
1 teaspoon vanilla
2 tablespoons bourbon
1½ cups milk
1 cup chopped pecans or black walnuts
2 large egg whites, stiffly beaten

Preheated oven temperature: 350°F.
1. Sift together the flour, baking powder and salt. Set aside.
2. Cream the butter or margarine in a large bowl until light and fluffy. Gradually add the sugar, 2 to 3 tablespoons at a time, and continue beating until the mixture is smooth and even in texture. Stir in the chocolate. Add the egg yolks and beat well. Stir in the vanilla and bourbon.
3. With a rubber spatula gently blend in the flour mixture alternately with the milk, beginning and ending with the flour mixture; this will be a thin batter. Stir in the pecans or walnuts.
4. Fold the egg whites into the batter lightly, with a down-up-and-over motion, gradually turning the bowl.
5. Pour batter into a well-oiled 13-x-9-x-2-inch pan or a 10-inch tube pan. Place in preheated oven and bake 25 to 30 minutes for the oblong pan and about 55 to 60 minutes for the tube pan, or until the cake shrinks from the sides of the pan or a cake tester comes out *almost* clean; this is a very moist cake and there will be a slight

stickiness remaining on the cake tester. Do not overbake, or the cake will not be of the desired texture.

6. Remove from oven and cool cake in pan on a wire rack 10 minutes; remove from pan. Cool and spread with Chocolate Bourbon Frosting (page 389).

Yield: 10 to 12 servings, or more.

Sour Cream Cake

This is a Southern recipe for a rich cake of fine texture, slightly moist and with an unforgettably delicate flavor. No frosting is necessary because the cake makes its own while baking.

3 cups sifted cake flour (sift before measuring)
1 teaspoon salt
¼ teaspoon baking soda
1 cup unsalted butter or margarine

3 cups sugar
1 teaspoon vanilla
1 cup sour cream
6 large eggs
⅔ cup walnuts or pecans, chopped

Preheated oven temperature: 300°F.

1. Sift together the flour, salt and baking soda. Set aside.
2. Cream the butter or margarine in a large bowl until light and fluffy. Gradually add the sugar, 2 to 3 tablespoons at a time, and continue beating until the mixture is smooth and even in texture. Blend in the vanilla and sour cream. Add eggs one at a time, beating about 1 minute after adding each. Gradually add the flour mixture and beat just enough to blend thoroughly.
3. Oil a 10-inch tube pan well on sides and bottom. Sprinkle the walnuts or pecans evenly on the bottom of the pan, not on the sides. Pour the batter over the nuts and bake in preheated oven 1 hour and 15 minutes to 1 hour and 30 minutes, or until cake shrinks slightly from the sides of the pan and a cake tester comes out clean.
4. Remove from oven and cool cake in pan on a wire rack 10 minutes; remove from pan.

Yield: 12 to 14 servings.

Variations: Sour Cream Cake with Rich Nut Topping

In Step 3 spread ¼ cup soft unsalted butter or margarine on bottom of pan. Sprinkle with walnuts or pecans and cover the nuts with ⅔ cup light brown sugar, firmly packed. Pour the batter over the brown sugar and bake as above.

Black Walnut Sour Cream Cake

In Step 2 after the eggs have been beaten into the mixture, stir in 1 cup chopped black walnuts. Continue with blending in the flour. Omit spreading walnuts or pecans on bottom of pan. Cool cake and dust lightly with confectioners' sugar.

Fresh Coconut Cake

The best time to make this cake is when coconuts are at their peak of freshness at the market. Both the liquid from the coconut and freshly grated coconut are incorporated into the batter. The cake is further enhanced with fluffy 7-Minute Frosting and generously sprinkled with additional freshly grated coconut. This cake keeps well and can be made several days ahead of party time.

3 cups sifted cake flour (sift before measuring)
1 tablespoon baking powder
½ cup unsalted butter or margarine
1¾ cups sugar
1 teaspoon vanilla
¾ cup milk combined with ½ cup of the liquid in the coconut (see note)
½ cup freshly grated coconut
Whites of 4 large eggs, stiffly beaten

Preheated oven temperature: 350°F.
1. Sift together the flour and baking powder. Set aside.
2. Cream the butter or margarine in a large bowl until light and fluffy. Gradually add the sugar, 2 to 3 tablespoons at a time, and continue beating until the mixture is smooth and even in texture. Stir in the vanilla.
3. With a rubber spatula gently blend in the flour mixture alternately with the milk mixture, beginning and ending with the flour mixture. Stir the grated coconut through the mixture.
4. Fold the egg whites into the batter lightly and quickly, half at a time, with a down-up-and-over motion, gradually turning the bowl.
5. Pour batter into a well-oiled 10-inch tube pan and bake in preheated oven 55 to 60 minutes, or until the cake shrinks slightly from the sides of the pan and a cake tester comes out clean.
6. Remove from oven and cool cake in pan on a wire rack 10 minutes; remove from pan. Cool and frost with 7-Minute Frosting (page 390). Sprinkle generously with freshly grated coconut.

Yield: 12 to 14 servings.
NOTE: Start with an unopened coconut full of liquid. Pierce eyes with a screwdriver. Drain off liquid and reserve. Place coconut in preheated

350°F. oven 15 to 30 minutes, or until coconut is cracked. Tap all over with hammer and then break open. Pry out meat and pare off dark skin. To grate meat, use a hand grater, blender or food processor.

Mix-Easy One-Egg Cake
(Basic Recipe)

For anyone accustomed to using mixes, this mix-easy batter is just as easy to assemble. No experience necessary. This is an old-fashioned "scratch cake," referred to by past generations as "busy-day cake." It is a moist cake of good texture that can be varied considerably by changing flavorings and adding nuts or raisins. Even the frosting is easy—just spread the ingredients on top of the cake and bake an additional 5 minutes.

Save time by premeasuring the dry ingredients in recipe quantities into plastic bags and labeling them for ready use. Each recipe makes 1 8-inch cake or 18 cupcakes.

½ cup unsalted butter or margarine

2 cups sifted all-purpose flour (sift before measuring)

2 teaspoons baking powder

¼ teaspoon salt

¾ cup sugar

¾ cup milk, combined with 1 teaspoon vanilla

1 large egg

Preheated oven temperature: 375°F.
1. Mix the butter or margarine lightly in a medium-sized bowl to soften.
2. Sift the flour, baking powder, salt and sugar over the butter or margarine. Add the milk mixture and mix until all flour is dampened; then beat hard by hand or with an electric mixer for 2 minutes. Add egg and beat 1 minute longer.
3. Pour batter into a well-oiled 8-inch square pan and bake in preheated oven 25 minutes, or until cake tester comes out clean. Bake cupcakes about 18 to 20 minutes.
4. Remove from oven and spread with optional Praline Topping. Return to oven and bake an additional 5 minutes.
5. Remove from oven and cool cake in pan on rack. Cut into squares and serve.

Yield: 1 8-inch cake or 18 cupcakes.

Praline Topping (optional)

⅓ cup brown sugar, firmly packed, combined with 1 tablespoon flour, ⅓ cup finely chopped nuts, 3 tablespoons melted unsalted butter or margarine and 1 tablespoon water

Variations: Chocolate Cake

In Step 1 use ⅓ cup unsalted butter or margarine and add 1 to 1½ squares (1 to 1½ ounces) unsweetened melted chocolate, depending upon taste.

Spice Cake

In Step 2 reduce amount of flour to 1⅞ cups and add 1 teaspoon ground cinnamon, ¼ teaspoon ground cloves and ¼ teaspoon ground allspice or nutmeg.

Raisin or Nut Cake

In Step 2 remove 2 tablespoons flour and mix with ½ cup chopped raisins or nuts (any kind); blend into the mixture with a spoon at the end of the mixing.

Honey Cake

In Step 2 decrease the sugar to ½ cup. Decrease the milk to ⅔ cup and stir in ½ cup strained honey.

Cottage Pudding

Omit Praline Topping. Serve warm or cold with lightly sweetened crushed berries.

Quick and Easy Pound Cake

During the colonial period, when extended families were the rule, this cake actually was made with 1 pound butter, 1 pound sugar, 1 pound eggs, and so on. The recipe below is more appropriate for smaller families.

2 cups all-purpose flour (sift before measuring)
¼ teaspoon salt
1 cup unsalted butter or margarine

1¼ cups sugar
1½ teaspoons vanilla
½ teaspoon almond extract
4 large eggs

Preheated oven temperature: 325°F.
1. Sift together the flour and salt. Set aside.
2. Cream the butter or margarine in a large bowl until light and fluffy. Gradually add the sugar, 2 to 3 tablespoons at a time, and continue

beating until the mixture is smooth and even in texture. Stir in the vanilla and almond extract. Beat in the eggs one at a time, beating well after each addition.
3. Gradually add the flour to the mixture and beat just enough to blend thoroughly.
4. Oil the bottom and about 1 inch up the sides of a 9-x-5-x-3-inch loaf pan. Pour in the batter and bake in a preheated oven 60 to 65 minutes or until cake shrinks slightly from the sides and a cake tester comes out clean.
5. Remove from oven and cool cake in pan on a wire rack 10 minutes. Run spatula around the sides of the cake to remove from pan.

Yield: About 8 servings.

Cornmeal Pound Cake

This is a Midwestern corn belt recipe that has been revised by omitting 1 cup of sugar and enhancing the cake with a light lemon glaze in deference to the traditional down-on-the-farm rich lemon buttercream frosting.

1½ cups all-purpose flour (sift before measuring)
1½ cups yellow cornmeal (sift before measuring)
½ teaspoon baking powder
¼ teaspoon salt
¼ teaspoon baking soda
1 cup unsalted butter or margarine

2 cups sugar
1 teaspoon vanilla
1 teaspoon grated lemon rind or lemon extract
6 large egg yolks
1 cup sour cream
6 large egg whites, stiffly beaten

Preheated oven temperature: 350°F.
1. Sift together the flour, cornmeal, baking powder, salt and baking soda. Set aside.
2. Cream the butter or margarine in a large bowl until light and fluffy. Gradually add the sugar, 2 to 3 tablespoons at a time, and continue beating until the mixture is smooth and even in texture. Stir in the vanilla and lemon rind or extract. Beat in the egg yolks one at a time, beating well after each addition.
3. With a rubber spatula gently blend in the flour and cornmeal mixture alternately with the sour cream, beginning and ending with the dry mixture.
4. Fold the egg whites into the batter lightly and quickly, half at a time, with a down-up-and-over motion, gradually turning the bowl.
5. Pour batter into a well-oiled 10-inch tube pan and bake in preheated oven 55 minutes to one hour, or until the cake shrinks slightly from

the sides of the pan and a cake tester comes out clean.
6. Remove from oven and cool cake in pan on a wire rack 10 minutes; remove from pan. Cool and spread with Lemon Glaze (page 391).
Yield: 10 to 12 servings.

Prune Cake with Buttermilk Frosting

The grandmother of a young lady I know from Georgia makes this traditional Southern cake to serve during the Christmas holiday season. It is a great spice cake with or without frosting and delicious any time of year.

1 cup cooked chopped prunes, well drained
2 cups sifted all-purpose flour (sift before measuring)
1 teaspoon baking powder
½ teaspoon salt
1 teaspoon baking soda
1 teaspoon ground cinnamon

1 teaspoon ground nutmeg
1 teaspoon ground allspice
1 teaspoon ground cloves (optional)
½ cup unsalted butter or margarine
1½ cups sugar
3 large eggs, well beaten
1 cup buttermilk

Preheated oven temperature: 350°F.
1. Prepare prunes following package instructions. Do not add sugar.
2. Sift together the flour, baking powder, salt, baking soda, cinnamon, nutmeg, allspice and optional cloves. Set aside.
3. Cream the butter or margarine in a large bowl until light and fluffy. Gradually add the sugar, 2 to 3 tablespoons at a time, and continue beating until the mixture is smooth and even in texture. Add the eggs and beat well.
4. With a rubber spatula gently blend in the flour mixture alternately with the buttermilk, beginning and ending with the flour mixture.
5. Pour into a well-oiled 10-inch tube pan. Place in preheated oven and bake 55 to 60 minutes, or until cake shrinks slightly from the sides of the pan or a cake tester comes out clean.
6. Remove from oven and cool cake in pan on a wire rack 10 minutes. Remove from pan. Cool and spread with Buttermilk Frosting.
Yield: 12 to 14 servings.

Buttermilk Frosting

1 cup sugar
½ cup buttermilk
½ teaspoon baking soda
¼ cup unsalted butter or margarine
1 tablespoon light corn syrup

1 teaspoon vanilla
1 cup shredded or grated coconut
5 slices canned pineapple, cut into small cubes, well drained
¼ cup candied cherries (optional)

1. In a medium-sized, heavy saucepan combine the sugar, buttermilk, baking soda, butter or margarine and corn syrup. Cook over low heat, stirring constantly. The mixture will foam considerably during the boiling. Cook until the mixture forms a soft ball in cold water (236°F.).
2. Cool slightly and stir in the vanilla, coconut and pineapple. Spread mixture over cooled cake immediately. If the mixture becomes too cool to spread easily, return to low heat for a few seconds. Garnish top of cake with optional candied cherries.

Yield: Enough frosting for 10-inch tube cake.

Banana Cake

For many years there was a small delicatessen at the corner of Second Avenue and 55th Street in New York City that was well-known for its delicious homemade banana cake. The cake was made by the proprietor's wife whenever there were overripe bananas on hand. Alas, the delicatessen no longer exists, but before it was sold the recipe was given to me exactly as it always was made by "Miss Bessie."

1½ cups sifted all-purpose flour (sift before measuring)
¼ teaspoon salt
1 teaspoon baking soda
½ cup unsalted butter or margarine
1¼ cups sugar

2 large eggs, lightly beaten
1 teaspoon vanilla
¼ cup sour cream
1 cup very ripe banana pulp
1 cup chopped walnuts or pecans (optional)

Preheated oven temperature: 350°F.
1. Sift together the flour, salt and baking soda. Set aside.
2. Cream the butter or margarine in a large bowl until light and fluffy. Gradually add the sugar, 2 to 3 tablespoons at a time, and continue beating until the mixture is smooth and even in texture.
3. Beat in the eggs and add the vanilla. Stir in the sour cream and banana pulp; blend until smooth. Gradually add the flour mixture and beat just enough to blend thoroughly. Stir in optional nuts.

4. Pour mixture into a well-oiled 9-inch square pan. Bake in preheated oven about 55 minutes, or until cake shrinks slightly from the sides of the pan and a cake tester comes out clean.
5. Remove from oven and cool cake in pan on a wire rack. Cut into squares and serve unfrosted.
Yield: 6 to 8 servings.

Mrs. Baum's Apple Cake

Mrs. Baum was well into her nineties when she baked this marvelously moist and nutritious cake for a DAR picnic, proving that good cooks stay forever young. The recipe belonged to her grandmother, who must have been a thrifty cook who used the leftover morning coffee as the liquid in the batter. The cake freezes very well.

1½ cups sifted all-purpose flour (sift before measuring)
1 teaspoon baking soda
¼ teaspoon salt
1 teaspoon ground cinnamon
¾ cup vegetable or corn oil
1 cup sugar

1 large egg
½ cup black coffee
½ cup chopped pecans or walnuts
2 cups peeled and chopped tart cooking apples
2 teaspoons sugar, combined with 3 tablespoons chopped pecans or walnuts for topping

Preheated oven temperature: 350°F.
1. Sift together the flour, baking soda, salt and cinnamon. Set aside.
2. Cream the oil and sugar in a large mixing bowl and beat 5 minutes, or until smooth. Add the egg and beat well.
3. With a rubber spatula blend in the flour mixture alternately with the coffee, beginning and ending with the flour mixture. Gently stir in the ½ cup nuts and the apples.
4. Pour batter into a well-oiled 11-x-7-x-1½-inch pan. Sprinkle top with sugar-nut mixture. Place in preheated oven and bake 40 minutes, or until the cake shrinks slightly from the sides of the pan and the center of the cake is firm to the touch.
NOTE: This is a very moist cake and the cake tester will come out slightly sticky.
    Remove from oven and cool cake in pan on a wire rack. Cut into squares and serve.
Yield: 12 servings.

Gingerbread

This is a firm-textured gingerbread that can be sliced and spread with butter to serve with tea or coffee. New Englanders dress up the simple cake with a topping of whipped cream, though many Southerners prefer a warm Kentucky Bourbon Sauce.

2 cups sifted all-purpose flour (sift before measuring)

1 teaspoon baking soda

½ teaspoon salt

1½ teaspoons ground ginger

1 teaspoon ground nutmeg

½ cup unsalted butter or margarine

1 cup light brown sugar, firmly packed

2 large eggs

1 teaspoon grated lemon rind or lemon extract

1 cup dark molasses or sorghum, combined with 1 cup boiling water

2 tablespoons bourbon (optional)

Preheated oven temperature: 375°F.
1. Sift together the flour, baking soda, salt, ginger and nutmeg. Set aside.
2. Cream the butter or margarine in a large bowl until light and fluffy. Gradually add the sugar, 2 to 3 tablespoons at a time, and continue beating until the mixture is smooth and even in texture. Add the eggs one at a time, beating well after each addition. Stir in the lemon rind or lemon extract.
3. With a rubber spatula gently blend in the flour mixture alternately with the molasses-water mixture, beginning and ending with the flour mixture. Stir in the optional bourbon.
4. Pour into a well-oiled 11-x-7-x-1½-inch pan. Place in preheated oven and bake 25 to 30 minutes, or until the cake shrinks slightly from the sides of the pan and a cake tester comes out clean.
5. Remove from oven and cool in pan on a wire rack. Slice into squares and serve.
Yield: 12 servings.

Angel Food Cake
(Basic Recipe)

This classic American cake was undoubtedly created by an early cook who overbaked a vanilla soufflé, thereby creating a new fluffy white cake good enough for angels.

This is a versatile cake and you can make many variations. The secret is to have all the ingredients at room temperature before you begin mixing. Make certain the tube pan is absolutely fat-free so that the batter can climb up the sides of the pan to rise to its full volume. Frozen egg whites are not recommended for this recipe.

There are two methods of mixing the batter: one is with granulated sugar and the other is with a combination of confectioners' sugar and granulated sugar. The latter is favored by blue-ribbon cakemasters.

1 cup sifted cake flour (sift before measuring)

1½ cups sifted confectioners' sugar (sift before measuring)

1½ cups egg whites (about 12 large eggs)

1½ teaspoons cream of tartar

¼ teaspoon salt

1 cup sifted granulated sugar

1½ teaspoons vanilla

½ teaspoon almond extract

Preheated oven temperature: 375°F.

1. Sift together the flour and confectioners' sugar. Set aside.
2. Beat the egg whites, cream of tartar and salt in a large mixing bowl until foamy. (Make certain that none of the egg yolk is present—even a smidgen will keep the whites from whipping to full volume.) Add the granulated sugar 2 tablespoons at a time, beating on high speed of mixer or by hand until stiff peaks form. Gently stir in the vanilla and almond extract.
3. Sprinkle the flour mixture over egg white mixture one fourth at a time, folding in gently with a rubber spatula just until the flour mixture is incorporated.
4. Carefully push the batter with a rubber spatula into a 10-inch tube pan. (Do not use a bundt pan for this purpose because the cake will stick in the creases.)
5. Pull a knife gently through the batter in a widening circle. This is important because it will break up any large air bubbles that may have developed while pushing the batter into the pan.
6. Place the cake in the center of the middle shelf of preheated oven. Bake 30 to 35 minutes, or until cake springs back when lightly touched.
7. Remove the cake from the oven and invert the pan on a funnel; keep in this position until completely cool. To loosen cake, insert a narrow spatula close against the inside of the pan, then pull it out and continue the motion around cake and tube. Serve the cake plain or frost as desired.

Yield: 10 to 12 servings.

Variations: Chocolate Angel Food Cake

In Step 1 substitute ¼ cup cocoa, preferably Dutch process, for ¼ cup flour. In Step 2 omit almond flavoring.

Orange Angel Food Cake

In Step 2 fold in 1 tablespoon grated orange rind. Substitute 1 teaspoon orange extract for almond extract.

Spice Angel Food Cake

In Step 1 sift 1 teaspoon ground cinnamon, ¼ teaspoon ground nutmeg and ½ teaspoon ground allspice with the flour and confectioners' sugar.

Tennessee Jam Cake

Jam cake is a delicious American fruitcake and is well-known in both Tennessee and Kentucky. The cake can be decorated beautifully for the Christmas season with a coating of Vanilla Buttercream Frosting and an edible wreath arranged on top of the cake. Use prepared frosting tubes to make holly leaves and red frosting gel to make shiny berries.

This recipe first appeared in print in 1968, after it was presented to me by a kindly lady from East Tennessee.

3 cups sifted all-purpose flour (sift before measuring)	2 cups sugar
1 teaspoon cocoa	4 large eggs, well beaten
1 teaspoon ground cinnamon	1 cup seedless blackberry jam
1 teaspoon ground nutmeg	1 cup buttermilk, combined with 1 teaspoon baking soda
¼ teaspoon ground cloves	1 cup chopped pecans or walnuts
1 cupunsalted butter or margarine	1 cup chopped seedless raisins

Preheated oven temperature: 350°F.

1. Reserve 2 tablespoons flour. Sift the remaining flour with the cocoa, cinnamon, nutmeg and cloves. Set aside.
2. Cream the butter or margarine in a large bowl until light and fluffy. Gradually add the sugar, about 3 tablespoons at a time, and continue beating until the mixture is smooth and even in texture. Add the eggs and beat well. Stir in the jam.

NOTE: Do not use blackberry jam containing seeds. The seeds impart a bitter taste to the cake.

3. With a rubber spatula gently blend in the flour mixture alternately with the buttermilk mixture, beginning and ending with the flour mixture. Coat the nuts and raisins with the reserved 2 tablespoons flour and gently stir them into the batter.
4. Pour into a well-oiled 10-inch tube pan. Bake in preheated oven 1 hour, or until a cake tester comes out clean.

5. Remove from oven and cool cake in pan on a wire rack 10 minutes. Remove and frost as desired.
Yield: 12 to 14 servings.

Carrot Cake

This nutritious cake is a product of the sixties. Unlike other variations frosted with cream cheese, this recipe is made with wheat germ, and pineapple is added to the batter for flavor. Serve for brunch with fresh strawberries. This is a quick-stir cake, using unsifted ingredients.

¾ cup wheat germ
1 cup all-purpose flour, unsifted
1 cup sugar
¾ teaspoon baking soda
½ teaspoon baking powder
½ teaspoon salt
1½ teaspoons ground cinnamon
¼ teaspoon ground nutmeg
¼ teaspoon ground ginger

1 8-ounce can crushed pineapple and juice
2 large eggs
½ cup vegetable or corn oil
1 teaspoon vanilla
1¼ cups grated carrots
½ cup chopped walnuts or pecans
Confectioners' sugar

Preheated oven temperature: 350°F.
1. Stir together the wheat germ, flour, sugar, baking soda, baking powder, salt, cinnamon, nutmeg and ginger in a large bowl. Add pineapple, eggs, oil and vanilla. Beat well with an electric mixer or by hand. Stir in carrots and nuts.
2. Pour into a well-oiled 10-inch tube or Bundt pan. Bake in preheated oven 45 minutes, or until a cake tester comes out clean. Cool in pan on a rack 10 minutes. Remove from pan and sprinkle with confectioners' sugar.
Yield: 10 to 12 servings.

Blueberry Cake

This is a simple-to-prepare blueberry cake recipe from the collection of a good cook in Cranbury, N.J.

2 cups blueberries
2 cups sifted all-purpose flour (sift before measuring)
2 teaspoons baking powder
½ cup unsalted butter or margarine
1 cup sugar

2 large eggs, beaten with ½ cup milk
2 tablespoons flour
¼ cup sugar combined with ¼ teaspoon ground nutmeg and ¼ teaspoon ground cinnamon for topping

Preheated oven temperature: 350°F.
1. Wash the blueberries and dry thoroughly on paper towels.
2. Sift the 2 cups flour with the baking powder. Set aside.
3. Cream the butter or margarine in a large bowl until light and fluffy. Gradually add the sugar, 2 tablespoons at a time, and continue beating until the mixture is smooth and even in texture. Blend in the egg and milk mixture; then add the flour mixture. Do not over-blend; this cake should have a muffinlike texture.
4. Coat the dry blueberries with the 2 tablespoons flour and stir gently into the mixture.
5. Pour into a well-oiled 13-x-9-x-2-inch pan. Sprinkle top with sugar, nutmeg and cinnamon mixture. Bake in preheated oven 35 minutes, or until a cake tester comes out clean.
6. Remove from oven and cool cake in pan on a wire rack. Cut into squares and serve.
Yield: 12 servings.

Strawberry Shortcake

Genuine old-time shortcakes are made with two layers of rich biscuit dough. With or without whipped heavy cream, these luscious cakes highlight the summer fruit season. Strawberry is probably the best known of all the shortcakes. After the strawberry season is over, you can make a filling of fresh blueberries, peaches or plums.

3 cups sifted all-purpose flour (sift before measuring)
4 teaspoons baking powder
½ teaspoon salt
3 tablespoons sugar
½ cup unsalted butter or margarine

About 1 cup milk
Unsalted butter or margarine
4 to 6 cups fresh fruit, cut into pieces and sweetened to taste (reserve ¼ cup fruit for garnish)

Preheated oven temperature: 450°F.
1. Sift the flour, baking powder, salt and sugar into a large bowl.
2. Cut the butter or margarine into the flour mixture with a pastry blender or electric mixer until it looks like coarse meal. While mixing with a fork, add enough milk to form a soft dough.
3. Knead the dough on a lightly floured surface for 30 seconds. Divide and pat ½ inch thick into 2 lightly oiled 9-inch round pans.
4. Bake in preheated oven 20 minutes, or until a cake tester comes out clean.
5. Remove from oven and immediately assemble the shortcake. Spread butter or margarine on top of each layer. (This will help prevent the

juices in the fruit from making the cake soggy.) Spread the top of each layer with prepared fruit. Place one layer on top of the other. Garnish top with reserved whole berries or fruit slices. Serve warm. **Yield: 8 to 10 servings.**

Cheesecake

This recipe came to me from a Southern family who call it "The only cheesecake." The texture is somewhere between that of a solid New York cheesecake and that of a lighter, whipped gelatin cheesecake.

This cake will not freeze well because it contains egg whites. However, it can be refrigerated for several days. Return cake to room temperature before serving.

The filling in this recipe will not crack on top if the oven is at the correct temperature, the pan is the correct size and it is not over-baked. To prevent cracking during the cooling period, run a knife around the just-baked cake while it is in the oven.

NOTE: Stirring the top of the batter with a spoon, just before the oven door is closed, will also help prevent cracking.

Crust

1½ cups finely crushed graham cracker crumbs
6 tablespoons melted unsalted butter

¼ cup sugar
1 teaspoon ground cinnamon
¼ teaspoon ground nutmeg

Filling

2 8-ounce packages cream cheese
3 tablespoons sugar
1 teaspoon grated lemon rind
1 tablespoon lemon juice
1 teaspoon vanilla

¼ teaspoon salt
5 large egg yolks, well beaten
2 cups sour cream
5 large egg whites
½ cup sugar

Fruit Topping

2 cups fresh strawberries, raspberries or blueberries
½ cup water

½ cup sugar
1½ tablespoons cornstarch

Preheated oven temperature: 350°F.

1. Combine all crust ingredients in a medium-sized bowl and mix lightly until crumbs cling together. Pat mixture in a 10-inch spring-form pan. Line the bottom and bring the mixture halfway up the

sides. Bake in preheated oven 10 minutes. Remove and cool while preparing the filling. Turn oven temperature down to 325°F.

2. Beat the cream cheese in a large bowl until light. Add the 3 table-spoons sugar, the lemon rind, lemon juice, vanilla and salt. Continue beating until light and fluffy. Add the egg yolks and beat with a fork to blend. Stir in the sour cream and mix well.

3. Beat the egg whites until soft peaks form; then gradually add the ½ cup sugar, a tablespoon at a time, until stiff peaks form. With a rubber spatula gently fold the egg whites into the cheese mixture.

4. Carefully pour the batter at once over the prepared crust. Bake in preheated oven 1 hour and 15 minutes. The middle of the cake may seem undercooked and soft at this point but it will become firmer as it cools. Turn off the oven and leave the door ajar. Cool the cake in the oven until it is almost room temperature. Refrigerate until cold.

5. Puree ½ cup of the strawberries, raspberries or blueberries, the water, sugar and cornstarch in a blender or food processor. Cook in a heavy saucepan over medium heat until clear and thick. Cool slightly. Add the remaining fruit.

6. Remove the cheesecake from the refrigerator and remove from pan. Spoon fruit mixture over top. Refrigerate until 45 minutes before serving time.

Yield: 12 to 14 servings.

Cake Frostings

From the countless cooked and uncooked cake frosting recipes in American cooking, I have chosen the most practical for the modern cook. The blender, food processor and electric mixer are handy appliances for making quick and easy cake frostings with good keeping qualities.

Most frosting recipes are interchangeable with one another, but bear in mind that they are meant to complement the color, flavor and texture of the cake.

Vanilla Buttercream Frosting
(Basic Recipe)

3 cups sifted confectioners' sugar
  (sift before measuring)
½ cup softened unsalted butter or
  margarine

3 tablespoons half-and-half
2 teaspoons vanilla

Place the sugar, butter or margarine, half-and-half and vanilla in a blender or food processor. Process until smooth. Stop motor as needed to scrape down sides.
Yield: About 1⅓ cups. Will frost a 10-inch tube cake or a 13-x-9-inch cake. Halve recipe for 9-inch square cake.

Variations: Chocolate Buttercream Frosting

Add 3 squares (3 ounces) melted unsweetened chocolate.

Mocha Buttercream Frosting

Omit half-and-half and vanilla; add ¼ cup strong black coffee.

Lemon Buttercream Frosting

Omit half-and-half and vanilla. Add 3 tablespoons lemon juice and a 1-inch square of lemon rind (no white), cut into strips.

Orange Buttercream Frosting

Omit half-and-half and vanilla. Add 3 tablespoons orange juice and 2 1-inch squares orange rind (no white), cut into strips.

Chocolate Bourbon Frosting

Use a food processor for this recipe, if possible. Otherwise, use a bowl because most blenders are too small to accommodate the ingredients.

1 pound (about 4¾ cups sifted confectioners' sugar (sift before measuring)
½ cup unsalted butter or margarine, at room temperature
2 squares (2 ounces) unsweetened chocolate
1 large egg, well beaten

1 teaspoon vanilla
1 teaspoon lemon juice
2 to 3 tablespoons bourbon, depending upon taste
1 cup chopped pecans or walnuts (optional)

Place the sugar, butter or margarine, chocolate, egg, vanilla, lemon juice and bourbon in food processor. Process until smooth. If not using food processor, place in a large mixing bowl and beat with an electric mixer until smooth. Stir in optional nuts.

Yield: About 1¾ cups. Will frost a 10-inch tube cake or a 13-x-9-inch cake. Halve the recipe for 9-inch square cake and use only the egg yolk. *NOTE: This is a generous amount of frosting for a 10-inch tube cake, but that is the way Southerners like it.*

7-Minute Frosting
(Basic Recipe)

This is a cooked frosting. For best results make on a day with low humidity so that the frosting will firm on the cake.

Whites of 2 large eggs

1½ cups sifted sugar

⅛ teaspoon salt

5 tablespoons warm water

1½ teaspoons light corn syrup

1 teaspoon vanilla

1. Combine the egg whites, sugar, salt, water and corn syrup in the top of a 2-quart double boiler. Mix well.
2. Place over rapidly boiling water. Beat constantly with an electric beater and cook 7 minutes, or until frosting stands in stiff peaks. (If making half the recipe, cook only 4 minutes.)
3. Remove from over boiling water; add vanilla and beat until thick and cooled.

Yield: Enough to cover a 10-inch tube cake or a 13-x-9-inch cake. One half of the recipe will frost a 9-inch square cake.

Variation: Strawberry 7-Minute Frosting

In Step 1 decrease sugar to 1 cup. Add ⅔ cup sliced fresh strawberries. In Step 3 remove from over boiling water and fold in an additional ⅔ cup sliced fresh strawberries.

Glazes

Glazes are low-calorie substitutes for frostings. Brush on while the cake, cookies or doughnuts are still warm.

Bourbon Glaze

1 cup confectioners' sugar, sifted (sift before measuring)
1 tablespoon boiling water

1 tablespoon bourbon
⅛ teaspoon almond extract

Combine all ingredients and stir well to blend. Brush on with pastry brush.
Yield: About 1 cup.

Lemon Glaze

1 cup confectioners' sugar, sifted (sift after measuring)

3 tablespoons lemon juice, heated
¾ teaspoon vanilla

Combine ingredients and stir well to blend. Brush on with pastry brush.
Yield: About 1 cup.

Honey Glaze

2 tablespoons granulated sugar
2 tablespoons light brown sugar, firmly packed

½ cup strained honey
2 tablespoons unsalted butter

Combine all the ingredients in a small, heavy saucepan. Bring to a boil and stir until sugars are dissolved. Brush on with pastry brush.
Yield: About ¾ cup.

Cookies

It can be said that eating cookies is an American national habit. Franchised bakery chains around the country are making a big business of emulating Grandmother by baking old-fashioned, wholesome cookies. Grandmothers from the beginnings of American baking have made it their business to keep cookie jars well filled and they have passed the tradition down to each new generation of cooks. As a result, cookie baking hasn't changed much through the years. The back-to-basics recipes in this chapter are traditional favorites, full of flavor and natural goodness.

Cookie Making Basics

Making old-fashioned cookies is not complicated. As in all other baking, unless the recipe specifies otherwise, the flour is always sifted before measuring. Any mild-flavored fat is acceptable for making cookies; I prefer unsalted butter or margarine, or solid white shortening.

For the recipes in this chapter we found in retesting the old recipes that rolling out the dough on a lightly floured board was an unnecessary step. For easier handling we chilled the dough and then shaped the cookies. This eliminated the possibility of incorporating too much flour into the dough while rolling. When making drop cookies, chilling the dough helps to keep it from spreading and flattening.

When placing cookies on the baking sheet, allow ample space of about 2 inches between cookies.

To Keep Cookies Crisp. Use a container with a loose-fitting cover. The cookies will remain crisp except in very high humidity (in which case they may be recrisped in a slow oven).

To Keep Cookies Fresh and Chewy. Store in an air-tight container.

Hermits

This is the original cookie carried to school in a tin pail by generations of New England schoolchildren.

3 cups sifted all-purpose flour (sift before measuring)
1½ teaspoons baking soda
1 teaspoon ground cinnamon
½ teaspoon ground ginger
1 teaspoon ground allspice
1 teaspoon salt
¼ cup unsalted butter
¼ cup solid white shortening

1 cup light brown sugar, firmly packed
2 large eggs, well beaten
¼ cup warm water
¼ cup dark molasses
1½ cups chopped raisins
1 teaspoon finely grated lemon peel (optional)
1 cup walnuts, chopped

Preheated oven temperature: 350°F.
1. Sift together the flour, baking soda, cinnamon, ginger, allspice and salt. Set aside.
2. Cream the butter, shortening and sugar in a large bowl until light and fluffy. Add the eggs, warm water, molasses, raisins and optional lemon peel; stir to blend well. Add the sifted dry ingredients and mix thoroughly. Stir in walnuts.
3. Lightly oil 2 baking sheets. Form dough into 2-inch-wide strips down the length of the baking sheet, allowing 2 lengths per sheet and keeping the strips 2 inches apart.
4. Bake in preheated oven 20 minutes, or until the dough is firm and baked through. Remove from oven and immediately cut into 2-inch lengths. Cool on rack.

Yield: About 28 cookies.

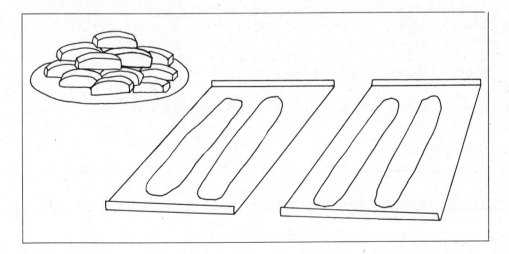

Gingersnaps

These are the old-fashioned spicy gingersnaps that used to be sold by the pound in country grocery stores.

2 cups sifted all-purpose flour (sift before measuring)	¼ cup solid white shortening
1 teaspoon baking soda	½ cup unsalted butter
1 teaspoon ground cinnamon	1 cup sugar
1 teaspoon ground cloves	1 large egg
1 teaspoon ground ginger	¼ cup dark molasses
	Sugar for coating

Preheated oven temperature: 375°F.

1. Sift together the flour, baking soda, cinnamon, cloves and ginger. Set aside.
2. Cream the shortening, butter and sugar in a large bowl until light and fluffy. Add the egg and beat well. Stir in the molasses. Add the flour mixture and stir until well blended. Chill the dough in the refrigerator until firm.
3. Form the dough into 1¼-inch balls. Dip tops in sugar. Place balls 3 inches apart on a lightly oiled baking sheet, sugar side up. Bake in preheated oven about 15 minutes, or just until set but not hard. The tops should be puffed up a little. Remove from oven and cool on rack.

Yield: About 30 cookies.

Mrs. Groves's Best-Ever Oatmeal Cookies

Mrs. Groves was a country lady from Cloverdale, Indiana, who sent her many children to school with the most delicious oatmeal cookies anyone had ever eaten, and this is how the recipe achieved local fame. The cookies originally were made with freshly rendered lard. In this recipe a combination of butter and solid white shortening has been substituted; the result is equally flavorful.

2 cups sifted all-purpose flour (sift before measuring)	1 cup granulated sugar
1 teaspoon baking soda	1 cup light brown sugar, firmly packed
½ cup unsalted butter	2 large eggs, well beaten
½ cup solid white shortening	1 teaspoon vanilla
	2 cups rolled oats (not instant)

Preheated oven temperature: 350°F.

1. Sift together the flour and baking soda. Set aside.
2. Cream the butter, shortening, granulated sugar and brown sugar

in a large bowl until light and fluffy. Add the eggs and beat well. Stir in the vanilla and oats. Let the mixture rest 5 minutes.
3. Stir in the flour mixture and blend well.
NOTE: This will be very stiff dough but do not add any liquid. The cookies will spread during baking.
4. Drop by teaspoonfuls about 2 inches apart on a lightly oiled baking sheet.
5. Bake in preheated oven about 12 minutes, or until lightly browned. Remove from oven and cool on rack.
Yield: 6 dozen cookies.

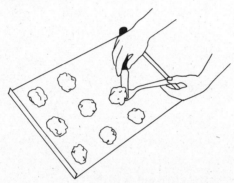

Chocolate-Chip Cookies

This is the original recipe for the famous Toll House cookies, first introduced to American cooks in 1939 through radio talks on "Famous Foods from Famous Eating Places." In 1939 chocolate bits or chips were not available and every cookie baker patiently chopped even-sized bits of semisweet chocolate bars for the amount required in the recipe. The baking soda can be sifted with the dry ingredients, but in the original recipe the soda was dissolved in warm water. This method of mixing gives the cookie a slightly chewy texture.

1½ cups sifted all-purpose flour
¼ teaspoon salt
½ cup unsalted butter
½ cup granulated sugar
½ cup light brown sugar, firmly packed

1 large egg, well beaten
1 teaspoon vanilla
½ teaspoon baking soda, dissolved in 2 tablespoons warm water
1 cup chocolate chips
½ cup chopped walnuts or pecans

Preheated oven temperature: 375°F.
1. Sift together the flour and salt. Set aside.
2. Cream the butter, granulated sugar and brown sugar in a large bowl until light and fluffy. Add the egg and vanilla and beat well. Add

the flour mixture alternately with baking soda and water mixture, beginning and ending with flour. Stir in chocolate chips and nuts.
3. Drop by teaspoonfuls about 2 inches apart on a lightly oiled baking sheet.
4. Bake in preheated oven about 10 minutes, or until lightly browned. Remove from oven and cool on rack.
Yield: About 36 cookies.

Chocolate Fudge Drop Cookies

These cookies can be served plain or made fancy with a topping of chocolate frosting.

2 cups sifted all-purpose flour (sift before measuring)
2 teaspoons baking powder
¼ teaspoon salt
½ cup unsalted butter or margarine
1¼ cups light brown sugar, firmly packed

1 large egg
½ cup milk, combined with 1 teaspoon vanilla
2½ squares (2½ ounces) unsweetened baking chocolate, melted
1 cup nuts (any kind), chopped (optional)

Preheated oven temperature: 375°F.
1. Sift together the flour, baking powder and salt. Set aside.
2. Cream the butter or margarine and sugar in a large mixing bowl until light and fluffy. Add the egg and beat well. Add the flour mixture alternately with the milk mixture, beginning and ending with dry ingredients. Stir in the chocolate and optional nuts.
3. Drop by teaspoonfuls about 2 inches apart on a lightly oiled baking sheet.
4. Bake in preheated oven about 10 minutes, or until no imprint remains when touched lightly. Remove from oven and cool on rack.
Yield: About 36 cookies.

Whole-Wheat Drop Cookies

These make very good lunch-box cookies.

1 cup sifted whole-wheat flour (sift before measuring)
1 teaspoon baking powder
½ teaspoon salt
¼ cup unsalted butter or margarine

½ cup light brown sugar, firmly packed
½ teaspoon grated lemon rind
1 large egg
3 tablespoons milk
½ cup chopped pecans or walnuts

Preheated oven temperature: 350°F.
1. Sift together the flour, baking powder and salt. Set aside.
2. Cream the butter or margarine, sugar and lemon rind in a large bowl until light and fluffy. Add the egg and beat well. Add the flour mixture alternately with milk, beginning and ending with dry ingredients. Stir in pecans or walnuts.
3. Drop by teaspoonfuls about 2 inches apart on a lightly oiled baking sheet.
4. Bake in preheated oven 20 minutes, or until lightly browned. Remove from oven and cool on rack.

Yield: 36 cookies.

Cornmeal Cookies

This is an East Tennessee recipe that dates back to the Reconstruction in the South, when cooks had to make do with whatever ingredients were at hand. The recipe has withstood the true test of time to become a kitchen favorite.

1½ cups sifted all-purpose flour (sift before measuring)
1 teaspoon baking powder
¼ cup unsalted butter
¼ cup solid white shortening
¾ cup sugar

1 teaspoon lemon juice
½ teaspoon grated lemon rind
1 large egg
½ cup white or yellow cornmeal
½ cup chopped raisins or nuts (optional)

Preheated oven temperature: 350°F.
1. Sift together the flour and baking powder. Set aside.
2. Cream the butter, shortening, sugar, lemon juice and lemon rind in a large bowl until light and fluffy. Add the egg and beat well. Stir in the flour mixture and cornmeal and blend well. Stir in the optional raisins or nuts.
3. Form the dough into a 1½-inch thick roll and chill until firm.
4. Slice the roll into ¼-inch rounds and place on a lightly oiled baking sheet.
5. Bake in preheated oven 12 to 14 minutes, or until lightly browned. Remove from oven and cool on rack.

Yield: 36 cookies.

Refrigerator Cookies
(Basic Recipe)

Before chilled cookie dough was readily available in supermarkets, every cookie baker kept a roll or two of chilled dough in the refrigerator for ready use. This recipe makes a large quantity of dough. For a smaller amount, halve the ingredients.

6 cups sifted all-purpose flour (sift before measuring)
4 teaspoons baking powder
½ teaspoon salt
¾ cup solid white shortening

¾ cup unsalted butter
3 cups light brown sugar, firmly packed
2 teaspoons vanilla
2 large eggs, well beaten

Preheated oven temperature: 375°F.
1. Sift together the flour, baking powder and salt. Set aside.
2. Cream the shortening, butter, brown sugar and vanilla in a large bowl until light and fluffy. Stir in the eggs and mix well. Add flour mixture and blend thoroughly.
3. Divide dough into 6 equal portions. Leave 1 plain and make the variations below with the remaining 5 portions, if you like. Shape each piece into a 1½-inch roll. Chill until firm. Slice off ¼-inch rounds and place about ½ inch apart on a lightly oiled baking sheet.
4. Bake in preheated oven 10 to 12 minutes, or until lightly browned.
Yield: 10 dozen cookies.

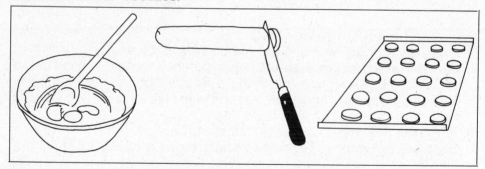

Variations: Chocolate

Add 2 squares (2 ounces) melted unsweetened chocolate to one portion of dough. Knead to blend.

Coconut

Add ½ cup shredded or grated coconut to one portion of dough. Knead to blend.

Dried Fruit

Add ½ cup chopped raisins, dates, figs or apricots to one portion of dough. Knead to blend.

Nut

Add ½ cup finely chopped almonds, pecans, walnuts or chopped peanuts to one portion of dough. Knead to blend.

Spice

Add ½ teaspoon ground cinnamon and ¼ teaspoon ground nutmeg to one portion of dough. Knead to blend.

Old-Fashioned Peanut Butter Cookies

These are a perennial cookie-jar favorite. To make fancy cookies, dribble the tops with melted semisweet chocolate after they have cooled.

1½ cups sifted all-purpose flour (sift before measuring)
1 teaspoon baking soda
½ teaspoon salt
½ cup solid white shortening
½ cup granulated sugar

½ cup light brown sugar, firmly packed
½ teaspoon vanilla
1 large egg, well beaten
½ cup creamy peanut butter

Preheated oven temperature: 375°F.
1. Sift together the flour, baking soda and salt. Set aside.
2. Cream the shortening, granulated sugar, brown sugar and vanilla in a large bowl until light and fluffy. Add egg and mix thoroughly. Stir in peanut butter. Add flour mixture and stir well to blend. Chill mixture in the refrigerator until firm.
3. Form dough into 1-inch balls and place on a baking sheet. Do not oil the baking sheet because there will be enough fat in the dough to keep the cookies from sticking. Press down on each ball of dough with the back of a fork to flatten the cookie to about ¼-inch thickness.
4. Bake in preheated oven 10 minutes, or until lightly browned. Remove from oven and cool on rack.
Yield: 4 dozen cookies.

Toffee Bars
(London Bars)

These cakelike cookies are a holdover from the sumptuous assortment of sweets that graced Victorian tea tables. The layered cookie is perfect to serve as a sweet ending to a dinner party and for gift-giving.

½ cup unsalted butter
½ cup light brown sugar, firmly packed

1 cup sifted all-purpose flour (sift before measuring)

Topping

1 cup light brown sugar, firmly packed
3 tablespoons all-purpose flour, unsifted
½ teaspoon salt

1½ cups grated or shredded coconut
1 cup chopped walnuts or pecans
2 large eggs, lightly beaten
1 teaspoon vanilla

Preheated oven temperature: 375°F.
1. Cream the butter and the ½ cup brown sugar in a medium-sized bowl until light and fluffy; add the 1 cup flour and mix well. Press the mixture evenly on the bottom of an 11-x-7-x-1½-inch baking pan. Bake in preheated oven 10 minutes. Remove and cool while preparing the topping.
2. Mix the 1 cup of brown sugar, the 3 tablespoons flour, the salt, coconut and walnuts or pecans in a medium-sized bowl; add the eggs and vanilla and mix well. Spread the mixture over the cooled layer in the pan. Return to preheated oven and bake an additional 20 minutes or until firm. Remove from oven and cool slightly. Cut into squares or bars while still warm.

Yield: About 24 cookies.

Quick and Easy Chocolate Brownies
(Basic Recipe)

These brownies are delicious served plain in the traditional manner or you can use the chocolate-rich batter as a base for bourbon brownies frosted lightly with a bourbon-flavored glaze. Bourbon-laced brownies are recommended as the perfect sweet to serve with coffee after dinner.

¾ cup sifted all-purpose flour (sift before measuring)
½ teaspoon baking powder
½ teaspoon salt
2 squares (2 ounces) unsweetened baking chocolate

½ cup unsalted butter or margarine
1 cup sugar
2 large eggs
1 teaspoon vanilla
1 cup chopped walnuts or pecans

Preheated oven temperature: 350°F.
1. Sift together the flour, baking powder and salt. Set aside.
2. Melt the chocolate and butter in a heavy, 1½-quart saucepan.
3. Remove from heat and add the sugar, stirring well to blend. Add the eggs one at a time, beating well after each addition. Add the vanilla and chopped walnuts or pecans. Add the flour mixture and stir to mix thoroughly.
4. Pour batter into a well-oiled 11-x-7-x-1½-inch pan and bake in preheated oven 25 minutes, or until the center is almost firm to the touch. Cool in pan and cut into generous 1-inch squares.

Yield: About 24 squares.

Variation: Bourbon Brownies with Bourbon Glaze

In Step 3 after the flour has been incorporated into the mixture, stir in 3 tablespoons bourbon. In Step 4 cool the brownies and spread lightly with Bourbon Glaze (page 391).

Coconut Macaroons

This is an excellent recipe for lovers of coconut. The secret of success is correct oven temperature, to keep the cookies from flattening out and sticking to the baking sheet.

¼ cup sifted all-purpose flour (sift before measuring)

2 cups confectioners' sugar, unsifted

6 cups freshly grated coconut or 1 pound dried coconut

1 teaspoon vanilla or almond extract

Whites of 4 large eggs, unbeaten

Preheated oven temperature: 350°F.
1. Sift together the flour and confectioners' sugar into a large bowl. Add the coconut, vanilla or almond extract and egg whites. Blend until thoroughly mixed.
2. Shape with the fingers into 1½-inch balls and place on a well-oiled baking sheet about 2 inches apart.
3. Bake in preheated oven 15 minutes, or until brown around the edges. Remove from baking sheet at once and cool on rack.

Yield: About 36 cookies.

Pies

America is known as the land of the pie. We have juicy fruit pies that follow the seasons, wonderful Thanksgiving pumpkin pie, pecan, lemon, strawberry, blueberry and all the others.

Sometime after the Revolution, thrifty New England cooks discovered that flat pies need less filling than deep-dish English pies. We make pies with 2 crusts or bake them in fluted shells; we dress them up with latticed tops or fluffy meringue.

Pie Making Basics

The basis for pie is good, flaky pastry. I mix my pastry in the Austrian manner, a method long associated with American farm-style pie making. For the beginner, it is a method easier than the more complicated French *pâté brisée,* made with five parts flour and four parts butter, and the crust is much flakier and more to the American taste.

Overhandling pastry dough during mixing and rolling is the cause of most failures. The warmth of the hands melts the fat and causes the pastry to be tough. I use an electric mixer to blend the shortening into the flour and I also chill the dough before rolling it to the desired size to fit the piepan.

Many professional chefs like to use fresh lard when they bake for themselves. I usually use half solid white shortening and half unsalted butter. For fruit pies I prefer the hearty flavor of a lard crust. Lard, like all pork products, will turn rancid if stored for an extended period. Always buy lard from a market with a high-volume turnover.

ROLLING SURFACE   Pastry can be rolled on any lightly floured surface. A pastry cloth and a pastry sleeve to cover the rolling pin are recommended for the beginner. The heavier the rolling pin, the easier it will be to roll the pastry.

PASTRY WHEEL AND CUTTERS   These are not essential, but the wheel is helpful for cutting dough into strips for lattice-top pies. Small cutters can be used to create fancy shapes for decorating two-crust pies.

PIEPANS   American piepans have sloped sides. Heatproof glass or dull metal pans are recommended; shiny surfaces reflect rather than absorb the heat.

OVEN TEMPERATURE   Proper oven temperature is essential to successful pie baking.

FREEZING PASTRY   There are two methods. The first is to bake several bottom crusts in metal pans and quick-freeze. Then they can be stacked, sealed in airtight plastic bags and returned to the freezer until needed. The second method is to shape the pastry dough into a ball and place it in an airtight plastic bag. Defrost in the bag before using and let return to cool room temperature. Sprinkle lightly with flour before rolling.

FREEZING BAKED, FILLED PIES   Fruit pies stored in air-tight plastic freeze reasonably well but the pastry may become slightly soggy when defrosted. To reheat, unwrap and immediately place in preheated 375°F. oven about 30 minutes, or until hot in the center. Cream and custard pies cannot be frozen successfully in home freezers.

Easy-Method Pie Pastry
(Basic Recipe)

Always remember, pastry making is easy! You too can produce a flaky and delicious crust comparable to that made by the best pastry chefs. I teach the following step-by-step method in my kitchen workshops.

1 large egg
1 teaspoon cider vinegar
5 tablespoons ice water
3 cups unsifted all-purpose flour

1 teaspoon salt
½ cup cold unsalted butter and ½ cup cold solid white shortening; or 1 cup cold lard

1. In a small bowl blend the egg, vinegar and ice water with a wisk or an electric hand mixer on lowest setting. Set aside.
2. Measure 3 level cups unsifted all-purpose flour and salt into a large mixing bowl.

3. Measure cold butter and shortening or lard onto a square of wax paper. Pinch or cut ½-inch pieces. If the fat starts to melt from too much handling, place in refrigerator for a few minutes to become firm.

4. With the mixer on medium setting blend the fat into the flour until the mixture looks like coarse cornmeal.

5. With a fork stir in the egg mixture. Continue stirring until the dough starts to form a ball. Then with the hands gather up and shape the dough into a flat round about 6 inches in diameter.

6. With a knife make a deep cross on top of the ball of dough. Wrap in wax paper and refrigerate at least 30 minutes. (Dough will keep in the refrigerator for 3 to 4 days, or it may be frozen up to 3 months.)

7. Remove the dough from the refrigerator and divide into thirds. Roll out amount needed for recipe and freeze remaining dough for future use.

8. Place one third of the dough on a floured pastry cloth. Set the remaining two thirds aside. With a floured rolling pin press down on the dough to flatten it into a circle about 6 inches in diameter.

9. Start rolling in each direction—always from the center out—to form a circle about 12 inches in diameter. The dough should be ⅛ inch thick. If the dough starts to tear—and this is usually because the kitchen is too warm—return to the refrigerator for 15 minutes.

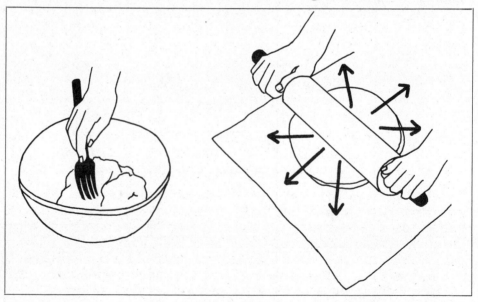

10. Fold the edge of the dough farthest from you over the rolling pin. Roll toward you until the rolling pin is encased in dough. Gently lift up the dough and place it at the edge of the piepan. Unroll the dough until it is centered and neatly covers the pan. Lift up the edges so that the pastry fits neatly inside the pan. Never stretch the pastry. Press the pastry gently against the rim and inside of the pan.

11. Using a knife or kitchen shears, trim the pastry to allow ½ inch of dough to hang over the pan, or if the pie is to have a top crust, trim the dough flush with the rim. Fold the extra dough under the crust to build up the edge. Flute the edge, using the forefinger and thumb to form a ruffled rim, or use the tines of a fork to crimp a design.

12. Place the unbaked shell back in the refrigerator for 30 minutes. This will rest and relax the dough if it has been stretched too much during the handling process, and it also will help prevent shrinkage during the baking. Bake following recipe instructions.

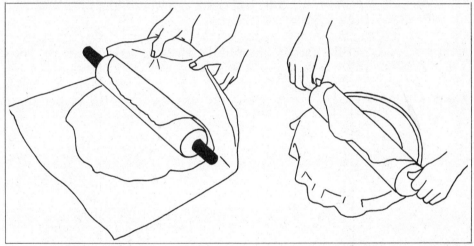

To Prepare Top Crust. Roll out second piece of dough as in Step 9. Cut slits in a decorative design in the middle of the rolled dough. If making several varieties of pies, initials identifying the filling contents are nice. The slits allow steam to escape during baking, and this also helps prevent the bottom crust from becoming soggy. Place the dough over the filled pie shell as in Step 10. Trim the top crust to allow ½ inch of dough to hang over the pan. Fold the extra dough under the edge of the bottom crust to build up the edge. Flute as in Step 11. Bake following recipe instructions.

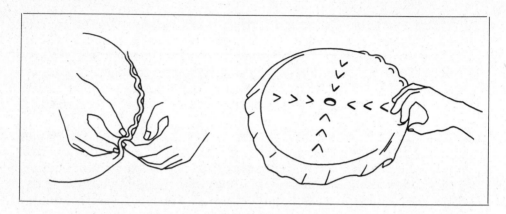

To Prepare Latticed Top Crust. Roll out second piece of dough as in Step 9. With a sharp knife or pastry wheel cut dough into strips ½ to ¾ inch wide. A ruler is helpful in keeping the strips straight and even. Place half the strips on the filled pie 1 inch apart. Do not pull the strips too tight because they will shrink away from the edge of the crust during baking.

To weave in the remaining strips, fold back alternate strips of dough already on the pie to the middle. Place a strip of dough, down the middle of the pie perpendicular to the strips already on the pie. Partially unfold the dough strips and weave in the strip of dough. Continue this process, working at right angles, until the lattice top is

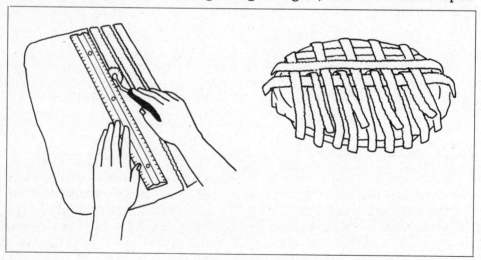

complete. Trim the pastry strips even with the bottom crust. Flute the edge as in Step 11.

To Prepare Prebaked Pie Shells. As a teacher, one of the most frequently asked questions is, "How do I keep my pie shells from shrinking when they are baked with no filling (*à blanc*)?" The following method is almost foolproof, provided that the dough has not been stretched too much during the rolling:

In Step 11 before trimming the dough, dampen the edge of the pan with cold water. Trim the dough and flute the edge. Prick the bottom of the crust in a few places with the tines of a fork. Place the shell in the freezer for at least 30 minutes. Remove from freezer and cut a piece of foil to fit over the crust and press down gently against the inside of the crust. Bake in a preheated 425°F. oven 10 minutes. Carefully remove the foil and bake an additional 12 to 14 minutes, or until the crust is lightly browned. Remove and cool in pan on wire rack. Fill as desired.

NOTE: A metal pan is recommended. If using Pyrex or porcelain, let the crust stand out of the freezer 20 minutes before baking, to prevent the pan from cracking.

Pie crusts made with crushed graham crackers or gingersnaps are basic to American pie-making. They are recommended as shells for chilled fillings if the pie is to be refrigerated more than a few hours.

Graham Cracker Crust

2 cups finely ground graham cracker crumbs

⅓ cup melted unsalted butter or margarine
3 tablespoons superfine sugar

Preheated oven temperature: 400°F.
1. Combine the cracker crumbs, butter or margarine and sugar; mix well to blend. Press mixture firmly on bottom and sides of a 9-inch piepan.
2. Bake in preheated oven 5 minutes; cool. Refrigerate until needed.
Yield: One 9-inch pie shell.

Gingersnap Crust

1½ cups finely ground gingersnap   ¼ cup melted unsalted butter or
   crumbs   margarine

Preheated oven temperature: 375°F.
1. Combine the gingersnap crumbs with the butter or margarine, and
   mix well to blend. Press mixture firmly on bottom and sides of a 9-
   inch piepan.
2. Bake in preheated oven 5 minutes; cool. Refrigerate until needed.
Yield: One 9-inch pie shell.

Meringue Topping
(*Basic Recipe*)

Soft meringue is the topping for many American favorites, especially
the custard-based pies.

Separate the eggs as soon as you take them out of the refrigerator.
It is critical that not even a trace of yolk find its way into the whites.
Eggs that have been refrigerated up to two weeks produce a fluffier
meringue than do those only a few days old. Be certain that the bowl
and beaters are free of fat. Use a stainless steel or copper bowl with a
rounded bottom for beating the egg whites.

The poultry and egg industry recommends spreading the meringue when both the filling and meringue are at room temperature.
Always spread the meringue completely to the edge of the filling.

Whites of 3 large eggs, at room tem-   6 tablespoons superfine sugar (see
   perature   note)
⅛ teaspoon salt   1 teaspoon vanilla
⅛ cream of tartar

1. Beat egg whites in large mixing bowl at low speed until foamy. Add
   salt and cream of tartar. Gradually increase mixer speed to medium-
   high until egg whites form soft, floppy peaks.
2. Beat in sugar 1 tablespoon at a time, beating well after each addition. Beat in vanilla, increase mixer speed to high and beat until
   mixture holds stiff peaks. To test, draw the flat side of a spatula
   through the whites; path of the spatula should remain without sag-
   ging. Spread immediately. Bake following recipe directions.
Yield: Enough meringue for a 9-inch pie.
*NOTE: Make your own superfine sugar by whirling granulated sugar
in a blender or food processor.*

Whipped Cream Topping

When whipped, heavy cream should be light, smooth and double in volume. To whip cream successfully, chill the bowl and beaters as well as the cream. Properly whipped cream will keep 1½ to 2 hours in the refrigerator.

1 cup heavy cream, preferably not ultra-pasteurized
½ teaspoon vanilla

1 to 3 tablespoons sifted confectioners' sugar to taste

1. Whip the cream only until it retains a firm shape but is still glossy. Do not overbeat, or the cream will turn to butter.
2. Stir in the vanilla and fold in the confectioners' sugar. Use according to recipe instructions.

Yield: About 2 cups.

NOTE: Any extra whipped cream may be frozen. Place small dollops, about 1 tablespoon each, on foil. Freeze uncovered. When frozen, wrap and return to freezer.

American Apple Pie
(Basic Recipe)

Served with a scoop of vanilla ice cream or with a wedge of fine Cheddar cheese, apple pie is the quintessential American favorite.

1 recipe Easy-Method Pie Pastry (page 403)
¾ cup sugar
2 tablespoons flour or 1 tablespoon cornstarch
1 teaspoon ground cinnamon
½ teaspoon ground nutmeg (optional)

6 cups peeled and cored tart cooking apples, sliced lengthwise into ½-inch wedges
1 tablespoon lemon juice
1 tablespoon unsalted butter or margarine

Preheated oven temperature 425°F.
1. Prepare and roll out the pastry as directed in the recipe; place in pan. Refrigerate the bottom crust and the unrolled top crust while preparing the filling.
2. In a large bowl combine the sugar, flour or cornstarch, cinnamon and optional nutmeg. Add the apple slices and lemon juice; toss to coat well.
3. Spoon the coated apples into the bottom crust, mounding them in the center. Dot the top of the apples with the butter or margarine.

4. Roll out the top crust according to Step 12 in basic instructions. Moisten the edge of the bottom crust slightly with cold water and place the top crust over the apples. Trim the overhang and flute according to Step 12 in basic instructions.
5. Bake in preheated oven 50 minutes, or until crust is brown and apples are tender when pierced with a knife through a slit in the crust. Remove from oven and cool on wire rack.

Yield: One 9-inch pie. Serves 6.

Variation: Frosted Apple Pie

Beat 1 tablespoon of egg white with a fork. Gradually beat in enough sifted confectioners' sugar (about ¾ cup) to make a medium-thick frosting. Add ½ teaspoon vanilla and stir well to blend. As soon as the pie is removed from the oven, brush the frosting over the top crust. Cool before serving.

Red Cherry Pie

The traditional cherry pie is made with sour red cherries and a latticed top. Because the fresh fruit has such a short season, the pie often is made with canned or frozen cherries.

1 recipe Easy-Method Pie Pastry (page 403)

Fresh or Frozen Cherry Pie Filling

1⅓ cups sugar
5 tablespoons flour or 2½ tablespoons cornstarch
½ teaspoon ground cinnamon
¼ teaspoon almond extract

4 cups fresh or frozen sour red cherries
A few drops red food coloring (optional)
4 teaspoons unsalted butter or margarine

Canned Cherry Pie Filling

1 cup sugar, or more to taste
¼ cup flour or 2 tablespoons cornstarch
¼ teaspoon almond extract
2 16-ounce cans pitted tart red cherries with juice

A few drops red food coloring (optional)
4 teaspoons unsalted butter or margarine

Preheated oven temperature: 425°F.
1. Prepare and roll out the pastry as directed in the recipe; place in pan. Refrigerate the bottom crust and the unrolled top crust while preparing the filling.

2. *To prepare the fresh or frozen cherry filling,* combine the sugar, flour or cornstarch, cinnamon, almond extract, cherries and optional food coloring in a large bowl; toss well to coat.

    To prepare the canned cherry filling, combine the sugar, flour or cornstarch, almond extract, cherries and juice and optional food coloring in a heavy, 2-quart saucepan. Cook over low heat , stirring constantly, until mixture thickens and boils.

3. Spoon the cherries into the bottom crust, mounding them in the center. Dot the top of the cherries with the butter or margarine.

4. Prepare the latticed crust according to Step 12 in basic instructions. Moisten the edge of the bottom crust slightly with cold water and complete the lattice. Trim the overhang and flute according to Step 12 in basic instructions.

5. Bake in preheated oven about 40 minutes, or until the crust is nicely browned and the juice begins to bubble through the latticed top. Remove from oven and cool on wire rack.

Yield: One 9-inch pie. Serves 6.

Wild Blackberry Pie

Blackberries have long been popular in rural cooking for making jellies and jams and for baking cakes, pies and cobblers. I remember when every farm family went berry picking in July, equipped with tin pails, large straw hats to ward off the brutal sun and kerosene-soaked kitchen string tied around the wrists and ankles to ward off the even more brutal chiggers that seemed to lurk in the choicest berry patches. A fresh blackberry pie was the reward.

    Blackberries and raspberries both are fruits of the *Rubus* genus and can be used interchangeably in most recipes. Cultivated blackberries are not recommended for pie-making because their seeds are so much larger than those of the wild variety.

    This pie is made with a latticed top to show off the luscious purple berries. The amount of sugar needed will depend on the sweetness of the fruit.

1 recipe Easy-Method Pie Pastry (page 403)	5 tablespoons flour or 2½ tablespoons cornstarch
5 cups blackberries or raspberries	⅛ teaspoon salt
¾ to 1 cup superfine sugar	2 tablespoons unsalted butter or margarine

Preheated oven temperature: 450°F.

1. Prepare and roll out the pastry as directed in the recipe and place in pan. Refrigerate the bottom crust and the unrolled top crust while preparing the filling.

2. Wash and drain the blackberries or raspberries.
3. Blend the sugar, flour or cornstarch and salt. Sprinkle 3 tablespoons of the mixture over the bottom of pastry crust. Spread the berries over the sugar mixture, mounding them in the center. Sprinkle with the remaining sugar mixture. Dot the top of the berries with the butter or margarine.
4. Prepare the latticed crust according to Step 12 in basic instructions. Moisten the edge of the bottom crust slightly with cold water and complete the lattice. Trim the overhang and flute according to Step 12 in basic instructions.
5. Bake in preheated oven 15 minutes. Reduce heat to 350°F. and bake 25 to 30 minutes longer, or until crust is nicely browned. Remove from oven and cool on wire rack.

Yield: One 9-inch pie. Serves 6.

Strawberry Pie

Both strawberries and blueberries are very delicate fruits. If they are baked in the shell, they will become the consistency of jam. Home cooks prebake the shell and then cook only a portion of the berries. This gives the pie a fresher flavor and a more attractive appearance. Serve cold, topped with whipped cream.

1 prebaked 9-inch pie shell
4 cups hulled fresh strawberries
¾ cup water
3 tablespoons cornstarch
About ¾ cup sugar, depending on the sweetness of the berries

1 teaspoon lemon juice
A few drops red food coloring (optional)
1 cup heavy cream, whipped and lightly sweetened with 1 tablespoon sifted confectioners' sugar

1. Prebake the crust as in Step 12 for Easy-Method Pie Pastry. Cool.
2. Line the pastry shell with 3 cups strawberries, reserving the remaining 1 cup.
3. Combine the water, cornstarch, sugar and lemon juice in a heavy, 1-quart saucepan. Stir to blend. Add reserved berries. Cook over medium heat until thick and clear. Add optional food coloring. Cool the mixture slightly and pour over the berries in the shell. Chill thoroughly. Top with whipped cream before serving.

Yield: One 9-inch pie. Serves 6.

Blueberry Pie

1 prebaked 9-inch pie shell
4 cups fresh blueberries
½ cup granulated sugar
½ cup light brown sugar, firmly
  packed
2½ tablespoons flour
½ teaspoon ground nutmeg

¼ teaspoon ground cinnamon
¼ teaspoon salt
1 teaspoon lemon juice
1 cup heavy cream, whipped and
  lightly sweetened with 1 tablespoon sifted confectioners' sugar

1. Prebake the crust as in Step 12 for Easy-Method Pie Pastry. Cool.
2. Line the pastry shell with 2 cups blueberries, reserving the remaining 2 cups.
3. Combine the granulated sugar, brown sugar, flour, nutmeg, cinnamon and salt in a heavy, 1½-quart saucepan. Mix well and then add the reserved berries, turning to coat. Simmer 5 minutes, stirring constantly, until the mixture thickens. Cool slightly and pour over the berries in the shell. Chill thoroughly. Top with whipped cream before serving.

Yield: One 9-inch pie. Serves 6.

Fresh Peach Pie

This is a beautiful open-face party pie—guests will be sure to ask for seconds. The recipe is particularly popular with cooks in western Pennsylvania, Ohio and Indiana when peaches are at their peak of flavor.

1 unbaked 9-inch pastry shell
4 to 6 firm ripe peaches, depending
  on size (about 1½ pounds)
¼ cup flour or 2 tablespoons cornstarch

½ to ¾ cup superfine sugar, depending on the sweetness of
  peaches
1 teaspoon ground cinnamon
1 cup heavy cream
Red food coloring (optional)

Preheated oven temperature: 425°F.
1. Prepare and roll out pastry shell, using Easy-Method Pie Pastry recipe (page 403). Place in the pan, trim the overhang and flute according to directions in Step 11. Refrigerate 30 minutes.
2. Bake the chilled crust in preheated oven 5 minutes. Set aside to cool while preparing the filling.
3. Peel peaches, cut in half and remove pits. Place the peaches on piecrust, cut side down.

4. Immediately combine the flour or cornstarch, sugar and cinnamon. Stir in the heavy cream to make a smooth mixture. Pour over the peaches.
5. Bake in preheated oven 40 to 45 minutes, or until custard is set and the crust lightly browned. Remove from oven and cool on wire rack. With the fingertip, lightly "blush" the rounded top of the peach halves with optional red food coloring.

Yield: One 9-inch pie. Serves 6.

Sour Cream Raisin Pie

With a hint of the flavor of mincemeat, this is the best-ever raisin pie. Serve plain or with a thin topping of sour cream.

1 unbaked 9-inch pastry shell
2 large eggs, lightly beaten
1 cup superfine sugar
1 cup sour cream
1 tablespoon flour
⅛ teaspoon salt

½ teaspoon ground cinnamon
½ teaspoon ground nutmeg
1 cup chopped raisins
½ cup chopped walnuts
Sour cream for topping (optional)

Preheated oven temperature: 425°F.
1. Prepare and roll out pastry shell, using Easy-Method Pie Pastry recipe (page 403). Place in the pan, trim the overhang and flute according to directions in Step 11. Refrigerate 30 minutes.
2. Bake the chilled crust in preheated oven 5 minutes. Set aside to cool while preparing the filling.
3. Beat the eggs and sugar in a large bowl; gradually stir in the 1 cup sour cream.
4. Mix the flour, salt, cinnamon and nutmeg; add the raisins and nuts and turn to coat well.
5. Gently stir the raisin mixture into the egg mixture and pour into the cooled crust.
6. Bake in preheated oven 10 minutes; then lower the heat to 350°F. and bake 25 to 30 minutes longer, or until the tip of a knife comes out clean when inserted into the center of the filling. Remove from oven and cool on wire rack. When cool, spread with a thin layer of optional sour cream.

Yield: One 9-inch pie. Serves 6.

Variation: Sour Cream Apricot Pie

In Step 4 substitute 1 cup chopped dried apricots for the raisins. Add ½ cup grated or shredded coconut.

Caramel Pecan Pie

There are many versions of pecan pie. This one is favored by those who prefer the flavor of brown sugar to that of dark corn syrup.

1 unbaked 10-inch pastry shell
1 pound light brown sugar, or 2¼ cups, firmly packed
¼ cup unsalted butter or margarine
¼ teaspoon salt

2 tablespoons flour
½ cup milk
3 large eggs, lightly beaten
1 teaspoon vanilla
1 cup pecan halves

Preheated oven temperature: 425°F.
1. Prepare and roll out pastry shell, using Easy-Method Pie Pastry recipe (page 403). Place in the pan, trim the overhang and flute according to directions in Step 11. Refrigerate 30 minutes.
2. Bake the chilled crust in preheated oven 5 minutes. Set aside to cool while preparing the filling.
3. Heat the brown sugar and butter or margarine in a heavy, 1½-quart saucepan over low heat. Stir until sugar is dissolved. Add salt, flour and milk, beating well to blend. Stir in the eggs, vanilla and pecan halves.
4. Pour mixture into crust. Bake in preheated oven 10 minutes; then lower heat to 350°F. and bake 30 minutes longer, or until the tip of a knife comes out clean when inserted into the center of the filling. Remove from oven and cool on wire rack.

Yield: One 10-inch pie. Serves 12 to 14.

Variation: Black Walnut Pie

In Step 3 substitute chopped black walnuts for the pecan halves.

Pumpkin Pie
(Basic Recipe)

Along with turkey and all the trimmings at Thanksgiving dinner, pumpkin pie is the traditional dessert. New Englanders sometimes make the pie with winter squash and Southerners are famous for their sweet potato pie. This basic recipe is used to make all three. Decorate the top with swirls of whipped cream if you want a festive-looking pie.

1 unbaked 9-inch pastry shell
2 cups cooked fresh, frozen or canned puree of pumpkin or squash
¾ cup light brown sugar, firmly packed
1 teaspoon ground cinnamon
¾ teaspoon ground ginger
½ teaspoon ground nutmeg
½ teaspoon salt
2 large eggs, lightly beaten
1½ cups half-and-half

Preheated oven temperature: 425°F.
1. Prepare and roll out pastry shell, using Easy-Method Pie Pastry recipe (page 403). Place in the pan, trim the overhang and flute according to directions in Step 11. Refrigerate 30 minutes.
2. Bake the chilled crust in preheated oven 5 minutes. Set aside to cool while preparing the filling.
3. Combine the remaining ingredients in a large mixing bowl and beat until smooth. (This can be done in the blender or food processor.) Pour mixture into the crust.
4. Bake in preheated oven 1 hour, or until the filling is completely puffed across the top and the crust is nicely browned. Serve warm or cold.

Yield: One 9-inch pie. Serves 6 to 8.

Variation: Sweet Potato Pie

In Step 3, substitute 1½ cups cooked puree of sweet potato for the pumpkin or squash. Add an additional ½ cup half-and-half, 3 tablespoons melted unsalted butter and 1 tablespoon dark molasses.

Caramel Custard Pie

Custard pie is a New England tradition. To please the palate, follow a highly seasoned main course with this caramelized-sugar version of an old favorite.

1 unbaked 9-inch pastry shell
3 cups half-and-half
½ cup plus 6 tablespoons sugar
3 large eggs, lightly beaten
¼ teaspoon salt
1 teaspoon vanilla

Preheated oven temperature: 425°F.
1. Prepare and roll out pastry shell, using Easy-Method Pie Pastry recipe (page 403). Place in the pan, trim the overhang and flute according to directions in Step 11. Refrigerate 30 minutes.
2. Bake the chilled crust in preheated oven 5 minutes. Set aside to cool while preparing the filling.

3. Heat the half-and-half to the boiling point and set aside. Heat the ½ cup sugar in a heavy skillet over very low heat, stirring constantly, until melted and light golden brown; this will take about 5 minutes. Remove from heat and immediately add to hot half-and-half, stirring constantly.
4. Combine the eggs, salt and 6 tablespoons sugar in a blender or food processor and process until well blended. Slowly add the half-and-half mixture. Process until smooth. Add the vanilla and blend well. Pour mixture into crust.
5. Bake in preheated oven 25 to 30 minutes, or until the tip of a knife comes out clean when inserted into the center of the filling. Remove from oven and cool on wire rack.

Yield: One 9-inch pie. Serves 6.

Shoofly Pie

The meaning of the name of this Pennsylvania Dutch pie is perfectly clear. In the days before screens were invented, it was a major task to keep the flies from swarming around the rich molasses pie.

There are two methods of mixing the pie filling. One is to layer the molasses and crumb mixture, beginning and ending with crumbs. The other is to pour the molasses mixture into the crust and use the crumbs as a topping, as in this recipe. This is called a "wet-bottom pie."

1 unbaked 9-inch pastry shell	⅛ teaspoon salt
1½ cups sifted all-purpose flour (sift before measuring)	½ cup unsalted butter or margarine
	¾ cup dark molasses
½ cup sugar	¾ cup cold water
1 teaspoon ground cinnamon	½ teaspoon baking soda
½ teaspoon ground nutmeg	

Preheated oven temperature: 450°F.
1. Prepare and roll out pastry shell, using Easy-Method Pie Pastry recipe (page 403). Place in pan, trim the overhang and flute according to directions in Step 11. Refrigerate 30 minutes.
2. Bake the chilled crust in preheated oven 5 minutes. Set aside to cool while preparing the filling.
3. Sift the flour, sugar, cinnamon, nutmeg and salt together into a medium-sized bowl. Add the butter or margarine and blend with an electric beater until the mixture resembles coarsely ground cornmeal. Set aside.
4. Combine the molasses and cold water in a small bowl; pour into the pastry shell. Spoon reserved crumb mixture on top.
5. Bake in preheated oven 15 minutes; lower heat to 350°F. and bake 35 minutes, until the filling is set. Serve warm or cold.

Yield: One 9-inch pie. Serves 6 to 8.

Lemon Meringue Pie

There are many types of lemon pie fillings in American cookery. But when we speak of the one made by our mothers and grandmothers, we usually mean a pie with a clear, tart filling, topped with mountains of delicately browned, fluffy meringue. This is an Indiana recipe that has been awarded many county fair blue ribbons for best of its class.

1 prebaked 9-inch pie shell, or 1 prebaked 9-inch graham cracker crust
1⅓ cups cold water
¾ cup sugar
5 tablespoons cornstarch
¼ teaspoon salt

1 teaspoon grated lemon rind
Yolks of 2 large eggs, well beaten
1 tablespoon unsalted butter or margarine
6 tablespoons fresh lemon juice
1 recipe Soft Meringue (page 408)

Preheated oven temperature: 325°F.
1. Prebake the pie shell as in Step 12 for Easy-Method Pie Pastry (page 403) or use basic recipe for preparing graham cracker crust (page 407).
2. Combine water, sugar, cornstarch, salt and lemon rind in a heavy, 1½-quart saucepan. Stir until cornstarch is dissolved. Cook over low heat, stirring constantly, until mixture thickens and turns clear. Boil 1 minute. Remove from heat and cool slightly.
3. Quickly whisk the egg yolks into the mixture. Stir in the butter or margarine and lemon juice. Pour mixture into prepared crust. Cool to room temperature.
4. Prepare the meringue and immediately spread over the pie, making certain that it touches the crust all around. Bake in preheated oven 15 minutes, or until lightly browned. Cool and serve.

Yield: One 9-inch pie. Serves 6.

Key Lime Pie

Necessity provided the inspiration for this famous pie. A Key Lime Pie is not authentic unless it is made with native limes from the Florida Keys and sweetened condensed milk. During the Reconstruction period after the Civil War, condensed milk was imported into the area in large quantities. The pie was originally made with a pastry crust. However, since the high humidity of the Keys causes this type of crust to lose its flakiness, local cooks have substituted a graham cracker crust, which keeps better.

1 prebaked 9-inch graham cracker crust
½ cup fresh lime juice
1 teaspoon grated lime rind
1 14-ounce can sweetened condensed milk

Yolks of 2 large eggs
1 recipe Soft Meringue; or 1 cup heavy cream, whipped and lightly sweetened with 1 tablespoon sifted confectioners' sugar

1. Prepare graham cracker crust using basic recipe (page 407). Refrigerate until cold.
2. Combine the lime juice and lime rind in a medium-sized bowl. Gradually stir in the condensed milk. Add egg yolks and beat until well blended. Pour into chilled crust and cool to room temperature.
3. If desired, spread meringue and bake according to directions in Step 4 for Lemon Meringue Pie. If whipped cream is desired, refrigerate pie until serving time and then spread with topping.

Yield: One 9-inch pie. Serves 6 to 8.

Variation: Lemon Pie

In Step 2 substitute lemon juice and lemon rind for lime juice and lime rind.

Chiffon Pie
(Basic Recipe)

Chiffon pie is a light and airy version of an old-fashioned custard pie. This is a perfect party pie because it can be flavored as desired and refrigerated, allowing the cook the freedom to concentrate on other last-minute details in the kitchen.

Chiffon pie has a silky, smooth, gelatin-based texture. For best results, avoid the quick method of dissolving gelatin, that is, dissolving the gelatin in hot liquid. For some reason when the filling is chilled, small bits of gelatin tend to reappear.

1 prebaked 9-inch graham cracker crust
2 cups milk
1½ tablespoons cornstarch
¼ teaspoon salt
½ cup sugar
3 large egg yolks, well beaten

1 tablespoon (1 envelope) unflavored gelatin, softened in 1 cup cold water
1½ teaspoons vanilla
3 large egg whites
½ teaspoon cream of tartar
6 tablespoons sifted sugar
Whipped Cream Topping

1. Prepare the graham cracker crust, using basic recipe (page 407). Cool.
2. Heat the milk in a heavy, 1½-quart saucepan to just below the boiling point.
3. Mix the cornstarch, salt, ½ cup sugar and the egg yolks in a medium-sized bowl, beating well to blend. Slowly add the hot milk, stirring constantly, until mixture is smooth.
4. Return mixture to saucepan and cook over low heat about 15 minutes, stirring constantly, until thick. Stir in the softened gelatin.
5. Remove from heat; stir in the vanilla and cool until mixture is almost set.
6. Beat egg whites until foamy; add cream of tartar. Continue beating and add the sifted sugar 1 tablespoon at a time, until stiff peaks form.
7. Stir one fourth of the egg whites into the chilled mixture. With a rubber spatula gently fold in the remaining egg whites. Spoon the mixture into prepared crust. Spread with Whipped Cream Topping (page 409). Chill several hours.
Yield: One 9-inch pie. Serves 6.

Variations: Orange Chiffon Pie

In Step 2 substitute orange juice, 1 teaspoon grated orange rind and 2 tablespoons unsalted butter or margarine for the milk. In Step 3 omit ½ cup sugar; in Step 5 omit vanilla. In Step 7 garnish the topping with fresh orange slices.

Chocolate Chiffon Pie

In Step 2 add 6 to 9 tablespoons cocoa, depending on taste.

Coconut Chiffon Pie

In Step 2 add ¾ cup grated or shredded coconut. In Step 3 decrease the ½ cup sugar to ⅓ cup. In Step 5 decrease the vanilla to 1 teaspoon. In Step 7 sprinkle topping with toasted coconut.

Pumpkin Chiffon Pie

In Step 2 decrease milk to ½ cup. In Step 3 add 1¼ cups cooked puree of pumpkin, ½ teaspoon ground ginger, ½ teaspoon ground cinnamon and ½ teaspoon ground nutmeg. In Step 7 garnish topping with pecan halves.

Black-Bottom Pie

Use gingersnap crust instead of graham cracker crust. In Step 4, after the mixture has thickened and before adding the gelatin, remove 1 cup to a small bowl. Stir in 1½ squares (1½ ounces) melted unsweetened baking chocolate and ½ teaspoon vanilla; spread this mixture on the bottom of the chilled crust and refrigerate. Add the gelatin to the remaining cooked mixture and proceed with recipe. In Step 7 garnish the topping with shaved unsweetened baking chocolate.

DESSERTS

Desserts in American cooking run the gamut from homelike simplicity to high sophistication. Choosing the right dessert is an art. Cooked correctly and served attractively, even a plain dessert can be enticing.

Always choose a dessert that complements the rest of the menu. If the entrée has been light, choose a rich dessert. On the other hand, choose a light dessert when serving a rich main course.

Desserts can be used to great advantage in rounding out the need for essential nutrients. Rice pudding and custards are good examples.

Rice Pudding

This is an old New England recipe. Serve plain with hot maple syrup or dress it up a bit with whipped cream and a topping of crushed fresh fruit.

½ cup long-grain white rice	½ cup seedless raisins
2 cups cold water	Yolks of 3 large eggs
¼ teaspoon salt	2 cups half-and-half
4 cups milk	2 teaspoons vanilla
½ cup sugar	1½ cups heavy cream (optional)

1. Combine the rice, cold water and salt in a heavy, 2½-quart saucepan. Bring to a boil and cook 5 minutes. Pour into a colander and rinse under cold running water. Drain well and return to saucepan. Add the milk and ½ cup sugar; bring to a boil. Lower heat and simmer uncovered about 45 minutes, or until almost all the milk is absorbed. Stir in the raisins during the last 5 minutes. Stir occasionally to keep mixture from sticking to bottom of pan.
2. Beat the egg yolks lightly and blend in the half-and-half and vanilla. Stir in a few tablespoons of the cooked rice; then slowly incorporate mixture into rice, stirring until well mixed.

3. Cook gently about 3 minutes just under the boiling point, stirring constantly, until the mixture has thickened. Cool to room temperature and then refrigerate. Serve cold with hot maple syrup.
4. To serve with whipped cream, whip the cream until soft peaks form; fold in the confectioners' sugar. Fold this mixture into the chilled pudding. Serve with desired topping.

Serves 8.

Bread Pudding

Bread pudding figures prominently in American desserts because in the days of home baking the stale bread was used. Grandmother would not recognize this recipe however, a dessert she never would have thought to serve company. This version has lovely layered texture. First one encounters a bottom of soft creamy custard and then a layer of bread cubes elegantly glazed with carmelized sugar. The pudding can be baked in a shallow casserole or in 1-cup portions.

2 cups milk
¼ cup unsalted butter or margarine
3 cups soft ½-inch bread cubes
½ cup sugar
2 large eggs, lightly beaten

¼ teaspoon salt
1 teaspoon ground nutmeg
½ cup seedless raisins
About ¾ cup sifted confectioners' sugar

Preheated oven temperature: 350°F.
1. Heat the milk and butter or margarine to the boiling point. Remove from heat and set aside.
2. Spread the bread cubes evenly on the bottom of a well-oiled, shallow, 1½-quart baking pan or use 6 individual baking cups.
3. Combine the sugar, eggs, salt, nutmeg and raisins with the milk mixture. Pour over the bread cubes and stir well to mix.
4. Place the pan in a larger pan and pour boiling water into larger pan to measure halfway up the side of the pudding pan. Bake in preheated oven 40 to 45 minutes, or until a knife inserted in the center comes out clean. Halfway through the baking stir the mixture thoroughly to moisten the bread cubes. Bake 1-cup portions 30 to 35 minutes.
5. Remove from water and sprinkle top generously with confectioners' sugar. Glaze under the broiler until lightly browned. Serve warm or chilled.

NOTE: The pudding can be served with a fresh fruit topping.
Serves 6.

Woodford Pudding

This is an old Virginia recipe, which traveled to Kentucky and is served with bourbon-flavored hard sauce. It is an interesting dessert to serve with Thanksgiving or Christmas dinner.

½ cup unsalted butter or margarine
1 cup sugar
3 large eggs
1 cup seedless blackberry jam
½ cup sifted flour (sift before measuring)

1 teaspoon baking soda, dissolved in 1 tablespoon buttermilk
½ teaspoon ground cinnamon
¼ teaspoon ground nutmeg
Bourbon Hard Sauce (page 247)

Preheated oven temperature: 350°F.
1. Cream the butter or margarine and the sugar in a large bowl until light and fluffy. Beat in the eggs one at a time, beating well after each addition. Stir in the blackberry jam and then the flour. Mix well. Add the buttermilk mixture, cinnamon and nutmeg; blend thoroughly.
2. Pour into a well-oiled 1-quart baking dish. Bake in preheated oven 40 to 45 minutes, or until firm in the center. Serve warm with Bourbon Hard Sauce (page 247).
Serves 6.

Hoosier Persimmon Pudding

The early Jamestown colonists were introduced to the wild persimmon by the Indians. In his first letters back to England, John Rolfe made note of this small, pulpy fruit which is unbelievably astringent when green.

Wild persimmons are not edible until after the first frost. My mother's family made much of this seasonal event. White sheets were spread under the laden trees to receive the frostbitten persimmons, which turned overnight into deliciously sweet fruit. As soon as possible, the persimmons were gathered in buckets and taken to the kitchen. The soft fruit was worked through a large colander to produce enough pulp to make the traditional Thanksgiving pudding. This is a cakelike pudding and should be served with a Southern Lemon Sauce. In the opinion of the purists, sweetened whipped cream topping is much too sweet and heavy for a pudding of this consistency. The following is my Grandmother's recipe. Cultivated persimmons can be substituted; however, they should be almost excessively ripe for full flavor. This is a large family recipe. It may be halved.

2 cups sugar
2 cups persimmon pulp
2 large.eggs, well beaten
1 teaspoon baking soda, combined
with 6 cups buttermilk
2 cups sifted all-purpose flour (sift
before measuring)

⅛ teaspoon salt
1 teaspoon ground cinnamon
1 teaspoon ground ginger
½ cup melted unsalted butter or
margarine

Preheated oven temperature: 325°F.
1. In a large mixing bowl add the sugar to the persimmon pulp. Stir
   in the eggs, mixing well. Add the soda and buttermilk mixture; stir
   thoroughly to blend.
2. Sift together flour, salt, cinnamon and ginger. Add to the persimmon
   mixture and beat well. Blend in the butter or margarine.
3. Pour into a well-oiled 13-x-9-x-2-inch baking pan. Bake in preheated
   oven 1 hour. The pudding should be soft to the touch but not runny.
   Remove from oven and cool in pan on wire rack. Cut into squares
   and serve.
Serves 12.

Baked Indian Pudding

Several modern quick-method recipes were tested for this book by a
New England cook well acquainted with making Indian pudding. In
the final kitchen results we all agreed that there is no comparison
between the short and longer cooking times. The longer produces a
creamy, full-flavored pudding not to be equaled. As in Colonial times,
to save energy we suggest baking the pudding alongside New England
baked beans.

4 cups milk
½ cup dark molasses
2 tablespoons sugar
2 tablespoons melted unsalted
butter
¼ teaspoon salt
⅛ teaspoon baking powder

½ teaspoon ground cinnamon
¼ teaspoon ground nutmeg
⅛ teaspoon ground ginger
1 large egg, well beaten
½ cup yellow cornmeal, preferably
stone-ground

Preheated oven temperature: 450°F.
1. Mix 1½ cups of milk with all the rest of the ingredients. Beat vigorously with a whisk and pour into a well-oiled, deep, heavy, 3-quart
   casserole, preferably of stoneware. Bake in preheated oven until
   mixture boils, stirring often with a whisk to keep mixture from
   lumping.

2. Turn oven temperature down to 225°F. and bake 7 hours. Halfway through the baking time, whisk in another 1½ cups milk. Toward the end of baking time, whisk in the remaining 1 cup milk. For proper consistency, the pudding should be stirred several times during baking. Near the end of baking time the pudding should form a nice crust on top. Serve warm with sweetened whipped cream or vanilla ice cream.
Serves 6.

Grossmutter's Plum Pudding

This Christmas plum pudding recipe has been in the Wille family of southern New Jersey for four generations. Unlike the traditional plum pudding of English origin, this recipe requires no special steaming utensil. The pudding is baked like a cake and has a lighter texture than when made with beef suet. This pudding should be sliced and served with a light covering of warm brandy. It is an old custom in the Wille family to pass a pitcher of warm sweetened milk to pour over the brandy-coated pudding. Or this pudding can be flamed with warm brandy and sliced for serving. It is delicious either way.

The recipe is large and it will make four generous puddings. It may be halved or the extra puddings may be used for gift-giving.

2 1-pound loaves stale home-style white bread	1½ teaspoons baking powder
3 cups milk	9 large eggs, well beaten
1 cup unsalted butter or margarine	Juice and rind of 3 lemons
3 cups sugar	4 pounds raisins
1½ teaspoons ground cinnamon	1¼ cups chopped blanched almonds

Preheated oven temperature: 300°F.
1. Crumble or cube the bread and cover with the milk. Set aside.
2. Cream the butter or margarine and sugar in a large mixing bowl until light and fluffy. Blend in the cinnamon and baking powder. Add the eggs and beat until well mixed. Stir in the lemon juice and all the rind (no white pith), the raisins, almonds and bread mixture. Stir until thoroughly blended.
3. Spoon mixture into 4 well-oiled 8-x-8-x-4-inch loaf pans. Bake in preheated oven 1 hour, or until a cake tester comes out clean. Remove from oven and cool in pans on wire racks. Remove from pans and wrap in foil. Store in a dark, cool place until needed.
Yield: 4 loaves.

Egg Custard

This is an easy method for preparing egg custard, which has a tendency to separate and become watery if not cooked properly. Too much sugar also will make custard watery. Unmold, if desired, and serve with a topping of lemon, fruit or bourbon sauce.

Yolks of 3 large eggs
3 tablespoons sugar
3 cups light cream or half-and-half

1 teaspoon vanilla
½ teaspoon ground cinnamon
¼ teaspoon ground nutmeg

Preheated oven temperature: 250°F.
1. Combine all ingredients and beat with a whisk or wooden spoon until well blended. Do not use the electric mixer, blender or food processor because this will alter the desired texture.
2. Pour mixture into 6 lightly oiled 1-cup custard cups. Place cups in a 13-x-9-x-2-inch baking pan. Fill pan with warm water to measure halfway up the cups. Bake in preheated oven 1 hour, or until a knife inserted in the center comes out clean. Remove from water and cool to room temperature. Refrigerate until serving time.

Serves 6.

Peach Crisp

A crisp is a pie without a bottom crust. This recipe has a delicious flavor because it is spiced with many of the good things used by fine New England and Southern cooks.

5 cups peeled fresh ripe peach slices

2 tablespoons lemon juice

Crumb Mixture

½ cup granulated sugar
½ cup light brown sugar, firmly packed
½ cups cold unsalted butter or margarine, slivered
¾ cup sifted flour (sift before measuring)

¾ teaspoon ground cinnamon
½ teaspoon ground cloves
½ teaspoon ground nutmeg
2 tablespoons brandy or bourbon (optional)
⅔ cup slivered almonds

Topping

1 cup heavy cream
1 teaspoon grated lemon rind

1 tablespoon sifted confectioners' sugar

Preheated oven temperature: 300°F.
1. Place peaches in a well-buttered 13-x-9-x-2-inch baking pan. Sprinkle with lemon juice and turn to coat well.

2. Combine the granulated sugar, brown sugar, butter or margarine and flour. Crumble with the fingertips until mixture barely clings together in lumps. Spread the mixture evenly over the peaches. Over this sprinkle the cinnamon, then the cloves and last the nutmeg. Pour the optional brandy or bourbon evenly over the top. Cover with the almonds.
3. Bake in preheated oven 1 hour, or until lightly browned on top. Remove from the oven and serve warm with whipped cream topping.
4. *Whipped Cream Topping.* Whip the cream until soft peaks form. Fold in the lemon rind and confectioners' sugar. Serve immediately.
Serves 10 to 12.

Variation: Apple Crisp

In Step 1 substitute peeled and sliced tart cooking apples for the peaches.

Peach Cobbler

A cobbler is a deep-dish fruit pie with a thick biscuit crust and a long history. It undoubtedly originated with the Scotch-Irish who brought the idea from Scotland in the early 1700s. A cobbler can be made with any fresh fruit in season, such as cherries, blackberries, raspberries, plums and even apples. However, peach is probably the best-known of all the fruit cobblers. Serve warm with Southern Lemon Sauce (page 245).

1 cup sugar
4 teaspoons flour
4 cups peeled fresh ripe peach slices
½ teaspoon almond extract
¾ teaspoon ground cinnamon

½ teaspoon ground nutmeg
2 tablespoons unsalted butter or margarine
1 recipe Southern Baking Powder Biscuits (page 358)

Preheated oven temperature: 425°F.
1. Combine the sugar and flour in a heavy, 2-quart saucepan. Add the peach slices and cook over low heat 5 minutes or until fruit is tender, stirring occasionally. Remove from heat and add almond extract, cinnamon and nutmeg. Spoon mixture into a well-buttered 9-inch-square baking pan. Dot with butter or margarine.
2. Prepare biscuit dough and roll out to a thickness of ½ inch. Place on top of the peaches, make slits for steam to escape and bake 25 to 30 minutes, or until nicely browned.
Serves 6 to 8.

Frozen Rum Pudding

This recipe was given to me by friends from New Orleans. It is a most unusual dessert.

2 cups milk
2 large eggs
½ cup sugar
¼ teaspoon salt
2 cups finely chopped dates

¼ cup dark rum
2 cups heavy cream
2⅓ cups almonds, lightly toasted and chopped
2 cups chopped pecans
Dark rum for topping

1. In a heavy, 2-quart saucepan heat the milk to the boiling point. Set aside.
2. Beat the eggs lightly in a large bowl; add the sugar and salt. Stir until well mixed.
3. Gradually pour the milk into the egg mixture, stirring constantly until smooth.
4. Pour the mixture back into the saucepan and cook over low heat, stirring constantly, until the mixture thickens slightly and coats the back of a spoon. Add dates and cool to room temperature.
5. Stir in ¼ cup rum. Whip the cream until soft peaks form and fold into the cooled mixture.
6. Pour into two refrigerator ice-cube trays or metal loaf pans and freeze until mushy. Turn out into a bowl and stir in the almonds and pecans. Refreeze in trays or pans until serving time. To serve, slice the pudding and serve on small plates. Pass a small decanter of rum to allow each person to pour a little over the pudding.

Serves 16. Recipe may be halved.

Apple Dumplings

This is an old-fashioned dessert worth reviving. The pastry-enclosed apples are baked in boiling syrup, which reduces to serve as a sauce. Brandy or bourbon may be added to the syrup for flavor.

8 6-inch squares pie pastry
8 small cooking apples
1 teaspoon ground cinnamon
½ teaspoon ground nutmeg
Flour for coating
1½ cups granulated sugar

1½ cups light brown sugar, firmly packed
3 cups water
¼ cup unsalted butter or margarine
½ teaspoon vanilla
¼ cup brandy or bourbon (optional)

Preheated oven temperature: 375°F.
1. Prepare pastry squares, using Easy-Method recipe (page 403).
2. Peel, core and slice the apples, allowing 1 apple for each pastry square.
3. Place the apple slices in the middle of the pastry squares. Sprinkle lightly with cinnamon and nutmeg. Dampen the edges of the pastry and seal by crimping the edges together to enclose the apples in a 4-sided pyramid. Coat pastry lightly with flour and make a few slits for steam to escape.

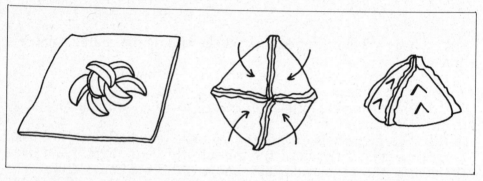

4. To make the syrup, put the granulated sugar, brown sugar, water, butter or margarine, vanilla and optional brandy or bourbon in a baking pan large enough to accommodate the apple dumplings. Bring to a boil over high heat and stir until sugar is dissolved.
5. Place the apple dumplings in the boiling syrup. Bake in preheated oven 45 minutes, basting often, until apples are cooked and the pastry is nicely browned. Serve warm with sauce.
Serves 8.

Homemade Ice Cream and Sherbet

Nothing evokes pleasant memories like homemade ice cream. One smooth, frosty mouthful more than compensates for the time and effort involved.

Part of the fun of making ice cream is to start with a basic vanilla recipe and create your own flavors by adding chocolate, nuts, coconut, crushed fruit or whatever combinations suit your fancy.

Ice Cream Making Basics

Making ice cream involves three basic steps: preparing the custard mixture; cranking, which beats air into the mixture while freezing; and ripening, which blends the flavors and hardens the ice cream (this waiting period is the hardest for most people).

TO PREPARE THE CUSTARD   The best ice cream is made with a cooked custard that should be made several hours in advance so that it has plenty of time to chill and develop flavor. If you substitute light cream or half-and-half for heavy cream, the mixture will freeze but the frozen cream will not be as smooth and fluffy.

FREEZING INSTRUCTIONS　　For best results, carefully follow the instructions that came with your freezer. These vary considerably, depending upon the capacity of the freezer and whether it is electric or the old-fashioned hand-crank. Even the composition of the material used by the manufacturer makes a difference.

Here are some tips to ensure successful ice cream making:

1. Protect all work surfaces with plastic. Salt is corrosive and it will kill surrounding vegetation.
2. Use heavy rubber gloves to protect hands from salt and cold.
3. Use a 1-quart pan for measuring ice.
4. Use a glass or plastic measuring cup for rock salt; salt pits metal.
5. Make certain the ice is chopped fine; it will melt more evenly and provide uniform cold. Otherwise, the ice cream is likely to turn out grainy, icy or mushy.
6. Freezing should not be too slow or too fast. Too large an amount of salt in proportion to the amount of ice will melt the ice too fast. The result is likely to be coarse-grained ice cream. Slow freezing causes a buttery texture.
7. Use a wooden spoon for stirring and repacking ice cream to retard melting.

HOW TO KEEP HOMEMADE ICE CREAM　　Homemade ice cream can be kept up to 30 days if packaged properly for freezing. After it has hardened about 3 hours, transfer it to plastic freezer containers, cover the ice cream with plastic wrap and seal the container with freezer tape.

Country-Style Vanilla Ice Cream

This recipe also is known as French vanilla ice cream.

1 quart milk, combined with 1 cup sugar	½ teaspoon salt
	3 cups heavy cream
3 large eggs	2 tablespoons vanilla
1 cup sugar	

1. Bring the milk and sugar mixture to a boil in a heavy, 2½-quart saucepan. Set aside.
2. Beat the eggs, sugar and salt until light and creamy; add slowly to the milk mixture, stirring constantly with a wire whisk to blend.
3. Cook mixture over low heat, stirring constantly, until mixture is slightly thickened and coats the back of a spoon. Make sure that the mixture does not boil, or it will curdle.

4. Remove from heat and cool to room temperature. Add cream and vanilla. Chill several hours. To freeze, pour into freezer container and freeze according to manufacturer's directions.
Yield: 4 quarts.

Variations: Chocolate Ice Cream

In Step 1 heat 3 squares (3 ounces) grated chocolate with the milk and sugar mixture. Reduce amount of vanilla to 2 teaspoons.

Banana Ice Cream

Force 3 large ripe bananas through a ricer or sieve and add to mixture just before freezing. Reduce amount of vanilla to 1 teaspoon.

Fresh Peach Ice Cream

Substitute 1 teaspoon almond extract for the vanilla. Halfway through the freezing add 2 cups sweetened crushed ripe peaches.

Fresh Strawberry Ice Cream

Omit vanilla. Halfway through the freezing add 2 cups sweetened crushed strawberries.

Watermelon Sherbet

Beautifully pink, deliciously flavorsome and certainly American, this is one of the coolest possible desserts to serve on a hot summer evening.

1½ cups sugar
1 cup water
4 cups watermelon puree

½ teaspoon salt
¼ cup lemon juice
2 tablespoons lime juice

1. Combine the sugar and water in a saucepan and boil 5 minutes, stirring until sugar is dissolved. Cool to room temperature.
2. Cut a very ripe watermelon into cubes, removing seeds. Puree in blender or food processor; add salt, lemon juice, lime juice and cooled syrup. Mix well, pour into freezer container and freeze according to manufacturer's directions.
Yield: About 2 quarts.

Buttermilk Sherbet

Mounds of buttermilk sherbet piled into footed crystal compotes make a stunning presentation, especially if decorated with orange slices and pineapple wedges.

¾ cup sugar
½ cup water
½ cup finely grated orange rind (no white)

½ teaspoon finely grated lemon rind (no white)
½ cup canned pineapple juice
⅛ teaspoon salt
2½ cups buttermilk

1. Combine the sugar and water in a saucepan and boil 5 minutes, stirring until sugar is dissolved. Cool slightly. Add the orange rind, lemon rind, pineapple juice and salt. Mix well and then chill several hours.
2. Pour mixture into freezer container and freeze according to manufacturer's directions. Halfway through the freezing add the buttermilk and stir well, scraping from the sides and bottom of the freezer container.

Yield: About 2 quarts.

RELISHES

Relishes are foods that offer a contrast in flavor to the main course—pickles and brandied fruit are good examples.

Apple Butter

Apple butter can be used as a spread for hot biscuits or it can be served as an accompaniment to curry dishes.

In the Ozarks apple butter is still made in the old-fashioned manner, that is, in large quantities in a copper kettle over an open fire, while grandmother sits patiently stirring the mixture until it reduces to the desired thick consistency. This is a modernized recipe to be cooked on top of the stove. Apples are purchased at the orchard by the peck, half bushel or full bushel; one peck is equal to one fourth of a bushel. The recipe may be halved, using 6 pounds of apples.

1 peck Winesap apples	1½ teaspoons ground allspice
½ cup water	5 cups apple cider
5 cups sugar	⅓ cup cider vinegar, combined with
1 tablespoon ground cinnamon	⅓ cup water

1. Quarter and core the apples but do not peel. Pour the water into a heavy, 5-quart kettle and add the apples. Simmer over low heat until apples are very tender, about 30 minutes.
2. Run the apples through a food mill or sieve. You should have 10 cups pulp.
3. Return the pulp to the kettle and stir in the sugar, cinnamon, allspice and cider. Simmer over very low heat about 5 hours, stirring frequently, until thick. Add the vinegar mixture a small amount at a time during the cooking. Allow the mixture to thicken to desired consistency, but keep in mind that some thickening will occur during cooling. Mixture should be of spreading consistency.
4. Remove from heat and spoon into sterilized jars and seal.
Yield: 8 half-pint jars.

Pear Honey

Pear honey is a traditional early American jam that is used as a spread for buttered toast.

4 cups coarsely ground Kieffer pears or any firm unripe pears

4 cups sugar

1 cup canned crushed pineapple, drained

1 lemon, with juice and rind (no white)

1. Peel and core pears. Put pears through a food grinder, using the coarse blade, or use a food processor.
2. Combine the pears, sugar, pineapple and lemon with juice and rind in a heavy, 4-quart kettle. Cook 30 to 35 minutes, or until the mixture thickens and pears are translucent.
3. Remove from heat and spoon into sterilized jars and seal.

Yield: About 8 half-pint jars.

Brandied Peaches

Whole peaches preserved in brandy-flavored syrup are used by Southern cooks to garnish baked ham. The syrup can be poured over vanilla ice cream to make a delicious quick dessert.

For best results use cling peaches in this recipe. These are the early peaches of summer with pits that "cling" to the flesh of the peach.

4 pounds cling peaches

4 pounds sugar (8 cups)

2 cups water

2 cups brandy

1. Place the whole peaches in boiling water for a few minutes. Remove and rinse under cold water. Remove skins and set peaches aside.
2. Combine the sugar and water in a heavy, 4-quart kettle and bring to a boil. Stir well to dissolve sugar and add the peaches. Boil 5 minutes. Carefully remove peaches and set aside.
3. Boil syrup 15 minutes, or until it thickens to a heavy syrup. Add brandy and remove from heat at once. Pour the hot syrup over the peaches and turn to coat well.
4. Spoon into sterilized 1-pint jars and seal.

Yield: About 5 pints.

Cranberry-Orange Relish

This relish is often served as a side dish to accompany chicken and turkey.

1 medium-sized orange
1 cup sugar

2 cups fresh cranberries, washed and stemmed

1. Trim 4 one-inch squares of peel from orange (no white); cut into thin strips. Peel the orange and slice; remove seeds.
2. Combine the orange peel and ½ cup of the sugar in blender or food processor. Process until rind is chopped fine. Add cranberries, orange slices and the remainder of the sugar. Process until coarsely chopped. Refrigerate overnight or several hours to blend flavors.

Yield: About 2 cups.

Midwestern Corn Relish

Almost every farm cook plans to put by several jars of corn relish during the canning season, using corn that has become a mite too firm to use for other purposes.

The secret of making good corn relish is to avoid scraping the corn off the cob. If the cob is scraped, it will impart a musty flavor to the cooked relish. Use a very sharp knife to cut off the corn, leaving a generous amount of the lower part of the kernel on the cob. Frozen or canned corn may be substituted in this recipe.

8 cups yellow corn (about 14 ears of corn)
2 cups chopped sweet red peppers
2 cups chopped green peppers
4 cups chopped celery
4 cups distilled white vinegar
1 cup finely chopped onion

1 cup sugar
2 teaspoons salt
2 teaspoons celery seed
2 tablespoons dry mustard
2 teaspoons turmeric
¼ cup flour
½ cup water

1. If using fresh corn on the cob, cook in boiling water 5 minutes. Drain and rinse under cold, running water. Cut corn off the cob to measure 8 cups.
2. In a heavy, 5-quart kettle combine the corn, red and green peppers, celery, vinegar, onion, sugar, salt and celery seed. Boil uncovered 20 minutes over medium heat. Stir often to keep mixture from sticking to bottom of kettle.

3. Combine the mustard, turmeric, flour and water in blender or food processor and process until smooth or beat with a whisk until smooth; add slowly to the corn mixture, stirring constantly to blend. Boil an additional 5 minutes.
4. Spoon mixture into sterilized jars and seal.
Yield: About 5 pints.

Classic Bread and Butter Pickles

Before fresh produce was readily available in the northern climes, a side dish of pickles served as a wintertime salad. This is an easy home-style recipe for pickles with a nice crisp texture.

15 medium-sized pickling cucumbers, cut into ⅛-inch slices
4 large white onions, sliced thin
1 large green pepper, sliced thin
¼ cup salt

2½ cups cider vinegar
2½ cups sugar
1 tablespoon mustard seed
1 teaspoon turmeric
¼ teaspoon ground cloves

1. Combine the cucumbers, onions, green pepper and salt in a large bowl. Cover with a tray of ice cubes. Let stand 3 hours.
2. Combine the vinegar, sugar, mustard seed, turmeric and cloves in a 5-quart kettle. Bring the mixture to a boil, stirring constantly; continue stirring until sugar is dissolved. Drain the vegetables and add to the boiling liquid. Heat thoroughly but do not boil.
3. Spoon into sterilized 1-pint jars and seal.
Yield: About 6 pints.

Watermelon Rind Pickles

One often wonders about the ingenious cook who discovered a use for discarded watermelon rinds. But no matter who the inventor was, the result is a traditional American side dish.

Watermelon rind
2½ tablespoons salt
4 cups cold water
4½ cups sugar
1½ cups cider vinegar

¾ teaspoon whole cloves
¾ teaspoon whole allspice
1 stick cinnamon
½ lemon, sliced thin

1. Trim the green skin and pink flesh from watermelon rind and cut
   into 1-inch squares to measure 6 cups; place in a large bowl.
2. Dissolve the salt in the cold water and pour over the watermelon
   rind. Cover with foil and let stand in a cool place overnight.
3. Drain the rind well and place in a 4-quart kettle with fresh water
   to cover. Bring to a boil, lower heat and simmer 15 minutes. Drain
   and set aside.
4. In a 2-quart saucepan combine the sugar, vinegar, cloves, allspice
   and sugar with the lemon. Bring to a boil and stir until sugar is
   dissolved. Cook at a rolling boil 5 additional minutes.
5. Pour mixture over the watermelon rind and simmer 15 minutes, or
   until the rind appears translucent.
6. With a slotted spoon ladle the rind into sterilized jars, adding a slice
   of lemon to each. Pour syrup over fruit to within ½ inch of top of jar
   and seal.

Yield: About 6 ½-pint jars.

WINES OF
AMERICA

In 1980 and 1981 more wine than spirits was sold in the United States. As sales of hard liquor continue to decline, the trend toward drinking more wine seems to be continuing. People from every class of society are searching for affordable and good American wines to drink on a day-to-day basis and for those that show promise to store for future enjoyment.

      Very few people in this country today are qualified to evaluate American wines, myself included. It is my good fortune to have as a friend and neighbor Harold E. Applegate, one of the charter members of the American Wine Society, and a regional Vice-President of the society from 1967 to 1978. This kind gentleman has graciously contributed an unpretentious and practical guide to American wines, their use and their potential. Enjoy!

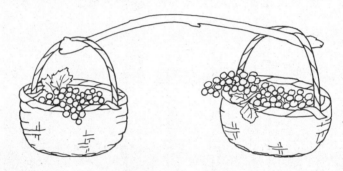

The Historical Perspective

Table wines have been a part of the American way of life since the earliest days of the colonial settlements. Wild grapes were found in abundance, and one of the very early agricultural projects was the establishment of vineyards, using varieties from the homeland to produce beverages the colonists had known there. There were many attempts. Some of them were large in scale and under the supervision of professionals such as Dr. Philip Mazzei, who was employed by Thomas Jefferson at Monticello. The results were always the same—utter failure. The vines would grow well for three years or so and then they would slacken and eventually die. The answer to the question "Why?" had to wait for the discoveries in microbiology by Louis Pasteur in the mid-nineteenth century. Nevertheless, the European vines had been around long enough to supply pollen to fertilize the flowers of the native vines; and a few of these accidental hybrids were found and propagated by amateurs. These became the foundation on which the wine industry east of the Rocky Mountains was built, by such pioneers as Nicholas Longworth and "Captain" Paul Garrett. Their work was paralleled on the west coast by the pioneering efforts of "Count" Agoston Haraszthy, who used the classic European varieties.

However, it was not a profitable business. America developed as a nation of beer and hard-liquor drinkers. It was only at the beginning of this century that some very fine wines were first made. Then came the disaster of Prohibition. The industry was ruined, and the road back after 1933 was slow and painful. Gradually the vineyards were replanted with premium varieties and the quality began to return. Finally, in the mid-1960s there was evidence of a definite change in the public's taste for wine, and that taste has developed and expanded countrywide.

At the present time, the United States produces more varieties of wine than any other country. These wines are divided into three main categories: vinifera, native and hybrids. Unless otherwise noted, all the varieties discussed are commercially available.

Vinifera

This is the term used to describe the varieties of wine from Europe and the Old World. Originally, the cultivation of these varieties was limited to California in this country, but pioneering efforts of Dr. Konstantin Frank, a farsighted immigrant from the Ukraine, have enabled them to spread to the eastern half of the country in the last two decades. The varieties are as follows:

Red Wines

Cabernet Sauvignon. This is the great grape of the Bordeaux reds, and the finest of the California varieties. The color is deep ruby, the bouquet expansive and the flavor many-faceted and full. When aged for five to ten years, these wines lose the hardiness and astringency of youth and smooth out to the mellow richness of maturity. Compared with the French Bordeaux reds, they bear a closer kinship to the rich wines of St. Emilion than to the seductive and delicate ones of the Médoc.

Merlot. A first cousin to the Cabernet Sauvignon, this is a fine grape in its own right. While beginning to be used to a small extent as a varietal, it is used largely both here and in France in blending with its cousin to soften the austerity of the latter and to shorten somewhat the aging period. It in no way lowers the quality of the wine.

Pinot Noir. This is the grape of the great French Burgundies. A contrary prima donna in both its viticulture (cultivation) and vinification (the actual wine) it is truly at home in France and nowhere else in the world. Though a fine wine, a California Pinot Noir is usually a mere caricature of a true Burgundy. Only on rare occasions is a great one produced. There is hope that we may be on the verge of finding a few of those spots where specific soil and micro climate will allow this grape to rise to its greatness. There is also a spark of hope in the east, in the Finger Lakes region of New York State, which will be discussed later.

Zinfandel. This grape had been grown in heavy tonnage for winemaking in California for many years and yet remained a sleeper. Only recently has it come into its own in the cool coastal counties—and in a big way. Its wines are of two types. The first is a relatively light-bodied, fruity wine with a deep, zesty, "guzzle me" flavor and a raspberry aroma. It could be called our Beaujolais. The second is a development of the last 15 years. It is a powerful, inky giant that needs years to mature and has the possibility of becoming one of the world's great wines.

Petite Sirah. This relative newcomer to the California scene comes from France's Rhône Valley. Its wines are big, dark, full-flavored and astringent when young but smooth out to a soft richness in maturity.

Gamay Beaujolais. There is confusion about this grape which comes from the Beaujolais region of France. Apparently it is not the Gamay à jus blanc, which yields the light, fruity and delicious young Beaujolais wines of France, but a clone of the Pinot Noir. Although it does not resemble a Beaujolais at all, the wine is fine nevertheless.

Napa Gamay. This is the other part of the Gamay confusion and still may not be the Beaujolais grape. The wine is good, not great. It is, however, often vinified into a fine, flavorful *vin rosé*.

Barbera. This import from northern Italy has taken to the coastal California climate like a duck to water, yielding big, full-bodied wines of deep color and full yet soft flavor. It is an excellent wine with pasta.

Grignolino. This is another northern Italian import but is little grown. Its wine, though not great, is pleasant "quaffing wine," with a heady, strawberry-like aroma. The most distinctive feature is its light color, more orange than red.

Grenache. This grape comes from southern France, where it is the dominant one in the blend known as Tavel, one of the finest of all rosés. Its red wine is uninteresting, but vinified as a *vin rosé* it is fresh, fruity and delightful, one of this country's best.

Charbono. This is another producer of big, dark, full-bodied wines, not unlike a good Côte Rhone.

Tinta Madeira and Tinta Cao. These grapes are the dominant ones of a group used in Portugal to produce the world-famous Ports. They are used here in the same way—to make a fortified dessert wine known as California Port. Most Ports are made from any old black grape that is handy at the time, and are cheap, rough and utterly without merit. However, the small production from the true Port varieties is of high quality, perhaps a little peppery on the tongue compared to the Portuguese product, but if they are made with care and are given the all-important element of time, they someday may stand toe to toe with the original.

Generics and jug wines. These are blends sold as Burgundy, Claret, Chianti and as just red wine. They are America's *vin ordinaire* and on the whole are vastly superior to those of Europe.

White Wines

Chardonnay. One of the world's great wine grapes, which creates the famous white Burgundy, this grape yields California's finest white wine and one of the finest in the east. The wines can vary widely in character, from a steely dryness and delicate bouquet like, but not identical with, the rare, genuine Chablis to the deep, rich flavor and heady aroma of white Burgundies from the Côte d'Or.

White or Johannisberg Riesling. Another of the world's great wines, it has not been entirely at home in California's climate. In the last several years, with very careful culture and choice of site, there have appeared a few fine wines, perhaps not the equal of the great German Rieslings but fine nevertheless. At their best they possess a pronounced, flowery fragrance and an almost overwhelming volume of fruity flavor that lingers on the palate. Watch for it in the east, where it can be great.

Pinot Blanc. The Pinot blanc grape, a cousin of the Chardonnay, being difficult in both viticulture and vinification, is little grown. The wine is barely inferior to Chardonnay and is dry and fresh, yet with a fruity richness.

Semillon. This third white grape among the world greats is currently out of fashion in chic circles in America. In the Bordeaux area it is blended in the proportion of 70 percent to 75 percent with Sauvignon blanc (20 percent-25 percent) and Muscadelle (5 percent) to produce the famed bottled sunshine known as Sauternes, one of the greatest of wines. Twenty years ago or less there was produced in California a small amount of wine made according to the Sauternes blend, from grapes grown in the Livermore area. It was concentrated in the warm, autumnal sunshine to yield a golden, luscious nectar. It was not a duplicate of Sauternes, although it came as close as possible and was a very fine wine. Now that some new areas are being found in California where the micro climate is conducive to the growth of the "noble mold" (*Botrytis cinerea*, which concentrates the grape in a magical way), it is hoped that there will be produced a wine that will be a nearly perfect reproduction of Sauternes, with its wonderful perfume and rich, figlike flavor that spreads over the palate and leaves a haunting memory.

Gewürztraminer. From the Alsace and neighboring German Palatinate this grape in the right location and handled with even more care than the Johannisberg Riesling yields a truly fine wine, even though it is not to everyone's taste. The spicy fragrance and almost perfumed flavor give the wine a sweet character even when it is dry. In the east it ranks with the best.

Sauvignon Blanc. The Sauvignon *blanc* grape, when allowed to ripen fully or become overripe, gives a rich, lusciously sweet wine with an almost overpowering character. This too is out of vogue. However, a resurgence has occurred in the form of a dry wine with far more body than its Pouilly Fumé French counterpart.

Chenin Blanc. The Chenin *blanc* grape, sometimes called Pineau de la Loire, is really more at home in California than in its native Loire Valley in France, where it is used to make Vouvray with its springlike freshness and only occasional rich sweetness. In California it develops its richness much more readily. Its future is a good one.

Folle Blanche. This grape was at one time the source of all the great cognacs in France. The wine that was distilled from it was so acidic as to be virtually undrinkable. In California the wine is delightful, fresh and crisp, a perfect summer luncheon wine. I hope that in the near future some fine American brandies will be produced from this grape rather than the mediocre so-called brandies that are now made from surplus table grapes.

Grey Riesling. The grape is not a Riesling at all but the **Chauché gris** from France. The wine is soft and pleasant with some spiciness in its flavor, but rather without distinction.

Muscat. This heading covers several types of wine made from three different grapes, all possessing a distinctive and almost overpowering aroma and flavor characteristic of all Muscat grapes. They frequently are referred to as "ladies' wines." Nearly all are made from the Muscat of Alexandria grape and sold as Muscatel—cheap, coarse and utterly without merit. From the same grape is made, in miniscule amounts, a very special wine, very sweet, low in alcohol, and sparkling. It is made and stored under refrigeration and sold as Moscato Amabile. Also made in small quantities from a grape known variously as Muscat Frontignan, Muscat Canelli and Muscat *blanc* are two high-quality wines, one fortified and the other at table strength. The third wine is made in a tiny amount in the east from the Muscat Ottonel, in both fortified and table-strength styles, and is the finest of them all.

Generics and jug wines. Most of these are not up to their red counterparts in quality for a single reason: more than half of all the white wine made in California has been made from the enormously productive, cheap table grape, Thompson Seedless. The wine, which is sold straight and also is used to stretch better wines, is characterless and without merit. Some wine is made from Sylvaner, Colombard and other standard grapes; it is good and an excellent buy.

Sherry

Huge quantities of sherries have been and are still being made in this country, but they are cheap and indistinguished. They bear only a small resemblance to true Spanish sherries and are far closer to Madeiras. This is understandable, considering the process by which they are made. Most are made by the heating, or Tressler, process, which is altogether unlike anything in Spain. Also almost any grape except those used by the Spaniards has been used. Now some wines are being made from the traditional Palomino grape, using the proper flor yeast, *Saccharolmyces beticus*. They are excellent examples of sherries.

Natives

The native grapes usually are thought of as representing the wild species indigenous to this country. Actually almost none of them are. Most are natural crosses of more than one native species with some vinifera. These grapes are higher in acid and lower in sugar content than the vinifera grapes, and if much labrusca "blood" is present, there will be a pronounced aroma, called foxiness. This is caused by the presence of methyl anthranilate in the skins and is very foreign to the European taste. The entire wine industry in the eastern half of the country was built and operated on the basis of these grapes until a generation ago. Some of the varieties are:

Red Wines

Concord. This is grown in larger quantities than all other eastern grapes combined and is responsible for much of the bad reputation of eastern wines. Dry table wines made from it are unpalatable. Only when sweetened with cane sugar it is passable. While of no interest to the serious wine lover, large quantities of this red wine are made, much of it kosher.

Ives. The red wine made from this grape has more body than Concord. In general, what is said about the Concord applies also to the Ives.

Norton (Cynthiana). Whether or not these two names refer to the same grape is a question of long standing for the botanists to settle. The Norton was long regarded as the best native grape for dry red table wines. It requires a long growing season and its culture is limited to the upper tier of the southern states. When properly handled and aged, the dark wine is quite acceptable. Its production today seems to be limited to northwestern Arkansas, where it is made lightly sweetened with sugar.

Isabella. Dark red and quite foxy, it is no longer made. However, there is some production as an Isabella Rosé.

Noble. The Noble is a black Muscadine grape of the south. The wine is dark and usually made semisweet, with the heavy flavor and aroma characteristic of the Muscadines.

White Wines

Delaware. This fairly small, thin-skinned, pink grape is the preeminent native grape. No vinifera has a richer flavor or a lovelier aroma. The aroma is highly perfumed and definitely "Yankee," though not at all foxy. The wine fits the same description and is one of the foundations of the eastern champagne industry. Little really good Delaware still wine is made.

Iona. The grape and its wine are in no way inferior to the Delaware. The vine, however, is very capricious in its culture, so that there is very little of the wine available.

Dutchess. A white grape, it yields a fragrant, almost frosty dry wine that is excellent with seafood.

Niagara. This wine is very popular with people who like sweet wines and is a big seller. It has a heavy flavor, is very foxy and is made sweetened to the semisweet level.

Catawba. The purple-red grape is a late ripener and fairly foxy. More than 150 years of usage has taught eastern winemakers how to handle it to get good results. Though its dry table wine is too austere for most tastes, Catawba and Delaware provide the base for fine eastern champagne. There is also a large amount of semisweet, fairly foxy Pink Catawba made.

Diamond (Moore's Diamond). An old, controlled hybrid originated by Jacob Moore, the Diamond is among the prettiest of all grapes. When not allowed to get too ripe, it yields a wine of good body, a spicy dryness and fairly pungent bouquet.

Scuppernong. This grape is a Muscadine native to the south and dear to the hearts of my "rebel" friends. There is considerable production of wine from it, nearly all of it very poor in quality. There is a small amount of pure Scuppernong wine that is made beautifully; it is redolent of the characteristic muskiness of the Muscadines, semisweet and heavy with a unique flavor. These wines are not for everyone but are highly admired by those who like them.

Carlos. This is another southern Muscadine; its wine is much like the Scuppernong.

Hybrids

These are products of scientific breeding by researchers in France and the United States (here largely at the New York State Agricultural Experiment Station at Geneva). Philip Wagner, the now-retired editor of the *Baltimore Sun*, has been the prime mover in the dissemination of the French hybrids. Attempts have been made to combine the quality of the vinifera fruit with the disease and climate resistance of the native species. The results have so far yielded no Chardonnay-quality fruit on a riparia-quality vine, or anything even close to it. However, the research has a good future.

Red Wines

The eastern wine industry eagerly looked to the red wine hybrids as a way to become competitive with the California vinifera reds. They are still looking. Although some varieties are better than others, on the whole the reds have been a little thin and lacking in charm. I think they are better blended than as varietals. As we learn more in our viticultural and vinification practices, perhaps the picture will improve. Among the varieties that can be found are Maréchal Foch, Leon Millot, de Chaunac, Baco Noir, Chancellor, Chelois and Chamborcin.

White Wines

The picture with the hybrid whites is considerably brighter. Experience is beginning to bring results.

Seyval Blanc. The Seyval blanc variety is head and shoulders above the rest of the pack. It is a productive variety with not too many viticultural problems. The wine varies widely according to soil and climate, from steely dryness to a full richness with a little residual sugar.

Aurore. This is another productive, though not foolproof, variety that is grown in considerable quantity in the New York Finger Lakes area, where it has found its way into some of the champagne blends. Its wine is light and to my taste lacks sufficient character.

Cayuga White. This productive new grape from the Geneva station is commanding attention, with others to follow from this source.

Other varieties of the French hybrids used to some extend are Vidal, Villard Blanc, Vignoles and Verdelet.

The Wineries

I shall not attempt to list the producers of the wines I have discussed, or anything approaching that. Listed will be the sources of those wines you have some chance of finding. Generally eliminated will be the tiny "boutique" wineries that sell only at retail from the winery. Standard quality, bulk-produced wines from large vintners are available almost everywhere nationwide. As for the much smaller producers of premium-quality wines, if you are in an area somewhere near the source or in an area of some affluence, you have a reasonable chance of finding at least some of them. If you are in an area where you have a state monopoly of all wine and liquor distribution, the outlook is bleak indeed; the people are the losers. The wineries are listed by area.

CALIFORNIA—NORTH OF SAN FRANCISCO BAY

Alexander Valley. Very good Chardonnay.

Beaulieu Vineyard. Created in 1900 by Georges de Latour, this has long been one of the greatest wineries in the country. It is now owned by the Heublein Company. In 1938, de Latour performed a tremendous service to the wine lovers of this land when he secured as his wine maker André Tchelistcheff, a wine-making legend in his own lifetime. The Georges de Latour Private Reserve Cabernet Sauvignon is one of America's greatest wines and a bright star anywhere in the world. Their Pinot Noir generally is excellent. What wonderful memories I have of their great Pinot Noirs of the '46 and '48 vintages! The Muscat Frontignan dessert wine is a fine one, just as the sweet Sauvignon Blanc used to be. Today I am told they are making a tiny amount of a bortytized (grapes concentrated by the "noble" mold) Sauvignon Blanc that is great. Their Chardonnay and champagne are also excellent.

Beringer. Now owned by the Swiss firm of Nestlé; they produce a line of standard wines or a cut better.

Buehler. Cabernet Sauvignon and Zinfandel.

Burgess. Excellent Cabernet Sauvignon and Petite Sirah, good Chardonnay.

Cakebread. Very good Cabernet Sauvignon and Chardonnay.

Carneros Creek. Chardonnay.

Chappellet Vineyards. Chardonnay, Cabernet Sauvignon and excellent Chenin Blanc.

Charles Krug. Good Cabernet Sauvignon, Pinot Noir, Chenin Blanc and bulk wines for the jug trade.

Château Chevalier. Cabernet Sauvignon, Chardonnay, Johannisberg Riesling.

Château Montelena. Excellent Zinfandel, Cabernet Sauvignon, Chardonnay.

Château St. Jean. Very fine Johannisberg Riesling, excellent Cabernet Sauvignon, Chardonnay, Fumé Blanc and Gewürztraiminer.

Christian Brothers. Large-scale producers of good wines of standard quality or better.

Clos du Bois. Pinot Noir, Johannisberg Riesling, Cabernet Sauvignon, Chardonnay and Gewürztraminer.

Clos du Val. Fine Cabernet Sauvignon and Zinfandel, very good Merlot and Chardonnay.

Cuvaison. Very good Chardonnay.

Diamond Creek. Very good Cabernet Sauvignon.

Dry Creek. Cabernet Sauvignon.

Far Niente. Excellent Chardonnay.

Freemark Abbey. Very good Chardonnay, Cabernet Sauvignon, Pinot Noir.

Grgich. Johannisberg Riesling, very good Chardonnay.

Gundlach-Bundschu. Fine Chardonnay.

Hacienda. Chardonnay, Cabernet Sauvignon, Gewürztraminer.

Hanzell Vineyard. Tiny, legendary winery created by former Ambassador James D. Zellerbach, producing small amounts of great Pinot Noir and Chardonnay.

Heitz Cellars. Quality as great as the production is small. Joe Heitz's Martha's Vineyard Cabernet Sauvignon in a good year is among the greatest wines of this nation. His Chardonnay and Pinot Noir are excellent, and the Grignolino is the only one made in California of which I am aware.

Italian Swiss Colony. Good, standard wines produced on a large scale.

Joseph Phelps. Pinot Noir, Zinfandel, Johannisberg Riesling, Gewürztraminer and excellent Chardonnay and Cabernet Sauvignon.

Louis M. Martini. American wine lovers owe him a vote of thanks. His policy was to produce top-quality wines that do not have to be aged 10 to 20 years to be drinkable and are sold at a very moderate price. The Cabernet Sauvignon, Pinot Noir, Zinfandel and Gewürztraminer are top rate. The Barbera, Johannisberg Riesling, Merlot and Folle Blanche are excellent. The refrigerated Moscato Amabile is sold only at the winery. The Dry Sherry is among the best produced in America. Perhaps the most noteworthy are the jug wines. Mountain Red Wine and Mountain White Wine are excellent and, to my mind, are the best wine values anywhere.

Mayacamas. The Chardonnays and Zinfandels are fine, big wines. The Cabernet Sauvignon and Chenin Blanc are not far behind.

Pedroncelli. Jug wines and very good Pinot Noir, Zinfandel, and Cabernet Sauvignon.

Robert Mondavi. This is one of the showplaces in California. The Cabernet Sauvignon is outstanding. Not far behind are Chardonnay, Fumé Blanc, Pinot Noir, Johannisberg Riesling and a delightful Gamay Rosé.

Sebastiani. This winery has been considerably upgraded in recent years, to become a producer of premium-quality wines sold at reasonable prices. The Cabernet Sauvignon and Chardonnay are very good; the Zinfandel and Barbera, first rate.

Silver Oaks. Very good Cabernet Sauvignon.

Simi. This is another winery upgraded from standard bulk to premium level and it produces good Chenin Blanc, Chardonnay, Pinot Noir, Zinfandel, and excellent Gewürztraminer, Gamay Beaujolais and Cabernet Sauvignon.

Sonoma Vineyards. Excellent Chardonnay and Cabernet Sauvignon.

Spring Mountain. Chardonnay, Sauvignon Blanc and Cabernet Sauvignon.

Stag's Lean. Cabernet Sauvignon and Chardonnay.

Stonegate. Sauvignon Blanc, Pinot Noir, Cabernet Sauvignon and very good Chardonnay.

Stony Hill Vineyard. The tiny but famed creation of Fred McCrea, making top-flight Chardonnay, Gewürztraminer and Johannisberg Riesling.

Sutter Home. Moscato Amabile and excellent Zinfandel.

Trefethen. Johannisberg Riesling, Pinot Noir, Cabernet Sauvignon and very good Chardonnay.

Veedercrest. Cabernet Sauvignon, Johannisberg Riesling and very good Chardonnay.

CALIFORNIA—SOUTH OF SAN FRANCISCO BAY

Almaden. Owned by National Distillers and a large-scale producer of nearly everything. Their Grenache Rosé is one of California's best rosés.

Callaway. Chardonnay.

Chalone. A tiny, isolated winery in very dry country. I have tasted a great Pinot Noir and a great Chardonnay from here. Chenin Blanc, Pinot Blanc and Cabernet Sauvignon also are produced.

Concannon. In the Livermore Valley, this is one of the state's historic wineries. Their Cabernet Sauvignon, Muscat Frontignan, and Petite Sirah are excellent. The Chenin Blanc, Sauvignon Blanc, Semillon and Zinfandel are not far behind.

David Bruce. Chardonnay.

Estrella River. Very good Chardonnay and Cabernet Sauvignon.

Firestone. Cabernet Sauvignon, Chardonnay, Pinot Noir, Johannisberg Riesling.

Martin Ray. This is the tiny winery of the late Martin Ray. The Cabernet Sauvignon, Chardonnay, and Pinot Noir were often among the best.

Mirassou. The Chardonnay, Chenin Blanc, Fumé Blanc, Gewürztraminer, Cabernet Sauvignon, Gamay Beaujolais, Petite Sirah, Pinot Noir and Zinfandel are among the state's best wines.

Monteviña. Fine, big Zinfandels and Barberas.

Paul Masson. Another large-scale producer owned by Seagram Distillers.

Pendleton. Cabernet Sauvignon, Chardonnay and Sauvignon Blanc.

Ridge. Cabernet Sauvignon, Petite Sirah and Zinfandel—all fine, big, powerful wines.

Ventana. Excellent Chardonnay.

Wente Bros. This has long been one of California's great wineries. The late Herman Wente was one of its finest wine makers and certainly one of its greatest gentlemen. Famous for their white wines, among the best have been the Chardonnay, Pinot Blanc, Gewürztraminer, Sauvignon Blanc and Semillon. I am told that they are making a small amount of their Chateau Wente (a true Sauternes blend) from botrytized grapes—that is great! They also have the popular Grey Riesling and several red varietals.

CALIFORNIA—CENTRAL VALLEY   This hot valley is the source of a tremendous volume of wine from a number of large-scale producers. The largest in the U.S. and the largest in the entire world is the *E. & J. Gallo Co*. Their Gallo Hearty Burgundy is a creditable wine in any league and an excellent buy.

Ficklin Bros. This small winery is devoted to one specialty product, the best port wines in this country, made from the true port varieties of grapes.

CALIFORNIA "CHAMPAGNE"   In Napa and Sonoma Counties, *Beaulieu Vineyard* and *Domaine Chandon Schramsberg* produce outstanding champagnes. Not far behind are *Korbel* and *Hans Kornell*.

PACIFIC NORTHWEST   In Washington, the following wineries are marketing wines from vinifera grapes: *Bingen, Cedar Ridge, Château St. Michelle, Hinzerling* and *Preston*. I have tasted creditable Johannisberg Riesling and Cabernet Sauvignon from *St. Michelle*. From Oregon come wines from *Adelsheim, Amity, Cotes de Colombe, Eyrie, Hillcrest, Oak Knoll and Tualatin*.

NEW ENGLAND   Because of a generally shorter growing season, winery activity is very limited. In the Narragansett Bay area of Rhode Island there are two wineries: the first is *Prudence Island*, producing only vinifera wines; the second is *Sakonnet Vineyards*, selling both vinifera and French hybrid wines. I have tasted only Sakonnet white blend, which was good, fresh, crisp and full-flavored. On Martha's Vineyard, *Chicama* is devoted entirely to vinifera. Connecticut has two wineries: *Stonecrop*, devoted to hybrids; and *Haight*, devoted to Chardonnay and Johannisberg Riesling.

NEW YORK   New York always has been the giant of the wine industry outside California, and is just as old. In fact, the Bonded Winery #1 license is held by the Pleasant Valley Wine Co., now a part of the Taylor Wine Co. The scene is dominated by four large wineries: *Widmer's Wine Cellars*, now owned by British interests; *Taylor Wine Co.*, now owned by Coca-Cola; *Gold Seal Vineyards*, owned by Seagram; and the *Canadaigua Wine Co*.

As in California, when the large- and medium-sized wineries are gobbled up by giant conglomerates, a horde of small ones, some of high quality, take their place. At the head of them is the *Vinifera Wine Cellars of Dr. Konstantin Frank.* A German-Russian viticulturist from the Ukraine, Dr. Frank escaped from Russia during World War II and eventually found his way to the United States. When told that vinifera could not be grown in the eastern climate, he refused to believe it. With the support of Charles Fournier, the distinguished head of Gold Seal, he proceeded to cultivate the grapes and make wines—with great success. His vineyard, primarily experimental, is devoted to Johannisberg Riesling, Chardonnay, Pinot Noir, Cabernet Sauvignon, Gewürztraminer, Aligote, Gamay Beaujolais, Pinot Gris, Sereksia and Muscat Ottonel. The Pinot Noir 1963, Muscal Ottonel 1964 (a fortified dessert wine) and Gewürztraminer 1979 are at this writing superb.

In the same Finger Lakes area are:

Bully Hill. Owned by Walter S. Taylor and using French hybrids.

Glenora. Some excellent wines: Chardonnay, Johannisberg Riesling, Delaware and several hybrids.

Gold Seal. Vinifera and a broad line using natives and hybrids. Their Charles Fournier champagne is among the best anywhere.

Herman Wiemer. New vineyard using vinifera.

Heron Hill. Chardonnay, Johannisberg Riesling and several hybrids.

Villa d'Ingianni. Chardonnay and excellent Delaware.

Wagner. Excellent Chardonnay, Johannisberg Riesling, Gewürztraminer, Delaware and three hybrids, including a fine Seyval Blanc.

Widmer. In a broad line, several native varietals are still being produced. Look for the Lake Delaware. Their sherries, weathered in barrels on the winery roof for four years, are among the best in the country.

Elsewhere in the state at *Benmarl*, Mark Miller produces both hybrid and vinifera wines in the Hudson Valley. In the Lake Erie area are *Johnson, Merritt* and *Woodbury.* The *Alexander Hargrave* vineyard on Long Island is devoted solely to vinifera.

MID-ATLANTIC   In New Jersey there is only one winery worthy of attention: *Tewksbury*, a small producer and new. Across the Delaware in Pennsylvania there is a flurry of activity with many small wineries operating but rarely under professional control. I have tasted several good wines from *Mazza, Naylor* and *Adams County.*

MIDWEST   Considerable wine is produced in Michigan from native and hybrid grapes by *Bronte, Warner* and *St. Julian. Fenn Valley, Leelanau* and *Tabor Hill* also add vinifera to their lists.

Ohio has two standout personalities. The first is Arne Esterer at *Markko* Vineyards, which produces a small amount of excellent viniferas. The second is Dr. Thomas Wykoff, well-known ear, nose and throat specialist, whose fine Au Provence restaurant and its associated Cedar Hill Wine Co. are the source of well-made vinifera and hybrid wines under the *Chateau Lagniappe* label.

Indiana has *Banholzer* struggling to make a name for himself with his list of well-made viniferas and hybrids.

Missouri was a major producer before Prohibition and in recent years has started to show activity again with *Rosati, Green Valley, Mt. Pleasant, St. James* and *Stone Hill* using hybrids and natives.

Wiederkehr Cellars in northwestern Arkansas has a lengthy list of all types.

SOUTH OF THE MASON-DIXON LINE   Maryland is the home of the established *Boordy Vineyards*, created and until recently owned by Philip Wagner, whose hybrid wines are well-known, good and reasonably priced. Nearby is *Montbray*, where Dr. "Ham" Mowbray is a producer of very good vinifera and hybrid wines.

Virginia has had a burst of activity recently with the establishment of *Piedmont, Meredyth, Farfelu*, and *Barboursville*, all of which give considerable attention to vinifera wine production in the rolling foothills of the Blue Ridge. I have had the privilege of tasting a well-made and very good Chardonnay from Piedmont. Also at the *Woburn* winery there is a tiny production of very good native and hybrid wines.

The South is the home of the muscadine grapes. Of all the Scuppernong wine made, I have tasted only one good one. It was from *Duplin Wine Cellars* in North Carolina—a beautifully made wine. In South Carolina *Truluck* has started a new venture using vinifera, muscadines and several hybrids.

Service

Wine should be stored in a dark, cool place with the bottle on its side to keep the cork from drying out. The rules for using wine are few. Reds should be served at room temperature for best flavor balance, uncorked for several hours before using and allowed to breathe in order to release the bouquet and flavor. Whites should be chilled, but *not* ice cold—one to one and a half hours in the refrigerator is sufficient. There are no absolute rules for matching wine with food. Generally, reds are considered ideal with red meats and whites with fish and white meats. However, the only rule is your taste. If you like it, use it. Wine enhances food and food enhances wine. What a joy!

The Wineglass

In order for a wine's appearance to be examined thoroughly, the glass should be absolutely clear, with no design or coloration that might disguise how the wine looks. Members of the American Wine Society use 10-ounce glasses when they gather for tastings of still wines. The sides should be tulip-shaped or at least have sides that slope inward near the top, so that the wine can be swirled around inside without spilling. Swirling releases aroma and "nose." (See glossary.) As red wine flows back down the sides of the glass it forms "church windows" or streaked coloration referred to as "legs." The richer the wine, the more colorful the streaks. Swirling clears white wines of residual sulfur dioxide. Glasses of this type, sold as all-purpose wine glasses, are available everywhere in inexpensive clear glass. The ideal champagne glass is long and narrow rather than bulbous. However, any tulip-shaped stem glass that narrows at the top will serve the purpose. If several wines are to be on the table at the same time, it is appropriate to use different shapes of glasses. This enables both the pourer and the tasters to avoid confusing the wines.

Glossary of Terms in Wine Tasting

Aroma: The smell of the grape.
Big: Intensely flavored, full-bodied, textured. Having a weighty quality that can be sensed in the mouth.
Body: Texture, weight, flavor intensity.
Bouquet: Vinous perfume of mature wine.
Buttery: Having the flavor of butter; evident in some Chardonnays and white Burgundies. Also creamy.
Complex: Challenging and interesting, with several dimensions.
Dry: Absence of sweetness from residual sugar. Lacking in fruit.
Earthy: Taste of the earth where the grapes grew.

Elegant: Displaying great finesse and balance. Lacking intensity but complex and interesting.

Fat: Heavy but lacking in complexity and firmness.

Finesse: Having great balance and harmony.

Finish: Aftertaste; sensation that remains after swallowing.

Flowery: Having an intense aroma of lilacs, honeysuckle or other flowers.

Forward: Mature before its time, soft and pleasant at a young age.

Fruity: Having the flavor of grapes and sometimes suggesting other kinds of fruit. Erroneously used to mean sweet.

Green: Young, immature, undeveloped.

Hard: Green, acidic, harsh.

Intense: Having strong, well-defined flavor and texture; robust.

Ladies' Wine: Sweet wine.

Light: Low in alcohol, lacking in body, dull.

Nose: Very pronounced bouquet.

Oaky: Aroma and flavor of oak barrels used for aging. Also woody.

Off: Turned bad.

Oxidized: Deteriorated from exposure to air, often indicated by brownish color and the odor of rotting hay.

Robust: Intensely flavored, full-bodied, strong.

Short: Lacking in aftertaste, not firm.

Soft: Lacking texture and firmness; sometimes, low in alcohol.

Spicy: Displaying nuances of spices; peppery, minty.

Sweet: Containing unfermented grape sugar that creates a sugary impression.

Tannic: Burdened with tannic acid, which is derived naturally from grape solids and from wooden aging barrels. Astringent, very dry.

Texture: Tactile quality, or how the wine feels in the mouth, sometimes suggesting solids and tannic acid.

Vegetal: Tasting and smelling of freshly mowed grass or hay.

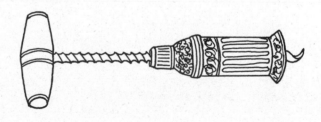

INDEX